Praise for John Hailman's *Thomas Jefferson on Wine*

"A fascinating look at our third president
and the evolution of his lifelong love of wine."
—*The Wall Street Journal*

"The book is a must for anyone interested in both
the favorite son of Virginia and the fruit of the vine.
Those who love both should read it twice."
—*The Washington Times*

"Exhaustively researched and entertaining."
—*City Journal*, New York

"If your idea of a good evening is sitting down to a Simon Schama
history program with a bottle of claret, then this is the book for you."
—*Decanter Magazine*, London

"John Hailman brings out the most epicurean side
of the most celebrated of American Francophiles."
—*The Figaro International*, Paris

"Hailman has done an exhaustive study and provided
a valuable window into who Jefferson really was."
—*The Wine Spectator*

"A fascinating exploration of the early days of the modern global
wine trade as experienced by one of the most significant figures
in United States history. Hailman has produced an admirable work
portraying Jefferson in vivid complexity while also illuminating
the joys and frustration of the eighteenth-century wine-lover."
—*Gastronomica, The Journal of Wine & Culture*

"Hailman really knows his wines."
—*New York Times Book Review*

From

MIDNIGHT

to

GUNTOWN

From

MIDNIGHT

to

GUNTOWN

True Crime Stories from a Federal Prosecutor in Mississippi

John Hailman

University Press of Mississippi / Jackson

www.upress.state.ms.us

The University Press of Mississippi is a member
of the Association of American University Presses.

All photographs courtesy of the author, unless otherwise noted

First printing 2013

∞

Library of Congress Cataloging-in-Publication Data

Hailman, John.
From midnight to guntown : true crime stories from a federal
prosecutor in Mississippi / John Hailman.
p. cm.
Includes bibliographical references and index.
ISBN 978-1-61703-800-6 (hardback) — ISBN 978-1-61703-801-3
(ebook) 1. Crime—Mississippi—History. 2. Criminals—
Mississippi—History. I. Title.
HV6793.M7H35 2013
364.1092′2762—dc23   2012044379

British Library Cataloging-in-Publication Data available

This book is dedicated to

Wayne Tichenor
Special Agent, Federal Bureau of Investigation
First Lieutenant, United States Marine Corps, Vietnam
The Best Investigator I Ever Met
My Partner in Over 100 Cases
Taken from Us Too Young by Lou Gehrig's Disease

Charles Overby
Friend and Mentor
CEO of the Freedom Forum and Newseum of Washington, D.C.
And the Overby Center at Ole Miss
Without Charles, This Book Would Not Exist

To the Women in my life:
Regan McGrew Hailman, my loyal wife of 44 years; and to Our Daughters
Dr. Allison Hailman Doyle, Lt. & Sr. Medical Officer, U.S. Navy
Lydia Hailman King, French Teacher extraordinaire

And to Our Beautiful Granddaughter,
Abbey McGrew Doyle
Smart as a Whip and Quick as a Cat
Our Hope for the Future.

The United States Attorney is the representative not of an ordinary party to a controversy but of a sovereignty whose obligation is to govern impartially, and is as compelling as its obligation to govern at all, and whose interest in a criminal prosecution is not that he shall win a case, but that justice shall be done.

As such he is in a peculiar and very definite sense the servant of the law, the twofold aim of which is that guilt shall not escape nor innocence suffer. He may prosecute with earnestness and vigor; indeed, he should do so. But while he may strike hard blows, he is not at liberty to strike foul ones. It is as much his duty to refrain from improper methods calculated to produce a wrongful conviction as it is to use legitimate means to bring about a just one.

—Mr. Justice Sutherland in Berger v. U.S., 295 U.S. 78 at 84 (1935)

Contents

Preface

The idea for this book came from a good source: singer/songwriter Willie Nelson. Several years ago, I was attending a seminar in Austin, Texas, when my old friend and fellow prosecutor, James Tucker, said, "Meet me at the back door of the hotel at precisely 6:00 P.M., and don't tell anyone where we're going." The second part was easy—I had no idea where we were going. At the appointed hour, James ushered me into his rental car with two other old friends: Lee Radek, chief of the Justice Department's Public Integrity Section, and Marshall Jarrett, head of the Office of Professional Responsibility, the dreaded ethics watchdog of DOJ.

Was I in trouble? Somehow I didn't think so. James said, "We're headed to Willie Nelson's ranch for a barbecue. My daughter married Willie's nephew." It was a memorable evening. Willie and his nephew played speed chess on a lighted board while we ate barbecue under the stars and his sister and his wife and their two little boys kept things lively. One thing did worry me at first: How would Willie Nelson feel about being surrounded by Feds after his well-publicized troubles with the IRS? Turns out it was no problem. We began swapping courtroom war stories. Willie liked my stories about incompetent bank robbers like the one whose getaway car wouldn't start and the one who wrote his demand note on the back of his personal check.

The next day, as we were leaving, Willie told James, "That fellow from Mississippi who tells those stories. Bring him back. He should write a book." That comment got me started. I began to keep records of our more interesting cases—not only the bank robbers, but the scam artists, hit men, protected witnesses, colorful informants, defendants with funny nicknames, over-the-top investigators, and those defendants who had a certain roguish charm. Civic clubs and book clubs began to invite me to tell them war stories. By the time I retired in 2007, I had more than thirty-five boxes of files full of trial stories—some funny, some tragic, all unique in a Faulknerian way. Several of the characters have since had whole books written about them like Dickie Scruggs, Emmett Till, Chicago gang leader Jeff Fort and Paddy Mitchell, leader of the most successful bank robbery gang of the twentieth century, the guys who wore rubber masks of ex-presidents like Mitchell in the Nixon mask proclaiming during a robbery, "I am not a crook." That part of their act was portrayed in the movie *Point Break* with Patrick Swayze.

I first started telling bank robber stories earlier when Bill Ferris, director of the Center for the Study of Southern Culture at Ole Miss, asked me to give a talk on them. For a title I suggested "Bank Robbers I've Known." Bill said, "Oh, no, no. It has to be *academic*-sounding." He said, tongue-in-cheek, "They think we are a *serious* University department, you know." The next day I proposed, "Prologomena to a Cultural Study of the Southern Bank Robber." He liked it. Bill loves stories and is himself a great storyteller which led to his being named Director of the National Endowment for the Humanities. From that post, he gave great support to my first book, a biography of Thomas Jefferson and his love of fine wines.

The basic thesis for the Southern Culture lecture was to contrast northern and southern bank robbers, a takeoff on President Kennedy's famous remark about Washington, D.C., being a combination of "southern efficiency and northern charm." In my experience, the typical northern bank robber would enter a bank, rudely cut in line, curse the tellers, and threaten to kill anyone who resisted. He would then successfully escape with the loot. The typical southern bank robber, by contrast, would walk calmly into the bank; wait politely in line; say, "Please give me all your money"; thank the teller; leave quietly; and get into his old broken-down getaway car—which wouldn't start. Variations on that theme are recounted throughout this book.

The title *From Midnight to Guntown* came to me in 1989 when the Justice Department assigned me the task of writing a history of our office for a volume commemorating the two hundredth anniversary of the U.S. District Attorneys. In compiling the history, I was shocked at how few records remained of the thousands of cases tried by our office. After ten years, many U.S. Attorney files are simply shredded. Similar rules apply to files of federal court clerks. Later, while reading the histories of the other ninety-three U.S. Attorney's Offices, I was amazed at the characters, from Jesse James to John Dillinger, that U.S. Attorneys have dealt with, and decided some of our stories should be preserved. Besides, I figured when I retired the reminiscing itself would be a pleasure. My mentor, former chief judge William C. Keady, said in his own book, *All Rise: Memoirs of a Mississippi Federal Judge*, that retired lawyers and judges should do three things: read, write, and reminisce. I decided to do all three.

Looking over a map of our district, I saw at the southwest and northeast corners the names of two towns that captured the colorful spirit of our district: Midnight, a predominantly black town deep in the plantation country of the Mississippi Delta, and Guntown, in the last foothills of the Appalachian range just north of Tupelo, birthplace of Elvis. Together, Midnight and Guntown seemed to capture the vital elements of the region's intertwined cultures.

The story of how Midnight got its name is typical. In the 1870s, the Delta was largely a primeval swamp of cypress groves still inhabited by native panthers and black bears and known more for yellow fever and malaria than moonlight and magnolias. After the Civil War, huge tracts of rich, virgin land were still available for settlers bold enough and desperate enough to risk death and disease on this frontier by clearing the land for cotton plantations, which often changed hands in late-night, whiskey-soaked poker games. The accepted legend on Midnight is that on one such evening, a group of planters were playing high-stakes poker using as collateral the deeds for thousands of acres of rich Delta land. As potential fortunes kept changing hands, the gamblers finally agreed on how to end the game. When the clock struck twelve, the game would be over, and whoever held the deed to the plantation they were playing for at that moment would be the owner. The happy winner, reflecting on how he gained his prize, decided right then to name his new plantation *Midnight* for the way he won it. Over the years, the plantation commissary and cypress cabins grew so much the place got its own post office, and the town of Midnight, Mississippi, was born.

The origin of the name *Guntown* is more controversial but equally colorful. The romantic version is that a beautiful Chickasaw princess who owned the land married a white man named Gunn and that the town was simply named for their family. One problem with that legend is the extra *n* in *Gunn*. The alternative story, only slightly more prosaic, is that because the town was a major railway depot during the Civil War, it became the storage place for enormous stockpiles of firearms. This story is supported by solid historical fact. Famed Confederate general Nathan Bedford Forrest took thousands of guns from Union forces there, and both General Grant and General Sherman considered Guntown a key strategic outpost in their march to Vicksburg. The town later became quite prosperous and even had its own newspaper, the *Guntown Hot Times*, whose archives faithfully preserve the town's colorful past.

For some years, the most important Civil War battle fought between Shiloh and Vicksburg was referred to by soldiers in letters home as the "Battle of Guntown." Only later did historians select a much less poetic title for the battle, Brice's Crossroads. A small museum there commemorates the history, complete with an audiotape narrated by Shelby Foote analyzing the intricate strategy of that battle. Of course, to us in the U.S. Attorney's Office, Guntown is better known for the colorful modern crimes committed there. My favorite involves our seizure of a fancy house, complete with indoor swimming pool, from a Chicago drug dealer. We forfeited it to the Mississippi Bureau of Narcotics for use as its regional office and used to run wiretaps poolside, much more pleasant than the sweaty little cubicles normally employed for that purpose.

A Sense of Place

South Mississippi got the Gulf Coast with its beaches and hurricanes as well as the state capital at Jackson and the romantic antebellum towns of Natchez and Vicksburg. But our district in north Mississippi got most of the Delta, with its infamous Parchman prison farm, one important home of the Delta blues, and its famed Highway 61 with its unrivaled variety of colorful human characters who combine high drama with low comedy. North Mississippi spawned not only William Faulkner, Elvis Presley, and John Grisham but B. B. King, Howlin' Wolf, and Fannie Lou Hamer. Its towns have names both cheerful and positive like Olive Branch and Holly Springs, and foreboding ones like Dark Corner in DeSoto County. It is also home to the darkest civil rights legend of all, the murder of fourteen-year-old Emmett Till of Chicago after his trip to

Money, Mississippi, where he allegedly whistled at or touched a white woman in a store before riding home on Dark Fear Road, a real place. As recounted here, our office, the FBI, and the local DA reopened that fifty-year-old case to resolve the false rumors that surrounded it and prosecute anyone still living who was involved. We succeeded in the first part at least.

North Mississippi is still a unique place where one regularly encounters a diverse universe of colorful and disturbing characters, not just bungling bank robbers and psychopathic killers but humorous informants, thoughtful judges, traumatized victims, scheming bureaucrats, brilliant investigators, eloquent witnesses with second-grade educations, outraged citizens, and sleeping jurors. People here like to give each other funky nicknames like "Cat Daddy" and "Hard Time." The cast of characters is easily as varied as the nineteenth-century London of Charles Dickens. Outsiders may call Oxford "Mayberry on the Yocona," but we cherish our eccentricities. This book tries to recapture the spirit of our place, which even now finds its past continually reincarnated in its present. Just as Faulkner and Grisham took their characters from real lives lived by real people in this region, the stories told here contain the same odd mixture of beauty and grace, tragedy and farce, played out before its natural scenic splendor at odds with its recurring acts of random, senseless violence but redeemed by moments of nobility and self-sacrifice. The book is by necessity episodic, like a weekly TV crime drama, but like *Law and Order* has consistent themes and characters.

All the stories in this book are true. They are public record, for now. In some cases, the victims are indentified by initials only. Certain towns, counties, and witnesses are also left unidentified to protect privacy. Out of respect for the deceased and their living descendants, some names have been omitted and dates and places obscured to protect innocent bystanders. For the really curious, citations to case names and numbers are supplied in endnotes for each chapter. For errors, omissions, and failures of memory, I apologize. I did not try to "enhance" these stories but just told them as the remaining official records tell them, supplemented by my own fragile human memory and those of other players I've interviewed. I studiously avoided trying to settle any old grudges and just told the stories, as nearly as possible, "with malice toward none and charity for all," as Lincoln famously said.

One challenge in putting these stories together was finding a structure. I first tried the lawyerly way, telling all the stories in chronological order, but that proved confusing. Then one day I spied in Oxford's Square Books a little paperback entitled *Careers in Crime*. Written in mock-serious style, it ranked the top fifty "careers" for people seriously considering a life of crime. From my own experience, "normal" criminals like thieves become criminals mostly by chance, starting with minor thefts and petty drug deals and graduating to greater financial rewards and harsher punishments. Violent criminals, by contrast, often seem to have endured childhoods as victims of violence and then internalize it and pass it on, as it were, as adults, often ending up in the worst of our prisons with the worst people of similar backgrounds.

The author of *Careers*, Michael Weinberg, took a different approach. He assumed criminals start off as practical, entrepreneurial sociopaths who lucidly seize upon crime as a profession both easier and more profitable than a dull eight-to-five job working in a cubicle for someone else. Weinberg then did a detailed statistical study of the pros and cons of various criminal "careers," assuming that successful criminals would do better by specializing in a single area of criminal expertise.

After considerable research, Weinberg came up with his fifty hottest criminal occupations. It would not be proper to call them the "Top Fifty" because several, such as "snitch," rank low on any cost/benefit scale. His observations were useful to me in coming up with an organizational scheme. The wildly different natures of the cases I saw as a general crime prosecutor at first seemed to be a random hodgepodge of wrongdoing. Looked at by the Weinberg categories, however, dividing criminals into bank robbers, killers, crooked cops, and so forth, the criminals seemed to group themselves into a series of logical "career choices," reinforcing my own rough conclusions from a lifetime of personal experience. Most bank robbers are such bungling amateurs that the rare "professionals" really stand out. Drug dealers are easily the laziest and least reliable of criminals, constantly cheating their customers, running out of product, or forgetting to show up for drug deals altogether. Out of fifty criminal careers, Weinberg ranked bank robbery as forty-seventh worst and drug dealing as fortieth. Only white-collar criminals made the Top Ten.[1]

Why North Mississippi has produced such colorful characters and stories is perhaps best explained by quotes from Mississippi writers engraved in large letters on the walls of the Overby Center at Ole Miss, where I was a fellow for two years during the writing of this book. The first quote is from an old friend who strongly encouraged me to write the book. He says of Mississippians:

> We are talkers. We talk about ourselves, each other, our ancestors, events, the funny and quirky and bizarre things people do. True stories, more or less, and the richer and more plentiful the detail the better.
> —Willie Morris

The second quote is a subtle one by the soft-spoken southern lady who tried for a whole year at Millsaps College in Jackson to teach me how to write:

> Long before I wrote stories, I listened *for* stories. Listening *for* them is something more acute than listening *to* them.
> —Eudora Welty

The stories that follow are the ones I listened for and listened to in the forty years I spent as both actor and observer in the courtrooms and jails of Faulkner country.

Common Law Enforcement Abbreviations and Acronyms

ADA   Assistant district attorney.

ATAC   Anti-Terrorism Advisory Councils, task forces formed right after 9/11 and similar to JTTFs (see below), headed by the U.S. Attorney for each federal district.

ATF&E   Bureau of Alcohol, Tobacco, Firearms, and Explosives, now part of the Justice Department but formerly in the Treasury Department where it was called simply the ATF, the term still used by most of law enforcement.

AUSA   Assistant U.S. Attorney, formerly Assistant U.S. District Attorney.

Beast, The Section 666 (see Revelations) of the Code makes bribery of state officials a federal crime if more than ten thousand federal dollars are involved.

Bitch, The A "three-strikes" law which makes an offender a "habitual offender" subject to a life sentence without parole, known as "real life."

CCE   Continuing criminal enterprise, a criminal drug gang of at least five members, subject to punishment by up to life in prison. The "drug kingpin" law.

CI   Confidential informant, usually a criminal cooperating with law enforcement for a reduced sentence.

CID   The dreaded Criminal Investigation Division of the Internal Revenue Service, recently renamed, confusingly, just the CI.

DA	State district attorney. In Mississippi, each elected DA has jurisdiction of from two to seven counties.
DEA	Federal Drug Enforcement Administration.
DOJ	Department of Justice in Washington, D.C. Also often called "Main Justice."
FBI	Federal Bureau of Investigation.
ICE	Immigration and Customs Enforcement (the sometimes unhappy merger of the former U.S. Customs with the former Immigration and Naturalization Service).
JTTF	Joint Terrorism Task Forces, district-wide groups headed by the FBI with members from all federal, state, and local law enforcement agencies, including U.S. Attorneys.
JP	Justice of the Peace.
LECC	Law Enforcement Coordinating Committee. A special task force in each district composed of federal, state, and local officers, headed by the LEC (law enforcement coordinator), a U.S. Attorney employee, usually a former deputy sheriff or police officer, whose job is to conduct joint training and to prevent law enforcement turf battles. A little-known but highly effective force.
Mailing, The	The key jurisdictional element of 90 percent of our federal fraud and corruption cases; a scheme to use the U.S. mails to defraud someone of something.
MBI	The Mississippi Bureau of Investigation, formerly the Criminal Division of the Mississippi Highway Patrol.
MBN	Mississippi Bureau of Narcotics, an elite statewide anti-drug agency.
MHP	Mississippi Highway Patrol.
OCDETF	Organized Crime Drug Enforcement Task Force, a team of federal, state, and local drug agents, commonly referred to as the "Oh-suh-deff." I was lead prosecutor for this group for five years.
RICO	Racketeer-Influenced and Corrupt Organizations, a federal law originally designed to combat traditional organized crime such as the Mafia but that DOJ and the courts have greatly expanded to reach just about

any organized criminal group, even if loosely organized. See our case *U.S. v. Bright*, 630 F.2d 240 (5th Cir. 1977).

SAC   Special Agent in Charge of a federal investigative agency.

SCIF   Secure Compartmentalized Intelligence Facility, known to viewers of the old TV show *Get Smart* as the "Cone of Silence" room.

SO   Sheriff's Office.

SS   The Secret Service. The oldest federal investigative agency. Not at all secret, this elite agency not only is responsible for protecting the president and other key federal officials and political candidates, but also investigates the counterfeiting of U.S. currency and all thefts of federal checks.

Supervisors   In Mississippi, as in California, we refer to our highest elected county officials as Supervisors, unlike Arkansas where they are referred to as "Judges." Some states call them Commissioners. Other states name them for their original function "road supervisors." In Mississippi the supervisors and their statewide organization still exert enormous power and influence under their unofficial name "the Courthouse Crowd."

UC   Undercover operative in an investigation.

USM   U.S. Marshal's Service. Often thought of as primarily assigned to guard courtrooms and prisoners, the marshals are the primary agency responsible for the Federal Witness Security (Protection) Program and the apprehension of federal fugitives and bail-jumpers. They have their own investigators known as inspectors.

USPIS   Little-known but highly sophisticated and effective criminal investigative arm of what Benjamin Franklin named simply the "Post Office." Postal inspectors enforce the critical white collar crime statutes against frauds committed by use of the mails.

From

MIDNIGHT

to

GUNTOWN

Prologue
The Making of a Career Prosecutor

For years, it never really occurred to me why I enjoyed being a prosecutor so much, but I knew I did. In my office, we used to say, "If I didn't need the money, I would do this job for free." What we all enjoyed most were the jury trials, which were like sports, full of intense competition performed before an audience of jurors. Our Anglo-Saxon system is clearly a modern form of deadly combat, mental and moral, with the underlying motives of violence and revenge focused and controlled.

My daughter Allison, now a medical doctor, caused me to think seriously about my subconscious motivations for enjoying trials so much. When she was fifteen and going through a period of adolescent rebellion, she did not think very highly of me. One day she introduced me to a teenage friend with the comment, "This is my father. He puts people in prison for a living." Looking at it that way caused me to ponder.

Most federal prosecutors take the job to gain experience, then move on after two or three years to more lucrative careers in private practice. Most find the job too stressful to consider long term for the modest salary it pays. A recent survey called the job one of the five most stressful jobs in the American workplace, up there with air traffic controller and pro quarterback. Yet a handful of us have made careers of it. Over time, as my daughter's words sank in, I began a sort of Freudian review of my motives.

I vividly recall my first encounter with law enforcement—the police officers who would later be my career partners. When I was little, my father was on the road all the time. One weekend we were playing in the backyard when a big, strange-looking dog approached, swaying from side to side. His mouth was covered with white foam. Just after my father said, "He is sick," there came the biggest explosions I had ever heard.

3

There were red and yellow flashes and blue smoke, and the dog collapsed. Two officers walked up to the dead dog and started to carry him away. The officers apologized to my father for my having seen them shoot the dog. My father explained to me that they were helping the dog because he was too sick to live and suffering a lot of pain. It was a good explanation and gave me a positive image of officers that has never left me—even though I've had to prosecute a few.

Maybe my love of cops-and-robbers was partly genetic and partly family history also. My father's favorite uncle was a Pinkerton detective and used to regale us with stories about cases he'd had. In retrospect, there was another event that impacted me even more strongly. When I was in second grade, our school had two bathrooms (one for boys, one for girls) in the basement for all twelve grades. A couple of sixth-grade boys had a favorite sport: holding us little boys upside down by our ankles and dunking our heads in the toilet. We would put our little hands on the seat and push back with our little arms as hard as we could, but always ended up sucking toilet water.

One day a heroic rescuer appeared, a high school athlete named Larry Payton. When he saw me getting dunked, he grabbed the sixth-grader who was doing it, slammed him against the wall, and choked him till his eyes bugged out. He told him in front of the other evil-doers that if he ever caught the little felon or anyone else dunking us, he would hold their heads under water in the toilet until they drowned. My feeling of relief is still palpable.

Years later, Marty Russell of the *Tupelo Daily Journal* asked me why I liked prosecuting. The dunking story suddenly came back to me, and I blurted out, "Prosecutors are there to remove the bullies from the playground." There is now a movement to combat bullying, but back then no one talked about it. We were expected to look out for ourselves as part of becoming men.

Later, sports were a huge influence. The camaraderie of the team soothed our painful adolescent egos and our need to be accepted as part of a gang. Our coach, a just-retired Marine Corps drill instructor, used many of their techniques on us. His practices were like boot camp, except you got to go home at night. His favorite way to end basketball practice was something he called Last Man Standing. He'd put us all in the foul circle and tell us the last one in the circle could go home. No punching or kicking was allowed, just pushing and pulling, but it was exhausting. The last two or three guys out were almost too weak to walk back to the locker room.

But it was really my father who was the key to my life as a prosecutor. A hard-nosed Amish German, he believed people learned things only through hard work. When I was sixteen, I told him I needed a car. He said I could have one as soon as I could pay for it myself. I spent the next two summers baling hay for local farmers. By the summer of 1959, before my senior year I had enough money to buy an old red Plymouth convertible. The first day I had the car, I baled hay all morning and had a long, hot baseball practice all afternoon. Wasting no time showering, I hosed myself off with my clothes on and let the wind air-dry my T-shirt and blue jeans as I drove to an outdoor dance. It was in a field full of pretty girls in thin summer dresses dancing barefoot on the grass to a live band. I asked the first girl I saw to dance with me. When people began tapping guys on the shoulder, I assumed they were cutting in. The pretty brunette and I danced without a break and were having a really good time when I noticed there were only three or four other couples still dancing. "Where did everybody go?" I asked her. "Silly, this is a dance contest," she said. "The rest of them have been eliminated." Even though we did not yet know each other's names, we somehow won the dance contest.

I asked if she would go out with me that weekend. "Of course, but you have to meet my mother first." I should have noticed she was driving a new Cadillac convertible that made my old Plymouth look pretty bad. But I was young. When we got to her house, a big one on a hill with columns and a manicured lawn, her mother greeted us on the tall, graceful front steps. I thought I made a good impression with my muscles and suntan, and forgot about all the hay in my hair and holes in my clothes. I should also have noticed the personal questions she asked me but was blinded by the dance experience and the girl's beauty and enthusiasm. Once back home I called her and asked what time I should pick her up. She was crying and said, "I'm so sorry. I cannot go out with you. My mom says you're too countrified." After I hung up, my mother asked what was wrong. I explained. My usually quiet mother called out to my father, "Dear, we're sending Johnny to Paris. We need to knock off his rough edges. Nobody calls *my son* countrified."

After two years of college French, a summer school in rural France, and another at Laval University in Quebec, I was accepted to the Sorbonne in Paris to have my rough edges knocked off. I enjoyed my first year in Paris so much that I refused to come home. My father said, "You can stay if you can pay for it. I'm not paying another dime." I got a job as a gofer with Air France, worked my way up to a gig as an interpreter, and stayed a second full year at the Sorbonne. By the time I returned home, I was fluent in French. Unfortunately, I never saw the girl's mother again to thank her for inadvertently giving me such a wonderful present.

Courtroom Rat in Paris and London

One day a French friend took me to one of his law classes and then to court. The class was as boring as the Sorbonne, but the court case was fascinating. Soon I was going nearly every day to what the French call the "Palace of Justice." The bailiffs and attorneys would tip me off to interesting trials. I became a "courtroom rat," hanging out daily to watch trials. I lived that year with French students in a boardinghouse with one eighteen-year-old English student who had just graduated from Eton and was taking a year off before college. When he moved on to Oxford, he invited me to visit several times. Tickets were cheap, so I went often. Each time I would stop in London, eat Indian food, and watch criminal jury trials all day at the Old Bailey. Despite my days as a courtroom rat, it never occurred to me that I might one day be a lawyer myself. My father had so drummed into my head how boring and commercial the law was and how shady lawyers were that the idea never seriously crossed my mind.

Upon my return from Paris in 1964, I met my future wife, Regan, at Millsaps College in Jackson. A small Christian college (for small Christians, some said), Millsaps had strict rules for young women, who had a 10:00 P.M. curfew. One night I let the time slip away and could not get Regan back to the dorm on time. Her absence was reported. The next day the dreaded Women's Council of grim-faced, aspiring matrons convened and, invoking their puritan code, sentenced Regan to be "campused" for the rest of her last semester, a medieval punishment which meant she had to be in her room by 6 P.M., 7 days a week. This was too much injustice.

For the first time the aggression of an advocate awakened somewhere deep inside me.

I was angry not just about being deprived of her company, but because she had been humiliated and I felt responsible. Our good friend, Professor Bill Baskin, told me that there was some procedure for appeal of the vestal virgins' decision. I searched student manuals and found that the Faculty Senate could appoint a three-person panel to review student-imposed punishments. Our allies on the faculty got a friendly committee appointed, including our two philosophy/religion professors who were too kind to impose such a cruel punishment. We thought it best that I not be a witness at the hearing, so I wrote what turned out to be my first legal brief, a statement of facts for Regan to read. She was too shy at the time to make a forceful oral presentation (those were the good old days). The panel rejected the Women's Council decision entirely and Regan was a free woman. I had won my first case.

New Orleans

As my Millsaps years wound down it became necessary to do something to avoid being drafted and sent to the jungles of Vietnam. In 1965, I managed to obtain a one-year Woodrow Wilson Fellowship for prospective teachers at Tulane in New Orleans. After getting my M.A. in French, I was looking for my path. Excited by friends who'd seen adventure in the earlier, easier years of the Vietnam War, I thought seriously about going after all. My coach advised I join the Marine Corps. When I told my father the good news, he went ballistic at the idea of his only son going into combat in what he thought was a foolish war. My line that I would be "missing the adventure of my generation" did not persuade him, nor did my idea that I would return and write a best-selling memoir of the war. He said firmly, "Unless you give me your word you're going to forget about Vietnam, I will fly down there and personally stomp you till you cannot even crawl to the recruiting station." I knew he would never do that, but I was moved by his passion. My father always gave me lots of freedom and good advice, so his violent reaction impressed me. Maybe Vietnam was not such a great idea. But what would I do?

Just then Don Stacy, an old friend from Millsaps, called and asked me to meet him at the Napoleon House, my favorite café in the French Quarter where I often studied. Don had, like me, gotten an M.A. on a Woodrow Wilson and had also not enjoyed it much. He had gone on to law school, however, and loved it. He urged me to take the LSAT, the entrance exam. I signed up to take it the next weekend, not knowing you were supposed to study for it. My scores came back surprisingly strong. Stacy told me what to do next: "Apply to four or five law schools, and we'll get them in a bidding war over you. Friend Hailman, we'll make a happy, healthy, wealthy lawyer out of you." Stacy had a strange vocabulary and a voice like a power saw. He once accurately called himself an eighteenth-century man trapped in the twentieth. Later, dissatisfied with his own progress, he committed suicide, leaving a nice wife and two little boys. But in his brief life he had a huge positive influence on me, and got me a full three-year scholarship to Ole Miss. As he said, pitting competing offers from Tulane, Duke, and Virginia against each other and Ole Miss did the trick.

Law Clerk

I loved all three years of law school, working twenty hours a week for Legal Services doing chancery court cases like divorces and defending misdemeanors every Monday in city court. One afternoon in 1969, as I neared graduation, I was walking down the hall of the law school swinging my tennis racket. I saw behind a desk in the dean's office a big man with a long mane of white hair sitting in a tall chair looking impressive. He said "Come on in. Sit down." He began asking questions and telling me little stories. We got along well for about five minutes. Then he said: "Why do you want to be my law clerk?" I said abruptly "I'm sorry sir, but I don't want to be your law clerk. The word clerk sounds boring and menial to me." He couldn't stop laughing. "You are certainly the most unusual applicant I've ever had. Tell me your name again." I told him my name and explained that I was not an applicant. He said, "But you're on my list," and showed me my name. He picked up the phone and called two of my professors. I could hear his end of the conversation. He kept chuckling. "I just talked to my friends, Professors Paige Sharp and Frank

Maraist. They said they recommended you as a law clerk applicant, and I put you on my list, but apparently you never took the trouble to apply. However, I'm going to disregard that and interview you anyway."

The judge asked me a lot of questions, then leaned forward and said, "This is my last question: What is the role of reason in human life?" Luckily, I had been a philosophy major for a while so his question did not surprise me. I told him that Plato had said that reason in human life is like a charioteer driving a chariot with two horses. One horse, representing the appetites, is pulling the chariot toward one ditch. The other horse, representing the passions, is pulling the chariot toward the other ditch. Like horses, the appetites and passions of human beings can easily pull them into the ditch. Only the charioteer—reason—can keep them in the road. At that point Judge Keady stood up and said, "I will be in touch with you to tell you who I've selected."

The following morning I received a call from Judge Keady. He said, "I have interviewed the other candidates. All are highly qualified and want the job. I understand you do not want it, but I'm going to make you the offer anyway. Drive over to Greenville tomorrow and we'll spend the day together. Frankly, I think you should be my clerk because you *need* it more than the others. You have talent, but you need direction." In Greenville we spent a couple of hours in his chambers talking law. Then he showed me his old office, where his senior partner had been Delta planter/lawyer William Alexander Percy, who wrote the classic memoir *Lanterns on the Levee—Recollections of a Planter's Son*. I was hooked. Whether I liked the title or not, for the next two years I was going to be a law clerk.

Life with a Federal Judge

So oblivious had I been to the world outside law school that I'd never suspected Judge Keady was the most respected judge in Mississippi, a legal lion on the level of Frank Johnson of Alabama. Unfortunately for Judge Keady, his renown came mainly through his enormous docket of school desegregation and other civil rights cases. From 1969 to 1971, while I was his clerk, he ordered the integration of half of all public schools of all thirty-seven counties of the northern district. The great irony of

Judge Keady's fame as the "civil rights judge" was that he was personally on the conservative side, loving the law as an institution and enforcing it whether he agreed with it or not. His dream was to be a legal scholar who raised the reputation of the Mississippi judiciary and made law more rational and fair to ordinary citizens and lawyers alike. He loved to write precedent-setting opinions, fifty-pagers, loaded with scholarly references to the wisdom of the great legal treatise writers. His subject matter was broad and deep, thanks to a crowded docket of varied cases left by his deceased predecessor.

Law school had not prepared me for the real legal world. Our first trial was a labor case involving violence during a secondary boycott. Then came complex tax cases, medical malpractice, legislative reapportionment, and admiralty cases with Mark Twain–like characters who worked towboats on the Mississippi River. The weeks in the library depressed me. I told Judge Keady I was a courtroom rat, not a library rat. He wisely made me an offer I couldn't refuse: Bring my law books in the courtroom so I could watch and listen to all the trials while doing my research and writing draft opinions. For two years I observed Mississippi's finest trial lawyers practice their trade.

Georgetown Law School

After two happy years, Judge Keady helped me receive a prestigious fellowship to Georgetown Law School in its two-year master's program. The program called for us Prettyman Fellows (Greta Van Susteren is the best-known) to act as defense attorneys the first year, then to serve as federal prosecutors the second year while taking one class in Supreme Court practice and writing for the *Georgetown Law Journal*. Our L.L.M. would qualify us for either a lucrative job with a good law firm or a teaching slot at a prestigious law school. To supplement my fellowship, I got a job as a clerk/consultant at the Wine & Cheese Shop in Georgetown, and my wife soon joined me in the cheese department. Within a few months, I landed another part-time job as the regular *Washington Post* wine columnist, thanks again to my French and the lady who called me countrified.

The program at Georgetown Law included a series of visits to local legal institutions. Our first stop was the chloroform-scented office of the

D.C. Medical Examiner. Our tour was chilling, not just because it was cold to keep the bodies from rotting, but because there were so many of them. With typical gallows humor, the dapper little medical examiner, who sported a bow tie and clipped moustache, cheerfully showed us his "clients," as he called them. My most vivid memory is of all the tags on the big toes of the rows of corpses. Someone asked if these bodies were recent homicide victims. "Yes, all of them." Asked if it was not depressing to deal with dead bodies all day, he said, "Not really. Some are challenging to diagnose, there is a lot of variety, and it's less stressful than dealing with live patients. These guys can't complain that my stethoscope is cold."

Then he showed us the other side. "There are some that bother me, however. This tiny one here is a year-old baby whose stepfather decided to pick him up by the foot and bash his brains out against a brick wall. The appearance of that soft skull was something I found pretty hard to leave at the office." Little did I suspect that I'd soon be appointed to help represent the killer.

The next day we visited St. Elizabeth's Hospital, the sort of place they used to call an asylum for the criminally insane. It was creepy. Patients babbled away with no one listening. A few were openly hostile. Our guide gave us a warning: "Do not interact with these people. You never know what will set them off. A few months ago, a visiting student started talking to a little guy who was just in here for observation. He had never given us a moment's trouble. We were about to send him back to the judge as competent to stand trial when he snapped and hit the student a vicious blow to the head with a piece of metal. The student is now a vegetable, so be careful."

My first client as a defense attorney was a parole violator less memorable for himself than for his sponsor, Washington, D.C., mayor Marion Barry. We met in a visiting room at the grim and notorious D.C. Jail. Barry, a handsome man with strangely hooded eyes and a mercurial disposition, greeted me coldly, no doubt seeing another white liberal do-gooder. Barry was from Itta Bena, home of Mississippi Valley State and Jerry Rice. When he heard I was from Mississippi, he blinked. When he learned I'd worked three years for Rural Legal Services and two years for the famous Judge Keady he laughed. It wasn't that he liked me any better, just that he found the situation a little more familiar. He asked point-blank why I would do such a lousy job. My honest answer, to get experience and see the real world, seemed to satisfy him. Mayor Barry said not to worry about the hearing—he had helped the judge get appointed, and my client was nonviolent and a good candidate to go back on parole. In an hour, my client was back on the street. I had won my first big-city case, though I could hardly claim much personal credit for it.

Senator Stennis

After less than one semester, I knew I did not want to be a defense attorney. Judge Keady called to ask how I was doing, and I told him. He said he didn't know if I would be interested, but Senator John Stennis had just called him seeking a lawyer for his Washington staff. The judge suggested I go see the senator. We hit it off right away, and I landed the job. The senator told me that my work would be as a problem-solver and troubleshooter and that I could choose my own job title. I chose "legal counsel" as a title for my business cards but ended up being more of a speechwriter, sounding board, and traveling companion for the quintessential old-time southern senator. On my first day, his secretary ushered me into a large, high-ceilinged conference room with a marble fireplace over which hung a portrait of Thomas Jefferson. In the center of the room stood an enormous mahogany table formerly used by vice presidents. Seated behind his desk, with the U.S. Capitol framed in the window behind him, the senator was an impressive figure. Already in his seventies, he was energetic and vigorous, with keen blue eyes and a booming but controlled voice. Because he thought like his constituents, he did not need to play games or try to deceive them. He was a wonderful storyteller.

Then-Senator Joe Biden of Delaware, in his 2007 memoir of his years in the Senate, *Promises to Keep: On Life and Politics*, aptly characterized Senator Stennis as the very model of a statesman. As for the difficult issue of his positions on race, the man who went on to be vice president said that Senator Stennis "was not like some of the others. He was not a hater. His heart was not in it."

My most enjoyable times with Senator Stennis occurred when he would pop in my office and say, "Come walk with me." I would follow his long, quick strides through the marble Senate halls or ride with him on the underground Senate railway to his private office in the Capitol.

He was a quick study with a phenomenal memory for detail. I never knew anyone who said fewer trivial things. We worked long and hard on bills to finish the Natchez Trace Parkway and on collecting his papers and establishing the Stennis Institute of Government at Mississippi State.

We traveled often to Mississippi by military plane to meet constituents, but my favorite trip was to Montana in September of 1972. Senator Stennis had been asked, as a member of the Senate's "inner club," to patch up a dispute between two fellow senators, Majority Leader Mike Mansfield of Montana and Harold Hughes, an eccentric former long-haul truck-driver from Iowa. The Senator never confided to me the nature of the dispute. All I knew was that we went trout fishing nearly every day, ate whole steers barbecued in pits in the ground at night and rode all over the state by jeep and small plane. The bonding worked. The Senators buried the hatchet. It was one of the great trips of my young life.

On our return to Washington my assignments were to attend and monitor the Senate Watergate hearings and to brief him on them thoroughly and then to work with him on the War Powers Act and on a proposal to amend the filibuster rule. He had me research thoroughly the procedures for a Senate impeachment, for Vice President Agnew, not for President Nixon. I was having the time of my life. Then in January 1973 everything changed. The senator was shot and gravely wounded in a street robbery and was hospitalized for months thereafter. I recount that trial in detail as the first case in Chapter Four, "Killers and Wannabes." My experiences watching the trial of his assailant certainly had a huge influence on my later decision to become a federal prosecutor.

Washington Lawyer

When it came time for me to leave Senator Stennis, he recommended me to friends at several Washington law firms. One boutique firm of a dozen lawyers invited me to interview over lunch at the Metropolitan Club. The managing partner was Gilbert Hahn Jr., the wealthy owner of the Hahn's shoe store chain who was also chairman of the D.C. City Council and founder of the Give a Damn Foundation, a liberal Republican group dedicated to improving the city government of the nation's capital. Richard Nixon soon fired Mr. Hahn for being too independent.

My first week at Hahn was interesting. The firm had split in half just a few months before I joined. One partner, Bruce Sundlun, went on to become governor of Rhode Island. Another partner, Bardyl Tirana, became head of the U.S. Civil Defense Agency. The firm was really wired politically. But it was Mr. Hahn who kept most of the trial business, and he needed lawyers quickly to handle all their court cases. It was an unusual firm in that nearly all our clients except my main client, the French embassy, came through referrals from other lawyers. As now, most Washington lawyers were lobbyists or commercial specialists or somehow affiliated with the government. No one seemed to do any trial work, and other lawyers sought us out to try their cases.

The first week we ate lunch every day at the same restaurant, a ratty little meat-and-three place on G Street called the Old Ebbitt Grill. (It has since moved around the corner near the White House and is now a fancy watering hole worthy of Georgetown.) On the first Friday, I asked Mr. Hahn, "Don't y'all ever eat anywhere other than the Old Ebbitt?" He looked at me strangely, then looked down the table at one of the partners and said, "Jack is Orthodox and the Old Ebbitt is kosher so—" He stopped in midsentence. "You're not a Jew, are you?" he said. "I never said I was. No one ever asked me." Our law clerk, Carl Bergman, started to laugh. Then everyone began to laugh. Carl said, "You're a goy. A fucking goy. Don't you know this is a Jewish law firm?" Then someone else said, "Hey, John can be our house goy, our designated non-Jew."

Mr. Hahn tossed me right into the fray of trial work, especially motion practice. I would arrive in the morning and Marjorie, the head secretary, would hand me a file and say, "John, you're due in Superior Court in thirty minutes. I've called you a cab. You can read the file on your way over." And they were challenging cases. The first one I recall involved an Italian restaurant allegedly owned by the Mob and represented by partner Mark Sandground, who owned several restaurants including the Palm steakhouse and a southern French place called La Nicoise. I was always representing French chefs who had drunk too much and tried to fight the police who arrested them. I tried everything from spite fences to Teamster violence cases and gamy society divorces.

Then one day, while I was carrying a stack of law books, my back suddenly seized up, and I fell to the floor, writhing in pain. The doctor diagnosed a ruptured disc. I ended up spending eleven days in traction in the hospital so sedated I had little communication with the office. One Sunday after I had recovered enough to be released from the hospital but before I had returned to work, my wife, Regan, drove me to our office in the Colorado Building to see what my desk looked like. I scraped slowly along the sidewalk with a cane and rode the elevator up to our office, but when I got there, my key wouldn't open the door. From the lobby I used the pay phone to call Marjorie at home. She said, "Oh, John, I'm so sorry. We didn't want to upset you in your condition, but a terrible thing has happened. The firm has broken up again. The partners have hired lawyers and are suing each other." Regan was seven months pregnant at the time. We had problems.

Providentially, Judge Keady called that very afternoon to check up on me. He had had a premonition. "John, I talked to Dean Parham Williams at the Ole Miss Law School and he has a slot made for you. It's only a one-year visiting professor assignment, but you would be teaching evidence and constitutional law, your favorite subjects." For the first time, I thought that maybe I just wanted to teach and get away from the stress and the endless "billable hours" of private practice. But I also had a sinking feeling. My hope had been to become a wealthy Washington lawyer and provide a really nice life for my wife and children. If I went back to Mississippi to teach, I would probably never make any serious money. I had offers from other D.C. firms, but my doctor told me the stress of law practice would probably put me back in the hospital. After agonizing over this decision for weeks, I just couldn't make up my mind, so I retrieved a beautiful old silver dollar given to me by my grandmother. I turned it over in my hand several times and decided I would commit my life to chance. If it came up "tails" I would stay in Washington. If "heads" I would return to Mississippi. I flipped the silver dollar high in the air. When it came up "tails" I was sad. I realized that I did not want to stay in Washington. I wanted to go back home to Mississippi. The coin flip had indeed decided my fate, just not the way I planned.

I flew to Oxford to interview for the teaching job and pick out my textbooks. At 6:00 in the morning before my interview with Dean Williams, I was awakened by a telephone call from U.S. Attorney H. M. Ray. He explained his own plan decisively: "John, I know you from your days with Judge Keady. You don't need to be a law professor. What you need to be is a trial lawyer. I'm offering you the best trial lawyer job in America, being a prosecutor in the most interesting U.S. Attorney's Office in the United States. I will beat any offer Parham Williams makes you."

The words had a prophetic ring, yet I feared being caught up in a federal bureaucracy. What would happen when Mr. Ray was replaced or retired? What if a real jerk came on as U.S. Attorney after I had been there too long to go anywhere else? H.M. insisted that I sign up for at least three years. After several agonizing hours, I agreed and told Parham that I still hoped to teach law in the evenings. The three years soon turned into thirty-three. I stayed with the U.S. Attorney's Office until I retired in 2007 and still teach federal trial practice, criminal trial practice, and law and literature at Ole Miss every semester after more than twenty-five years. It was a good choice I'll never regret.

I called my father to tell him I "might" take a job as a prosecutor in the U.S. Attorney's Office in Oxford. He quickly warmed to the subject: "Is that like a district attorney?" I told him "That's what they used to call them." He was jubilant. "I'm proud of you son. It is absolutely wonderful you're going to be a DA. They are not like those other lawyers. They do important work. When do you start?" I had to admit that for once I did not seek his advice in advance: "I started today."

I

BANK ROBBERS I'VE KNOWN

My Favorite Crime

We once took an informal poll in my office for our favorite crime to prosecute. The result was unanimous: bank robbery. Why? Well, a bank robbery is fast-moving and exciting, and even though there is an element of force and violence, physical injury is pretty rare, although there is often emotional trauma to the tellers and other victims. There is also no confusion about whether a crime was committed. In a white-collar case, there is usually no doubt who did it; the only question is whether what the accused did was a crime and whether he or she knew it was a crime. With bank robbery, the issue is the opposite: It's clearly a crime; the only issue is identity. Was the defendant the one who did it?

A bank robbery is also a kind of set piece, almost like a play with well-known roles and actors. There may be a getaway driver, a lookout, tellers trying to memorize the robber's appearance or tag number, and occasionally a pursuing posse. The robber usually has a disguise, whether a ski mask, a lady's stocking with eyeholes, even a Halloween mask. Normally there is a weapon, whether a pistol, bomb (real or fake), or a concealed sawed-off shotgun (that's why it's sawed off). Many robbers use some sort of demand note; others foolishly use their own voices, which can later be used to identify them.

Then there is the getaway vehicle or vehicles, usually a car, but occasionally a bicycle or even a scooter, which moves more easily through modern urban traffic. I have even experienced occasional old-time bank robbers who rely on foot speed. Others pick a rural bank near a swamp or a drainage ditch and hide their getaway car on the other side to fool old-fashioned tracking dogs.

Most bank robbers use what is known as a "switch car," i.e. a second car parked in a secluded spot not too far from the bank where they can ditch the first getaway car, whose tag number might have been recorded by an eyewitness. Bank robbers often steal a car just before the robbery to use for the immediate getaway, then ditch it and drive away in their own car (unobserved, they hope). I am always amazed how often amateur bank robbers borrow a car from a family member, making the family member an unwilling but crucial witness against them at trial.

One challenge that amateurs never seem to think of is how to safely spend the robbery proceeds, referred to in the trade as "the loot." Tellers keep stacks of marked bills to give to robbers. They are not really marked; the serial numbers are just recorded at each teller's counter. Those large-denomination bills are then fairly easy to trace. Nearly every bank now has surveillance cameras and dye-pack devices that look like stacks of bills but are actually trick bags with real bills on the outside concealing a pack of red dye and tear gas hidden inside along with a minor explosive that is set off by an electric charge hidden in the door frame of the bank. The dye pack soaks the robber and loot with dye just after he exits. Look through your wallet or purse and you will usually find a bill or two with small red splotches on the edges from a dye pack that went off.

Variations on these scenarios are endless. In Oxford, we once had a repeat offender who always used the same M.O. (modus operandi) and same disguise: He would "case," or surveil, a local bank, hide behind the back door, where he knew the first employee entered, rob the bank, and bind the employee with a pair of toy handcuffs from a store that sold theatrical supplies. His disguise was always the same: He covered his face with band-aids, leading to our name for him, the "Band-Aid Bandit." Researching old cases to see if anyone else had used the band-aid MO, I found a New York robber with horrible acne who got the nickname the

"Clearasil Bandit." When finally caught, he sued the police and media for emotional distress, claiming it was cruel to stigmatize him because of his zits. He lost.

Another unusual disguise was used by a lady bank robber I prosecuted who circled her eyes and cheeks with bright red lipstick. When caught, her car trunk was filled with Halloween masks which she said she never used because she "couldn't see out good enough," a dilemma with which most trick-or-treaters can identify. My favorite lady bank robber stuck up a bank down the road in Batesville in what became known in our office as the "boob job" bank robbery. The day before she robbed the bank, she made an appointment to have breast enhancement surgery. She had the surgery but was caught soon afterward. Who knows? Maybe it was worth it to her.

A law review article I read many years ago said that of all federal prisoners, bank robbers had the lowest average IQs. The bank robbers I've known tend to support such statistics. Since that law review article was written, I suspect that drug dealers have surpassed bank robbers as the lowest IQ inmates, but I'm sure it was true at the time. One bank robber in Holly Springs handed the teller a demand note that said, "I want money. Big bills. No exploding rubber bands. None of that shit." The teller, understanding what he meant, did not give him the dye pack, but as the robber exited, she turned over the note, which was written on the back of a check. The robber had "cleverly" obliterated the name on the check with black magic marker. He had forgotten, however, the account number at the bottom of the check. The teller gave the sheriff the name of the account holder, the robber's mother. When the robber arrived on foot at his mother's porch, the sheriff was sitting in a rocker waiting on him. That story made it all the way to the *New York Times*.

In Senatobia, one robber accidentally shot his partner, then shot out the bank surveillance cameras after first smiling into it. The film, which was not damaged, clearly identified him and resulted in his conviction. His partner was caught while seeking medical treatment. One deputy sheriff in Tallahatchie County wasn't razor-sharp either. After a bank robber got away, the deputy found what he thought were $20 bills outside the bank. Thinking he'd recovered loot, he carried it back into the bank. Unfortunately, it was an unexploded dye pack, which blew up inside and covered the bank's interior—and the deputy—with red dye and tear gas.

Another robber, eager to get going, grabbed a customer who was standing in front of him in line to push her out of his way. The lady, apparently accustomed to unwanted advances from strange men, thought she was being molested and threw the man to the ground, knocking him out. A teller called the police, who arrested the robber before he woke up. Even more incompetent was a fat robber who fell down outside the bank and couldn't get up because his pants were too tight. He thought he "looked good" though.

There was one bank robber I felt sorry for. At arraignment, Magistrate Norman Gillespie asked if the robber had money to make bond. "It doesn't matter," he said. Gillespie, strict but sympathetic, said "What do you mean it doesn't matter?" The defendant replied, "I don't want to make bond. I'm too ashamed to go home." He stayed locked up and pleaded guilty but got a shorter sentence due to his genuine remorse.

A bank robber walked into a Clarksdale bank one day looking distracted. He handed a bag to a teller and said, "Fill it up with hundreds." She told him she would get some from the back. Once in back she told the manager what was happening. He went out and asked if he could help. The robber reiterated his demand. The manager, seeing the man looked disturbed, asked what the would-be robber would give the bank in return. He said, "I have the keys to the city." The manager asked if he had a gun or a bomb. "No," he replied. The manager then told the man "Just leave then." He did but turned around and came right back in, cursing loudly. The manager turned stern saying, "We don't allow profanity in this bank. Now stand over by the door." Cursing loudly, the man went out the door where he ran into Clarksdale police, who arrested him. In a quick patdown, they found he had a loaded .38 revolver in his pocket. He was sent to a federal prison medical center for mental evaluation, found incompetent, and civilly committed. We have not heard of him since.

One incident several people claim to have witnessed involved FBI jargon. When a crime participant gets away without being recognized, he is called an "unknown subject," or UNSUB. If a subject is known only by his first name—say, Joe—he is referred to as "Joe LNU," for "last name unknown." Some say this case involved the late Joe Ray Langston, the prominent defense attorney from Booneville, although I've heard the story attributed to others. Joe Ray, a colorful trial lawyer with many colorful clients, was cross-examining a Chinese American FBI agent from

California about a suspect. "So you say you only know the first name of this man. Is that correct?" The agent replied in the affirmative. "How can you say that when your report says this man is an Oriental, just like you?" The agent replied calmly, "I never said anything like that." Joe Ray continued, "Your report says the suspect's name is Joe LNU, does it not?" When the witness stopped laughing, the trial judge let the agent explain to the jurors and Joe Ray that LNU was not an "Oriental" name but an acronym for "last name unknown." The incident became the stuff of local legend.

One bank robber had a really bad day. During the robbery, he forgot to pull his ski mask down over his face. Then, like many bank robbers, he stopped for a six-pack during the getaway to relieve the stress. Police followed his trail of empty beer cans and found him sitting beside a lake. When he saw the police, he tried to throw his sawed-off shotgun in the lake, but it went off in midair, so he just gave up. Sawed-off shotguns are easy to conceal and effective for intimidation. With their short barrels, they can spray the whole inside of a small bank if fired. One robber I prosecuted had successfully robbed a bank near Tupelo and never been caught. A year later he robbed the same bank with another sawed-off shotgun. As he ran out he tossed the shotgun behind some shrubs by the bank's front door. This time he was caught. When the FBI searched the bushes, they found not only the second gun but also the first, still lying there, badly rusted from the robbery the same robber had done a year before.

One creepy bank robber from Alcorn County at least had a neat name: Melvis Calvary. Trying something new in good luck charms, Calvary performed an amateur black mass, sacrificing a goat to ensure success, something he'd read about in a book. It didn't work. He was caught and convicted anyway. One case gave me a chill. It involved FBI agent Wayne Tichenor and former Marshall County sheriff Osborne Bell. As the first black sheriff of Marshall County, Bell was doing well. One day he and Wayne were sitting in my office preparing to testify in one of my bank robbery trials. Wayne told us about searching a defendant and not finding a small gun he had hidden in his boot. Luckily, the defendant decided to cooperate and told Wayne where to find it. The very next afternoon Sheriff Bell came upon a long-haired white drug user shooting up in his car along a rural Marshall County road. After deputies searched the man, Bell put him in the back of his squad car. The man had a tiny single-shot .22 derringer concealed in the palm of his hand and used the weapon to shoot Bell in the head at point-blank range. Bell died of the wound.

On the lighter side was a remark I heard defense attorney Rob McDuff make to a client about a stiff sentence he'd just received: "Well, you see, it's just that this judge takes bank robbery *so seriously.*" A student reporter heard the remark, and it made the Ole Miss paper, the *Daily Mississippian*, the following day.

Mississippi is now known as much for our casinos as for our magnolias, and casinos are robbed as often as banks since they have nearly as much money. But casinos are not good targets because their security is usually better than banks. One robber went into a casino and announced a holdup. Despite the man's mask, the casino clerk recognized him as a regular customer, because of his powerful, distinctive cologne, Vegas Nights. The clerk even called him by name. The man laughed, took off his mask, and started playing the slots, pretending it was all a joke. He was later arrested when guards noticed someone had cut all the phone lines to the casino. A search of his truck found wire cutters, the mask, and a gun hidden together. He received seven years.

Bulletproof bank windows are something else, and so are the tellers behind them. The sister of Judge L. T. Senter of Aberdeen was confronted one day at her drive-through window, which was bulletproof and had no opening. "Give me some goddamn money or I'll shoot," he said. "Give it your best shot," she replied. He did, and after several whistling ricochets nearly hit him, he drove away. Al Moreton had a robber once, whose name he has forgotten, who whispered to a teller, "This is a robbery," so no one else could hear him. The teller was a veteran of other robberies and was sitting behind a bulletproof window. She whispered back, "Show me your gun." When he shook his head no, she yelled out, "You little snot, get out of here." He did.

Another hapless bank robber was a man named Edward Earl Moore, who robbed a bank to get enough money to buy a bus ticket to meet his probation officer up north. He was caught and his probation revoked. Another hapless one robbed a bank to get money to pay for the drug treatment that was a condition of his probation. He didn't learn until too late that his probation officer had already paid the bill. A robber from the town of Independence carefully covered his license plate with cloth but forgot to remove the For Sale sign, which gave his home telephone number, from the back window of his getaway pickup.

AUSA Bob Norman had a robber once who used a carved tree limb painted black as a fake gun. Bob told the judge it was a "real *stick*-up." Another of our robbers, when identified for the jury by a teller eyewitness, whispered too loudly to his attorney, "She can't tell it was me. She couldn't see anything but my eyes." Another got bad news from a juror when he testified in a strong voice, "I did *not* rob that bank." One juror in the box blurted out even louder, "Yes, you did too." A group of robbers from the Gulf Coast came to our district to rob a bank far from their area so they wouldn't be recognized. They did fine till one dawdled and got left behind. His only way home was by Greyhound bus. He used a pay phone across from the bank to call his family collect. A witness recalled seeing a robber using the pay phone. We subpoenaed the phone records for the day and the robbers were all eventually identified and convicted.

A bank at Verona was once robbed by two "gentlemen" who got scared and tossed the loot out the window of their car. Two old ladies picked up the money and flagged the men down and gave it back to them. As they sat in their car a police car came up with blue lights flashing. They raised their hands and prepared to surrender, but the police car drove on by, being on another call. The ladies, noticing the men's demeanor, wrote down their tag number and, when they learned there'd been a bank robbery, called police and gave them the number. The police quickly found the robbers, who surrendered quietly. In 2000, a defendant left behind a bank robbery note on an envelope. In the envelope was a certificate—with his name on it—indicating he had successfully completed a Department of Corrections anger management course.

A robber in Kansas City, where my daughter was going to medical school, made a classic error. After robbing six banks, he finally left enough clues that police had enough evidence to search his house. They found a to-do list that had an entry "rob bank." He got ten years in federal prison.

When a defendant wanted in one district is caught in another, the court holds a Rule 40 probable cause hearing before he is "removed," or extradited, to the prosecuting district. One day I had such a hearing in Greenville on Michael George Malone, who was wanted for a bank robbery in Oklahoma. The Oklahoma FBI agent testified that this robber had used a truly unique way to keep tellers and customers from notifying police. Just before he went out the door, he made them gather in three groups and sing a round of "Row, Row, Row Your Boat . . . gently down the stream." He forgot you could push alarms with your finger while singing. Last I saw of him, he was in custody and headed for Oklahoma.

Peacelover Shabazz: The Nation of Islam Comes to Greenville[1]

Peacelover Shabazz, known as Percy Walker before joining the Nation of Islam, was the first bank robber I ever tried, right after I joined the U.S. Attorney's Office. Al Moreton handled the case but let me sit at counsel table to learn the ropes. The characters were something else. The defendant had a shaved head and sat up totally straight and immobile the whole time. He looked like the character from old Mr. Clean commercials. Like most converts, Shabazz was more fervent in his religion than someone raised in it. As my father used to say, "There's no prude like a reformed whore." Shabazz demanded a Muslim attorney.

Fortunately, a Muslim attorney had just graduated from Ole Miss, which was under pressure to admit minorities. Although his English was a little spotty, thanks to the state university diploma privilege, Iraqi immigrant Aqbar Deedeedar was admitted to the bar automatically without taking any bar exam. Aqbar was a gentleman with formal manners, calling everyone "Sir," even those who treated him as an unwanted foreigner and called him by the "N" word behind his back. He hung out a shingle in Greenville. He did not type and wrote his legal pleadings in longhand. Being used to Arabic script, which is highly stylized, his handwriting was a work of art, more like calligraphy than handwriting.

Aqbar could not afford a vehicle, and since court hearings in criminal cases were held in Oxford, where the U.S. Marshal, Probation Officer, and U.S. Attorney all had their offices, Aqbar was obliged to ride to court on a Greyhound bus. To protect Mr. Shabazz's right to counsel, the judge had to tailor his court schedule to fit Greyhound bus schedules between Greenville and Oxford. Thanks to the exquisite courtesy and seriousness of Mr. Deedeedar, however, things went smoothly in the case despite the bizarre behavior of defendant Shabazz. At the end everyone thought Mr. Shabazz received a fair trial, despite his unusual counsel and even more unusual examining psychiatrist, Dr. Harry Fain. Dr. Fain flip-flopped from first saying Shabazz was a psychotic paranoid schizophrenic to his final opinion that Shabazz was a sane "normal" bank robber who merely acted peculiar due to excessive religious zeal.

Shabazz had been apprehended by police while dancing naked on top of his new Cadillac in the middle of Highway 61, the old Blues Highway just north of Delta State University. Shabazz had heard on his car radio that the leader of his faith, the Honorable Elijah Muhammad, had just died. Beside himself with grief, Shabazz was desperate to express his emotions. At the time the arresting officers had no idea that Shabazz had robbed a bank. It took a thorough and insightful FBI investigation by veteran agent John Neelley to put it all together.

Back on December 10, 1974, a teller at the Commercial National Bank in Greenville saw a lone black male approaching the bank: "He had a green ski mask on his head, but not pulled down. There was hair sticking way out where the eyes are supposed to be." The teller told the others, "Hey y'all, here comes the Easter Bunny." The man stopped at the door, drew the ski mask down over his face, pulled out a revolver, and shoved it in the manager's face and told him to stand up. The manager heard the robber cock the pistol as he walked up to his desk. The robber pulled out a white cloth bag and told them to put the money in it. He kept telling them to hurry up or he would "blow their heads through the ceiling." The tellers noted that the robber "was very calm and in complete control of the situation. Everything he said was clear and distinct and easily audible." The robber got away clean with more than $47,000. No clues to his identity were found until two months later.

On February 14, 1975, Officer Nassar of the Shelby Police Department was on routine patrol. "Right in the middle of town, going south on Highway 61," he met a dark blue Cadillac pulling a U-Haul trailer. "It was blowing its horn." Nassar made a U-turn "to see if he was trying to flag him down or having trouble." When Nassar caught up with the car, it was stopped "right in the middle of the road. The defendant was yelling, trying to get the other occupants out of the car." The driver "got up on top of the car and started to jump up and down on the roof. He had stripped to the waist and had only his trousers on. When another motorist tried to pass, he swung his big belt buckle and shattered their windshield."

Officer Nassar told the Sheriff's Office he "had a man stopped that looked drunk or on drugs or something." When Deputy Ello Wren arrived, the defendant had stripped completely naked and "was lying facedown on an oriental-type praying rug. He walked around naked for a while, then got on top of deputy Wren's car in a squatting kind of mood, like he was fixing to stomp his car." The deputy told Shabazz to get down off the car, but "he just grinned and kept on."

Officer Nassar finally waved his shotgun at the man and told him, "You have showed out long enough, now get down from there. The man didn't say a thing, just came right off the car, didn't give a bit of trouble." The defendant "opened the tailgate of his U-Haul-It trailer and started rummaging through it." Nassar hollered at Wren, "You need to stop him. Maybe he has a gun. I don't know what he is looking for." Deputy Wren told the defendant "You'd better stop it, or the white man here is fixing to stop you." The defendant kept referring to officer Nassar, a Lebanese-American, as "the white man" and Deputy Wren "Black Brother."

Shabazz was charged with resisting arrest. In inventorying the contents of the handbag of his wife, a deputy found she had the sawed-off barrel of a shotgun in her purse. She also had a newspaper clipping of the December 1974 bank robbery in Greenville and a drawing of the bank.

Following the indictment of Shabazz for the bank robbery, attorney Deedeedar filed a motion for a psychiatric examination. The psychiatrist's report to the court said that the defendant was neither competent to stand trial nor responsible for his actions during the robbery "in the absence of overwhelming testimony of more *proximal* witnesses." At the hearing on his sanity, Shabazz vigorously challenged the finding of incompetency and tried to demonstrate that he was competent to stand trial. The court eventually agreed, over the objection of attorney Deedeedar.

At trial, a bank customer identified the defendant as "fitting the image of his recollection." The head teller, who had first called him the Easter Bunny, was also positive: "I know that man when I see him. I have nightmares about it. I can still see him now." Another teller who saw the robber before he pulled his mask down, testified, "That is the *nose* I saw that day—the eyes, the ears, the face, the cheeks. He fits the description all the way along every part." When pressed on cross-examination, she testified, "I feel sure if I could hear him talk I would know for sure." After the defendant was directed to speak, she said, "I feel you are him."

A justice of the peace testified that a writ for collection for unpaid rent had been served on the defendant in Greenville the day before the robbery and that the overdue rent plus costs were paid just two days after the robbery. Receipts in the wife's purse showed expenditures for the month after the robbery of more than $28,000. None of the $47,000 taken in the robbery was recovered. Other evidence showed that in January 1975, in Detroit, Shabazz had paid cash for a TV set, had had substantial work done on his 1973 Cadillac, and had paid cash for the purchase of a house in Kansas City.

The defendant called his wife as a witness. She testified that he was at home with her on the day of the robbery and that their expenditures were all from funds provided by a temple of the Nation of Islam in Kansas City. She said the diagram in her purse was planted there by police, along with the newspaper clipping about the robbery. The defendant then called Dr. Harry Fain, who testified as to his initial evaluation of defendant, saying that he had given him only a "tentative" diagnosis of paranoid schizophrenia at the time of the robbery. His first report was qualified, however, by a lack of serious information from "proximal" witnesses and was based almost entirely on the fact that Shabazz appeared so disturbed when he came in and because of the grandiosity of his religious claims. "Crazy people often think they're Jesus," Dr. Fain testified. With the additional information available to him from the evidence at trial, Dr. Fain dramatically reversed his opinion and testified that the defendant was sane and that he could "find no reason to believe defendant lacked the capacity to appreciate the wrongfulness of his conduct, and that he could have conformed his conduct to the requirements of law." Fain concluded that "most significant was his refusal to take the MMPI [Minnesota Multiphasic Personality Inventory] test which is specifically designed to detect malingering, or faking."

Peacelover Shabazz had, in large part, convicted himself despite the best efforts of his able, bus-riding Muslim attorney. The judge sentenced Shabazz to fifteen years in federal prison, and we never heard from him again. Attorney Deedeedar moved off up north, and we never heard from him again either.

Sorry about That Bum Rap, Johnny Paul[2]

Another of my favorite cases was technically not a bank robbery at all but the burglary of the post office in Victoria, Mississippi, in June 1974. A veteran criminal named Johnny Paul Washam and two accomplices did the burglary, netting 679 readily negotiable blank postal money orders. To meet the legal definition of *robbery*, the defendant must steal directly from another person, normally by use of a weapon or by intimidation, which is called a "strong-arm" robbery. In legal terms, *burglary* is the taking of property by breaking and entering a residence or business with no one present. If someone is present, it becomes robbery, punishable more harshly because of the danger to the victim.

In the Victoria job, the proof was slim and the witnesses few. For me, it was a training exercise in which I mainly sat and watched veteran prosecutor Al Moreton try the case. The proof was simple. A postal expert from the crime lab testified that shoe prints on envelopes found on the floor of the post office the morning after the burglary bore the imprint of an unusual shoe sole identical to one seized from defendant Washam, who claimed never to have been in that post office in his life. A search of the defendants' car yielded other evidence against Washam and the other two men, William Jan Hoover and Carrol Lee Wyatt. After their arrests, Washam jumped bond and was a fugitive for over a year, twice escaping from jails in Tennessee. In his absence, Judge Keady severed the trials of the defendants. Al Moreton first tried Wyatt in October 1974 and convicted him. Al then tried Hoover while Washam was still a fugitive. Wyatt had agreed to testify and gotten his sentence cut for agreeing to testify that Washam had planned the burglary and that all three burglars had broken in together and stolen the money orders.

In his usual calm, cerebral way Al Moreton first called his shoe-print expert, who was impressive and unshaken on cross-examination. Then he called the accomplice Wyatt, who described in great and convincing detail how the burglars planned the job and committed it. As he always did, Al questioned the witness slowly, holding back the most vivid facts till the end of his examination to heighten the jurors' interest. In this case, Al held back the names of the perpetrators, planning to close with a dramatic in-court identification of Hoover by Wyatt. When he reached that critical point, Al asked Wyatt whether he saw in the courtroom one of his partners in the burglary. Wyatt made a big point of looking all around the courtroom. "No sir, I don't." I looked up at Al, whose grip on the podium had tightened, but who looked calm as ever. "Look again," he said. The witness did. "Now do you recognize him?" Hoover replied, "No sir, sure don't."

Al tried a different tactic. "Alright then, do you recall the names of the men who were with you?" Wyatt replied firmly, "Yes, sir." Encouraged, Al proceeded: "Alright then. Would you please look at the jurors and tell them the names of the two men who broke into the post office with you?" Wyatt looked straight at the jury and said, "Yes, sir. Their names are Ray Blackwell and Harvey Crowell." This time I thought I saw Al's knees buckle, but he never showed any surprise to the jury. In excruciating detail, he took Wyatt right back through the case: the planning, discussions, execution, getaway, and apprehension of the burglars. Somehow, largely by his demeanor and grasp of details, Al seemed supremely confident of his case. Never did he raise his voice or accuse the witness of lying, but by his subtle sequence of questions he made it clear what had to have happened: With his sentence already cut in advance, Wyatt was lying to save his partner. The result: a hung jury. A month later, Al tried Hoover again. This time, Wyatt testified for the defense, and Hoover was acquitted.

In August 1975, Johnny Paul Washam was finally caught. Al immediately put him on trial, with Wyatt again testifying for the defense. This time I participated as Al's partner in examining witnesses and arguing to the jury. For the jurors, it had to be a tough case. They stayed out deliberating for two full days. When they returned, it was with a well-reasoned verdict that gave me an early lesson in juror wisdom. They found Washam guilty on the same evidence on which they'd found Hoover not guilty. One critical fact had apparently persuaded them: Washam's jumping bail. The judge had instructed the jury in the standard way that "flight of a person, when accused, may constitute proof of consciousness of guilt." That instruction, from a federal judge, who is often regarded by jurors as speaking with God's own voice, turned the tide.

At his sentencing, Washam recited a poem about freedom he had written in his cell. The poem centered on the beauty of spring, the budding trees, the blossoming flowers and fresh air that he, Johnny Paul Washam, as a habitual offender in his forties, would never breathe again if the judge gave him the expected sentence. Judge Keady, a kind and philosophical man with a soft spot for a good con man, whether defendant or lawyer, surprised me. "Johnny Paul Washam," he said. "You have a heart full of poetry and a lot of talent for persuading people of just about anything. But instead of using that talent for good, you have squandered it. You have become a menace to society." He then proceeded to give Washam twenty years plus four years plus four more years, all to run consecutive to each other and to two other state sentences Washam still had to serve. The sentences virtually guaranteed that Washam would die in prison. I always thought that Judge Keady was influenced partly by the calm determination of Al Moreton in overcoming insurmountable odds to convict the recidivist Washam. It was as if the old judge could not let the old prosecutor down, and together they would protect society.

On appeal, Washam's main issue was the way I "vilified" him in closing argument. Years later, while writing the first draft of this book, relying on my memory alone, Al had to remind me of this fact. At first I didn't even remember making the argument. When Al showed me the transcript, however, it was clear that the wording could only have been mine, not Al's. Despite my inflammatory insults to the defendant, the Fifth Circuit affirmed both convictions.

But that was not the end of the story. Years later, I was teaching a training course for new prosecutors in Washington, D.C. During a riotous time one late night, after lots of wine and trial stories, one of my instructors said, "You should play a little trick on Washam. Get an AUSA from Hawaii to send a postcard from Honolulu to Washam in the federal pen." I asked one of my Hawaiian friends to do it, and he did. At that time, I knew next to nothing about how much trouble inmates can cause prosecutors by claiming that their rights have been violated, but it seemed like a good idea at the time.

Anyway, I wrote out a little message for the AUSA from Hawaii to put on a postcard and send to Washam in federal prison in Atlanta. The postcard, which had a color picture of beautiful Hawaiian girls dancing the hula in grass skirts, said simply,

Dear Johnny Paul,
Having a wonderful time. Sorry about that bum rap you took."
Sincerely, Harvey & Ray

At first, I didn't tell Al what I'd done. When I finally did tell him, he worried for a couple of years that Washam would use the card as proof that Ray Blackwell and Harvey Crowell really existed. Even if I admitted what I'd done, Washam would claim prosecutorial harassment. For whatever reason, Washam never complained. Maybe the postcard never arrived. Maybe some lonely inmate clerk stole the picture and kept it for himself. Maybe Washam enjoyed the joke. Maybe he was too embarrassed to admit he'd been had. Who knows what happens in federal prisons?

A Running Robber: George of the Swamp[3]

If I had to name my favorite homegrown North Mississippi bank robber, it might be George House Jr. A stocky man of low intellect but much experience, House robbed many banks. I first learned of him from retired Greenville police captain Buddy Wilkinson, the bodyguard, or "court crier," for Judge Keady. In theory, a court crier's duty is to open court by heralding the judge's entrance with the loud, time-honored cry: "Hear Ye, Hear Ye, United States District Court is now open according to law. Chief Judge Keady presiding. God save the United States and this honorable court." A marshal at the U.S. Supreme Court, miffed by the Court's liberal, prodefendant rulings under former Chief Justice Earl Warren, once rephrased the cry to "God save the United States *from* this honorable court."

Federal courts are big on ritual. The judge enters in his black robe, ascends the bench, and invariably states, "Be seated, please." Another ritual takes place just before "Hear Ye" when the crier suddenly yells out, "All rise!" and the spectators are required to stand. After some of the heated trials I've seen, this intimidating ritual is a pretty good way for judges to enforce order before things get disputatious. The phrase is memorable enough that Judge Keady titled his book of memoirs *All Rise*.

Buddy often told me how he chased George House on foot through the streets of Greenville after one of his bank robberies. When Buddy crawled up under a shotgun house after him, House emptied an entire handgun at him but missed, and Buddy got his man. Before I arrived as a prosecutor, AUSA Al Moreton had already tried House for robbing the branch bank at Stoneville, a sleepy town near Greenville. Having no car, House paid a guy to drive him there. The driver later testified he figured House planned to rob the bank—there was not much else to do in Stoneville except work at the agricultural experiment station, where they studied boll weevils, and House had little interest in them. The driver said he was too scared of House to say no, but after he dropped House off and promised to pick him up in five minutes, the driver headed straight back to Greenville. He testified that although he was too scared to refuse to take House, he was even more scared of getting caught in a gun battle during the getaway and figured George would be caught and in prison and unable to retaliate.

It was a hot, quiet morning in the Delta when House entered the bank. He approached the one teller cage, which was empty. He yelled for service. No answer. He went back outside and saw a man tending rose bushes in front of the bank. "Can I get some service here?" House asked. "Alright," said the man, reluctantly laying down his hoe, putting on his jacket, and adjusting his tie. When the teller assumed his position behind the cage, House produced a pistol and announced it was a holdup. The teller calmly gave him the money and House rushed out to find he had no getaway driver. Being a practical man and an extremely healthy one, House started running the five or six miles back to Greenville. As he reached the city limits, a sheriff's car pulled up and arrested the breathless House without incident.

The first time I saw House was in the federal courtroom in Oxford, where I was to try him for robbing another federally insured bank. Al Moreton had told me to consult the state DA at Greenville, Frank Carlton, about what to ask House on cross-examination if he took the stand. Frank regaled me with George House stories. One was about his training regimen. While in the pen, House always kept in shape, running wind sprints in the prison yard. On one occasion, when confined behind a fence as punishment, he got a heavy cane pole and began practicing pole-vaulting over fences, which was otherwise unnecessary at Parchman, a plantation prison farm so remote that there were no other fences, just open land with swamps so impenetrable it was said that *almost* no one had ever escaped from there, though many had tried. One exception, a trusty, took advantage of the privileges he received and fled to Massachusetts. When asked if the prison was getting too lax, gaffe-prone Governor Ross Barnett explained, "If you can't trust a trusty, who can you trust?"

As in the prison in the movie *Cool Hand Luke*, which to me closely resembles Parchman, officers on horseback using bloodhounds could easily catch fleeing inmates before they ever got off the vast plantation. Frank Carlton's favorite story about House involved one of his more successful escape attempts. Somehow avoiding a head count, House made it through the swamps overnight all the way to Ruleville (home of civil rights pioneer Fannie Lou Hamer) some eight miles south, where he went straight to the town's only drive-in. Hunkering down on the ground beneath the drive-through ledge, House ordered five cheeseburgers, five fries, and five milkshakes. The waitress, seeing he was alone and on foot and covered with mud and that his face was swollen with mosquito bites, figured he was an escaped inmate. To keep him from leaving, she gave him his order and called the sheriff. By the time the sheriff got there, House had finished most of the meal and was too tired to run. "We got you now, George," a deputy said. Bold as ever, House said through a mouthful of cheeseburger, "You boys didn't catch me. You *rescued* me."

My own experience with George House was much tamer. Released once again, he robbed a bank in the Delta and fled into a swamp known as the Bogue Phalia [pronounced fuh-lie-uh] near Marks, where the famous Poor People's March on Washington began in 1968. FBI agent Wayne Tichenor called me at home to tell me that the famous bank robber was on the run and asked if I wanted to go along for the chase. DOJ rules discourage prosecutors from being on crime scenes for fear they will end up being witnesses and disqualified from trying the cases. But this case was special. Parchman was sending its best tracking dogs—bloodhounds to track on the ground and German shepherds to "wind" or sniff him out in the air above the swamp. The search leader was to be none other than Quitman County sheriff Jack Harrison, whom Wayne and I had just unsuccessfully prosecuted for beating up an inmate, a story told in detail in the chapter on *Civil Rights* (see chapter 3).

The search was exciting, with horses and dogs running everywhere. A mosquito-bitten and exhausted House meekly surrendered around noon the next day. The trial was pretty quiet except for the moment when I learned that the inmate dog trainer, who had been paroled and had absconded, was not available to testify. Harrison sarcastically asked me if I planned to call the dog to the stand. I refrained from saying the dog had a better criminal record than he did. We were, after all, brothers in law enforcement.

The main drama in the trial was the last day. Throughout the trial, House had worn heavy boots. On the last day, House persuaded the marshals to let him wear prison-issue tennis shoes. As Frank Carlton had warned me, tennis shoes were the sign George was going to make a run for it. In those more naive days, tenderness for the rights of defendants required that all defendants, however violent, had to appear in court unrestrained, lest the jury be prejudiced against them. Even back then, however, House's reputation prevailed. The judge ordered his hands and feet shackled to a heavy chair behind a blanket over counsel table, out of sight of the jurors, who were taken in and out of the courtroom and never saw him restrained. That avenue closed, House remained in court for the verdict and was sentenced to a long term in a federal pen; I never saw or heard of him again.

A Teller's Life Is Saved by Robber Incompetence[4]

On November 12, 1981, two men appeared on a used car lot in Helena, Arkansas, directly across the river bridge from the Mississippi Delta. One, a tall, fair-skinned black male in his late teens had freckles and a medium afro. His companion, a darker, heavier man in his mid-twenties, wore a long expensive black leather coat and a fancy homburg hat with the brim turned up, known in the area as a "go-to-hell" hat. The younger man told the salesman he wanted to test-drive a green Ford LTD and would "go by the bank to get some money." The irony of that statement did not become apparent until later that day. With business slow, the salesman reluctantly let them take the car, which they drove away in the direction of the bridge to Mississippi. The car bore no license tag at the time. The two men never returned.

At about 9:20 a.m., in nearby Lula, Mississippi, manager Kay Powell and teller Mary Alice Arnold were the only people in the bank. They saw three men drive up in a green Ford LTD and look around in a suspicious way. Two men got out of the car, then got quickly back in and drove around the corner when another car appeared. Mrs. Powell, who had been robbed before and had attended an FBI seminar on how to handle bank robberies, went to the door and called out the car's tag number to Mrs. Arnold, who wrote it down: Tennessee # AMA 151. How the Tennessee tag got on the car was never explained.

Shortly thereafter, a man entered the bank wearing a black homburg hat and long black leather coat, but no mask. When Mrs. Powell asked if she could help him, he said, "You're damn right. This is a stickup, and you better do what I say if you don't want to get hurt." The man held a black revolver in which Mrs. Powell could see the "little round chamber" with bullets in it. A second man, taller, thinner, and younger with fair skin, freckles, and an afro, entered and held another gun on the two women. The one in the black leather coat vaulted the teller's counter, threatening to kill the two women. He slapped Mrs. Powell and told her to "Open the damn drawers." He struck her again "real hard" when she stepped forward to put the money in a flowered pillowcase he was holding.

The first robber began grabbing money from the teller drawer, which also held the bank's alarm, a package of bait money with recorded serial numbers, and a dye pack concealed in what appeared to be a packet of $10 bills. The first robber filled his pockets, then stuffed the security pack down the front of his pants, unwittingly triggering the silent alarm, which went off in the Coahoma Bank directly across the street. As the second robber escorted Mrs. Powell to the vault, the phone rang next to Mrs. Arnold, who asked the first robber if he wanted her to answer it. "You're damn right I do," he told her, adding, "If you fuck up, I'm going to kill you." The caller was a teller from the bank across the street. The first robber placed his gun to the back of Mrs. Arnold's head, and she heard the gun make a metallic click. The caller asked if they had set off their alarm. Mrs. Arnold said, "No," hung up, and told the robber it was a wrong number. When the bait money was pulled, it had activated the bank's surveillance camera facing the teller cages; the camera took a series of remarkably clear pictures of the robbers, neither of whom was masked. After obtaining $26,242, the robbers made the women lie on the floor and fled. Mrs. Powell looked out the door and saw the same green car driving away about a block down the street when a big cloud of red smoke began to pour out of the car. The first robber got out and fled on foot.

Officers called to the scene included the town marshal, county sheriff, highway patrol, and FBI. An airplane and helicopter were called in for the chase. At the place where the first robber exited the car, officers found a loaded .32 H&R revolver beside the flowered pillowcase loot bag, as well as $21,798 in cash from the bank. One officer went north toward Tennessee and found the green Ford LTD, whose visible VIN plate identified it as the one stolen from the Arkansas car dealer an hour earlier. The keys were still in the car, and the seat belt warning buzzer was still buzzing. Inside were bills stained with red dye, money wrappers marked "United Southern Bank, Lula," and a surgical glove like the one that could be seen on the second robber's hand in the bank surveillance photos. There were red dye stains all over the abandoned getaway car.

Neighbors told officers that the robber on foot had headed toward a wooded area near Muddy Bayou north of Lula. Chuck Johnson, the son of the town marshal, whose family farmed some ten thousand acres, heard his mother broadcast the information about the getaway route on his CB radio and went to an abandoned tenant house near Muddy Bayou and waited inside. Shortly a dark object that Johnson thought was a coyote, common in that area, moved up a cotton row from the bayou. Johnson thought about shooting it but waited. When the helicopter flew over, however, the "coyote" raised up, and Johnson saw that it was a man wearing a homburg hat and a long black leather coat. The man began to run away. Johnson fired a warning shot from his rifle and the man stopped, raised his hands, and said he was not armed. His hands and clothes were covered with red dye stains.

Sheriff Jesse Bonner arrived to arrest the man. After being advised of his rights, the man gave his name as Robert Wilson but refused to answer further questions. He did, however, ask for medical attention, pointing to his crotch, where the dye pack had exploded. He was taken back to town to the doctor, photographed, and taken by FBI agent Wayne Tichenor to the bank, where he was made to stand outside the drive-through window for viewing. Mrs. Powell immediately made a positive identification, as did Mrs. Arnold. The first robber was identified as Tony Craft of Youngstown, Ohio, who was on federal parole following two prior bank robbery convictions. His brother, Mancy "Man" Craft, was apprehended a month later in Youngstown. The driver was never identified or apprehended.

Fearing prejudice and relying mostly on legal defenses, attorney Arlen Coyle waived a jury trial and asked Judge Keady to sit as both judge and jury. We agreed. Coyle also protested that Tony Craft's postrobbery identifications at the bank's drive-through window were unlawfully suggestive. Judge Keady found them "suggestive, but not unduly so."

Powell and Arnold testified that the robbery lasted about five minutes and that they had excellent opportunities to observe the robbers at close range. In open court, the two women positively identified Tony Craft as the first of the two robbers, noting his "high cheekbones" and "mean eyes." Hosia Nixon, owner of a record shop and clothing store in nearby Tunica, positively identified Tony Craft as the man who bought the black homburg hat a few days before the bank robbery. Nixon testified that when Craft bought the hat, he was already wearing the same black leather coat in which he was later apprehended. Fay Perkins, a shy, thin young woman, testified that in late October 1981, she rode from Youngstown to Tunica with her cousin Tony Craft in his new gray Lincoln Continental to attend a funeral. Tony went back to Youngstown but returned to Tunica the week of the robbery, this time with his nineteen-year-old brother Man, who stayed with Miss Perkins and her grandparents in Tunica. The night before the bank robbery Man left the house walking and never returned. Miss Perkins looked at bank surveillance photographs and courageously and unhesitatingly identified her cousins Man and Tony as the robbers.

In a dramatic ending, we closed our case by calling an ATF firearms expert, who testified that the seized H&R .32 revolver was loaded with .32 automatic shells rather than regular .32-caliber revolver ammunition. He concluded that the thinner rim on the automatic shells had caused a misfire, since the firing pin could not properly strike the bullet's primer and thus the primer did not ignite to fire the bullet. He testified that the firing pin mark on the unfired live shell found in the gun after the robbery was made by that gun. The metallic clicking heard by Mrs. Arnold, he testified, showed conclusively that the robber had tried unsuccessfully to shoot Mrs. Arnold in the head during the robbery and that she had survived only because the gun was loaded with the wrong ammunition. We knew this fact before trial but did not tell Mrs. Arnold, who was already scared to death about testifying. At the next recess, when I told her of her brush with death during the robbery, she was cooler than I expected: "When I heard that click, I thought he had tried to shoot me. It just wasn't my time, I guess."

No Further Questions in Mound Bayou

One of my personal favorite bank robber stories happened while I was Judge Keady's law clerk, long before I started at the U.S. Attorney's office. It involved the robbery of a bank in Mound Bayou, an old, all-black town in the Delta on Highway 61. Al Moreton tried the case, but neither he nor I can recall the name of the robber nor find a file that resembles it. As the story has evolved in retelling over the years, it goes like this:

In the 1960s, a bank in Mound Bayou decided it was a good idea to station an employee at a desk by the front door to greet customers as they came in, answer their questions, and direct them to the proper teller or bank officer to transact their business—sort of like a greeter at Wal-Mart today, but with more authority. A stern retired schoolteacher was hired for the position. She relished the authority, fitting somewhat the same role as Aunt Esther on Fred Sanford.

One day a young, impolite and decidedly unsouthern "customer" walked in and strode straight up to her. "Bitch," he said, "Give me some damn money and make it quick." Totally unfazed, the retired teacher addressed him dismissively: "Young man, don't take that tone with me. And by the way, if you're such a bank robber, where's your bag?" After a couple of menacing looks, the robber lowered his gun, snorted, and went on to the tellers, apparently concluding he'd get nowhere with the retired schoolteacher. The rest of the robbery was pretty traditional, featuring loot, cameras, eyewitnesses, and eventual apprehension.

At the trial, the retired teacher took the stand and clearly and distinctly identified and pointed out the robber. On cross-examination, the defense attorney tried some standard tricks. First he asked her about her age and her memory, an approach she obviously resented. Then he questioned her eyesight, again stressing her age. Finally he asked her if it wasn't true that she was so mad at the bank robber's rudeness that it had clouded her judgment and caused her to want to identify his client whether he was the robber or not. The teacher replied, "Would you please repeat that question?" After a rambling, repetitious question, the teacher replied in an outraged voice, "If you are trying to impugn my integrity, you can just forget about it!" The attorney quickly said, "No further questions" and withdrew from challenging her as fast as his client had.

A Preacher in a Volvo Robs an Oxford Bank[5]

One of my personal favorite bank robbers was Anthony Lewis, a suave and educated Seventh Day Adventist preacher from Chicago. I'll never forget his guilty plea after robbing a bank in Oxford. When a bored Chief Judge Neal Biggers came to the standard question about how far the defendant had gone in school, Lewis replied in clear, clipped diction, "I have a master's of divinity degree, Your Honor." The judge peered down over the top of his glasses at Lewis, briefly speechless. Lewis was definitely not your average bank robber, who normally can barely remember what grade he was in when he dropped out.

The preacher had come to Oxford on church business and had unexpectedly fallen in love with a beautiful young woman there. Desperate not to lose her and to have enough money to woo her successfully, Lewis devised a bank robbery plan only a bookish man would believe in: Using his gray, church-owned Volvo station wagon, he decided to rob a bank in the old Kroger shopping center, thinking he could make a quick getaway up nearby Highway 7 to Memphis.

Lewis's disguise was fairly effective—a pair of dark shades and a hat with the earflaps down like on that old Johnny Carson TV skit with a farmer from Minnesota wearing a heavy plaid jacket. Lewis, however, looked out of place in steamy Oxford in his odd costume. Lewis's weapon was better—a fake bomb made of a small cardboard box wrapped in duct tape with red and green wires sticking out all over. The fake bomb convinced the teller it was for real and she gave him her money. Luckily for Lewis, the bank was loaded with Kroger receipts ready to be picked up by armored truck, so Lewis netted more than $30,000. But he was not destined to keep it long.

As he drove away, Lewis's problems began. A nervous amateur in a hurry, Lewis made a mistake and picked rush hour for the job. Being from Chicago, he probably thought Oxford didn't have rush hours. When he drove away from the bank, he tried to turn left up Highway 7 but was blocked by a long line of cars. Panicking, he turned right on University Avenue, which funneled this stranger, who knew no back streets, downtown toward the packed Oxford Square. Easily identified by his practical, professor-looking Volvo station wagon, he was quickly apprehended by police along with all his loot. The fake bomb he left behind in the bank was covered with his fingerprints.

Veteran defense attorney Ron Lewis (no relation) was appointed to represent Anthony Lewis. Ron himself is quite a story, being a graduate of both Dartmouth and Harvard, so Judge Biggers and I faced an unusually educated defense team. Ron dutifully filed motions for mental exams, which were denied by Judge Biggers, who rightly reasoned that stupid isn't crazy. When we learned from the probation officer's presentence report that Lewis's motive for the robbery was to get money to please a pretty young woman, his insanity claim seemed even less believable. When he lost his motions, Lewis tried briefly to fire Ron Lewis and bring down a Chicago lawyer, but the judge denied that motion, too, taking it for just a delaying tactic. After his guilty plea and sentencing, Lewis fruitlessly pursued from prison for over a decade various arcane legal technicalities and jailhouse appeals. All failed. In the year 2000 he was finally released on parole.

Of all his many pleas, one will remain with me forever. When Judge Biggers asked him at sentencing if he had anything to say, Lewis made the usual apologies and pleas for mercy. Then this black man from the North spontaneously gave one of the greatest compliments to the people of Oxford and our local Mississippi justice system that I've ever heard: "Your Honor, I've been treated with more courtesy and respect by people here in Oxford as a bank robber than I was ever treated in Chicago as a minister of the Gospel." Case closed.

Full-Service Bankers[6]

One day the high sheriff of Tippah County came to visit Buck Tatum Jr., president of the Bank of Falkner. The sheriff told Tatum that trusties in his jail were saying that an inmate had been bragging about how easy it would be to rob the bank at Falkner. The bank was a competitor of the bank founded by William Faulkner's grandfather. Tatum Jr. did not take kindly to people robbing his bank. Accompanied by the sheriff, he went straight to the jail and confronted the inmate, Dewayne Porterfield: "I hear you've been running your mouth about robbing my bank. If you do, I'll track you down and catch you myself and have you put away in

Parchman Prison forever." Experienced criminals like Porterfield dreaded Parchman, a hellish place on a fifty-thousand-acre plantation deep in the Delta where inmates worked every day, often in one-hundred-degree heat in the summer, and spent every night in open, un-air-conditioned, unheated barracks with dozens of violent and dangerous inmates. Tatum figured his threat would protect the bank's customers and employees from harm.

A couple of weeks later, Tatum received a phone call from the manager of a branch of his bank located several miles away in the tiny town of Walnut. The bank had been robbed. Tatum immediately said, "It's that damn, stupid Dee-Wayne (as everyone pronounced it). I guess I should have told him to stay away from Walnut, too." Tatum called the sheriff, who verified that Dewayne Porterfield had slipped out of the jail that morning with another inmate named Ross. The two men had been seen walking toward Walnut. The sheriff said his deputies were looking for the two and would probably catch them that same day. But Buck Tatum was not waiting. He called his brother-in-law, Woody Childers, board chairman of the Bank of Falkner, and said, "Woody, that damn Dee-Wayne has robbed our bank after I specifically told him not to. We need to get him." Childers was equally outraged: "Wait there, Buck Junior, I'll be right over." Childers picked up Buck Jr. in his yellow Cadillac, and they drove madly around Tippah County, looking for the robbers without success. After an hour or so, Childers's Cadillac overheated and started to smoke, so they switched to Buck Jr.'s pickup, which gave them a moment to stop and think. Tatum asked Childers, "If you were that damn, stupid Dee-Wayne and had robbed a bank, what would you do?" Childers, who knew Dee-Wayne, thought for a moment and said, "Head for the nearest beer joint?" Tatum thought some more: "And if those fellows were right who said they were on foot, which way would you go?" Childers wondered, "Try to hitch a ride to Memphis?" Buck Jr. agreed.

The brothers-in-law remembered a little beer joint on the shortest route from Walnut to Memphis and took off for it at high speed like something out of the *Dukes of Hazzard*. As their pickup topped a rise, they saw two men walking slowly along. One was tall and skinny like Dee-Wayne, the other shorter and stockier. "Surely it's not them," Buck Jr. said. But it was. Buck Jr. and Woody pulled up alongside the walkers. Tatum pointed his pistol at them and told them to stop. The shorter man, who was carrying a shotgun, laid it carefully on the ground. Buck Jr. said, "Put your hands up." They did. While Childers kept his own pistol pointed at them, Tatum patted both men down for other weapons, finding none, but discovered the loot from his bank on Porterfield.

The bankers did not quite know what to do next. It was before the days of cell phones and Buck Jr. cursed himself for not having a CB radio in his pickup. He also wished he had some handcuffs. Finally, he said, "You drive, Woody. I'll keep them in the back." Tatum lowered the tailgate and ordered the tired, dusty robbers into the back of his pickup. Then he stopped. Later Tatum told me what he was thinking at the time: "I don't want to screw this up. These citizen arrest deals can be tricky." So he proceeded to advise Porterfield and Ross of their rights, reciting them as best he could from TV crime shows he'd watched over the years. Both robbers pled guilty and to their relief were sent not to Parchman but to federal prison. Although the federal joints were air-conditioned and had better guards, the companionship was probably not much better. As noted in *Careers in Crime*, "prison wife" is the worst of all criminal careers, ranking #50.

After the sentencing of Porterfield and Ross, I figured I'd seen the last of Buck Tatum, but several years later I found myself confronting him in my office during a plea-bargaining session with his lawyers. We had some good laughs about Dee-Wayne and how the bankers had given the robbers a citizen's advice of rights. Then we got down to business. Through a series of bad business deals, Buck Jr. had gotten himself in a deep financial hole. His only way out was to embezzle from his own bank, which he did. His family members caught him with the help of the FDIC. The stress of the investigation caused him to have a major heart attack, and it was a much thinner and older Buck Jr. I faced in my office. We reached a plea agreement under which he would testify in other unrelated cases of which he had knowledge. One interested me especially because a bank bag with $50,000 had been found just sitting on the floor of the vault of the Bank of Falkner. The money was not in a safety deposit box and was not listed on the bank's books. Pinned to it with a simple safety pin was a piece of cardboard that said, "Property of Thurston Little." "Buck," I asked him, "What was that $50,000 for?" He replied, "Well, I don't know for sure. I just let Thurston keep it there in the vault as a favor. I didn't charge him for keeping it and didn't pay him any interest on it either. He would just go in now and then and put some in or take some out. I never asked him about it and didn't really want to know. But you know Thurston, he just had to tell me about it. I don't know if it's true, but he said it was to buy votes and pay off public officials, but that's just what he said. You know Thurston." Another prosecutor handled Buck's embezzlement case after that, and I haven't seen him since.

At Last a Professional: Presidential Mask Bank Robber Caught in Our District[7]

In 1992, the Canadian Broadcasting Company did a prime-time special on a fugitive said to be the most "professional" bank robber of the twentieth century, a Canadian named Patrick Michael Mitchell. A book about his robberies, *The Stopwatch Gang*, was already a best-seller, and the gang's MO of wearing presidential masks was featured in the movie *Point Break* with Patrick Swayze.

Born in a poor Irish neighborhood in Ottawa, Paddy Mitchell was an unusual fellow: a bank robber competent in his chosen profession. Although he remained all his life basically a thief, he managed to give bank robbers a brief aura of glamour, at least until he was caught in 1994 by Southaven chief of police Tom Long and his officers and sent to prison for the rest of his life by federal prosecutors Charlie Spillers and Chad Lamar of our office.

Mitchell began quietly enough. He went straight to work from high school, married, had a son and drove a soft-drink truck. But he also kept bad company, hanging out in Ottawa bars. Using his natural ability for scheming, Mitchell began his "career" planning heists for other people in exchange for a cut of the loot. Soon he wanted more of the profits for himself. Finally, when he netted more from hijacking one liquor truck than he would have made in a year delivering soft drinks, he turned to robbery full time. In 1973, he formed a three-man gang with Stephen Reid, a hippie, and Lionel Wright, a reclusive newspaper clerk. The strange fact that his partners were named *Reid* and *Wright* should have been an omen this was not an average group. Reid later became a published writer of novels about bank robbers. What are the odds of that?

The trio began robbing banks in unusual ways. They always called attention to themselves, which is usually unwise, however gratifying it is to the ego. Mitchell carried a large stopwatch around his neck during robberies. He insisted his jobs be so well planned that his gang could be in and out of the bank in one hundred seconds—less than two minutes. For a few years, Mitchell robbed for a living while telling his wife he was going to his humdrum job every day. Eventually, however, there were too many absences and too much to explain, so he simply abandoned her and his young son and went on the road for good.

With Reid and Wright, he went on a robbery spree across Canada that reached its height in 1974 with the Great Gold Heist, in which the trio stole $1.8 million in gold bars from an armored truck at the Ottawa airport. Errors in this flamboyant caper finally resulted in their arrests and convictions, with Reid sentenced to ten years in prison, Wright seventeen, and the mastermind, Mitchell, twenty. Within two years, however, all three had escaped from prison. Wright went first, simply walking away through a hole in a prison-yard fence. Reid's prison break required more planning, but he finally got away while on a field trip for rehab training in woodworking.

Shortly thereafter, Mitchell made a much more challenging escape that is still a legend among prison inmates across the U.S. and Canada. Learning that it was possible to fake a heart attack by swallowing liquid nicotine leached from cigarette butts soaked overnight in water, Mitchell overdid it. Instead of one cigarette, Mitchell soaked a whole pack of cigarettes in a big glass of water, then ran three miles around the prison exercise yard before drinking the nicotine solution. It nearly killed him. His heart attack symptoms were so real that guards rushed him to a nearby hospital, where his old partners Reid and Wright were waiting for him disguised as emergency-room workers. All three got away and hid out for days in a nearby basement while Mitchell recovered from his near-death experience. His heart had nearly exploded.

Mitchell and his Stopwatch Gang decided to move operations to the United States, believing that they were too hot in Canada. South of the border they began a spectacular spree of bank robberies, glorying in their m.o. as the "stopwatch gang." They enjoyed women, drugs, and life on the beach, not to mention fine cigars and the best champagne. But most of all they loved the adrenaline rush of the robberies themselves, which

Mitchell compared to a long cocaine high. Over the next twenty years they robbed, by Mitchell's count, more than 140 banks, netting over $8 million, all of it soon spent on riotous living.

Their favorite region was the American Southwest. In 1980, they successfully robbed a series of banks in San Diego, the high point being a Bank of America branch where they got $280,000 but were caught on a surveillance video wearing their presidents' masks and using their stopwatch. The FBI put the pieces together and found them at their favorite hideaway, the beautiful little city of Sedona, Arizona, a sort of New Age party town where Mitchell was known as a generous millionaire businessman. On Halloween 1980, Reid and Wright were arrested for the San Diego robbery, but Mitchell slipped away and kept on robbing, both solo and with new partners. In 1983, robbing solo, he was caught robbing a business in Arizona. The Stopwatch Gang was no more.

Wright served his time and went to work as a reclusive accountant for the Canadian prison system, which took him back. Reid did his time, married and moved to Vancouver, where he began writing novels, including *Jackrabbit Parole*, a gritty, lightly fictionalized version of the gang and its escapes. Looking much older and with neatly trimmed facial hair, he built a career doing TV interviews about his life of crime. Later he was caught again, this time in a drug deal, and went back to prison for good. Mitchell soldiered on. Sentenced to seventeen years for the Arizona robbery, he promptly conned another team of prison guards. Mitchell got a job cleaning inmate visiting rooms and gained the trust of the guards. In later TV interviews they still seemed captivated by his Irish charm which caused them to forget about his previous prison escapes and his years as a successful fugitive. By 1986, Mitchell had determined the prison's weak point, a duct system that opened out near the back fence. He talked his way into a job cleaning the area beside the warden's office, where a large duct was exposed. He was able to cut into it with homemade tools fashioned from his cleaning equipment. One night he crawled out the duct, climbed the fence, and walked away.

It was 1986 and time to consider a new career path, without of course giving up bank robbery. He moved to the French Quarter in New Orleans, adding the French-sounding alias *Richard Landry* to his existing list. By 1988, after a long string of successful bank robberies, some alone, some with a partner, Mitchell had saved enough money to retire. Because his face was featured on wanted posters around the country, he had plastic surgery done "so my own mother would not have known me."

He boarded a plane in Seattle and flew to the Philippines, where he met a beautiful but poor woman named Imelda in a Manila shoe store where she was working. She believed his story that he was Gary Weber, a rich American insurance executive. He moved her to a mansion on a hill overlooking the beautiful, secluded Trinidad Valley 150 miles north of Manila. They married and Mitchell fathered a son by her in November 1989. Imelda trusted him completely. Mitchell put Imelda's brothers through college and set her father up in business. He became a local philanthropist, helping earthquake victims. Mitchell exercised and even became a vegetarian. But he could not stop robbing banks. On his yearly "business trips" to America, he kept on robbing.

Mitchell at first seemed unable or unwilling to tell me in an interview why he could not retire as he'd planned. He also had difficulty explaining why he kept leaving his Filipina wife, their son, and what he called his "Garden of Eden on the island," but he did. Finally, he admitted it was probably a mixture of his spendthrift way of always blowing his loot on flamboyant gestures and his love of the score, the addictive adrenalin excitement of the robberies themselves. Whatever the reason, he headed back yearly to the U.S. in the Philippine rainy season to rob a bank or two for thrills and cash. By 1990, he was No. 3 on the FBI's Most Wanted List. His face was on posters all over the U.S.

In 1994, his notoriety finally caught up with him. After he was featured on a segment of *America's Most Wanted*, someone in the Philippines recognized Paddy Mitchell as the same person as Gary Weber. He heard that authorities were coming for him. He told Imelda the truth and kissed her and their son good-bye forever. With $11,000 in hand, he planned to fly to Vancouver and on to Juárez, Mexico, knowing as an Anglo he could easily slip into the U.S. among the hordes of returning American tourists while the border guards looked for illegal Mexicans.

But there was one problem: He discovered his U.S. passport had expired. No problem for Paddy. He simply stopped by the U.S. consulate in Manila on his way to the airport, got his passport renewed, and flew off to Vancouver. When he got to Vancouver, there was another problem. While waiting for his flight to Mexico City, he heard an announcement directing Gary Weber to report to the Canadian immigration desk. Rather than fleeing as anyone else would have, Mitchell headed straight for the desk and calmly answered all their questions. He told them he was visiting his sister in Mexico City before going home to the United States. After twenty nervous minutes, Canadian immigration officials bought the story and Mitchell had escaped again.

When he reached Juárez, Mitchell simply walked across the border back into the United States. But he had only $6,000 left. As he said later, "Money doesn't last long when you're on the run." His shortage of cash led to a career-ending decision when he skipped his usual careful planning and "rushed into this thing looking for some fast cash." But he did not act entirely without planning. Just inside Texas he retrieved his old .32 caliber pistol, which he'd stashed, knowing he would return to do another bank job. He paid $700 in back rent for an old Ford LTD he'd left at the El Paso airport, knowing he'd need it for his next job. From there he drove straight to Southaven, Mississippi, a booming suburb of Memphis with thirteen banks.

Mitchell had cased a likely bank in Southaven the previous year while gambling at the dog-racing tracks across the Mississippi River in Arkansas. He knew when several large stores, including Wal-Mart and Kroger, had large cash receipts delivered to the bank by armored car. He also had a plan to fool the police, which proved to be fatally flawed. From a pay phone he called the local hospital and said, "Some people I kidnapped last night are in the trunk of a green car in your parking lot. They may be dead." He then called City Hall and said in a crazed voice, "I just put a bomb in your building and it's gonna blow you all to bits, you SOBs." Then he overdid it. Using an Irish brogue, which in a later interview I heard him use several times, Mitchell called Trustmark Bank and said, "You're about to get robbed. There's two guys coming in two minutes. They're going to kill everybody in the bank."

Little did Mitchell know what he had blundered into. The Southaven Police Department was no amateur outfit. It was located in a luxurious suite of offices with leather chairs and plush carpets that had formerly belonged to a wealthy medical practice forfeited to the city after narcotics were illegally dispensed there. Chief of police Tom Long was a longtime friend and ally of our office. His department was probably the most sophisticated and well-staffed police department in the state, and its officers were accustomed to being challenged by big-city criminals from Memphis, a large city with a crime rate equal to that of Detroit.

There was another fact that Paddy Mitchell could never have suspected: a decade earlier, another robber had called in bomb threats to two local stores to lure police away from the bank they planned to rob. I remember that robbery well because I handled it. One of the robbers bore a striking resemblance to former Washington Redskins quarterback Sonny Jurgensen. Chief Tom Long remembered the incident too. Mitchell's phone calls sounded like a diversion. Long immediately sent an officer to every bank in town and personally headed for the Deposit Guaranty, which had the most money and was the best target.

It was a rainy Tuesday. Flamboyant as ever, Mitchell was outside the bank wearing a blond wig and dark sunglasses festooned with distracting green and pink ribbons. He waited for the lunchtime crowd of customers to disperse and walked into the bank alone carrying his old .32 pistol loaded with four rounds and a fake bomb concealed in a green shaving kit. He had followed a Loomis armored truck from business to business and knew that the bank was flush with cash. Still, as he later admitted to us, he almost backed away. Experience had honed his instincts. Something didn't feel right. A voice in his head kept saying, "Something is wrong. Get the hell out of here." He started to leave, then thought of how badly he needed the money and of how he'd never have a better opportunity for a big, quick kill. He'd be broke before he could plan another such lucrative job.

Mitchell pulled his green turtleneck over the bottom of his face, walked into the large, beige bank, and pointed his gun at the first teller's head. He screamed to intimidate her. "Don't set the alarms or I'll kill every one of you. Where's the bags?" She motioned him to the vault. "Open the door or I'll kill you." A teller opened it, and he ran in and filled his blue duffel bag with as many hard-to-trace tens and twenties as it would hold. He took no conspicuous hundreds, and there was no time for tellers to slip in bait bills or a dye pack. The job was going perfectly. For a moment, Mitchell thought his premonitions were wrong and he was on his way back to New Orleans and the French Quarter.

As he exited, he laid the green shaving kit in the middle of the lobby and announced, "This is a bomb. If you come after me, it will go off." He cleared the bank safely—in less than ninety seconds by his stopwatch—and was backing out in his old Ford LTD when two police cars rammed him from the back and side, knocking him across the seat. When he raised his head, he was looking into the face of a burly cop and down the barrel of his gun. Chief Tom Long was on the other side, blocking his escape. Mitchell later said he was suddenly so depressed that he thought of reaching for his own gun to provoke the cops into killing him. But that was with the benefit of time and hindsight, and also made a better story. At the time he simply said, "I give up. Please don't kill me." Paddy Mitchell, perhaps the most famous bank robber of the twentieth century, was caught—most people thought for good. But he had not given up. He still had one more trick up his sleeve.

The following day, Greg Weston, the Ottawa reporter who helped make Mitchell famous with his book *The Stopwatch Gang*, managed to get a quick telephone interview with Mitchell, and on February 25, ran a four-column story on him and his latest job. For me 1994 promised to be a busy year. We had just indicted the warden and a dozen other officers at the Parchman penitentiary for beating a handcuffed inmate almost to death. I was to try that case and was also on a DOJ team scheduled to fly to Haiti to give training to Haitian prosecutors, hoping to help quell the unrest there. Nevertheless, I could not resist the Paddy Mitchell case. As criminal chief for the office, I assigned all cases and selfishly assigned Mitchell to myself and a talented and gung-ho young assistant named Chad Lamar to try it with me. Ron Lewis, the former Wyoming cowboy with a B.A. from Dartmouth and a master's in French from Harvard, was appointed to represent Mitchell, now a pauper entitled to free counsel at taxpayer expense.

To the surprise of us all, Mitchell insisted on pleading guilty. He said he always pled guilty. That put us on alert, reminding us that he also had always escaped. Lafayette County sheriff Buddy East had been a friend of mine since the 1960s when I was a law student. We talked with Deputy Marshal Eddie Rambo about the likelihood that Mitchell's "defense" to the charge would be to escape again. The FBI notified us that Mitchell was also under indictment in the Northern District of Florida for an armed bank robbery there in 1987. When Mitchell was informed, he told Ron Lewis that he wanted to plead guilty to that one, too. Under Federal Rule 20, a defendant can waive his right to be tried where the crime was committed and plead guilty in the district where he is arrested. A second guilty plea made us even more suspicious. Nevertheless, Mitchell entered guilty pleas to both bank robberies and to using guns in both robberies. His maximum punishment was thirty-five years on each robbery, making us even more sure he would try to escape.

He did, of course, and he might have made it. He began his scheme in typical fashion, sending a note through the prison grapevine with an article about him as an escape artist to inmate Horace Colonel. Together they recruited a colorful team of would-be Houdinis: Colonel, who was in for drug trafficking; Thomas Dwayne Combs, a state inmate awaiting transport to Parchman to serve a forty-year sentence from Circuit Judge Henry Lackey on eight counts of sexual battery; and James Carpenter, an unemployed professional wrestler who went by the name "Handsome Jimmy" Valentine. I had just convicted him for a violent extortion in which he poured gasoline on a gambler in Greenville (a tactic Carpenter blithely called "Exxoning him") and threatened to "light him up" with a match if the victim did not pay his gambling debts. Instead, the victim whipped the overweight wrestler and called the police, who put Carpenter in jail. All of Mitchell's accomplices faced long sentences and had plenty of motive to escape from the ultramodern, high-tech three-hundred-bed jail in Oxford that inmates called the Buddy East Hotel.

Despite the heightened security, Mitchell managed to coordinate an escape plan that got way too far along. He got a friend of Combs to smuggle in hacksaw blades, which Mitchell used to saw through the heavy cell bars covering the heating duct in Cell 304, on the top tier just below the prison roof. From there, Mitchell planned for the escapees to climb down on ropes made from prison sheets, just like in the movies. To cover the sounds of the sawing, Mitchell played his TV loud, which was not uncommon. Hanging sheets over the front of his cell was more suspicious, but other inmates and trusties figured there was sexual activity going on and didn't want to watch. To solve the biggest security problem, the absence of bars over the mouth of the duct, Mitchell showed his accomplices a trick he'd learned in the pen in Arizona. He mixed dried toothpaste with black cigarette ash and made a paste to hold the sawed-out bars back in place. For a while it worked well.

Then Horace Colonel became impatient, fearing he'd be shipped off before the escape plan got a chance to work. Colonel suggested a far more vicious approach: Mitchell would fake another heart attack, and as accomplices helped him toward the ambulance, they would kill the marshals guarding him and all get away. Colonel knew the marshals' procedures because they had taken him to the hospital when he got particles of steel in his eye while sawing with the hacksaw blade. Apparently no one realized at the time where the metal had come from. Mitchell nixed the shooting plan, not because he opposed violence but because the marshals were "too professional and sophisticated" to fall for it and the inmates would never pull it off. "Those marshals are hard core," Mitchell insisted.

Informants inside the jail eventually ratted them all out and Sheriff East and the marshals searched Mitchell's cell and found the cut bars and hollowed-out air duct. This time, Mitchell did not plead guilty; he went to trial. Colonel's lawyer offered us his client's testimony in return for some leniency on his drug sentence. Much as I wanted to try this historic bank robber with Chad Lamar, I was out of the country on a DOJ mission at the time and could not be there. To take my place, I chose veteran AUSA Charlie Spillers, who had prosecuted Colonel and had a rapport with him and could handle him as a witness. As Charlie and Chad recall it, the trial was a hoot. "Handsome Jimmy" testified for us and made a good witness. Combined with Colonel, some photos, and the marshals' testimony, it made an overwhelming case.

Mitchell of course had total confidence he could talk his way out of it so he took the stand, allowing Charlie Spillers to cross-examine him about his previous escapes to prove his criminal intent. Mitchell had a novel story: Yes, this escape plan sounded like what he had told the testifying inmates about his prior escapes. But his version was that this time it was only to protect himself from violent inmates, especially Horace Colonel. He said it was obvious that the other inmates had simply copied his old escape plans from the newspaper articles. He testified he personally knew nothing of their plan to escape, this time.

As Mitchell himself admitted in later interviews, Charlie Spillers destroyed him on cross-examination. Playing to Mitchell's monstrous ego, Charlie got Mitchell to boast about his earlier escapes. Charlie was even able to show the jury the Canadian Broadcasting video about Mitchell's robbery "career" and get him to brag about it too. The colorful Mitchell had such a unique way of thinking that the jury understood that he was behind the escape. The others were not smart enough to have conceived this plan without him. The jury convicted Mitchell in short order. Judge Biggers sentenced Mitchell to another five years in prison, the legal maximum for the escape, to be "stacked," or served after all his other sentences in all courts. That sentence guaranteed Mitchell would die in prison. As Mitchell said later, "I'll be 123 years old when I get out."

On June 30, 1995, when all possibility of appeals had run out and Mitchell was about to be shipped to a maximum security prison to serve his time, he and his attorney agreed to an interview. Present were several marshals, the prosecuting and defense attorneys, and reporter Jonny Miles from the *Oxford Eagle*, who later did a fine feature story on Mitchell for *GQ* magazine. We all satisfied our curiosity, asking Mitchell all the questions we'd wanted to ask but could not ask in court. He was quite a storyteller. We asked him for insider tips on bank robbery. I naively asked if he ever got ideas from other bank robbers he met in prison. Adopting his Irish brogue, he said, "Those aren't bank robbers, God bless 'em. Anyone who hands a teller a note is not a bank robber; he's an amateur. The only real American bank robbers are in Atlanta, and I haven't been there yet." He said he was afraid of guns and never had one except to use as bluff in a bank robbery. He told of one job where an accomplice accidentally fired his gun while drawing it and shot himself through the arm and Mitchell in the buttocks with a single bullet.

Mitchell reflected with considerable insight but no remorse on his life of crime: "I'm not smart. I can't spell, I can't do math. I have no skills. In a way I had no choice. And I'd rather be in prison than work in a car wash." He talked of the other inmates in the Oxford jail. "Carpenter trusted me. He told me he was a snitch and trusted me not to tell. I didn't tell on him, and he didn't tell on me. He only testified because he had to." He ruminated on the others also: "Colonel, now he was scary. He told me about all the people he'd killed. I didn't like to look him in the eye. He had a very cold look straight on." U.S. Marshal David Crews gave a fair assessment of Mitchell that agreed with mine: "He has no moral underpinnings. He is sinister, but he does have a certain style." Chad Lamar put it subtly: "There are so many conflicts in Paddy's character and philosophy. He's a walking conflict. Paddy is really a party boy who just happens to be damn good at robbing banks."

Once in federal prison, Mitchell continued to try to manipulate the system. For years he petitioned to be sent back to Canada to serve his time and even conned the U.S. State Department into supporting him under a U.S.-Canadian treaty. But our office opposed it vehemently to the end. His claim of wanting to be closer to his first family rang hollow to us. After all, he said the same thing about his first wife and young son he did about his second wife and young son: "I missed them all right—for a while." We figured that what he really missed was his freedom and that he planned to get it back by escaping from whatever Canadian prison he went to.

Over the years, Mitchell found a new avocation in prison as a blogger. With his usual pizzazz, he pontificated online on everything from prison conditions and chemotherapy to war in the Middle East and "The Bank Robber's Life." But he never robbed another bank. Patrick Michael Mitchell died in the Medical Center for Federal Prisoners at Butner, North Carolina, at 8:43 A.M. on Sunday, January 14, 2007, of lung cancer metastasized to the brain, which caused heart failure. As the official notice from the Bureau of Prisons stated in standard bureaucrat speak, "His projected release date was December 21, 2033." It was a commonplace end for an uncommon man.

Try It Again, Frank[8]

Justice was almost defeated in one bank robbery case because of my overconfidence. Although frequently warned of racial solidarity among jurors, I had had so much success convicting black defendants with mostly black juries that I grew complacent. One of the most vigorous defense attorneys in those days was Charles Victor McTeer, a soft-voiced three-hundred-pound ex-football player from Maryland who moved to Greenville to be a civil rights lawyer. The big difference between Victor and other civil rights attorneys was that he also intended to make lots of money and as the saying went "do well while doing good." He succeeded richly, driving a new Mercedes and flying his own plane. His daughter, Heather, also a lawyer, was for several years mayor of Greenville.

One day, a young man named Nathaniel Johnson robbed a bank on South Main Street in Greenville just a block from where I once lived on the south end of Arnold Avenue. The robbery was a violent one and the black victim teller suffered a miscarriage and lost her late-term baby as a result, so we took the case especially seriously. One of our best FBI agents, John Canale of the prominent Memphis family, was assigned to the case. John did a brilliant job lining up evidence, including a unique candlestick from the defendant's house whose bottom unscrewed. Inside, the defendant had rolled up and hidden several hundred dollars in bait bills. The case looked like a lock, but Victor refused a plea agreement and confidently announced ready for trial. With equal confidence, I also announced ready, and using hardly any challenges picked a jury that was mostly black. The marshals, always our best allies, warned me right away from what they heard in the hallways that I was in trouble with my jury. They were mesmerized by Victor McTeer and his civil rights reputation.

In criminal trials, prosecutors try to keep things serious. Humor usually favors the defense. One sign I always look for is what happens when defense attorneys try to make a joke. If jurors don't laugh, I'm on solid ground. But if they laugh with the defense attorney, I am usually in trouble. In his opening statement, McTeer ridiculed the idea that his client would be so stupid. He called the loot from the robbery "chump change," a phrase I had never heard till then. But the jurors clearly knew it and laughed aloud along with Victor. Their minds soon seemed made up and closed to all our evidence. I began to feel bad for John Canale, who had really suffered along with the victim bank teller through her miscarriage and poured his heart and soul into the case. I couldn't stand the idea that this violent criminal might go free to rob again. Near the end of the trial, local district attorney Frank Carlton came in to watch. I told him at a recess how things were going.

As I fretted, Frank took action. When the jury returned with the stunning but not unexpected "not guilty" verdict, Frank was ready. As the defense celebrated and the jurors smiled, Judge Keady tried to gavel the crowd to order. Frank approached the bench. "Your Honor, as an officer of the court, I'd like to know how you want me to proceed. I have a state arrest warrant for this defendant for armed bank robbery." Judge Keady chuckled: "Has he robbed another bank already?" Carlton smiled. "No sir, this one. This verdict was pure and simple jury nullification of a good case, and we don't intend to tolerate it. Shall I arrest him here or wait and take a chance he'll escape out a back door?" Judge Keady never hesitated: "Arrest him where he stands." The judge, a racial moderate vilified by what he called "confederates" as a liberal on racial matters, amazed me with his next statement, made right in the presence of the acquitting jurors: "This man clearly robbed a bank right here in our city, abused the poor black teller, and does not need to go free to rob again. Take him away." The jurors looked surprised, then embarrassed, hearing the judge stress the loss to the teller, not the bank.

The sheriff took Johnson down the street to the state courthouse, where he was arraigned and Victor McTeer was again appointed to represent him. Since the witnesses were still around and Victor was clearly prepared, a new trial began the next morning. I was too embarrassed to go watch, but Frank called me the next day and told me the jury had convicted in less than an hour and the state judge had given the defendant a long sentence on Parchman Farm, a much worse place than any federal prison.

But what about double jeopardy? Doesn't the Fifth Amendment say that no one shall be twice put in jeopardy for the same offense? Yes, but there is an important exception. If the prosecution is by another "sovereign," as in the federal vs. a state government, the Double Jeopardy Clause does not apply. In federal court, the principle is called dual prosecution. If a defendant has been acquitted in state court, say for a bank robbery, he cannot be reprosecuted in federal court for the same robbery unless the Attorney General in Washington personally approves the second prosecution. But state prosecutors are not so limited. This exception to double jeopardy law has been challenged several times in the U.S. Supreme Court, but always without success. Thanks to that strange twist in the law, the bank teller received justice after all, and state-federal cooperation did its work.

Thunder Eagle Ghost Dancer Launders His Loot[9]

James Keith Johnson was a veteran incompetent bank robber. His main claim to fame was his use of the fake but colorful pseudonym Thunder Eagle Ghost Dancer. He was white with no Native American ancestry but apparently just liked the name. He robbed two banks in north Florida on successive days in March 1995. As he was escaping from each bank, dye packs given him by the tellers exploded. Because the money was stained red by the dye, Ghost Dancer drove all the way to two casinos in faraway Tunica to "launder" it by feeding the red money into slot machine bill validators and "cashing out," in effect exchanging dirty bills for clean ones. It didn't quite work out that way.

Several people at each casino observed Ghost Dancer playing the slots. At Fitzgerald's, he hit a jackpot, winning $1,600 from one machine. Because of tax reporting requirements, casino employees made him sign an IRS report of his gambling winnings. He foolishly used his real name, James Keith Johnson, and his real social security number. The next day's soft count of currency found several thousand dollars in dye-stained money. Both casinos reviewed their surveillance videos for anyone having a connection to the red-stained money and soon identified a man and woman who matched the descriptions of Ghost Dancer and his girl-friend, Cat Dancing, playing the machines where the dyed bills were discovered and taking large amounts of tokens to the cashiers.

Ghost Dancer testified at trial to both his gambling methods and his past legal entanglements, which included being in prison most of his adult life "for protecting women and children at Wounded Knee, South Dakota." He also claimed he was shot "through both eyes" by a sniper in Alabama, that he was the personal bodyguard for a U.S. magistrate, and that he had suffered seventy-two broken bones while being "roasted" by federal agents. Strangely, he denied he was crazy. He also claimed he was a registered Shaman for the Creek Indian Federation and requested that he be allowed to enter the courtroom for trial in "a cloud of ritual smoke." The judge rejected that request, along with Ghost Dancer's proposed alibi witness, Danny "Snakeman" Schertz, a Satanist priest I had recently convicted of kidnapping and rape. The judge sentenced Ghost Dancer to five years on top of his two lengthy Florida sentences. The Court of Appeals affirmed, and Ghost Dancer was through dancing for many years.

A Stuttering Bank Robber[10]

At around 11:30 one morning in November 1983, bank teller Bonnie Tate saw a man wearing a jacket and baseball cap walk very fast past her drive-in window toward the front of the Bank of Commerce in Amory, though she could not see his face. Moments later, the man entered the bank through the front door. He had placed a towel with a bright flower pattern over his face. The man stuttered badly. She finally realized that he was saying, "Give me all your money or I'll blow your goddamn brains out." The man took the money and asked for her car keys. She claimed she didn't have them, and he left. She watched him cross the street toward a Fred's Store and a Big Star grocery, and rang the alarm.

Eyewitness Loretta Cribbs testified that while washing dishes by her kitchen window behind Fred's Store she saw a man run in the direction of Fred's and pull off a jacket and cap as he went by. Mrs. Tate later identified the red baseball cap and dark blue windbreaker as items worn by the robber. Records at the police department proved the alarm call was received at 11:34 A.M.

Eyewitnesses Charles and Mary Nix testified that for several months they had supervised defendant James Earl Kelly at a local furniture factory. They saw Mr. Kelly across from the drive-in window of the bank around 11:30 A.M. on the morning of the robbery. Kelly was close enough to their car that Mrs. Nix could have touched him. Kelly was wearing a cap and a dark jacket and walking fast. They testified that Kelly stuttered and that his speech was hard to understand, particularly for a stranger.

Eyewitnesses Elmer Walton and his brother Harvey and Harvey's wife, Judy, all testified that at lunchtime on the day of the robbery they were in Fred's when Kelly approached Elmer, whom he knew from the furniture factory. Kelly asked for a ride to a plant located half a mile from Fred's. Elmer agreed to take Kelly for $10. Judy Walton noticed Kelly had a *plain* towel, dirty white, hanging from his pocket. When the Waltons had driven less than a block from Fred's, Kelly told them he wanted to get out because "the police was hot on him and he had to get out of town." He told them he had about $3,000 in cash on him from selling drugs. The Waltons did not know at the time that the bank across the street from Fred's had just been robbed, but when they heard the news later that evening, they reported Kelly's unusual behavior to local police.

FBI Agent Wayne Hardy interviewed James Earl Kelly the following day with local sheriff Pat Patterson and chief of police Carl West of West Point, where Kelly resided. Kelly gave Hardy an elaborate alibi for his activities on the day of the robbery. Kelly first told Hardy that he had driven from West Point to Aberdeen, where he arrived around 1:00 P.M. at a club called the Conspiracy Club or the Burning Spear. Kelly claimed he left the Conspiracy Club about 2:00 and went on to the Rainbow Bar to look for a dice game. Kelly told Hardy he was never in Amory at all on the day of the robbery. Hardy testified Kelly was unemployed and badly in need of money from August 1983 until the robbery in November 1983. Kelly was way behind on his car payments before the robbery but made up all his payments as well as late charges right after it.

Defense attorney Dudley Williams presented several witnesses in Kelly's defense. His wife, Beatrice, testified that she went with him to pay bills before the robbery and arrived back at her mother's house at 11:00 A.M. She claimed to remember the time because she did not want to miss her favorite TV program, *The Young and the Restless*, which came on at eleven. Jessie Moore of Aberdeen testified he too always watched *The Young and the Restless*, in his case because there was a character on the program nicknamed "Jazz" who supposedly resembled him. He testified that on the day of the robbery *The Young and the Restless* was not very interesting, so he stopped watching it about 11:15 and went to a club called the Red-Hot Pot, across the street from the Conspiracy Club. Moore claimed he saw James Earl Kelly on his way and stopped with him at a bootlegger's place and stayed with Kelly at the Red-Hot Pot for two hours drinking.

Kelly took the stand and testified more or less along the lines of the alibi he originally gave Agent Hardy. The most notable fact about Kelly's testimony was not its content, however, but that he stuttered and was very hard to understand. His speech pattern was identical to that described by the victim teller and the Nixes and the Waltons, and the judge had to keep asking him to repeat himself because no one could understand him. Kelly testified that he quit his job at the furniture factory after a dispute with Charles Nix and that Nix had a motive to lie against him. In an unparalleled whopper, Kelly testified he had had a sexual affair not only with the wife of Elmer Walton but also with Judy Walton, wife of witness Harvey Walton, even after he heard all of them testify that neither woman had ever met or even heard of James Earl Kelly. On cross-examination, Kelly denied that he had an unusual speech pattern saying, "I c-c-can t-t-talk f-f-fast and I c-c-can t-t-talk s-s-slow." He insisted that he carried a towel around only to wipe off his car after going through a car wash and stated, "I n-n-never even r-r-robbed a p-p-piggy b-b-bank."

On the night after the defense rested its case, we were all a little worried about how the jurors looked. I wondered if they thought I'd humiliated Kelly about his stuttering. The evidence was powerful to us as veterans, but to this group of mostly uneducated factory workers, we figured it was possibly confusing. I was mainly concerned that the robber's towel had bright-colored flowers on it while Kelly's was plain white. I asked FBI agent Hardy to try to figure out some explanation for the discrepancy overnight. He did so beautifully.

On our rebuttal case the next morning, Sheriff Patterson took the stand and blew the defense away with a towel agent Hardy had purchased the night before at Wal-Mart. Patterson first showed the jury that the towel was white on one side. Then with a dramatic flourish, he quickly flipped it over to reveal a flowered pattern on the other side, and how you would not notice it if you saw only one side hanging from his pocket and saw only the other side across a robber's face as a mask. Several jurors gasped and began looking at each other and nodding.

The jury worried us a little by staying out for more than four hours. We had presented twenty witnesses and the defense eight, and the jurors had sent in two different notes with questions about the jury instructions, especially about what "reasonable doubt" meant. But they finally returned with a unanimous verdict of guilty.

Another Aberdeen Soap Opera and a Pair of Girbaud Jeans[11]

One bank robbery case I vividly recall was that of a nineteen-year-old high school graduate named Frederick Franks. His father was a successful, highly paid executive at a local factory. As the son of an affluent black family in rural Aberdeen, Franks was resented by his peers and sought to impress them. Franks was a good athlete, but that was not enough. He was educated, but as for many teenagers, that was more detriment than blessing. You had to hide your interest in ideas to fit in. To be a big man in town, Franks decided to become a drug dealer, since drug dealers had fine cars and plenty of money and women, while college graduates were something vague and far away and not quite real. To set himself up in the drug business, he needed money, but his father wouldn't give him any unless he went to college.

Franks also needed firearms to be credible as a drug dealer and to defend himself, so he resorted to a foolish plan of financial self-help. He robbed a bank just a few miles from his house. The FBI agent assigned to the case was way more than a match for him. Leonardo "Leon" Floyd was nearly as bright and ingenious as the man he was named for. A former professional football player and Atlanta policeman, Leon was one of my all time favorite FBI agents. After interviewing the victim bank tellers, Leon and I met with local police chief Brent Coleman, who checked his informants and got a tip that Franks was the robber and why he had done the robbery. From tips out of local clubs we learned what happened. Franks had made a clean getaway in his mother's car, hid out at home for a while, and then started buying drug-dealer clothes and guns. He treated friends to several pairs of expensive, deep-pocketed Girbaud jeans from France, then the drug dealer pants of choice. Leon and I interviewed the sales clerk who sold the jeans. She recognized Franks's picture. The store still had some bait bills from the bank robbery in its cash register. A local prostitute also testified, fearfully, about Franks's sudden free-spending ways. Even without a positive teller ID or a fingerprint, we got an indictment with our scared witnesses and circumstantial evidence.

At trial, Franks actually made a good witness when he took the stand and denied the robbery, claiming he was at home all morning watching TV with his ten-year-old brother. In an interview his mother refused to alibi for him, which was unusual. Franks claimed she had emotional problems, and we decided not to put her through the ordeal of trial, not knowing what she would do under pressure. We also didn't have the heart to use an honest woman against her own son. Franks therefore called his little brother to the stand to alibi for him instead. The little fellow was clean-cut and clear-eyed and not nervous. Yet some instinct told me something was not right about his testimony.

Leon Floyd had carefully timed the route from the Franks house to the bank and back, finding that Franks could have made it to and from the bank and done the robbery in less than twenty minutes. Thus, the time he needed for his alibi was short, but it also tied him to a time frame on which I could cross-examine him. And just one mistake on the time-line would probably be fatal to his alibi defense, given our witnesses and the fact that jurors tend to disbelieve alibis from family members anyway. They always somehow sound wrong.

The little boy surprised me from the stand when I asked him a standard question: "What programs did y'all watch on TV that morning?"

He recited calmly a one-hour kid show I'd never heard of followed by a one-hour episode of *Days of Our Lives*. "Do you remember what happened that day on *Days*?" I asked him. "Was Stefano on that day?" He couldn't remember. "What about Bo and Hope?" He couldn't remember that either and didn't seem to really know anything about *Days*, hardly a kid show. The men on the jury looked at me blankly, but the women gave me knowing looks as if they appreciated that a mere male knew something about daytime soap operas. I gave silent thanks to my daughters for watching the program while we were home for lunch. I actually used to enjoy *Days*. My wife was appalled, however, and thought we were all low-brows for watching it, but you never know what esoteric knowledge a trial lawyer may need.

The kid show was another matter. I'd never heard of it and hesitated to cross the little boy because he clearly had watched it at some point and seemed to know it. Using a normal trial lawyer tactic, I stalled till the lunch hour, hoping I would think of something to ask if given a little more time. As soon as we recessed, Leon and I talked about what to do. The newspaper! The *Daily Journal* in nearby Tupelo ran a TV schedule every day. I called a reporter at the *Journal* and he faxed me the TV schedule for the day of the robbery plus the other days of that week. Miracle of miracles, the boy had not been prepped well enough. The kid program he was talking about was on an hour after the robbery and was not even playing on the day of the robbery but the day after. It was sad to see the little boy's pathetic, apologetic expression as he looked over to his big brother at counsel table, admitting with his eyes that he'd let him down and gotten the alibi wrong.

Closing argument was emotional. Rather than stressing the facts of the robbery, I touched on them just enough to remind the jury of them, then focused all my energy on the little brother. Who could blame him for trying to help his big bubba? I stressed the betrayal by Franks of his little brother's innocence. That cynical act was worse than the robbery itself, I argued, worse even than his plan to betray his family by setting himself up as a drug dealer. If these selfish and destructive acts did not show the heart of a bank robber, then nothing could. The jury convicted on both the robbery and firearm charges in less than an hour.

When Leon and the chief and I got through celebrating, I drove triumphantly back to Oxford. I stopped at the edge of town at my favorite used clothing store, Carol's Thrift Shop, referred to locally as "Chez Car-ole." I asked if she had any Girbaud jeans. She had one pair in my size for $10. They were comfortable and well cut, with deep pockets almost down to my knees. They were even the right length. I wore them for years.

You Busy This Weekend?[12]

A most unusual bank robber I prosecuted was a homesick young Ger-man named Kai Reinhold. His mother had married an American named Webb and moved with him to West Point, home of famed bluesman Howlin' Wolf. Lonely and friendless, the teenage Reinhold tried to find some bluesmen but ended up with a bad crowd of crackheads instead. One of them, who held court in the backroom of a local pool hall, was so professional at cooking crack that he was nicknamed "the Chef."

One day, Kai (pronounced like "sky") was especially despondent and appeared suicidal to the sympathetic crackheads. All he wanted was to return to his homeland. "Ain't no problem," said a new associate, who seemed to know the legal system quite well. "Just get yourself arrested for some federal beef and they'll ship you home. Don't rob no liquor store or nothin' or the state will slap you down on Parchman Farm." Persuaded, Reinhold decided to rob a bank, figuring if he got away with it, he would buy a one-way plane ticket to Germany. If he got caught, the government would deport him there for free. It seemed a foolproof plan.

Reinhold asked his associates for the loan of a gun, believing from American movies that you needed one to rob a bank properly. "Oh no," they said. "A gun is a ten-year rap stacked on the robbery. The Feds don't like those guns. They'll send you off to the pen." Trusting his new friends, Reinhold accepted the loan of an old rusty butcher knife to use as his weapon. The next day, Reinhold calmly walked into a bank in West Point and approached the teller. "I want $2,000," he said. "Do you have an account with us?" she inquired politely. "No, this is a robbery. I need the money to fly to Germany." Smiling, the teller said she could not help him unless he had some collateral. He pulled the butcher knife from his sleeve and said, "I'm serious. I won't hurt you, but I'm desperate." The teller realized he was not joking and thought he might be crazy. Still, he looked so young and harmless, handsome even.

Reinhold began to notice the teller more closely. She was young, blonde, and quite attractive. As she handed him a stack of bills that enclosed an exploding dye pack, she activated a silent alarm that rang at the police department. Smiling, he looked at her more closely. "You look really good. Would you go out with me this weekend?" The teller was not scared but puzzled and said calmly, "I don't think that would be a good idea under the circumstances." He continued his wooing. Finally, as Reinhold reluctantly left the bank, local police caught him with both the loot and the knife. My friend, Assistant U.S. Attorney Vernon Miles had the case but was transferring from our Oxford office to the U.S. Attorney's office in Puerto Rico to "chase women" as he explained it, so Vernon willed the case to me, knowing my love of quirky bank robberies.

After an appropriate but unsuccessful mental exam found that Reinhold was merely foolish rather than crazy, he pled guilty to unarmed bank robbery. His entire take was $556.77, not enough for a ticket to Germany, not even right after the 9/11 plane bombings. An amused Judge Michael P. Mills gave Reinhold the sentence required by the Federal Sentencing Guidelines of forty-one months in prison, much of which he had already served in custody between November 2001, when he was caught, and August 2003, when his mental exams were over and he was finally sentenced. According to the court docket, he never paid his lawyers. I still wonder what happened to him.

Would You Like Biscuits with That?[13]

My all-time favorite victims in a bank robbery case were an eighty-eight-year-old lady in Itawamba County named Euple and her sixty-year-old caretaker, Earnestine. While the ladies were minding their own business early one Wednesday morning in March 2006, three fleeing bank robbers broke into their home near the Tennessee-Tombigbee Waterway. The ladies had heard of a robbery on TV the night before. When the caretaker heard someone forcing open the front door, she said, "I bet it's those bank robbers."

She was right. Three men from Memphis had robbed the Renasant Bank in Smithville in nearby Monroe County and were fleeing back to Memphis. Going way too fast in their gold Pontiac Grand Am, they ran right off the end of an unfinished approach road into the swamp near the waterway. The men waded all night through ten miles of marshes and mosquitoes until they saw the ladies' house at first light and decided to take shelter there. "They were wet and dirty and smelled bad, but they were very nice and respectful and treated us well," said the caretaker. "They were tired and hungry so we cooked them breakfast." Although legally the ladies were hostages, their cool and caring demeanor seemed to soften the young bank robbers. The men "politely" asked for the car keys. "They said they just wanted the car and would not hurt us. They even offered to buy us gas and refill the tank. They took the car, but ran it right away into the ditch before they could even get out of the yard," she said.

Then the ladies' steel magnolia side came out. They saw officers hiding in the woods and figured their house was surrounded, which it was. They also figured the robbers might not continue to be so nice. Unbeknownst to them, the FBI, police and sheriff's deputies were meeting at the nearby Ozark Baptist Church and seriously considering rushing the house with a SWAT team, not knowing that things inside were going so well.

The older lady finally made the robbers an offer: "I'll get my son to come pull you out. I'll tell him you just got stuck." The robbers agreed. "I'll need to explain it to him though, so he won't be suspicious. I also need to get my morning paper. I really miss my *Daily Journal* each day, and you shouldn't be going out there." The robbers fell for it.

The older lady whispered the whole situation to her son when he got there, and he pretended he could not get the car out of the mud. The robbers finally realized they were surrounded by officers, and a tense standoff ensued for an hour or so. Then they released first the caretaker and finally the 88-year-old lady. After a further three-hour standoff the robbers decided to surrender. The ladies' cool courtesy under extreme stress probably contributed greatly to the happy outcome. After it was over, the president of the Renasant Bank of Smithville gave some sound advice for bank robbery victims: "A robbery is something you hope never happens, but unfortunately it does. The way our people handled it was outstanding. They just did it by the book, stayed calm. Let the professionals handle it. Nobody should try to be a hero."

But it was the ladies, amateurs trained only in good manners, who turned out to be the real heroes—and the real professionals. The robbers were prosecuted and convicted in state court for bank robbery and kid-napping. The prosecutor was assistant Tupelo district attorney Clay Joiner, who has since joined the U.S. Attorney's Office in Oxford and at the time of this writing is serving as U.S. Legal Counsel in Kirkuk, Iraq, for two years.

The Honey Bun Bandit[14]

In September 2003, Kevis "K-Money" Wilson organized a group to rob the Caesar's Grand Casino at Tunica. K-Money first approached Jason Godown, whom he had picked up hitchhiking and who was living with K-Money in nearby Walls looking for either work or "a good score." K-Money told Godown he had someone inside the Grand Casino who would help them with a robbery, a cashier, who like K-Money, was Afri-can American. K-Money told Godown he figured the robber needed to be white, reasoning people would be less suspicious of an inside job if a white person robbed an African American cashier. K-Money probably thought too much. Amateur sociology is not helpful to real robbers.

Godown approached his fiancée, Linda Stevenson about the rob-bery. Stevenson was an attractive twenty-three-year-old blond stripper who had performed at various establishments across the country, includ-ing Platinum Plus, a notorious "gentlemen's" club in Memphis. Steven-son agreed to participate. Godown and K-Money traveled to the Grand to case the area where the insider, Nataisha, worked at the "transaction point," where patrons cashed in their winnings. K-Money made plans for Linda to meet Nataisha so they would recognize one another during the robbery.

Godown, Stevenson, and K-Money met at Nataisha's apartment and discussed what should be said during the robbery. Nataisha agreed to call on the phone to signal she had a "full bank" for Stevenson to rob. Casino procedures required cashiers to comply with all of a robber's demands. Stevenson was told to say "This is a bomb. Don't make any sudden moves. Give me all your big bills and give me ten minutes to get out. If you don't, there's a man over there who will detonate the bomb."

On the day of the robbery, Godown, Stevenson, and K-Money's girl-friend met at K-Money's apartment. When Nataisha called to signal that it was time to rob the casino, they started to leave. But K-Money asked that everyone go inside, where he had them kneel. Stevenson later testified she feared something sexual was about to happen, but no. Instead, K-Money led the group in a prayer for the success of the robbery, sort of reminiscent of some people's belief that God cares who wins football games.

Stevenson entered the casino and approached Nataisha's cage wearing a big dark wig and long coat. She pulled out a gift-wrapped box, placed it on the counter, and told Nataisha it was a bomb. In their haste, the only box the robbers found in K-Money's kitchen to use as a fake bomb was an old box of Honey Buns. Later, when a bomb squad opened it and found the box, reporters matched the box with the blonde Stevenson and began calling her the "Honey Bun Bandit."

As planned, Nataisha handed Stevenson all the money in the drawer—more than $65,000—and Stevenson fled. Nataisha began shaking and acting as if she were having a seizure. Another cashier alerted the shift manager. Another teller heard casino guests hollering, "She got robbed; she got robbed." A check of Nataisha's bank revealed there was no money in it. Since the alleged bomb was still on the countertop, casino security took the threat seriously, saying, "It would have been unwise to assume it was a hoax." Casino patrons near the cage were evacuated, and all casino restaurants were shut down. The Memphis Bomb Squad arrived and ordered a full evacuation: "Every human being in the place has to be removed." The casino security chief said such evacuations are extremely rare because casinos operate twenty-four hours a day, seven days a week, and evacuations are very costly for the casino. The robbery had occurred at approximately 10:00 P.M., and the casino was closed until approximately 5:30 A.M. the following morning.

After robbing the casino, Stevenson fled with Godown north on Highway 61 to a Memphis hotel where they had rented a room. K-Money divided the stolen money: Nataisha got $11,000, Godown and Stevenson approximately $27,000. K-Money kept the rest.

Due to several slip-ups, the robbers were all quickly caught. Stevenson pled guilty and agreed to testify in return for a reduced sentence. Due to her good looks and the nature of her fake bomb, the press was all over her case as the "Honey Bun Bandit." At trial, a defense attorney confronted a nervous Stevenson about her "sweet deal." She replied, "It's not sweet to me, I'm going to the pen." The defense attorney tried again: "You don't like being seen in a jail uniform, that orange jumpsuit, do you?" The question seemed to settle her nervousness a little: "Actually, I always thought I looked pretty good in orange." No further questions.

2

CORRUPTION IN POSITIONS OF TRUST

Lawyers, Judges, Supervisors, Sheriffs

Introduction

Prosecuting public officials and other prominent citizens for corruption brings conflicting reactions from the public. For some, it deepens their cynicism about government: "They're all crooks—I told you so." Other times, a few public officials criticize us prosecutors: "Every time y'all prosecute another sheriff or county supervisor, it makes the rest of us look bad." The latter view has a grain of truth, but to me it is a price worth paying. If you don't prosecute corruption, you end up with a national reputation for immorality in public life like New York City for sex scandals, Chicago for rigged elections ("vote early and often"), or our fun-loving neighbors in New Orleans, which is not called the Big Easy for nothing.

My favorite Louisiana corruption story, surpassing even the scandals of Governors Huey "Kingfish" Long and Edwin "Vote for the Crook" Edwards, allegedly involved a grand jury in Jefferson Parish, home turf of alleged Mafia boss Carlos Marcello. For many years, grand jurors there had a tradition of throwing lavish dinners to celebrate the end of their yearlong term fighting crime. One year things got out of hand. People say that jurors not only ordered the finest dishes and wines and capped off the evening with the usual expensive cognacs and Cuban cigars but decided to share the experience with families by putting cases of champagne and boxes of cigars on the parish tab to take home with them. When new grand jurors were sworn in and reviewed the outrageous dinner bill of their predecessors, they indicted its predecessor grand jury for corruption. In Mississippi, we've seen corruption, but we will never really rival our beloved neighbors, who know how to throw a party.

In the wake of our own corruption scandals, the Mississippi Legislature has tried several times to enact reform laws. Many say our core problem is our propensity to elect rather than appoint nearly all of our public officials. No other state has as many elected officials as Mississippi. We elect everyone from constables to Supreme Court justices. Our highway commissioners are elected, as are our insurance commissioners and transportation commissioners. Some school superintendents are elected. Statistics can, of course, always be misleading, but using our own small sample, it does seem that we have prosecuted more elected officials for corruption than appointed officials.

Not all of our cases were predictable crimes. One police chief was supervising an attractive young female probationer/informant. When he informed her that she would have to have sex with him to continue on probation, she reluctantly complied, but carried a tape recorder in her purse and taped their sessions. One fine evening when the chief demanded "the usual," she played him one of the sex tapes and told him, "My lawyer has a copy, so don't even think about grabbing this one." She demanded a weekly cash payoff or else she'd inform the FBI and the chief's wife. He paid but soon ran short of cash and looked for a new source of funds. As head of the local Crime Stoppers fund, he controlled its finances and promptly bled it dry to meet her demands. When caught by a routine audit, he pled guilty, resigned, and went to federal prison. She went on to become the bartender at our favorite watering hole.[1]

Corruption among sheriffs was more routine and predictable. Although the great majority of Mississippi sheriffs are upright and honorable (and don't have beer bellies), we convicted over a dozen during my years as prosecutor. Most of these cases involved bribes received in return for not enforcing laws against crimes like running gambling houses and beer joints in dry counties, which a substantial minority of citizens thought should be legal. The antics of some of the more colorful ones, such as Harvey Hamilton of DeSoto County and Don Spradling of Itawamba County, are recounted here in some detail. The case of Sheriff Johnny Nunnally of Tishomingo County was more unusual. When a local convenience store owner who didn't like Nunnally put up a big flashing electric sign mocking the sheriff, Nunnally had an informant plant drugs in the store owner's home and busted him for possession. We then busted the sheriff for planting them. After his release, he became a highly successful fundamentalist preacher.[2]

Sheriff Steve Shuffield of Water Valley, just south of Oxford, was a sadder case. After a serious back injury, he became addicted to prescription narcotics and started obtaining large doses from inmate trusties and began exhibiting bizarre behavior. Despite heroic efforts by loyal friends like highly respected sheriff Buddy East of Oxford, all attempts at intervention failed, and we finally had to prosecute Shuffield for prescription drug fraud, forcing his resignation.[3] Other sheriffs prosecuted included Bud Michael of Prentiss County (meth)[4] and two consecutive sheriffs and their deputies from Tunica County, John Pickett and Jerry Ellington, for corruption.[5] It seems like the second sheriff would have learned from the downfall of his predecessor, but human nature is a strange thing.

In one election, Randy Roberts of Pontotoc thought his secretary was working for his opponent. Roberts wiretapped the secretary's phone, leading to a federal conviction and his resignation.[6] Roberts was apparently not much impressed by his conviction, however. At the next election, in a field of twenty candidates (must be a great job), he again ran for sheriff but was defeated. More fortunate was the macho John Alan Jones of Humphreys County, who was caught and convicted for receiving bribes to allow illegal honky-tonks to operate wide open in his county and for failing to pay federal taxes on his income from the bribery. When informed that his sentence was only eighteen months in federal prison, Jones pronounced himself unimpressed: "I can hold my fist up a bear's ass longer than that." Upon his release, despite being barred as a convicted felon from carrying a gun, he ran for sheriff again. The forgiving voters reelected him, gun or no gun, apparently believing in old school, bare-handed law enforcement. People said his opponents were offering more law enforcement than voters really wanted and voted the honky-tonk ticket.[7]

The sheriff of Montgomery County, caught with an odd mix of moonshine and counterfeit money in the trunk of his patrol car, had a deputy's sister put a voodoo hex on the jury. It didn't work.[8] One especially good corruption case came from Red Banks in Marshall County, where the FBI opened an undercover beer joint/pool room complete with a boogie-woogie piano player as the undercover operative. That operation, called Dirty Pool, was launched to catch truck thieves coming out of Memphis, but it quickly blossomed into a sweeping corruption/drug sting when the DEA meshed its undercover cocaine operation, Mojave Desert Snow, with Dirty Pool. Before the agents were through, we had convicted not only several national-level drug dealers and local truck thieves, with more than forty convictions in all, but also several local public officials, including a county supervisor, a notorious constable called "Big Jerry," and even a local school board member, for receiving bribes to protect drug deals.[9]

A most unusual defendant in Dirty Pool was Sherrie Miller Daly, former wife of colorful professional golfer John Daly.[10] Sherrie Daly had never been one of our suspects until, as one agent who liked to fish expressed it, "She just jumped in our boat." It all happened quickly. Part of the undercover operation involved flying drug suspects to South Florida on an undercover FBI plane to wow them with what big crooks the agents were. When the regular FBI plane broke down, they had to rent one on short notice. The rental plane's pilot, who knew nothing of the undercover, was dating Sherrie Daly at the time, after she was divorced from John. When she heard of the trip, Sherrie volunteered to come along for the ride to Miami. When she heard the suspects' conversations with the FBI agents posing as Colombian drug dealers, she volunteered to launder their money for them, just as she had laundered money for her father through his trucking company. She was caught on tape so red-handed that she had to plead guilty. Because of her former husband, the news quickly went viral worldwide. One of my daughters was Googling my name right after that and said, "Pop, your case on Sherrie Daly is all over the Internet. It's in Japanese and Chinese and Russian."

It was typical irony that my name should be associated with that case, since I did not handle it. The only real work I did other than supervising it as criminal chief was to write the press release as our press officer.

THE FEDS: aka "Mississippi's Untouchables" during the FBI's Operation Pretense—a statewide undercover investigation into corruption by county supervisors. Clockwise from upper left: Bob Whitwell, U.S. attorney for the Northern District; James Tucker, criminal chief, Southern District; the author, criminal Chief for the Northern District; George Phillips, U.S. attorney for the Southern District. (Courtesy of *The Clarion-Ledger*, J. D. Schwalm, photographer)

Reunion of former law clerks of Chief Judge William C. Keady. Front row from left: Martin Kilpatrick, Frances Griffin, the judge's loyal secretary, and Judge Keady. Back row from left: Dan Webb, Jerry Read, the author, Will Ford, Wayne Drinkwater, and Charles M. Powers.

Life-size official portrait of brilliant U.S. District Judge Neal Biggers, which hangs on the wall of his courtroom in Oxford. Counsel for the Scruggs defendants referred to him, unfairly, as "Maximum Neal."

Beloved U.S. Senator John C. Stennis, center, flanked by the author, the Senator's legal counsel and speechwriter during Watergate, and the brother of Stanley Kimmitt, Secretary of the Senate, during a visit to Montana in September 1972.

Statue of William "Cousin Will" Faulkner on his bench in front of the old Oxford Federal Courthouse, now City Hall, where the author tried some of his first cases.

A statue honoring James Meredith, the first black student at Ole Miss, which now stands in a special plaza between the Lyceum and the Library. As Chancellor Robert Khayat stated in dedicating it: "We are committed to respect the dignity of every person, and this monument stands as tangible evidence of that commitment." (Photo by Nathan Latil, University of Mississippi photographer)

Hailman honored

Assistant U.S. District Attorney Al Moreton (left) and U.S. District Attorney Robert Q. Whitwell present longtime Assitant U.S. District Attorney John

Hailman with a plaque signifying Hailman's promotion to Senior Litigation Counsel.
—EAGLE Staff Photo by Bruce Newman

Hailman joins elite nationwide group

John R. Hailman of Oxford is among 20 Assistant U.S. District Attorneys nationwide who were recently nominated to serve as senior government litigation counsels.

The announcement was made by William P. Tyson, director of the Justice Department's Executive Office for U.S. Attorneys. The Senior Litigation Councel Program was created to recognize outstanding U.S. attorneys based on their litigation careers, their performance and their commitment. Nationwide, only 63 of the more than 2,450 assistant U.S. District Attorneys have achieved this career honor.

To be eligible a federal prosecutor must have at least five years of experience, most of it in litigation, hold a GS-15 employee rating equivalent and have commendations for their courtroom performance. A recipient also must be available to serve on a rotating basis as a faculty member of the Attorney General's Advocacy Institute.

Hailman has served as an Assistant U.S. District Attorney here for more than 12 years, nearly all of which has been the preparation and trial of government cases. He has been especially active in bringing to justice complex and lengthy public cor-

ruption, white collar and drug cases, as well as cases dealing with bank robbery, murder and kidnapping. Throughout his tenure with the Northern District federal courts he has handled all civil rights cases and numerous class action lawsuits.

Included in his litigation are several precedent-setting cases and has been very active in the area of public corruption and narcotics litigation. Hailman is the supervisory attorney for the FBI's statewide Pretense undercover investigation which revealed widespread corruption on the county level.

Hailman holds a Master's Degree from Tulane and a fellowship in trial advocacy at Georgetown University. He also spent two years at the Sorbonne in Paris, where he served as an interpreter. His legal skills and command of French led him to handle the first case under a treaty with Switzerland involving mutal assistance in criminal proceedings which resulted in a guilty plea from a Swiss banker accused of fraud in the Northern District.

Hailman served as a law clerk under U.S. District Court Judge Willaim C. Keady, was a legal counsel to Sen. John Stennis and was in private practice in Washington D.C.

National Advocacy Center of the U.S. Justice Department at the University of South Carolina Law School where the author taught for many years.

The faculty of the Justice Department's Advocacy Institute or "school for prosecutors" in Washington before it moved to its current quarters in South Carolina. The author is on the left front beside current U.S. District Judge Ginny Grenade of Mobile and in front of U.S. Magistrate Richard Dean of Atlanta.

The author as a student at the Sorbonne in Paris where he spent two years constantly watching trials as a "courtroom rat" at the Palais de Justice in Paris and the Old Bailey in London.

Regan, the author's wife, at the Barnes and Noble homestore in New York where the author's book *Thomas Jefferson on Wine* was a "staff selection."

The author as a high school basketball player. His coach, just-retired Marine Corps drill instructor, instilled a love of competition and teamwork much needed for future prosecutors.

The Oxford Anti-terrorism Task Force. Left to right: FBI agent John Lavoie, Chief of Police Steve Bramlett, Sheriff Buddy East, the author, Detective Andy Waller, and FBI resident supervisor Rich Calcagno.

The author with his daughters, Dr. Allison Doyle, left, and Lydia King, right, in front of a painting of them as little girls aged three and eight.

The author, with his wine-tasting cup, receiving an award for his nationally-syndicated column on wine, food, and travel.

Unfortunately, my name appeared on the release as our contact person. Despite all our efforts to protect John Daly's reputation by repeatedly mentioning in the release and in open court that John Daly knew *nothing* about what his ex-wife did, he still trashed us in the press anyway, perhaps just out of chivalry to his ex-wife. She did not return the favor, publishing in 2011 an outspoken exposé on the life of a golf-wife called *Teed Off.* Not surprisingly, she did not mention her little brush with federal law.

Federal versus State Prosecution

Perhaps it would be useful to explain at this point how some cases come to be federal crimes, while others are state crimes. Not only lay persons but many lawyers have no idea how the system works. Many crimes can be prosecuted in either state or federal court. A bank robbery in Mississippi is an armed robbery in state court, just like the robbery of a convenience store. Bank robbery is also a federal crime if the victim bank is FDIC-insured, as most banks now are. Drug cases are similar. Nearly every sale of drugs that violates state law is also a federal crime. It is basically up to state and federal prosecutors whether such cases go to federal or state court. Since there are plenty of cases to go around, whichever prosecutor wants the case can usually have it. Practicality usually prevails.

If a drug dealer operates in multiple counties, it is easier to handle him in federal court, since state DAs have to try their cases county by county, while federal prosecutors can try them in any county where the dealer made one of his sales. If a case crosses state lines, as many do, federal prosecutors usually handle it due to their nationwide subpoena powers, whereas state DA subpoena powers stop at the state line.

Other considerations can come into play as to who will prosecute when crimes violate both federal and state law. The cost to one county government can be too high; single-county juries are easier to influence by media or defendants compared to federal court, where members can come from several counties—all thirty-seven counties in the case of our federal district. Politics can also play a role. Mississippi DAs and judges are elected and are more subject to pressures of public opinion, while federal judges and prosecutors are appointed by the president and confirmed by the U.S. Senate. For that reason many sensitive cases investigated by local sheriffs and police are brought to us by them with the agreement of local DAs. On occasion, state DAs up for reelection ask us to let them handle "hot" cases, when they need voters to see them doing the big cases rather than "giving everything to the feds," as their opponents would charge.

Most violent crimes like murder, rape, and burglary are exclusively state crimes. In fact, over 90 percent of all crimes in the U.S. involve state law only. Such cases become federal crimes only if they cross a state line or when a federal facility such as the U.S. mail is involved. Uniquely federal crimes are rare, limited to things like treason, the counterfeiting of U.S. currency, or crimes committed on federal lands like national parks. Mississippi has a large number of such parks.

Our system of shared prosecutions sounds complicated, but in my experience it works surprisingly well, as stories throughout this book will show. Our biggest problems have come when Congress and some federal judges have tried to limit federal jurisdiction in political corruption cases, as discussed here.

Some of the falls from grace recounted here involve judges—mainly Justice Court judges—and of course lawyers, the most flamboyant of them Richard "Dickie" Scruggs, the only billionaire we have prosecuted. As a class, however, no group of public officials can compare to Mississippi's powerful county supervisors, of whom we convicted five dozen statewide in cooperation with our southern district counterparts in a case featured by Mike Wallace on *60 Minutes* as Operation Pretense. In a separate case, we quietly convicted the unfortunate, financially strapped father of our world-famed crime novelist John Grisham, which some observers say altered the nature of his novels from local to national and gave him a certain hostility toward the power used by the FBI and some federal prosecutors portrayed in his fiction.

Harvey Hamilton: The Old Peg-Legged Sheriff Meets RICO[11]

One of the pleasures of being a trial lawyer, especially a prosecutor, is that you never know when the best case of your life may suddenly fall in your lap. For me it happened early, in 1976. I'd had fun putting away bank robbers, car thieves, convicted felons caught with firearms, and even an honest-to-God Ku Klux Klan leader. My investigators had mostly been experienced veterans, always older than me and certainly wiser. I'd never had a corruption case, and my general impression was that North Mississippi had pretty straight public officials, especially its law enforcement officers. I'd yet to meet a bogus one. But when I finally did, he was a doozy.

In those days, all of us Feds had our offices in the same building, the federal courthouse in Oxford, a block west of the Square and its stately antebellum courthouse, hub of William Faulkner's fictional Yoknapatawpha County. The ATF was on the first floor, the marshals and judges on the third, and we were on the second floor with the FBI and the probation officers. We were not only close physically but also partners psychically. The FBI agents were then all hard-core Hooverized, with white shirts, narrow ties, and short haircuts. They were the real thing: grown-up Boy Scouts.

One day the straightest arrow of them all, resident agent in charge Kenneth P. Hughes, knocked loudly on the door of my private office. Hughes did not know how to knock softly and was not eager to learn. He had a deep, commanding Boston brogue and a cold stare. Hughes could intimidate defendants into confessing just by the menacing way he read them their rights.

That day, Ken had his game face on and was all business. Following in his wake was a skinny, wide-eyed rookie with gold-rimmed glasses. Ken, who called me "John" when we drank beer together on Friday nights after work, was in full Hoover mode that day: "Mr. Hailman, I'd like you to meet our newest special agent, fresh from the academy. His name is Wayne Tichenor, and he is a Marine." Not *was* a Marine but *is*, as in forever. The "academy" is of course the FBI Training Academy at Quantico, Virginia, about forty miles south of Washington, D.C. The academy is surrounded on all sides by a Marine Corps base. I later taught there several times. It is a stern place but rich in camaraderie.

"Agent Tichenor, being low man on our Bureau totem pole, has been assigned by me to handle DeSoto County, which in case you hadn't noticed, has started to attract all the worst thugs from Memphis. But since he is just back from a combat tour in Vietnam with the Marine Corps, I'm sure he can handle them. I know you will treat Agent Tichenor right and show him the ropes. He already has his first case for you."

Before Wayne or I could say a word, Hughes was out the door. I invited Wayne to sit, and we began to chat and swap sports stories. It was as if we'd played ball together or double-dated together for years. He had gone to Memphis State and knew both the dark and funny sides of that big country town. He'd just gotten a call out of the blue from a man named David Baker, who said he needed help with a little legal problem, mentioning up front that he was a professional gambler. "Gosh, I hope the FBI's not harassing you," Tichenor told him sarcastically. Baker appreciated the approach. "I'm glad you're not one of those tight-assed Hoover guys," Baker said. "I'm pretty loose, but I can't lend you any seed money if that's what you want," Tichenor replied. Baker asked to meet someplace they would not be seen together. "Why don't I just come to your joint," Tichenor said, wanting to get a free look at his gambling den. Baker agreed. "It's called the Matador Lounge."

Baker came right to the point: "The new DeSoto sheriff, that fellow Hamilton who ran as Mr. Clean, the guy who was going to clean up corruption, is already shaking us down for payoffs." Tichenor found it amusing: "And you want us, the FBI, to protect your illegal operation against the sheriff?" Baker persisted. "Look, I understand. But don't you think a crooked cop is worse than a little gambling? After all, we're just giving people what they want. But gambling is not all of it."

Baker offered to introduce Tichenor to his partners. "I figured I might as well get to know as many of my local criminals as I could," Tichenor told me. Baker's first partner arrived in five minutes. "He was a big, handsome business-looking guy built like a linebacker with blond hair and blue eyes and wearing an expensive blue blazer with brass buttons. His name was Danny Owens, and he was not at all what I had expected. There was something cold and crazy in his eyes. They had no feeling." As a native Memphian, Tichenor knew all too well who Danny Owens was. He ran a chain of drug-infested high-end "gentlemen's" strip clubs notorious for drugs and violence. Owens had recently been acquitted in state court on a murder charge. During a hand-to-hand battle with pool cues, a motorcycle gang leader had bled to death from a deep stomach wound allegedly inflicted by Owens. No knife or other weapon was ever found. Owens's able defense attorney was Bob Gilder, another colorful character who later became a good friend. Bob had persuaded jurors that the gang leader died from falling through a plate glass front door during the fight, earning Gilder the nickname "Door" because in his closing argument in the case, he had argued, "The door did it."

I asked Wayne if he had any other criminals I could call to the witness stand to corroborate the testimony of these distinguished criminals against the newly elected reform sheriff. "Oh, yeah, there's my star witness. Her name is Fran Jenkins. She's Baker and Owens's partner in the Matador Lounge, but her real business is a massage parlor called the Camelot. Classy name, huh?" At that point, with most agents I would have just made up an excuse, another meeting or something, and ended the matter by telling him to submit me a full, written report detailing the laws violated and the evidence we would use to prove our case. But there was something different about Wayne Tichenor, so I asked him to tell me more about Fran Jenkins.

"Well, she's a redhead from Kentucky in her thirties, very funny and charming. She's got a lot of miles on her, but if she had taken a couple of different turns, she could have been a good wife for a banker or maybe even a U.S. senator." Only Wayne Tichenor could have said that with a straight face. "So now we're helping not just the gamblers but also the prostitutes, right?" Tichenor ducked my question. "We've got to start somewhere. These guys are just informants. I don't see them as our main witnesses, but we can get our suspects on tape. From what I know, most of the DeSoto County government is crooked, law enforcement included, and I think we should take them on."

There was something about this skinny young agent's mixture of passion and calm that hooked me. "Where do we start?" I asked. "Well, Ken Hughes has already agreed to let me meet with the guys running the Organized Crime Task Force in Memphis. They're working corruption cases that bleed over into DeSoto County, and they're trying to break up Danny Owens's sex and drug businesses, but can't do it because it's protected by too many corrupt officers. They have a small, separate unit totally detached from the others, and they'd like us to work with them." It was all going too fast for me. "So we're going to work with our victims and then we can bust them later?" I liked Tichenor's answer: "That's about it. We don't owe them a damn thing. Who do they think they are, anyway, asking us to clean up law enforcement so they can commit their crimes in an honest environment?"

My memo to the file about our conversation was the strangest I'd ever dictated. My secretary asked, "Who is this guy Tichenor? I like him." I told her I guessed we'd find out as we went along. It was a couple of weeks before I heard back from Wayne. He had not been idle. By some act of FBI legerdemain, Wayne and Ken had persuaded their boss in Jackson to open a Level I undercover operation against the sheriff. They'd already recruited a veteran Memphis police undercover agent to play the role of an organized crime foot soldier who was testing the waters for a national syndicate to take over gambling, prostitution, and drugs in DeSoto County.

It was always my rule (based on some bad early experiences) never to allow any UCs to operate in our district without first meeting them face-to-face and making sure I was comfortable with them. Too many were either cop-groupie cowboys or criminals themselves. But most bureaucrats who supervise federal investigators have always discouraged this. They insist that prosecutors never interact with informants. Their unhealthy mantra is "We investigate. You prosecute." When you read in the paper about some blown trial, this self-defeating theory is often behind it. To me, prosecutors and investigators are natural partners, not competitors. At their very best, they are brothers, and that is how things developed with Wayne Tichenor and me. Best of all, it was Wayne who first suggested that I meet his UCs before we began.

Baker was about what I figured, a seedy gambler type. I was to meet Fran Jenkins next, but she had the flu and sent her bookkeeper Debbie in her place. Since Debbie would handle the tape recordings of the sheriff and his bagmen, I figured she'd be just as good and probably a better witness. A divorced blonde bank teller with a little girl to support, Debbie told me her story. A good-looking classmate of hers from high school had told her at a school reunion that she was working at a "spa," the euphemism for a massage parlor, which was the euphemism for a whorehouse. Debbie, who had been doing bookkeeping at a bank for a decent salary, was shocked yet intrigued at her friend's career choice. "Do you really give them massages?" she asked. "Well, we massage parts of them," she was told. "Why don't you come and visit?" After a Saturday night hanging in the lobby, Fran Jenkins told Debbie she needed a helper, a strictly legal one, one night a week. No sex, just bookkeeping. Business was brisk, and Fran and the other girls had no time to keep up with paperwork. Debbie agreed to try it. To her surprise, within a week she was servicing occasional clients as well as keeping books. She soon found she could make more in one night having sex with acceptable strangers than she could make on her bank job in a month. Fran let her pick her customers, telling undesirables she was "just a bookkeeper."

I tried not to ask Debbie, "How did a nice girl like you end up . . . etc." She put me at ease. "It was safe. It was easy. I *liked* it. Most of the guys were more scared than I was, just fumbling country boys. Fran ran a tight ship: no drunks, no drugs, no danger. For some reason I just took to the job. Before I knew it, Fran put me in charge of "special services." Before I could embarrass myself by asking what that was, Debbie explained, "Some guys can only get off if it's kinky. They wanted me to paddle them, wear black leather, and verbally abuse them. It never turned me on, but it was easy to do and they tipped like crazy. I ended up with whips and the whole nine yards. Everything was great till one night the new sheriff, Hamilton, sent a guy by who said we'd have to start paying him $500 a week or he'd shut us down."

Fran and Debbie quickly decided that they had to pay off the sheriff to survive. Then one day they got a visit from another sheriff's man saying that the first guy had been stealing from the sheriff and they needed to pay the new man instead. Not knowing who to believe, Fran went to Baker and Owens for advice, and they decided to go to the FBI, a curious choice under the circumstances, but you never know why people do what they do. Before Wayne Tichenor could even ask, Fran volunteered to carry a hidden tape recorder in her purse and record the payoffs and conversations. Debbie would write down in advance the serial numbers of the bills Fran used for the payoffs and hand the tapes and the lists to Wayne Tichenor at anonymous shopping malls right after they occurred. Soon a third bagman appeared, a suave businessman from south Louisiana named Houston Morris. He was polite and funny and treated the girls with so much respect that a couple of them offered him a "freebie." He politely declined, saying he had a beautiful young wife and a new baby and didn't need the risk no matter how tempting the offer was.

In the meantime, Sheriff Hamilton was getting his countywide corruption machine cranked up. Working with his campaign manager and "right arm," auto parts salesman John Harter, Hamilton began tapping the many sources of illegal income accessible to a sheriff. Mississippi sheriffs held vast discretionary powers. They are still referred to by old-timers as the "high sheriffs," as in old Mississippi blues songs. The sheriff, not a judge, would usually decide whether someone arrested would be allowed to make bond and how much it would be. They often helped pick the grand jurors. If a sheriff wanted you indicted, you got indicted. Local district attorneys, who are also elected, cross sheriffs at their peril. A hostile sheriff could put a DA back in private practice at the next election.

Wayne introduced me to Sergeant Jim Kellum, a stocky, bearded Memphis detective with a quick wit and lots of undercover experience. To our surprise, running a corruption sting was much like running a drug sting. You just act your part, offer the target the opportunity to do what he already wants to do, and you're off to the races. Kellum, keeping it simple, took the undercover name Jim Smith, saying, "Why complicate things?" He was to play the role of an agent of an Oklahoma organized crime syndicate who'd heard law enforcement south of Memphis was "not too vigorous." Kellum had gotten an introduction to John Harter and asked to meet the sheriff personally. Harter immediately showed a weakness Kellum figured he could exploit: Harter asked Kellum for $5,000 in cash for the introduction, saying, "The old man don't need to know about this." Knowing that disloyal confederates are always useful, Kellum gave Harter a $500 "down payment," saying he'd get the rest after the meeting if he found he could trust Harter. One key to good UC technique is to always get the target to prove to you that he is reliable, and not the other way around.

Things moved quickly. Harter took Kellum to his residence, where Kellum waited by the pool whistling "Danny Boy," much to the amusement of the agents listening in on the wire. Hamilton arrived, and the three of them went straight to the 301 Club, the large pink-stucco mansion just a mile from Memphis that Elvis Presley had built for Priscilla as a getaway in the early years of their marriage. Set up as an elegant supper club downstairs, the upstairs had been converted for VIP guests into a regular illegal casino, complete with slot machines, high-stakes poker tables, and dice games. Fran Jenkins's prostitutes were to join them later.

Hamilton immediately offered to cut Kellum and his syndicate in on the deal, of course for a substantial investment. Kellum feigned enthusiasm but said "his people" operated alone and never had partners, saying "people talk." His organization would hire and fire all employees and account to no one. As a criminal syndicate, this setup seemed reasonable to Hamilton. He praised Kellum's "professionalism." Of course from Kellum's perspective, he had to have complete control so his officers could gather evidence, video, and audiotapes, and make sure that what looked illegal was actually a legal undercover operation. The bookkeeping and security for such deals are much tougher than they look. After all, if things went wrong, the headlines would read, "FBI Runs Beer Joint, Gambling Den, Condones Rampant Prostitution."

Just as Hamilton was getting comfortable, gremlins appeared. A friend of Harter's saw Kellum at the 301 Club and thought he recognized him. Harter confronted Kellum about how he learned of their operation. Kellum said through a local bunco artist who'd been running the 301 Club and picking up payoffs from the Camelot. Harter had checked some more and even heard that "Jim's" real name might be something like "McKellum." Harter, not a clever man, again confronted Kellum: "Have you ever worked with the police?"

Our cover was almost blown before we got started. Luckily for us, greed prevailed. Somewhere in the criminal underworld, the myth persisted that officers are not allowed to lie about being officers. With ultimate cool, Kellum boldly asked Harter, "Jeez, the sheriff don't think I'm the heat or nothing, does he?" Harter was fooled and persuaded Hamilton to go along. We were back in business, but it had been a close call. Kellum was too local. Someone else might recognize him. With his agreement, we phased Kellum out.

To act as the next mobster above Kellum in the chain of command, the FBI chose a smooth, suave agent from headquarters named Les Davis, who was sent to Oxford to pose as Les Daniels, a capo in the Oklahoma mob. Davis had previously spent a year in Mississippi and understood just enough of our unique culture to read situations and fit in. Kellum introduced Davis to Harter and Hamilton and left the stage, telling the crooked law officers that he was going back to Oklahoma. To further enhance the dark side of the supposed OC connection, the FBI also sent in Gene "Gino" Stephens, a tall, burly agent of Portuguese descent who really looked the part of a mob enforcer. With Gino as the muscle and the suave Davis as the front man, our team looked ready for prime time. Hamilton took an immediate shine to Davis, calling him at all hours to ride around the county with him, showing him how local corruption worked. When Davis suggested that some people might not welcome organized crime in their midst, Hamilton was adamant: "We're the poorest state in the nation, and you are just what we need."

Things started off well. The FBI rented a series of suites at the Memphis Hilton and loaded them with legal bugs and video cameras. The UC agents played their mobster roles to the hilt. But when they suggested using a bank account to transfer payoffs, the streetwise Hamilton balked: "I don't like to put my John Henry on nothing. Let's just use play money (cash)." Hamilton vouched for Harter: "He's my right hand, my quarterback. His mouth is my mouth." The agents smiled inwardly at his trust, knowing that Harter had been cheating Hamilton behind his back. Wanting Hamilton on tape rather than just Harter, Davis said, "We understand. We trust him, too, but our bosses say deal only with Number one." Flattered, Hamilton agreed.

He briefed them on his operation. "We got thirty-eight honky-tonks in the county running wide-open. No hours, no rules. They pay $150 a week each. We control all the gambling machines in all of them, too." He explained how a father-son team, the Robert Harbins, Sr. and Jr., paid him for the entire county gambling machine concession, saying they had run out all the little nickel and dimers. "We're about to take over gambling in Tunica County and Marshall County, too." When Stephens asked about constables, elected officers who serve as bailiffs for justices of the peace, Hamilton said, "Put a quarter [$25] a week on them and you'll have no problems." When Stephens asked about the justices themselves, Hamilton said, "If there's no one to arrest you, where's the problem?"

At their next meeting, Hamilton took on the role of consigliere, warning the undercover FBI agents about FBI stings: "Watergate started off in Washington and got the president himself and now it will move down to your lowest-titled man in the state." He said each "spa house" paid him $500 a week, but the slot machines were the most lucrative. "That is where you're going to really rake it in." Hamilton handed Davis a special DeSoto County deputy sheriff's badge (just like Elvis once had), authorizing him to carry a gun at all times. Hamilton then launched into a series of homey aphorisms on corruption. When Stephens asked how the prostitution business would get known since it was illegal to advertise, Hamilton said, "I don't have to tell you how a coon finds a tree." He told them to let gamblers win some on the front end to build up business, saying, "You gotta feed the pig if you want to eat it." He also warned them that not all law enforcement was corrupt, saying, "Your federal boys and your state ABC alcohol boys, they don't tell me when they're coming. They got a right to come in here just like you've got a right to drive down Broadway."

Hamilton concluded his little seminar on corruption with a message: If caught, he would never tell on them, and they'd never tell on him: "When the heat gets on my ass, you can nail my nuts to a sycamore tree and I ain't tellin' a goddamned thing. And if a son of a bitch squeals on me, he's a dead motherfucker. That's just how simple it is. Now I may go to Parchman, but that SOB who sends me, he ain't going to be out there eating cake and ice cream." This prophecy later came back to haunt Hamilton. Unbeknownst to him, FBI undercover agent Les Davis had once been a cartoonist, and he later drew a picture of Hamilton with his privates nailed to a tree while Wayne Tichenor stood by eating cake and ice cream.

Harter drove Davis around the county looking for a good spot for an illegal twenty-four-hour gambling/liquor/prostitution joint. When Harter suggested they call it the Dew Drop In, Davis sniffed, "We were thinking of something a little classier." The FBI didn't want just any old beer joint. After several false starts, Davis found a nice former supper club in a secluded location not far from Interstate Highway 55. The FBI agents, fond of using puns as names for their UC operations, called it the Pump House. By January 1977, the slot machines and dice tables were in place, and Davis was ready to open.

He had also solved another little problem. Hamilton and Harter kept offering him his choice of the best-looking prostitutes at the Camelot. The agents, being agents, had already taken an informal poll and elected a brunette named Jenna as the Camelot "queen." But Davis was happily married, and hanky-panky was the last thing he needed. The FBI solved the dilemma by assigning special agent Gail Denman, an agent from New Jersey, to pose as Davis's girlfriend.

All through January things went great. Hamilton showed up almost every night at the Pump House, took his payoffs in person, and incriminated himself all over the tapes. He did the same thing at the Camelot massage parlor. The next month, problems began. A constable named Macon Campbell came by and told Davis that his wife had him going to church and he'd decided he would take no more payoffs, saying, "I have to look at myself in the mirror in the morning." Davis peeled off several bills and offered them to Campbell, who said, "I'm not asking for *more* money. If you do that again, I'll arrest you." A week later, Campbell reappeared and arrested Davis, who told me later he wondered how the incident would look in his FBI personnel file. Tichenor, who never worried about anything, said, "That should just enhance your reputation as a real criminal for other UC operations." Davis was not amused.

Davis met with Hamilton and told him he was paying for protection and he'd better start getting it—or else. Hamilton replied with one of his little parables, saying Davis was "going too fast, too wide-open." He stressed that corruption needs to be subtle: "It's just like this coat I've got on. You can take it and throw it in that puddle and it will be all wet, just like that, and everybody will know it. Or you can take one drop of water at a time and put on it and slowly get it wet, but nobody will notice it even when it is thoroughly wet."

Embarrassed at his inability to give Davis protection, Hamilton dug himself in deeper, boasting of his statewide ties, saying, "me and the Governor are close as chocolate is on a cake." He said Davis could still get whatever he wanted: "Just pull the cord and the bell will ring." But Hamilton was not all confidence. He warned Davis that he'd heard that the Feds were snooping around and that the state grand jury was about to meet, so the Pump House needed to "close for repairs" till they were out of session since Hamilton admitted he could not control local DA Gerald Chatham Jr.

Another interesting character, Chatham was the son of Gerald Chatham Sr., the courageous young DA who had prosecuted the men who murdered Emmett Till back in 1955. Much praised by the national media for his courage, Gerald Chatham Sr. had died of a heart attack while still in his thirties just after the Till trial ended. Gerald Jr. was cut from the same cloth. He was one of only three public officials in DeSoto County we informed of our undercover operation.

As Hamilton had predicted, he could not control the local grand jury, and distinguished FBI Special Agent Les Davis was indicted, fortunately under the name "Les Daniels." Gerald Chatham got it dismissed, but Les was worrying what his OPF (Official Personnel File) would be like. For our case the worst was yet to come, and from a most unlikely source. Some FBI bureaucrat in Washington had reviewed Davis's personnel file and noted that he had never attended the official FBI undercover-agent training course, which lasts a month. Davis was ordered straight to Quantico, potentially blowing our whole case. I went ballistic, ranting and screaming till my wife feared I'd have a stroke.

Wayne Tichenor stayed cool but could not calm me down. That took Ken Hughes. "Mr. Hailman, the sheriff himself told us to shut it down. Les Daniels, an important syndicate man, has been indicted. It is only natural for him to leave town." It was as simple as that, and it worked fine.

In the meantime it was business as usual at the Camelot massage parlor until one night Sheriff Hamilton called and told Fran Jenkins, "The heat is on," and he would not be coming any more but was sending an old and trusted friend named "Jack." Hamilton said "once you see him, you'll always know him." That night a big green Buick with an Arkansas tag pulled up out front. The three-hundred-pound man who got out had not previously been a customer, and Jenkins immediately knew he had to be the sheriff's man. One of the girls slipped out and wrote down his tag number. It came back to a Jack Briggs of West Memphis, Arkansas, just across the river.

Briggs went right up to Fran Jenkins, who boldly said, "I only deal with one man, and you ain't him." Briggs, who not only spoke in a whisper like the old actor Sidney Greenstreet in the movie *The Maltese Falcon*, also physically resembled the actor. He told her the sheriff could not come because "there is so much heat on, the Feds and all." Briggs explained he was "Harvey's best friend" and was the first one who had put Hamilton in alcohol rehab, joking it was a challenge because Harvey kept smuggling in half-pints of whiskey in his artificial leg, which caused him to refer to himself as "the old peg-legged sheriff." Fran Jenkins coolly played her role: "What if a Fed was to come here and ask me questions? What do I say?"

Briggs was ready. "I'm a businessman. I made you a loan. You're paying me back." Briggs said he would always call before coming and they would use a sort of oil company code since that was one of his businesses. "I'll call you well No. 9. A hundred barrels of oil will equal $100." Briggs, who saw himself as a real, if somewhat obese, James Bond, told Fran to call him No. 14, because "that's the middle number of my social security number." Not to be outdone, Fran Jenkins said, "You can call me No. 33, because that's my age and I can remember that." After each of his visits, agents would videotape Briggs going to a nearby restaurant, where he always met right away with Hamilton. Tichenor would then meet with Fran Jenkins and go over the tape recordings with her and receive the serial number lists from Debbie, information that later proved crucial at trial.

From the tape recordings of Hamilton, Harter, Briggs and their cronies, we figured we had a pretty good case. But some problems remained. Most of the laws they were violating were state laws, not federal. Our proof of the gambling was mostly talk, the prostitution normally did not cross state lines, and the after-hours booze cases were misdemeanors. The bribes were all of state officers, not federal. Since then many of those laws have changed, but in 1976, our arsenal of legal weapons was pretty slim. We needed more law to go with our facts.

One thing we could not figure out was what Hamilton was doing with all the money he was receiving. We had planned to use the IRS to bring tax-evasion charges, but there too lay a problem. Hamilton only had two bank accounts, one checking and one savings, and none of the payoff money had gone into either account. Nor was any money coming out of either account. As his attorney later said at trial, he was just "ratholing" it. He was living off his cash payoffs and banking his salary. Then, in one lucky tape, Hamilton helped us out by telling Les Davis why he didn't trust banks—he knew too many crooked bankers. He kept all his money at home and suggested Davis do likewise. With that evidence as probable cause, we got search warrants for Hamilton's house, car, and person. Teams of FBI agents served the warrants one day right after Fran Jenkins had paid off Briggs. On the shelf in Hamilton's bedroom closet they found a Fran Jenkins payoff bill. In his wallet they found more payoff bills. Having just seen him hand something to his wife, a nice innocent lady, right before they searched him, they received her permission for a female agent to search her purse. Among her grocery money they found several more payoff bills from Fran Jenkins. Hamilton's poor wife was buying her groceries with the prostitutes' money.

Simultaneously with the searches, pairs of FBI agents began serving subpoenas for the next federal grand jury on every gambling den, honky-tonk, and massage parlor. Most cooperated right away. Several were brought in for me to interview personally. One I remember vividly was the mother of Dr. Leslie McLemore, political science chair at Jackson State University and for many years the president of the Hinds County Board of Supervisors and a vital leader in Mississippi's era of racial reconciliation. Leslie's mother ran a popular café in the town of Walls, totally legal, but Hamilton had threatened to shut her down if she didn't pay him anyway. He encouraged her to stay open after hours and sell liquor illegally, which she refused to do. Leslie came in my office and got right to the point: "My mother needs no lawyer, she's done nothing wrong, but I want to know one thing. Are you really going to do something this time? DeSoto County is desperate; it's always been like this, for blacks and whites alike. All I want is your word that you will go all the way."

Of course I said we would, but in my heart something changed that day. Before that, the case had been an adventure, a well-meaning game. But what Leslie McLemore said brought home to me just how much this case meant to so many people and the suffering and despair it would cause if we lost. After they left, I *really* went to work. Leslie's comments had motivated me like a football coach at halftime, and this game was now for keeps.

Hamilton immediately went on the attack, asking a state senator to "silence" one of his employees, who ran a little honky-tonk. The senator immediately called me and offered to come to the grand jury with his employee, saying they would both testify. Then Hamilton got even bolder and talked directly to Warren "Tut" Sullivan, one of the biggest and richest of the Delta cotton planters, asking him to get one of his employees to deny that Hamilton had shaken him down. Sullivan immediately called Tichenor and reported it. The good guys were lining up on our side. So was the press.

But we still had the legal issues to deal with. Ken Hughes suggested what was then the magic word in law enforcement, RICO, the punning title of a new federal anti-Mafia law. RICO stood for the "Racketeer-Influenced and Corrupt Organizations" law. Intended originally only for use against traditional organized crime, federal courts had ruled such an application would be discriminatory and anti-Italian and that RICO could be used against any organized group of five or more persons whose primary purpose was to make money from crime. The special appeal of RICO was that it federalized most state crimes. A RICO indictment would solve all our legal problems. But we could not just indict for

RICO like any other federal crime. The FBI first had to ask Main Justice to approve it, and then the attorney general himself had to sign off on it. Our own local FBI signed off enthusiastically on our proposal. I was flattered when U.S. Attorney H. M. Ray had enough confidence in me as a young prosecutor to send me to Main Justice in Washington alone to plead our case.

Not knowing what to expect, I was led into a small but well-furnished office with one big blonde guy built like a tight end sitting behind the desk. In a real Yankee brogue, he started off, "I like your case, I really do, but you've got a lot to learn about RICO." To my surprise, he sat right down with pen and paper and over the next six hours, not even stopping for lunch, he radically changed and improved my indictment. When he finished it was like a combination jury argument and press release and made Hamilton and his cronies sound like the return of Al Capone. When his secretary finished retyping it, he stamped it and signed it approved, writing his name as large as John Hancock on the Declaration of Independence. I was to hear his name many times in later years. It was none other than John Dowd, the prosecutor of Pete Rose and many other famous cases.[12]

I had never had better or more intense mentoring. What a great experience this was getting to be. The first RICO case in the history of the state of Mississippi. I flew back to Oxford elated. We brought Fran and Debbie to the grand jury the day before the other witnesses who were subpoenaed, so they would, we hoped, remain unnoticed. It didn't work. The press was there with flashbulbs popping. Wayne also told me something else he had just learned. Fran Jenkins had been addicted to heroin for years, but since the investigation started was trying to kick her habit, largely without success. When she showed up, she looked years older and shook visibly. But she got through her testimony fine, her memory was excellent, and she refused all Wayne's offers to have agents guard her house for the next few weeks, saying, "Harvey's all mouth. He'd never hurt me. I know men and I know his kind." Unfortunately, it was not Harvey she had to worry about, as we learned too late.

The next morning, as I presented witness after witness to the grand jury, I got a call from Wayne: "Fran is dead. Shot with her own gun. The coroner has ruled it a suicide, but I don't believe it." I didn't either, yet somehow I also didn't feel in my gut that Hamilton would do it. We subpoenaed anyone and everyone who might have had a grudge against Fran or might know who did. We got nowhere. One surprise was a call we got from Bob Gilder, the jolly, high-living DeSoto County lawyer who had represented both Harvey Hamilton and Fran Jenkins in the past. His office abutted the Camelot, and he had once shown an agent a peephole behind a framed law certificate where he could watch proceedings in one of Fran's rooms, with her permission of course. He considered Fran a good but unfortunate woman, and he was furious with us: "You got Fran Jenkins killed over nothing. You had no right to take advantage of her." He was especially mad at Wayne, whom he accused of "using Fran, using her all the way to her death."

We were impressed with Bob's sincerity but curious about what he seemed to know that we didn't. Then one day I realized why. Bob knew everything that happened in DeSoto County and Memphis. One afternoon, while I was leaning pretty hard on some witnesses about Fran's death, Wayne Tichenor stepped into my office. "Your next interview is here. He's probably the most important. It's Danny Owens. Last night they played me the tape from Fran's answering machine. The last voice on it was Danny Owens. He said he had to meet with Fran urgently the night she died."

When Owens stepped into my office, the look in his eyes gave me a physical chill, unusual for me. He was maybe the scariest guy I'd ever encountered. The coldness in his eyes and voice were unlike anything I'd seen outside a movie. I lost my macho. No way could I intimidate this guy. I started differently: "Fran Jenkins was your friend?" His reply fit his demeanor: "No, just a business partner." I asked him who could have wanted her dead. Did she owe money? Have any stalkers? "I don't know anything," was his only answer. Feeling stupid and helpless, I tried to sound tough but failed. "We'll be in touch." He walked out without saying another word.

Then I got one of those hunches and called Bob Gilder. "Bob, you know I'm sick about this. You know all the players. Is there any chance Danny Owens was Fran's heroin supplier and thought she might have testified to all she knew, not just Hamilton?" Bob pleased me by his reply: "John, you and I are going to be friends. I know you are hurting over what happened to Fran. This is between counsel and you can never use it, but I've been thinking just what you're thinking. It may have all been a tragic mistake, but we'll probably never know."

But we all knew that it was not a suicide. Fran Jenkins was left-handed and had one of those writing bumps on the inside of her left middle finger. The gun she was shot through the mouth with was found in her right hand. Someone had obviously planted it there. Suddenly the rest of our big-time case seemed trivial. Our desire to make a big legal kill had resulted in the real killing of a real person, a good person if a sad one. Wayne Tichenor was devastated, but resilient as always. "We've got to win this one for Fran."

With Fran gone, our only real witness on the massage parlor payoffs was Debbie. With the photographs of Hamilton meeting the girls, one of which actually showed his hand taking a wad of bills from Fran's hand while sitting in his patrol car with his SO-1 tag on the back, we had some evidence. Better yet, Debbie had talked personally with Jack Briggs and could identify his voice along with Fran's on the tape recordings of the payoffs, with all their incriminating details. Then there were the bills Debbie had marked that were found in Hamilton's wallet, house, and wife's purse. Debbie was now our crucial witness. Obviously other people knew that too. One night Wayne got a call from Debbie, who lived on an upper floor in a Memphis high-rise. She was half-hysterical: "Wayne, when I got home, the babysitter said my daughter had been crying because she couldn't find her tricycle. I went out on the balcony where we kept it. I looked over the railing, and the tricycle was lying on the concrete walk, all mangled up, several stories down. I wondered how a five-year-old could have done it, but she said she didn't, and I believe her. A few minutes ago a man with a deep voice I didn't know called and said, 'Next time it won't be the tricycle. It will be your daughter splattered on the concrete.'" Wayne was calling me from a pay phone on his way to Memphis. "What do you know about the Witness Protection Program?" I told him not much, but on our office chart I was the "witness security" officer. I called the DOJ Operations Center emergency number and told the duty officer I had a critical threat to the life of a witness in a RICO case. "I'll patch you through," he said. It was then around 11:30 P.M. A raspy voice answered within seconds: "This is Gerry Shur. What's happened?"

Gerald Shur was one of the unsung heroes of Main Justice. An old mob prosecutor with a thick New York brogue, he had almost single-handedly created the Witness Protection Program and ran it in a personal, hands-on way. Against overwhelming opposition, he got it going and kept it going, using a specially trained squad of U.S. Marshals to physically move and guard the endangered witnesses while his tiny staff handled the difficult task of creating whole new identities for witnesses and their families. My fear was that, like most big-time DOJ programs, this one would take months, and we would lose Debbie while we waited. I outlined our problems: the murder of Fran, the tricycle, Danny Owens, the web of local law enforcement corruption. I even dropped John Dowd's name as a supporter to give the case credibility.

Gerry did not mince words: "Sounds like a righteous case. We'll take it on." Still worried, I asked when Debbie might be accepted in the program and what kind of paperwork he would need. His reply astonished me: "She's in the program now, by my authority. Have your agent call the local U.S. Marshal to pick her up right away and we'll take it from there. Tomorrow you can start filling out the forms. They're all in the U.S. Attorney's Manual (which I rarely opened). Here's my private number. Call me personally, at any hour, if you have any problem of any kind."

Never in my life had I felt more proud of my own U.S. government. How decisive, how clear, how sensible this guy Gerry Shur was. I felt more than relieved; I felt grateful. Fortunately, I was later able to pay him back by representing him twice in civil cases when disgruntled criminals and others sued the Witness Protection Program and Gerry personally. I tell these stories in detail in chapters 4 and 5.

With Debbie protected, we slung out more subpoenas and persuaded nearly every victim of Hamilton's extortion to testify. One of the most interesting was a Delta Chinese guy who ran a beer joint and was known locally as a famous high school football player named B. B. Tong. At his interview, he refused to answer any questions at all: "I ain't sayin' nothin' about nothin'. I got to live here. You can go back to Oxford." On the day that he was scheduled to appear before the grand jury, I was putting on witnesses like there was no tomorrow. The witness rooms overflowed all the way down the hall with gamblers, prostitutes, and honky-tonk angels. But B. B. stood out even among the crowd. He stood about 6', 4" and probably weighed 260, really big in the pre-steroid era. I called his name and motioned him toward the grand jury door. I considered challenging him to "man up" as they say now, but that didn't seem quite right. Besides, I was scared of him just looking at him. He had small beady eyes in a big round face. He actually looked more Choctaw than Chinese. After debating how to approach him, I finally just said "Mr. Tong, a lot of people in DeSoto County look up to you as a football hero. You see all these poor, scrawny little people who are not afraid to testify. Are you going to let them down?" He never said a word, but I thought I saw something in his eye. He walked in, sat down, and gave some of the most devastatingly believable testimony I'd ever heard. He was even better at trial. Seeing a man of his size and strength cry, because he felt so helpless before the corrupt Sheriff Hamilton and his DeSoto County law-enforcement people, was a uniquely moving experience. "When you can't go to the police, who do you turn to?" he asked.

With a powerful RICO indictment in hand, we began answering boxes of frivolous defense motions. Judge Orma "Hack" Smith, a former Ole Miss football star also known for his dancing skills and charm with the ladies, was the presiding judge. There was intense media interest. The story was front-page news every day in both Memphis papers and led the TV news on all stations every night. Never had I seen so many reporters cover a trial. They rarely needed to ask us for quotes. There were so many colorful witnesses and human-interest stories that they had more than they could ever have space to write anyway. Everything was pro-prosecution. We were on offense and stayed that way the whole time. Hamilton's first defense was that the whole thing was "politics," but since no one had announced to run against him, that story rang wildly false.

One final thing that made the trial uniquely enjoyable was the color-ful cast of defendants and their attorneys. My wife gets nervous when she gets near a courtroom, and never once had she seen me try a case or argue an appeal. But she did agree, at my insistence, to come for the jury selec-tion in Hamilton, just to see the lineup of defendants and attorneys I had described to her. From the side they resembled a row of Alfred Hitchcock or W. C. Fields look-alikes, with their bulging bellies and prominent noses. The first thing she later said was "They all have such big noses. Big bellies I expected, but those noses are special." Of course not all fit that profile. Bob Gilder, who represented both Harter and Hamilton, was the smallest and also most colorful. His appearance was like the anti-FBI. His white shirt had ruffles at the collar and cuffs. Court rules required him to wear a tie, but he refused to knot it and wore it simply flipped over once so it constantly bounced as he moved. I wondered if he really projected the kind of image a law-and-order sheriff needed before a jury, but it wasn't my problem.

Next most-colorful counsel was the Rumpole-like Murray Williams, a brilliant advocate whom jurors always loved. He often appeared unprepared and hung over with bandages covering wounds he'd suffered in late-night drinking bouts during trial. His Mondays were the worst. An even odder couple was the slim, handsome former U.S. Attorney from Memphis, Warner Hodges, and his client. Hodges would have made a perfect representative for Hamilton. Instead, Hodges represented Bill Chaney, Hamilton's fat bagman who had already been convicted of two major felonies and was the main face most of the black honky-tonk owners had dealt with. After one of Warner's smooth, sneering cross-examinations of one of my terrified black witnesses, which I felt was racially tinged, I did something I have never done in court before or since. As Warner swaggered confidently behind our counsel table, I eased my chair around as if to talk to my secretary and deliberately tripped Warner, sending him sprawling in a full-length pratfall in front of the jury. Jurors chuckled. I was glad I did it at the time and was completely at ease apologizing to the judge and the jury for the "accident." I swear Judge Smith gave me a little wink.

Representing the obese Jack Briggs was local attorney Mel Davis, an old friend with little federal trial experience. He mainly deferred to the other lawyers, but he did have one bad moment cross-examining Houston Morris, the Louisiana contractor/bagman. To avoid having the defense bring it up first, I had made Morris tell the jury that he had once been the leader of a Ku Klux Klan klavern in Denham Springs, Louisiana, where he had held the titles of Kleagle and Grand Cyclops, positions of importance in such circles. On cross Mel Davis asked Morris if he could prove where he was on the day Dr. Martin Luther King Jr. was assassinated. We objected vociferously at this slur, there being four blacks on the jury. Back in chambers Judge Smith asked Mel, "Mr. Davis, do you have any factual basis for making such an inflammatory insinuation?" Mel had to admit that he didn't. Judge Smith went right back on the bench, chewed out Davis in front of the jury, and told them to "rub this remark out of your minds entirely." Unbelievably, our Klansman had come off as a victim.

The most intriguing of the defense attorneys was a tall, expensively tailored New Orleans attorney named Cecil Burglass. I hated to think how much his handmade English shoes cost. He represented the Harbins, father and son, but they clearly could not have afforded him, and we all knew the Bally gambling machine company was footing their bill. Cecil took the bull right by the horns in his voir dire during jury selection. "Ladies and gentlemen, I don't want you to hear this from someone else as a rumor. I represent, and have for many years, a New Orleans resident named Carlos Marcello, an immigrant from Italy who has been rather successful in business. Some have unfairly accused him of ties to organized crime, even calling him the 'Godfather.' But he has never been convicted of anything in his life other than not paying enough taxes, and we can all identify with that."

Cecil's bold, unorthodox approach worried me. In courtrooms where small-town Mississippi lawyers compete to convince jurors who is the most countrified, I had personally seen the big-city lawyer approach work. Some jurors seem to think that's what lawyers are supposed to be like. Cecil's office in New Orleans, which I later visited, was as colorful as he was. Located in the old neighborhood called Faubourg Marigny just below Esplanade, his was the only white law office at that time in a virtually all-black neighborhood of middle-class families. Cecil had style to go with his money. Rather than staying in a motel, he rented a beautiful furnished house from a professor on sabbatical, and he partied every night of the trial.

Cecil's most memorable day came during the sixth and final week of the trial. By that time it was clear that our case was overwhelming, and the defense attorneys knew it. Even their cross-examinations were becoming perfunctory. Bored, Cecil invited Judge Smith's attractive courtroom clerk to lunch, unusual but no real ethical violation. Margaret, a vivacious divorced blonde with a keen sense of humor, went along. As tired of the trial as the rest of us, Judge Smith gave us an unusually long two-hour lunch "hour" that day.

As their lunch was ending, Cecil asked Margaret if they shouldn't cap off their meal with a fine brandy. She demurred, then said, "Oh, what the hell." Margaret stuck to her one snifter, but Cecil ordered another and then another. Margaret later told me she thought of leaving him there, but that would have been rude. Besides, by then he probably could not have found the courthouse alone, so she walked him back after his fifth brandy. Cecil had figured that since he was last in line of eight to cross-examine my next witness, he'd be sober by the time his turn came. But for some reason, perhaps fatigue, my witness only took about ten minutes. The other defense attorneys took almost no time cross-examining him. Judge Smith turned to Cecil, who was giving off a brandy smell noticeable all over the courtroom, and said with a little smile, "Mr. Burglass, you may cross-examine."

Visibly startled, Cecil got shakily to his feet, obviously staggering drunk. Judge Smith kindly said, "I know things have moved pretty quickly here, Mr. Burglass. Would you like a brief recess to go over your plans for cross-examination?" Cecil slurred right back, "Thank you most kindly, Your Honor, but I'm fully prepared."

Steadying himself on the podium, open-handed and without a note, Cecil began to cross-examine. Judge Smith and every lawyer in the courtroom looked on in fear. We all dreaded a mistrial more than anything. If Cecil committed some error, a mistrial could be declared, and all our weeks of trial work would be lost. The judge was in the same position. Where would he find six free weeks in his loaded docket to retry the case? Even worse off were the defense attorneys. None of their clients had any more money. Everything they possessed had gone to pay their lawyers for this trial. If it had to be retried, by the rules the judge would appoint them all to retry the case for a pittance, seriously damaging their practices since several were solo practitioners. Everything was riding on a drunken Cecil not doing anything crazy.

To our amazement, either through sheer adrenalin, or just the acting skills of a supreme trial lawyer, Cecil Burglass launched into the finest cross-examination of the trial. He used logic and creative common sense to undercut my witness. He triumphed. For once in my life I was glad to see one of my witnesses lose. The jurors looked ready to applaud. Without the podium to support him, Cecil needed a little help from co-counsel to regain his seat at counsel table. Judge Smith mercifully called a recess, and after the jury filed out, smiling, prosecutors and defense attorneys alike swarmed around Cecil to congratulate him. He promptly dozed off, awakening only when Judge Smith reopened court thirty minutes later.

The court records show that we subpoenaed seventy witnesses for the trial and put fifty of them on the stand. Houston Morris and Debbie were both devastating, especially her testimony about her daughter's tricycle. Macon Campbell, one of the rare truly "Christianized" criminal witnesses I ever saw, tore them up, too. His lawyer, whom I had not previously met, was Bob Whitwell, later to become one of my favorite U.S. Attorneys. A couple of the honky-tonk owners were special favorites of the jury, too. Helton Saulsberry had a joint called Saulsberry Hill, named for Fats Domino's song "Blueberry Hill." He brought the jury to tears when he testified how he had first lied to the FBI about payoffs out of loyalty to the Sheriff, but when Hamilton sent Saulsberry's own cousin, a deputy sheriff, to threaten him about telling the truth to the grand jury, "That was the last straw." Saulsberry testified he paid Chaney for Hamilton every week "like clockwork." When asked by Hamilton's defense attorneys on cross-examination if Saulsberry actually saw the money go into Hamilton's hand, he coolly replied, "Well, I certainly didn't *go with* the money. I just gave it to Mr. Bill to give to him."

A touching part of the trial came when one bar owner approached me in the hall just before I was to put him on the stand. "There's something on my heart I should have told you long ago. I hear now they can ask you about being convicted before. Well, over twenty years ago I went to Parchman for statutory rape of a girl who was just fourteen but looked a lot older. I was just eighteen myself, but they sent me off anyway. Do I have to tell that? I thought you should know, because some of these defense lawyers might know it. They seem to know everything about everybody." I immediately reported the facts to Judge Smith, who called the witness and the defense attorneys into his chambers. "What is your position, gentlemen?" Of course, they all wanted to use it to impeach the man. We wanted to keep it out, saying it happened twenty years ago. The evidence rules back then left it pretty much up to the judge whether to let it in or not.

Judge Smith asked the man a question I had not thought of upon such short notice. "Does your family know about this?" The man wept, then said: "My wife does and she understands, but I have two daughters in their early teens. It would kill them to think I was a rapist and a jailbird." Judge Smith did not hesitate: "In my discretion, under Rule 403, I find that this old conviction would have insufficient probative value under these circumstances and could be severely prejudicial to this man's important relationship with his daughters. No mention will be made of this matter whatsoever. Is that clear?" Maybe it's just me, or maybe lawyers really were more honorable thirty years ago, but I swear it seemed to me the defense lawyers all looked pleased that the judge's ruling relieved them of the duty of "zealously" representing their clients by destroying a man's family. Not one of them objected further.

The funniest witness, in a case already rich in comic relief, was Jessie Massey, an elderly man who "did a little gambling" and "sold a little beer" at his country store. When Al Moreton asked him on direct if he'd ever paid off Bill Chaney for the sheriff, he said, "Yes sir, every week." On cross, Bob Gilder challenged him: "Now Mr. Massey, you're just saying what the FBI wants, aren't you?" The answer: "Yes sir." Gilder went on: "You never paid off anyone for anything, did you?" Answer: "No sir, never did." Gilder sat down. Al Moreton got back up and showed Mr. Massey his grand jury testimony. "Did you or did you not tell the grand jury you had to make payoffs?" Massey replied firmly, "Oh, yes sir, sure did make payoffs, sure did."

At that point, Judge Smith wheeled his chair along behind the bench so that he was eye to eye with the witness and said, "Now, Mr. Massey, you can't tell two opposing stories like this. You're under oath. Why are you doing this?" Massey, perturbed, said, "Well, Judge, to tell you the truth, I'm scared to death. Whatever I do, some of these men can come and hurt me, so my wife told me to just agree with everything anyone told me to say." Judge Smith didn't laugh or even smile: "Now, this is a court of law, and I'm the judge here. Now you tell *me* the whole truth right now, or I'll have you locked up for contempt. And you can go home and tell your wife I'll have her locked up for tampering with a federal witness. Now which story is the true one?" Massey seemed relieved. Someone was in charge. He said, "The truth is what I told the grand jury and that little fellow in the black suit there," referring to Al Moreton. Judge Smith asked forcefully if any attorney on either side had any further questions. No one did. "Go on home to your wife. And if she gives you any trouble, you call me. My telephone number is there on your subpoena."

When we rested our case late one morning, Al Moreton and I looked forward to another of those two-hour lunch breaks while the defense got ready to put on its case. Judge Smith asked defense counsel how many weeks it would take them to present their evidence. A spokesman for the group arose and said, "We plan to rest, Your Honor. We don't believe they've proved their case." It was apparent to Al and me that they had either given up or they had someone paid off on the jury who would hang it up. We leaned toward the latter theory because during jury selection certain jurors had reported in chambers that people acting for Hamilton had approached them and tried to influence them. We feared there had been other approaches which might have succeeded. Judge Smith said mildly, "Well, gentlemen, it seems to me an unusual tactic under the circumstances. In your opening statements, each one of you solemnly promised the jury that your man would take the stand in his own defense. Do you think the jurors can forget that?" The attorneys told the judge they felt sure if he would instruct them to do so that would do it.

Al and I were equally sure that someone had fixed the jury. Then Judge Smith gave us the scare of our lives. "All right Mr. Moreton, Mr. Hailman, I'll receive your proposed jury instructions at 1:30 P.M. and closing arguments will begin at 2:00 P.M. Who will open the arguments for the government?" I stammered, "M-m-m-may it please the court, I will, Your Honor. But could we have until tomorrow? We had not expected defense counsel to break their word to the jury." The judge was firm: "No, sir, I've had civil cases stacked up behind this case for six weeks, and they need a trial, too. I'll see you at 1:30 P.M." By some miracle, Al slung together a set of perfect jury instructions for some really tricky and novel legal points. I took the court's official witness and exhibit lists from Margaret King, drank some coffee, and winged it. In reality, our case was so overwhelming that argument was not that difficult.

The defense arguments turned out to be surprisingly good. Since that was all they had, they had spent all their time on them. They had spent far less time reading the ethical rules, however. Most were state court lawyers used to the old Mississippi rule that in closing argument a lawyer can "sail the seven seas"—that is, argue just about anything. They began with personal attacks on the FBI, claiming that agents had "planted" the marked bills and "made up the tapes." That was to be expected. But their praise of Sheriff Hamilton surprised the jurors so much that some laughed openly during argument. Hugh Cunningham, a tall, elderly attorney from Jackson, referred to Hamilton as a "one-man posse" and a "regular Marshal Dillon" who "clamped down on crime tight as a hat band." Others called the FBI agents "loathsome, like vultures feeding on the high sheriff." They accused Tichenor of having an affair with Fran Jenkins and Gail Denman of being Les Davis's paramour. We prosecutors were called "cruel and faultless" and "part of a scheme to convict an innocent man" by "tricking and sandbagging" the poor, hardworking defense counsel.

One said we had hidden most of the real evidence, saying, "this case is like an iceberg, most of it is hidden under the sea." The citizen witnesses who testified for us were called "stool pigeons," contrasting them to Hamilton, whom they characterized as "the old, peg-legged sheriff, standing out in the cold rain, bare-headed at a funeral." One said Hamilton had "had his hair combed by the winds of the ages, and his cheeks washed by the morning dew."

After the first day's arguments, which went on for more than four hours, the judge recessed to hear more of the same in the morning. When court reopened, Bob Gilder was wearing dark shades and asked if the judge would hear him briefly in chambers. When we got back there, Bob said, "Judge, I don't want my client to be prejudiced by this Hollywood look I've got, but my eye is blood-red. Would you mind explaining to the jury for me that I'm wearing these dark shades only because of a medical condition that makes my eyes hypersensitive to light." Judge Smith, with a twinkle in his eye and knowing Gilder's reputation for late nights and occasional fights with people who made fun of his ruffled shirts, said, "Mr. Gilder, I will, but only on the condition that you tell the court and counsel, off the record of course, what really happened to your eye." Turning to the court reporter he said, "Lee, don't take this down." Gilder stood. "Judge, it was just a little misunderstanding. Around 2:00 A.M. in the parking lot at the Ramada Inn, after conferring with counsel over a drink or two I was getting into my car. Some gentlemen nearby, seeing me removing my coat, thought the gesture was meant as an offer of fisticuffs." Gilder then pulled off his shades, revealing a beautiful shiner and a blood-red eyeball. "I'll explain to the jury you have an eye irritation and the dark glasses are worn for medical reasons with the court's approval," Judge Smith said.

Bob Gilder proceeded to make a very credible jury argument, downplaying a little friendly gambling, a few drinks, and stressing how poor working people needed to unwind sometimes without the FBI "morality police" interfering. He stressed how difficult it was for sheriffs and their deputies to break up fights at beer joints at closing time "when the women don't come out even," saying a "little tip" from the owner was no more than they deserved for doing their dangerous jobs. If our evidence hadn't been so strong, he might even have swayed some of the jurors.

But the argument to end all arguments was by the oratorical Murray Williams, a former federal prosecutor who asked the jurors to "apply the acid test of reason" to the evidence, pronouncing our case "the weakest case, in my judgment, I've ever seen," a personal opinion on the merits of the case expressed in blatant violation of all rules of ethics. But we didn't object, figuring we'd either already won the case or they had a juror fixed anyway. The closing arguments were mostly for show at that point. In conclusion, Williams flashed his red and gold Masonic ring to the jurors and delivered a chilling metaphysical sort of threat:

> If he who made the moon and the sun and hung the stars on high can be merciful and just, then so can you. If you convict Harvey Hamilton on the testimony of thieves, rogues, whores, and disgruntled politicians, then never again will the nightingale of a clear conscience perch upon your pillow to sing you to sleep at night, but the ghosts of the wicked and the perjured shall be your companions, until your dying eyes shall—at the last—turn to read the rapt and mystic meaning of the stars.

The jurors were not laughing. For a moment I thought a couple even looked fearful. But I figured it would pass, and it did. In a few hours, they came back with verdicts of guilty on all defendants on all counts. No one was ever charged in Fran Jenkins's death.

Jury Tampering 101: A Sheriff Solicits Help from U.S. Senator James O. "Big Jim" Eastland[13]

The RICO trial of Sheriff Hamilton had achieved such wide publicity that Judge Smith decided to conduct all the juror questioning individually in chambers. With over 150 jurors summoned, if each juror had answered all the questions in front of the others, there was too much risk someone would blurt out something they'd heard that was so prejudicial it would have caused the judge to have to dismiss the entire panel, summon another one, and reset his schedule for another six weeks.

At first we were not particularly worried about jury tampering, thinking it would be too risky considering that the jurors were summoned from all of our thirty-seven counties. We figured we could just knock off all jurors from Hamilton's home county, DeSoto, who probably had no desire to sit on a jury that might convict their own sheriff, a very powerful man to cross. Years later I read an article on jury tampering in the *Wall Street Journal* that changed my mind.[14] I wish I'd read it before the Hamilton trial. It said, in summary, that jury tampering was a good idea for guilty defendants for several reasons: First, contacted jurors rarely reported it; second, even if a defendant was caught and convicted of jury tampering, sentences were incredibly light, with judges often considering punishment for the primary offense sufficient. The average sentence nationwide for jury tampering was usually one year or less, even in cases like ours where a twenty-year sentence for the main offense was not unusual.

Most interesting was the article's insight into regional differences. In large cities, threats to jurors and their families were common. Money was usually offered, sometimes in large amounts. Convictions for jury tampering were rare in all regions but especially in the South, where a different culture appeared to prevail. In the South, the article said, money was rarely offered and threats almost unknown. The southern approach was to appeal for sympathy for the underdog. The juror contact was usually made at second- or even thirdhand by an intermediary for the accused. The intermediary would insist that the defendant was a good person and an old friend who would never have committed the crime. The intermediary would usually tell the jurors of false "evidence" the prosecution would use that was the product of some personal or political vendetta by some powerful person. Since no money or threat was involved, the contacted jurors did not feel too threatened and would simply deny the contact when asked by the judge, believing they were independent enough to make up their own minds and, like most of us, not wanting to end up in court and in the papers and on television as accusers. Most southern jurors apparently just took the path of least resistance and remained silent.

The article was remarkable in its accuracy as to our case. During voir dire questioning of jurors, three of the ladies were from Quitman County, adjacent to DeSoto County. Their county seat was Marks, known nationally as home of the famed Poor People's March on Washington. In our case, all three ladies first denied any contact by anyone. All three invented various excuses why they could not serve. Had they had better excuses, Judge Smith would no doubt have let them off and we'd never have known about the jury-tampering. But their excuses were so weak that the judge declined to excuse them. Hearing that, the first one to break volunteered to Judge Smith that, while she had not talked about the case with anyone, someone had approached her about it. Early on the Sunday morning before Hamilton's trial was to begin on Monday, a man had knocked on her door and said, "I am James Reed, your county supervisor for this beat, and this is my wife." Reed asked to come in while his wife waited on the porch. Reed got right to the point: "Sheriff Harvey Hamilton is my good friend. He goes on trial tomorrow in Oxford on false charges trumped up by political enemies. I know you've been summoned for jury duty and if you're selected, I just hope you'll give him a fair trial." It was blunt yet subtle. He didn't ask her to acquit Hamilton no matter what, but his intentions were clear. The woman told Reed, "I don't want to serve. It makes me nervous. I hope I don't have to." That drew Reed out a little more: "Oh, I hope you do serve, and remember, as your supervisor there's a lot I can do for you." That remark bore a not-so-subtle implication: "I'm powerful. There's a lot I can do for you and against you."

The other two Quitman County jurors, both women, were then called back individually and, when confronted by Judge Smith, testified to an almost identical contact by Reed using almost identical language. The three ladies did not know each other. It sounded like a desperate, last-minute attempt by Hamilton to save himself from what he knew was our overwhelming evidence. The immediate response of defense counsel was interesting. They of course denied knowing anything about the contacts, and we believed them. Then they said there was no proof that Hamilton had any idea his friend was trying to help him out.

Judge Smith asked the key question: "Did any of you gentlemen give your clients a copy of the jury list furnished to you by the Court for you to use in checking jurors' backgrounds for bias?" They all agreed they had. "Did you tell them this court requires that they must not contact, directly or indirectly, any juror?" The lawyers all nodded "Yes" vigorously. The judge then turned to us and asked another key question:

"Gentlemen, do you think there is too much risk to this trial by these improper contacts?" Al Moreton and I looked each other in the eye and, without even asking to consult, shook our heads. "No sir. Let's proceed. But we do ask that you re-question carefully each and every juror as to whether anyone has approached them." The defense attorneys competed with each other in jumping up like porpoises to object: "That's highly prejudicial, Your Honor, and will unduly suggest someone has been tampering." John Farese led the charge. "Well, Mr. Farese, should I dismiss this jury and start all over?" Judge Smith asked. Farese and the other attorneys asked to consult out in the hall and quickly came back and said, "Judge, this case has cost these defendants a lot of money. We can't afford to do it again. We'd rather go forward."

Al Moreton and I chuckled, knowing he really meant their clients had no money to pay more attorney's fees. Judge Smith said he would not go back and re-question the fifty or so jurors he'd already questioned, but would be more specific and pointed in questioning the hundred or so he'd not yet queried. We all agreed that this was a fair compromise.

As soon as we were out in the hall, Al and I started trying to figure out how we could smoke out any other jurors who had been illegally contacted. We decided to look most closely at the jurors who seemed the most nervous. We realized we had overlooked a key element in Harvey Hamilton's background. Before being elected sheriff, he had served two terms as county supervisor; he had been very active in the statewide supervisor organization and had contacts everywhere. With 5 supervisors for each of the 37 counties represented on the jury panel, there were more than 150 potential jury-tampering James Reeds out there.

Jury selection is the key to success or failure in every trial. We had asked for a district-wide jury to get jurors less likely to have private knowledge of the case and its players. The defense wanted jurors who had not read about the case in the Memphis papers or seen it on Memphis TV, but the case had received so much publicity and was so colorful that just about everyone still breathing in the district had heard something about it. Judge Smith directed us not to do any investigation as to the three ladies until our jury was selected but then asked for a thorough investigation, including personal interviews by the FBI of all jurors not selected to serve. The FBI did just as Judge Smith directed and scores of interviews were conducted.

One thing we learned later totally amazed us. Four male jurors who did serve on the jury all lived in Attala County, Oprah Winfrey's home—geographically as far as you could get from DeSoto County. Despite all the questioning by the judge and lawyers, however, and all the private investigations we had all done on the jurors, no one had learned the most important fact: All four of the Attala jurors had moved there from DeSoto County, and all knew Hamilton's reputation as a crooked supervisor. With all our hours of questioning, somehow that fact never came to anyone's knowledge until too late.

When Hamilton's trial ended with the conviction of all defendants, I drafted an indictment on James Reed. In an interview Hamilton's jailer told Wayne Tichenor he had overheard some of Hamilton's talks with Reed. The jailer claimed he knew of no other supervisors Hamilton had used, but did know of someone else Hamilton had talked to about the jury: United States Senator James O. Eastland. Wayne and I learned this in a Saturday morning interview just after Hamilton's RICO trial ended. At the time, James "Big Jim" Eastland was one of the most powerful men in the United States. As Chairman of the Senate Judiciary Committee, he controlled the fate of nominees for all U.S. Attorney and all federal judge positions, as well as all U.S. Supreme Court nominees. How would we handle this development?

Uncharacteristically, my first reaction was that of a timid bureaucrat: "We'll have to get DOJ approval to interview a U.S. senator, and my guess is they won't approve it." Tichenor took more of a Marine Corps approach: "What the hell, the SOB lives in Doddsville. I say I just go down there and interview him." My spine was stiffened by Wayne's reaction, and I offered to go with him. "No, you'll get your boss H. M. Ray in trouble. It's better if we limit it to an FBI investigative matter. The judge told us to do it. Besides, if you're a witness to the interview, you can't prosecute the case." I changed totally. "I don't give a damn about trying the case. I can help you. I know Eastland personally. We are on good terms. I used to run messages between him and Senator Stennis."

To persuade Wayne to let me go with him, I told him a couple of stories. "Senator Stennis and Senator Eastland appear to be opposites and have two very different camps of supporters in Mississippi. Stennis is the dignified statesman, former judge and state DA. Senator Eastland is a wheeler and dealer and backroom guy who speaks in monosyllables through a haze of cigar smoke. Stennis lets it be believed he's a teetotaler, although he's not, while Eastland loves to have a glass of Chivas Regal in one hand an expensive cigar in the other when he talks to the press. Eastland has had bad press in Washington but great in Mississippi and is tremendously effective behind the scenes. Stennis has a great reputation in both places, not just because he is great, but because he's such a good secret source for so many reporters of so many different political persuasions. They both have their own games."

Tichenor was curious: "So how do these guys get along?" My answer was that when Senator Stennis joined Senator Eastland in the Senate, they made a pact. Senator Stennis told me about it. Before every Senate vote, each would notify the other not only which way he would vote but the reason he would give in public for his vote. That way, even when they voted differently, each one protected the other's back with the press and the voters back in Mississippi. Eph Cresswell, the chief of the Senator's staff, usually handled these messages, but when he was not there, on several occasions Senator Stennis sent me to Senator Eastland's office to tell him about a vote. Eastland trusted me for that reason and also possibly because his son Woods was a classmate and friend of mine at the Ole Miss Law School. Successful politicians check people out. But what Senator Eastland really liked, I think, was that I wrote a *Washington Post* column about wine and food. Senator Eastland loved good food. Every time I saw him, we'd exchange restaurant tips.

Thinking I'd persuaded him, I told Wayne I was ready to go. "Are you going without telling H. M. Ray?" He had me. It would get H. M. Ray in trouble with DOJ whether I told him beforehand or not. It was not a case of acting first and seeking forgiveness later. No way I would go without asking H. M. first, and if he agreed for me to go, he'd be in trouble with DOJ, and his reappointment as U.S. Attorney would be coming up soon, a decision over which "Big Jim" Eastland would have veto power. Wayne was right. I should not go with him.

Wayne picked up the phone and called the senator's office in Washington. A secretary said he was in Mississippi for the weekend. When Wayne told her he was a Mississippi voter, which was true, the secretary gave him the senator's office number at his plantation in Doddsville. Wayne dialed it and the senator answered the phone himself. Wayne told him he was with the FBI and needed to talk to him right away. Agents doing background checks on judicial and other nominees no doubt talked to him all the time. "Come on down," Eastland said. I went home and waited by the phone. It was over a two-hour drive to Doddsville one way, but Wayne took advantage of law enforcement courtesy from the Highway Patrol and less than two hours later he called me. "John, that was the interview of my life. What a sharp, quick, cagey old guy that Eastland is." Wayne told me the senator had known right away from reading the papers why he was coming. It was not some background check on some federal judge nominee. "He volunteered it all. He started right off saying, 'You're here about that sheriff' before I could ask him anything." The senator said Hamilton had shown him a printed list of the jurors, with those from Sunflower County highlighted. "I knew them but didn't know much about them except one, a serious lady who works in a doctor's office. I told Hamilton he didn't want to take her, that she'd convict her own grandmother. And would you believe it, that fool sheriff left her on the jury, and she voted to convict him just like I said she would. The talk is all over the county."

Wayne said he asked Senator Eastland if they'd talked about the case other than the jurors. "Well, of course Hamilton, that's his name, said it was all politics. But he had this other fellow with him, his jailer, I believe it was, which he should never have done if we were going to talk seriously. I figured the fellow was some sort of bagman, so I turned to him and asked him how often 'the bag' went around, and he said, 'Every Tuesday.' I looked at Hamilton and told him I thought that was pretty stiff on some of those little people. Hamilton just shrugged. They left after about fifteen minutes. Didn't pay a blind bit of attention to anything I told them."

On Monday, Wayne came to our office, and we met with H. M. Ray and told him about the interview. H. M., always a team player, told Wayne he had handled it just right by going alone straight to the senator. I read that as meaning H. M. appreciated our office having deniability and that an informal shirtsleeve interview rather than a suit-and-tie FBI job made the senator feel trusted and respected and was probably the reason he was so open. Still, we hoped the case would plead guilty and we wouldn't have any need to go through all the hoops required to get a U.S. senator to testify. Nor would we ever have to tell the defense or the press about it, especially the part about the bag going around, which tended to show Senator Eastland was no babe in the woods when it came to local corruption. It reminded me of something Senator Stennis once told me. "You know, Jim and I take different approaches, different angles. I tend to go straight at things. But when Jim could do something easily and with entire propriety, he seems to love making it look like he did it by some shady backroom process. Both ways work, of course, but I'd have a mighty hard time doing it his way."

As we'd hoped, after we got Hamilton indicted, both he and James Reed pled guilty. At Reed's sentencing, I was amazed to learn that this rich Delta planter had dropped out of school in the second grade and could barely read or write. At Hamilton's sentencing, I argued hard for the maximum sentence, which was five years. Judge Smith gave me a fatherly look, as he often did, and noted that Hamilton was over sixty and already had many years of prison time to serve, and that one more year would be a sufficient deterrent. I disagreed but remained silent, thinking to myself later how the *Wall Street Journal* was right.

Several years later, given a weekend furlough to visit his family, Harvey Hamilton was arrested for getting drunk and using his artificial leg to kick in the door of a youngish girlfriend he wanted to visit. His chances for early release were extinguished. Years later, when Wayne Tichenor was dying prematurely of Lou Gehrig's disease but continuing to work, testifying from his wheelchair in a Memphis corruption case, Wayne mailed me Harvey Hamilton's obituary from the Memphis paper. In an accompanying note Wayne called it "The only obituary I ever read which reads like an FBI rap sheet. It's two whole columns mostly about all the crimes he committed."

As FBI undercover agent/artist Les Davis noted in his classic cartoon of Hamilton nailed to a sycamore tree, Wayne and I were not exactly out there eating cake and ice cream, but we had outlasted Harvey Hamilton. To his credit we had to admit that, as Hamilton had promised, he had never "squealed" on anyone. But he did unwittingly open a door for us. The years Wayne Tichenor spent investigating Hamilton's corruption in DeSoto County led us to our next big case: former pro football star Will Renfro and other members of the DeSoto County Board of Supervisors.

"Will Renfro, You Can't Hit an FBI Man!"[15]

While investigating Sheriff Hamilton, FBI agent Wayne Tichenor heard from many sources that corruption was, if possible, even worse among the local board of supervisors than in the sheriff's office. In those days, supervisors were even more powerful than they are today, being the basic unit of government for each county. Men often went into office as poorly paid road foremen and exited as wealthy landowners after just two four-year terms. Tradition allowed them extensive use of county equipment and labor for their own private purposes. Tradition also considered it normal for supervisors to build expensive taxpayer-funded barns on their private property, which they were then allowed to keep as their own property when they left office. Supervisors were little lords in their own domains, most counties having five districts with no centralized office for oversight or coordination. Each supervisor decided how to spend the money for his district, or beat, as they were called. In some states, these officials were more properly called *road supervisors* because that was supposed to be their primary function. In DeSoto County, easily the fastest-growing county in the state of Mississippi, road and bridge building were booming, spurred by white flight from Memphis and the lure of a quiet, suburban life.

The fastest-growing part of the fastest growing county in Mississippi was the area just across the state line from Memphis, which had over fifty thousand people but was unincorporated and had no government except the supervisors. Opportunities for corruption were almost unlimited. The area known as "Southhaven," was just across the state line from the Memphis neighborhood known as "Whitehaven," which when you consider the two names together gives you a pretty good idea what was driving the growth of the area. Supervisor for Southhaven was a former pro football star named Will Renfro. A 6', 6" true athlete, Renfro weighed 260 and was known from his stints as a defensive end with the Pittsburgh Steelers, Washington Redskins, and other teams as an excellent pass-rusher, feared by quarterbacks around the NFL. A local boy who had played at nearby Northwest Community College, Renfro was both admired and feared and was well known for his violent temper and his habit of using intimidation and physical force to get his way.

In dealing with informants and local criminals in the Hamilton case, Tichenor had gotten an earful about Renfro and his ways from around the district. People complained about Renfro's blatant misuse of public property and personnel and of how fast he was enriching himself with land deals, fat contracts, and healthy kickbacks from companies selling to the county. In a freak development that we did not learn of until later, an IRS agent named Bill Gibson, a vigorous investigator, went alone one day to the home of Renfro's elderly parents. Gibson asked them some really blunt questions about their son's dealings, which greatly upset the elderly parents. Gibson, a medium-height guy with a mustache, left after a few minutes without learning much from the parents and thinking the interview was of no importance. It turned out to be of great importance to the rest of us, however, especially FBI agent Wayne Tichenor.

Also a man of medium height with a mustache, Tichenor was checking some records the next day at the Chancery Clerk's Office in Hernando, the county seat, later immortalized as the courthouse of "Ford" county in John Grisham's crime novels. Tichenor, a naturally gregarious man who was popular in the county due to his genial way of dealing with witnesses and suspects alike, was walking down the hall when a very large man blocked his path. "The guy was shaped like a triangle, big and wide at the top and narrowing way down to his waist," Tichenor told me later. "We'd actually never met, but I knew from pictures of his scowling face I'd seen in the paper it had to be Renfro," Tichenor said. With an odd mixture of violent hostility and southern manners, Renfro said, "Are you *Mister* Tichenor?" As soon as Wayne said "Yes, sir," Renfro acted.

He sort of bull-rushed me. He came at me first with his head down, then raised it up and kind of butted me with his chest, like you might do with a quarterback. He grabbed me by my jacket and lifted me up over his head like a rag doll. I felt him turning me so my head was toward the concrete and felt sure he was going to slam me head-first into the floor. We had hand-to-hand combat training in the Marine Corps, but I'd never needed it in real life. I sort of twisted my body and he ended up throwing me flat on my back instead of my head. The look on his face was pure fury. He was twisting my head around when a lady's voice called out, "Will Renfro, you stop that. You can't hit an FBI man." Boy, was I glad to hear her. The look on Renfro's face changed suddenly when he heard her voice. He looked bewildered, as if he'd been in a trance. He said something about his parents and jerked me to my feet and walked away.

The witness, Beverly Allen of the clerk's office, ran up to help Tichenor, who was dizzy. "What was that all about?" she asked. "I don't know. I'd never met the guy." Down the hall Tichenor saw another big guy, this one with a beard, walking toward him. When it appeared that Tichenor was ok, the bearded guy sat back down on a bench just outside the courtroom.

Later that afternoon Wayne walked into my office. "Well, I finally met Will Renfro. He knocked me down right in the courthouse up on the second floor." I asked Wayne to tell me about it and he said it was hard to figure. "It was like the guy just snapped, and then he snapped back out of it. After he had knocked me down, he picked me back up and was tugging at my necktie. Beverly Allen said he cocked his fist to punch me in the back of the head but her screaming stopped him. She asked me why I didn't pull my gun. I told her it happened too fast and by the time I got my wits about me, he was gone."

My own first thought was that this unprovoked attack would make a good addition to our RICO indictment, which I was already drafting. Then Wayne changed my mind. "When I told the guys at the office about it, they called the SAC, and he will be calling you wanting Renfro arrested. But I don't think that's a good idea. This is just a sideshow and could delay us for months. I wasn't hurt, and I'm not scared of the guy. Next time I'll be ready. Prosecuting him would make me look like a crybaby."

I questioned Wayne for a good twenty minutes about what he remembered. He never saw Renfro's fist; nothing was broken. "Was there any blood?" I asked. "Just a couple drops on my cheek where his watchband scratched me as he was turning me." I worked on Wayne until he was convinced that even if it made him look weak, the FBI's honor and the safety of other agents were at stake. By the time the SAC called, we'd agreed to get a federal arrest warrant for Renfro for assaulting an FBI agent in the performance of his duties.

The SAC was happy but I was worried. Wayne's testimony so far was weak. Then I interviewed Mrs. Allen, who was a powerful witness. By checking court records we found out who the other witness was: a first-offender drug-dealer awaiting arraignment. I called DA Gerald Chatham and told him what had happened. Without my even asking, he dropped the charges on the young dealer so his character couldn't be impeached at Renfro's trial by his own conviction. The kid turned out to be a beautiful witness, lucid and with that gift of articulating small details that is so persuasive to neutral listeners like jurors. His strongest statement was:

> When the huge guy pulled on the little guy's necktie and twisted his head around and pulled back his fist, the big guy's fist was bigger than the little guy's head. If that lady hadn't screamed, one punch in the back of the head could have killed him. I was too scared to do anything and it was all over in seconds. As soon as the big guy saw there were witnesses, he ran off.

Now we had a case, with two strong, neutral eyewitnesses to reinforce Tichenor, the victim who couldn't see what happened to him.

Reporters were all over the story as soon as Renfro was arrested. Ken Hughes, supervisor of the Oxford FBI office and Tichenor's close friend, asked the U.S. Marshals to let him make the arrest personally. They agreed. Hughes took 6', 5" Joe Lattus, the biggest agent in the FBI office, with him. When Ken said something about hoping Renfro resisted, I told him not to provoke anything. "Our case is good, so don't mess it up with revenge." Ken agreed and said he was just saying he *wished* Renfro would resist but knew that any beating of Renfro would hurt Wayne's case. The arrest went well. Renfro was polite and offered no resistance, talking only about harassment of his parents and that Tichenor had slipped on some sawdust on the floor from repairs being made to the courthouse. Hughes did have one problem with Renfro, however. His wrists were so huge no FBI handcuffs would go around them. U.S. Marshal rules require that arrested subjects be handcuffed for transportation. Hughes did the only thing he could under the circumstances: he put leg irons on Renfro's wrists. They both laughed about it.

Media coverage of the case was heavier than usual because Renfro was up for reelection. Both Renfro and the women at the courthouse gave statements to the press, and when his story about Tichenor slipping on sawdust got out, his opponents started handing out dustpans with little brooms attached encouraging voters to sweep out the courthouse and Renfro with it. They had a field day with the story, with Renfro huge and menacing beside Tichenor, the 160-pound Vietnam veteran who had somehow fended off Renfro's attack.

The trial was set for a Monday in Clarksdale. U.S. Attorney H. M. Ray insisted on sitting with me at counsel table at trial to add the personal weight of his office to support the FBI agent, whom he felt the defense might unfairly attack. When H. M. and I got to the motel Sunday night, someone had left the windows open and the air conditioner off. The walls of our room were so covered with mosquitoes they looked black instead of motel beige. We asked to change rooms, but there were no empty rooms in town, reporters having gotten most of them. H. M. and I splattered the walls with dead mosquitoes for ten minutes or so until Wayne Tichenor arrived with bug spray. After meeting until late in the evening at the courthouse preparing for trial, we got back to the blood-splattered motel rooms, which smelled like cotton poison, but at least they were cool and we slept through the smell with no problem.

Our part of the trial went smoothly. Renfro had hired Oxford law partners Hal Freeland and Gerry Gafford, two good lawyers and friends of ours who we knew would not try any low tricks. Their only problem was keeping Renfro under control. The big man came to court looking even bigger than usual, foolishly wearing tight jeans and a "muscle" shirt with no sleeves, revealing his enormous upper arms. Our witnesses were excellent, and Judge Keady ruled that the defense could not question our drug dealer witness about why he was at the courthouse because his case had been dropped and such questioning would have been more prejudicial than probative. Then the defense took over.

Having little choice, there being no eyewitnesses favorable to him, Renfro's attorneys put the big man on the stand. His very presence, his intensity of movement and his angry expression seemed to unnerve the jury. Then they decided to do something which, ever since, I've always instructed my law students in trial practice never to do: They tried an obviously unrehearsed courtroom demonstration. Such scenes are highly persuasive if they work, but disastrous if they go wrong. With Renfro on the witness stand, Hal Freeland called for his partner to come forward, asking the judge for permission to act out the confrontation with Tichenor. H. M. and I were astonished. Renfro's appearance was menacing already, and it was a godsend for us for the jury to see his body in action.

Freeland said to his partner, "Gerry, go stand in front of the jury. How tall are you?" The answer was about the same height as Tichenor. It was evident Gafford weighed a good deal more, but we certainly had no objection. "Gerry, you lie down on your back on the floor in front of the jury in the position Mr. Tichenor said he was in when, as we contend, he slipped on the sawdust." Gafford looked surprised, convincing us this scene was as big a surprise to him as it was to us. He lay down on his back right in front of the jury box. "Now, Will, you show the jury how you helped Agent Tichenor to his feet." Renfro, cat-quick, walked forward and straddled Gafford with his legs. Looking right at the jurors, Renfro reached down with amazing quickness and strength, grabbed Gafford by both shoulders, and with a huge grunt like one of those modern tennis players, hauled Gafford high up in the air, with his feet dangling helplessly, then put him back down on his feet hard, glowering and scowling all the while. "That's just how it happened," Renfro volunteered.

The jurors were wide-eyed and pushing themselves back up in their seats. Rather than showing how Renfro's enormous strength allowed him to "help up" a fallen Tichenor, the image was exactly the man Tichenor had described: quick, unbelievably strong, and totally violent looking. Tossing his blonde hair and flexing his biceps, Renfro proudly returned to the witness stand. The jurors would not look at him. Several seemed plainly scared.

I personally felt the trial was over, but the defense had promised it would put on some "good character" witnesses to establish Renfro's reputation as a truthful man whose testimony should be believed and whose only violence had taken place on the football field. When we recessed the night after the demonstration, I asked Wayne if Renfro's reputation was really that good. "Hell no, it isn't. You want some people to prove it?" Wayne picked up the phone, made three phone calls, and in a couple of hours three middle-aged men appeared at our motel room. They were hard-working types still dressed in their work clothes. Each would testify that he had done work for Renfro and that he was not only angry and violent all the time but could not be trusted to be honest or tell the truth.

I knew that somewhere in the rules there was an anti-character-witness rule, but I'd never used it before. Under the rules, usually the only way you can attack a defendant's character for violence is if he injects it himself by his own witnesses, as Renfro had done. And the only way we could put on testimony that a defendant was not to be believed was if he took the stand. The Renfro case gave me my first chance to test the effectiveness of such testimony. It was devastating. The jurors shook their heads in disbelief at some of the deals Renfro had done, then nodded in agreement as each workman witness testified that he personally would not believe Renfro under oath. The jury went out and did not stay long, coming back with guilty verdicts on all counts.

We went back to the RICO case and finished the investigation and got that indictment even before Renfro was sentenced on the assault case. When Judge Keady gave Renfro eighteen months for assaulting Tichenor, we were satisfied. Then Renfro changed lawyers, hiring Billy Pace, the retired former ATF agent from the Tupelo Ku Klux Klan case, who'd retired and hung out a shingle. After reviewing our evidence on the corruption case, Billy asked if we'd consider a plea agreement. By then we were well into our investigation of other DeSoto County supervisors and didn't want to spend several more weeks trying a complex corruption trial on Renfro. We let Renfro plead to one count. Judge Keady gave him two more years of prison time in a consecutive sentence, and we moved on, convicting DeSoto supervisors Johnny Wallace and James Earl Riley.[16] We thought our days with DeSoto supervisors were over, hoping the voters would be more selective next time and elect some honest replacements. But there was still one DeSoto County case left. It was not the most important, but it was certainly one of the most unusual.

John Grisham Sr. and the Wobbly Wagon[17]

One of my oddest cases began, not surprisingly, in an odd way. One morning U.S. Attorney Bob Whitwell called me into his office to meet with state auditor Pete Johnson. Bob got right to the point. "John, Pete here just flew up on the state plane on an important matter. Pete, tell John the deal." Pete proceeded to explain that his office had just closed an extremely sensitive investigation on the father of John Grisham, whose first novel, *A Time to Kill*, I had just read and much admired. Little did I suspect at the time just how famous or how rich John would become—nor how modest and natural he would remain despite his wealth and fame.

Pete said he had heard that the case agent for his office was angry that John Sr. had been allowed to pay back some money he'd taken from DeSoto County and that there would be no state prosecution of him. According to the auditor's staff, the agent had delivered a copy of the case report to our office the previous day. As criminal chief, the file would have been given to me for assignment. If it involved corruption, I probably would have assigned it to myself. I told Bob I'd never heard of such a case but would of course tell him immediately if I heard anything about it. I was too busy the rest of the day to think about it, but when I skimmed my in-box before going home, halfway down the pile I saw a thick manila envelope with a note from Pat Williams, the secretary who sat outside my door. Dated the previous day, the note said, "Mr. Hailman, a gentleman left this and said to give it to you and asked you to call him after you read it." It was the Grisham file.

The first page said that John Grisham Sr., a DeSoto County supervisor who also owned a heavy equipment business, was in financial difficulty and had taken advantage of his situation as supervisor to sell the county some worthless equipment and charged them over $20,000 for it. Without reading it thoroughly, I took it straight to Bob. Always an emotional guy, Bob said, "John, this is horrible. John Grisham was my law clerk in private practice. He's a great guy. His father has lots of political enemies, but to me he's probably the most honest guy on the board. But I'm a Republican, and he and John are both big Democrats. If we pursue this case, it will not only look political but I could lose John's friendship, and I cherish that. I'm going to recuse myself from this case entirely. You study it and work with Al Moreton, and y'all do whatever you think is right." It was classic Bob Whitwell, sensitive both to what was personal and what was legal and how it would look to the public. I took the file home with me.

Reading the file would have been funny if it had not been about my friend John Grisham's father. Although we'd never gone to trial against each other, he'd defended a couple of my cases at the investigative stage, and I admired both his skill and his character. In one case, he represented a fellow member of the legislature suspected of burning his own business for the insurance money. When I asked him, John agreed to submit his client to a polygraph by my favorite examiner, Bob Campbell of the FBI. We promised John and his client we would show them all the questions in advance so there would be no misunderstandings that could skew the results. They agreed. We often used the polygraph to clear people and reduce the number of suspects, rather than hope the suspect would flunk the test and confess. Most agencies select agents to be trained on the polygraph from among their best interrogators. One of the most important uses of the polygraph is not only to clear the innocent but to take advantage of the critical moments just after a suspect fails the poly to use his fear against him and obtain damaging admissions or even confessions. In the case of John's client, my instinct was that he would flunk the test flat and might well confess. He was a nervous guy anyway, and all the circumstantial evidence pointed to him. The fire could have been an accident, of course, but no one else had a motive to burn his business.

The morning John and his client arrived, I felt we were in luck. The guy was sweating profusely. When Bob Campbell began to explain the polygraph process to him, the guy began to shake as well as sweat. Bob read the signs right away. "You took some sort of drug to try and beat my machine, didn't you?" The guy began to nod. "What did you take?" The guy shook some more and said, "Beta blockers." Bob asked if he was taking them under a doctor's supervision. "No—they're my wife's." When the guy told him how many he'd taken, Bob's eyes widened and he turned to John. "Mr. Grisham, I can't polygraph your client in this condition. There's no telling how he'd react, but he'd certainly flutter my needles and appear deceptive even if he told the truth. I strongly recommend you take him straight to his doctor on the way home. The way he's looking he may well overdose."

John asked to be excused and took his client into the office next door. I swear we heard a heavy thud, like a body hitting the wall. Bob and I thought his client had either fallen out against the wall or John had slammed him up against it. I always favored the latter theory, but never asked John what happened. He then knocked quietly and stuck his head in the door. "We're leaving. I won't be representing him anymore, but I'll see that he gets medical treatment if he needs it." It was the last time we would see John on that case.

The Grisham Sr. case being from DeSoto County, it went to Wayne Tichenor, who covered that county. After investigating and convicting Harvey Hamilton and Will Renfro and other supervisors from there, Wayne was loaded with sources. I gave him the auditor's report and told him its history. We met with the investigating auditor himself, a nervous guy who seemed depressed. A few weeks later, he committed suicide. In addition to that downer, Wayne felt just as I did about the case: "I really liked Grisham's book. It was very true to life in DeSoto County as I know it and pretty pro-law-enforcement for a defense attorney. I wish the case against his father wasn't so strong."

Wayne had already gone much deeper than the state auditor. All over DeSoto County people were laughing about the case. Mr. Grisham had apparently called on an old friend in Michigan named Richard Selander for a little favor. He obtained for Selander a license to sell equipment to the county and called him on the phone and told him of two pieces of junked equipment he had that they could pretend Selander owned and was selling to the county. Mr. Grisham assured Selander that the equipment was good and the county needed it, but it belonged to Grisham's company and under conflict-of-interest rules, he could not sell it to the county himself. Selander was to be a harmless straw man who would fly to Memphis, drive down to DeSoto County, pick up the equipment off-site and deliver it on a rented trailer to the supervisor's lot as if he had driven it all the way from Michigan.

Right away the plan went seriously wrong. Several county employees recognized the old junked equipment as local, not from Michigan. Worse, Selander rented a trailer that was too light, which wobbled the couple of miles to the county barn and nearly collapsed under the weight of the heavy diesel engine it was hauling. The matter was too notorious to ignore. We had no choice but to prosecute, whatever our personal feelings. We confronted Selander. He confessed, pled guilty, and with his testimony, we got an indictment against John Grisham Sr.

At arraignment, the father was harsh and rude to his son, who was representing him. We heard him say things like *naive* and *do-gooder* and "If I'd just denied it like I wanted to, we wouldn't be here." I made up my mind to tell John he needed to hire his dad another lawyer. Before I could, however, attorney Grady Tollison of Oxford called and said he would be defending the elder Mr. Grisham. We gave Grady our discovery documents, and when we met to discuss the case, he didn't waste time. A fervent Democrat, Grady said, "John, we need to plead this case, but are y'all out for blood? John seems to think this is some sort of political vendetta pushed by Whitwell and the Republicans." I assured Grady it was not political. I also asked him personally to try and persuade John to understand how bad Bob felt about it, but John remained convinced that Bob was behind it. For some reason, he never held it against me though, maybe because I'm politically neutral and possibly because of the plea agreement Grady and I worked out. The father would plead guilty to making an interstate phone call in support of a fraud on the county. No federal restitution was required, since he'd already paid the county back in full under the agreement with the state auditor. All that was left was how much time he'd have to serve. We had to insist on some prison time, not probation, as we did in all corruption cases, but Grady persuaded us that being gone from his business doing time would bankrupt his client and he would lose his business and his life savings.

I don't recall whose idea it was, but from somewhere we came up with a compromise. The defendant would serve his time, eight months, at night in the federal jail in Memphis, not exactly an easy place for a man in his sixties. Every day from 8:00 A.M. to 5:00 P.M., he would work at his business, which was located less than an hour from the jail. For once a deal worked as planned. The father resigned as supervisor, turned his business around, had no more legal problems, and successfully retired several years later to a quiet home in the Ozarks. His son, however, has held a lifetime grudge against Bob Whitwell, offering to finance his opponents if Bob went into politics, which he did, running for Congress after eight successful years as U.S. Attorney. Despite his deserved notoriety as a crime-fighter, Bob lost the election to former state senator Roger Wicker, who is now a United States Senator for Mississippi.

Many of John Grisham's best-selling legal thrillers have featured FBI agents and U.S. Attorneys as ambitious, heartless villains. As noted earlier, he never seemed to hold it against me personally, even agreeing to speak to my law and literature class at the Ole Miss Law School, patiently autographing the stacks of his books my students brought to him. Later his son Ty took my federal trial practice class and easily won the award as top student in the class. Only one thing remains to be said about this case. Rumors flew at the time that a Republican politician or politicians came to Bob Whitwell and urged him to pursue the case. That was false. Two politicians did come, but both were Democrats, and Bob turned them away.

Operation Pretense: We Become "Mississippi's Untouchables"

In 1985, a new FBI agent-in-charge arrived in Jackson. Weldon Kennedy, a Texan and veteran pilot, immediately energized law enforcement state-wide. Personally flying the three-seater FBI plane, he visited every sheriff and chief of police from Memphis to the Gulf Coast. He had one question for everyone: What is your biggest crime problem, and how can the FBI help solve it? Everyone's biggest problem turned out to be corruption, mostly by county supervisors, who were poorly paid and supplementing their income by demanding kickbacks on everything purchased by their counties, especially road-building supplies like expensive culverts, parts for bulldozers like grader blades, and the tar, gravel, and earth moving equipment used to build roads. Kennedy met with both U.S. Attorney's Offices, in Jackson and Oxford, and asked for our support. He proposed a statewide undercover sting operation.

Jackson U.S. Attorney George Phillips had just the idea for Kennedy. An equipment supplier named John Burgess had recently complained of being shaken down by supervisors for 10 percent on every sale he made to a county. Burgess, an ordained minister and devout fundamentalist, was fed up with the system and wanted action. After meeting with Phillips and Kennedy, he agreed to allow his business near Jackson to be used as a front by the FBI to run the sting. Two tobacco-chewing, down-home FBI agents were assigned to act as his salesmen, and his business was outfitted with video cameras and audio recorders, hidden in a back room where elaborate records of the kickbacks were also kept by an FBI agent-accountant. Crooked supervisors flocked to the business, renamed Mid-State Pipe and Supply, placing orders and demanding kickbacks. The agents obliged. Based on the percentage of the kickbacks and Brother Burgess's role, the sting was code-named Operation "Pretense," short for "The Preacher's 10 Percent." Under FBI and U.S. Attorney guidelines, we could not target public officials unless there was "predication"—some basis beyond mere suspicion that an official is corrupt. We had some predication for some supervisors but needed more.

After catching one statewide salesman on tape, agents hotboxed him. He "rolled over" and in return for a lighter sentence agreed to not only wear a wire and work with us, but to give us predication on dozens of supervisors statewide to whom he'd already paid bribes. The whole story is way too long to recount here but there is an excellent full-length book about it by Dr. James Crockett, retired Director of Accountancy at the University of Southern Mississippi entitled, appropriately, *Operation Pretense: The FBI's Sting on County Corruption in Mississippi.*

The first problem we faced in the case was an embarrassment of riches. We had so many targets that the FBI budget didn't include enough money to make all the payoffs the supervisors wanted. On the other hand, if we kept the payoffs too small, jurors might agree with defense attorneys who would argue we should spend our time chasing bank robbers and drug dealers rather than little $50 kickbacks. In the end, we compromised, taking only cases where the targets wanted at least several hundred dollars. We would not prosecute a supervisor until he had taken at least three payoffs to rebut the defense that these were just isolated one-time incidents, perhaps under pressure by the undercover agents.

The state auditor at the time was Ray Mabus, a Harvard Law graduate and later Mississippi governor, ambassador to Saudi Arabia, and Secretary of the Navy. Mabus gave us the full support of his agents, who knew the system intimately and were a huge help getting needed documents that might otherwise have disappeared from local courthouses. Within a few months we had enough evidence to indict at least fifty supervisors in the two districts, but decided to indict first just ten or so in each district to keep the cases manageable. In our district, we got indictments of all five members of the Pontotoc County board. Teams of FBI agents and auditors arrested them just before sunrise, when a defendant is most vulnerable. Within weeks they were all ready to plead guilty. To our pleasure and relief, the press supported us heavily, making the cases front-page news across the state for months. Every stage of every case led the evening news around the state.

One day while Bob Whitwell and I were visiting our prosecutor partners in Jackson, Jerry Mitchell of the *Clarion-Ledger*, who had strongly supported our sting, asked us to pose for a picture together. We usually never agreed to such apparent headline-grabbing and looked at each other to see who would say "No" first. No one did. Jerry asked us to stand in front of the judicial seal at the U.S. courthouse in Jackson, where we were meeting, and reached into a big plastic garbage bag and pulled out four 1930s fedora hats. To our further surprise, we agreed to put them on and pose together. To me we all looked either like gangsters (me) or bootleggers (James Tucker), but they snapped our picture anyway and the next weekend we were on the front page. Senator Trent Lott called Bob Whitwell the next day to chew him out for "showboating." The story began with a big, bold headline: "The FEDS: Their Jobs Tell the Story."[18]

> Mississippi 1985.
> A string of counties is ruled by powerful public officials who turn their heads at corruption and hold out their hands for payoffs—a jungle of deceit, bribery, and fraud.
>
> This is the story of four men—Mississippi's "Untouchables." Federal prosecutors waging war on a half-century of public corruption where "kickback" had become synonymous with "county supervisor." It is the story of U.S. Attorneys George Phillips and Robert Whitwell and Assistant U.S. Attorneys John Hailman and James Tucker, four men who have used the courts to smash lawless elements from the coast to Corinth, from crooked office-holders to drug dealers to professional gamblers.
>
> Combined, they have more than four decades with the U.S. Department of Justice. Their offices have prosecuted 57 supervisors and 14 equipment suppliers in 25 counties stemming from an FBI undercover probe called Operation Pretense.
>
> That's just part of their job.
> This is their story.
> By Michael Rejebian and Jerry Mitchell

My only regret about Operation Pretense was that it ended before we got to follow up on Weldon Kennedy's idea to set up a second sting with a lobbying firm as its front to accept requests for bribes from members of the Mississippi legislature. We had predication on several, and it looked like a target-rich environment, but we could never get Washington to approve it. If they had, Mississippi would have had its own equivalent of the sting called ABSCAM successfully worked against members of the U.S. Congress. But you can't have everything. And when Weldon Kennedy was transferred back to Washington, he soon became deputy director, number two man in the whole FBI, where he was invaluable to the whole country, not just our little district.

Courtroom Observers Attend the Trial of a Black Supervisor[19]

The first defendant in Operation Pretense in our district to go to trial was county supervisor Larry Miller of Winston County. Miller was hardly our choice for the first Pretense trial. He was the first black supervisor ever in Winston County and the only black supervisor indicted in our district. As the potential jurors were filing into the courtroom, two busloads of NAACP members from Winston County also walked in en masse, led by a 6', 8" preacher. There were also numerous black persons among the jurors. Race would clearly be a factor in the trial.

I decided to take the bull by the horns and walked straight up to the lead preacher and introduced myself and told him we were glad he was there. He seemed wary and more than a little surprised and replied bluntly but honestly, "We're here to see Larry gets a fair trial." I told him we were glad of it, thinking to myself that his group looked middle-aged and serious and that when they heard the powerful audio tapes we had of their fellow church member Miller asking for bribes, they would go home and dispel the rumors that there was some racial motive behind it. It was one of our stronger cases and would have an extra moral appeal to this religious group of jurors because of the *way* Miller had handled his corruption. The only thing that bothered me was that Miller's wife, the mother of his children, was in the audience and would hear the dirt that was at the heart of his case. Our evidence would reveal that the county purchasing clerk, a pretty young black woman, was also Miller's mistress and had been helping him rip off the county.

In picking the jury Al Moreton and I followed our experience with newly enfranchised black jurors. Leaving only one black person on a jury tended to leave them feeling isolated. We had even experienced eleven-to-one hung juries, so we accepted five black jurors, mostly male and mostly young. They all had good records, good jobs, and good reputations based on our background checks. It did worry us a little that two were from Marshall County, for many years a center of militancy and boycotts. As far back as Reconstruction, when the federal court had to leave Oxford temporarily because the Ku Klux Klan was so strong there, it was moved to Holly Springs in Marshall County, which was heavily black. A certain racial tension had long existed there. Nevertheless, we went for it.

After two days of hearing their trusted supervisor and his girlfriend discuss on tape ripping off their county, the NAACP members walked out of the courtroom at the end of the day. Their leader, who towered over me, walked up and said to me very simply, "Larry has lied to us all along. We hope you convict him." I had checked out Winston County and knew Miller represented a predominantly black district, so I replied, "And we hope you elect a straight supervisor you can be proud of." We shook hands and they left.

Later that week, when the jury came back with a verdict, we saw that one of the young black men, a factory worker from Holly Springs in his twenties, was carrying the verdict forms, a sign he was the foreman. He and other jurors looked at us positively and avoided looking at Miller and the defense table, always a good sign for us. The verdict was guilty on all counts. The lead defense attorney, Johnnie Walls of Greenville, with whom I'd once worked at Legal Services in Oxford, shook hands as always, but said something unusual this time. "John, I'm not wasting my time or your time or Larry's money filing an appeal. You've got him cold, and there's no point."

I felt good about what Johnnie said except for one thing: When there's no appeal, no briefs are written, no opinion is published by the Court of Appeals, and in most cases not even a transcript of the trial testimony is typed up. Therefore, discussion of this case rests entirely on what I kept from our own files, including the indictment, witness interviews, a copy of the verdict, and my own personal notes of the trial. But one thing is certain: it was a meaningful trial for all of us, black and white, and I will never forget it. And the voters of Winston County did elect another black supervisor to replace Miller and we've never had another corruption complaint against a supervisor from Winston County.

Opposing Former Chief Judge J. P. Coleman before His Own Court[20]

After the last supervisor pled guilty, we began using convicted supervisors as cooperating witnesses against crooked providers of goods and services to counties, commonly known as "vendors." One tricky decision in each case was to decide whether the money a supervisor got was the result of extortion by the supervisor or bribery by the vendor. It was often difficult to tell. Sometimes the parties themselves hardly knew. When a vendor did not want to pay but the supervisor threatened to cancel all his county business unless he was paid off, that was clearly extortion by the supervisor and the vendor was a victim. If, however, the supervisor did not ask for money, but the vendor insisted, then that was bribery. We found cases of both.

When Operation Pretense began to make national news, I was asked to teach how to prosecute corruption cases at DOJ and at private seminars nationwide. In 1987 assistant attorney general William Weld, later governor of Massachusetts, asked me along with several AUSAs, including Rudi Giuliani and Eric Holder, to write a chapter for the DOJ *Manual for Prosecution of Public Corruption* (1988). It was in 487 large-format pages. I later taught the same subject in over a dozen countries, from Morocco to Indonesia, most of which had much worse corruption problems than we did. In writing my monograph, I sought an analogy for the bribery/extortion issue that would catch the attention of case-hardened prosecutors. Finally I settled on humanity's favorite subject, sex. If, for example, a supervisor forced a vendor to give up a thing of value such as cash, that was extortion, which is like rape. It has a clear perpetrator and a clear victim. Bribery, on the other hand, is more like illicit but consensual sex: either party can initiate it, both parties can enjoy it, and neither party is likely to report it since both are involved regardless of who initiated the idea.

Before I wrote that chapter Judge Biggers once told his secretary, before taking a guilty plea from a chief of police for accepting sex as a bribe from a female CI, "Watch this. I'm going to get Hailman good." In federal court, after a defendant has admitted his guilt, the judge always turns to the prosecutor and asks for a summary of our evidence to show we really have a case and are not bluffing. In this case I stated that the defendant received as his bribe "sexual relations with an attractive young female." The Judge then asked me with a straight face if I was saying that sex was a thing of value. My equally straight-faced reply surprised him. "Absolutely, Your Honor. Sex is, without a doubt, a thing of value."

Of all the vendors we looked at, the company most clearly guilty of bribery was an Alcorn County company called North Mississippi Supply. It was run by Bobby Little, brother of Thurston, whom I'd already convicted twice of defrauding the United States. In the North Mississippi

Supply case, however, the only brother involved was apparently brother Bobby. All five supervisors from Pontotoc County testified that Bobby Little paid them kickbacks on every county purchase. Two supervisors from Monroe County, Bud Faulkner and John Alan Cockerham, said the same.

Our only dilemma was when to seek an indictment. Travis Little was running for the state senate during the month after we completed our investigation, when we would normally have sought an indictment. Travis Little was a Democrat, and with Republican Bob Whitwell being U.S. Attorney, we finally decided that indicting another of Travis's brothers just before the election would look political, even though it wasn't, so we held off for a month. In hindsight, it was definitely the right thing to do. Several defendants had already spoken loud and long on TV about Pretense being political. In the end, Travis Little was not only elected but served several successful terms in the state senate, finishing his career as president *pro tem* without a hint of scandal, so we felt vindicated in holding off on indicting his brother to avoid politics.

When Bobby was indicted, we had a different dilemma. Our witnesses had identified hundreds of documents reflecting hundreds of bribes paid to them by Bobby Little and his company. President Jimmy Carter, during his final year in office, had instituted a rule in the *U.S. Attorney's Manual* arbitrarily limiting all indictments to just fifteen counts, thinking as a non-lawyer that was plenty, and apparently fearing we might abuse some poor, helpless defendant. Since most of Bobby Little's deals involved small amounts, often under $100, we were concerned that if our charges were limited to just fifteen deals the case would seem too trivial to jurors. Worse, our own Judge Keady had recently ruled that we could not offer proof of any transactions that were not alleged in the indictment, thus cutting out about 99 percent of our proof in the Little case.

In the end, we asked ourselves, what is more important, Washington or local justice? Should we consider Jimmy Carter or justice for our citizens in our own local corruption cases? We decided to go for broke, charging Little with every last bribe we could prove, figuring, as the old saying goes, it would be easier to seek forgiveness than permission. We figured DOJ might yell at us but would not likely throw out important local corruption convictions for which we'd already won national recognition.

Our next dilemma was how to charge a conspiracy in the case, since only such a charge would allow us to put in all the otherwise hearsay statements of Little and others. We finally decided to indict the company itself as a defendant. Indicting a company can be useful. Even though you cannot dig up a corporation's buildings and equipment and put them in jail, you can ask the judge to put such heavy fines on them that it will put them out of business, not to mention making them pay back their profits to the victim counties on all their crooked deals.

When you indict a company, it actually appears in court through one of its chief officers, usually its president or CEO. Since North Mississippi Supply was mostly a one-man show, we were basically charging Bobby Little with conspiring with himself. What would President Carter say about that?

My indictment ran to 310 counts and 327 pages, alleging patterns of violations of four different federal laws. I decided the jury would need some sort of index, I but didn't want to call it that. The thing was so flamboyant that Al Moreton refused to have anything to do with it, so I went over the top again and entitled the outline a "Concordance," telling the boys Jimmy Carter might even appreciate the biblical tone I claimed it would give the document. It was so thick we had to have it bound by an outside printing company, it being too big for our office's machines.

Bobby Little surprised us with his choice of defense counsel. Apparently he still thought there was something political about Pretense. My opponent at trial was to be none other than the renowned J. P. Coleman, who was not only a noted legal scholar, but had previously been elected district attorney, state attorney general, and governor of Mississippi. He had also been a judge on the Fifth Circuit Court of Appeals in New Orleans, where he retired as its highly respected chief judge. I had argued many cases before Judge Coleman and had always won. Seeing him down in the pit with me at opposing counsel table was quite a shock. I knew he was not only a fine legal scholar and writer but a real fighter who enjoyed trying jury cases. This case would be no exception. Throughout the case we exchanged some pretty hot written motions and responses, always writing each other heartfelt private letters of apology and mutual praise thereafter.

As we expected, Judge Coleman demanded a jury trial, and we vowed to give him one. There was never, with him, any suggestion of a guilty plea, but he was surprised at how strong our evidence was, especially our supervisor witnesses. My favorites were the two from Monroe County, the skinny and sarcastic Bud Faulkner and the chubby and cheerful John Alan Cockerham. John Alan had invited me to go crappie fishing with him before trial, which I would otherwise have enjoyed, but declined because of how it would have looked. He understood. I still think the offer was genuine and he would not have tried to drown me or influence me, but if someone had seen us or heard about it and he had gotten a light sentence, it would have sounded mighty strange.

My next-to-most favorite moment of the trial was when John Alan was telling where and when Bobby Little handed him bribes. Usually it was at John Alan's barn or some other isolated location where there would be no witnesses. One day, however, Bobby Little asked John Alan to meet him for lunch at the Shelaine Motel in Aberdeen, which had an excellent buffet and where lawyers often ate for a change from my favorite place, Tony's Greek restaurant, run by my friend Chris Provious and his wife Frankie. Off premises, Chris and his father Tony made an excellent red wine from Greek grapes in the high-walled courtyard between his restaurant and his home. The fact that Aberdeen was in a dry county always seemed somehow beside the point during our enjoyment of his wine.

The only drawback to the Shelaine restaurant was its men's room, which was tinier than the restroom in the cheapest French hotel. John Alan testified at trial that Bobby Little was in a hurry one day and insisted that since Bobby "owed" him several hundred dollars in kickbacks, he would just pay him right there, suggesting they step in the men's room, a big mistake. The two rotund men became stuck in the restroom and had to call the manager to help them get out. Judge Coleman had real trouble doing a serious cross-examination of John Alan while the jury was still laughing about the bathroom incident.

My favorite trial incident involved convicted Pontotoc County supervisor Theron Baldwin whose nickname was Boss Hog because of his striking resemblance to the rotund politician on the *Dukes of Hazzard*. Baldwin had testified unequivocally to the grand jury about all the bribes Little had paid him over the years, reciting times, places, and exact amounts. He had been a perfect witness. When I called him at trial, however, I thought there was a hint of a smirk on his chubby little face. Then in his late seventies, Baldwin walked arthritically to the witness stand to take the oath. He stated his name clearly enough, but when I asked him about his dealings with Bobby Little, he "spun" me as trial lawyers say. "Mr. Hailman, you probably haven't heard this. It's been a long time since that grand jury, and I've had a stroke, and it has totally wiped my memory clean. I can't remember anything about Bobby Little other than that I knew him."

I looked over at Judge Coleman. He had a twinkle in his eye and a broad smile on his face. I'd been spun this way before by "cooperating" drug case witnesses, but never by a politician. They usually didn't want people to think their minds were gone. But Mr. Baldwin had retired after his felony conviction, so he no longer cared. I asked him if he remembered testifying before the grand jury, and he said he did. I asked him if he had told the truth. Again he said he did. Seeing where I was going, Judge Coleman rose and objected, arguing loudly that I was picking on this poor old man. But the judge also saw where I was going and over-ruled him. "So," I concluded, "You're telling this jury that everything you told the grand jury back when your mind was still good was absolutely true and correct?" He replied unhesitatingly, "Yes, sir." I glanced over at Judge Coleman. His head was down. He knew what was coming.

I told Judge Keady we offered in evidence Baldwin's grand jury testimony as his "past recollection recorded" because in his current mental state, he was now an "unavailable witness." Judge Keady turned to Judge Coleman and called us up to the bench. "Mr. Coleman (he refused to call him "judge") do you have any objection?" Judge Coleman responded: "Your Honor, this is unfair. It deprives my client of the right to have me cross-examine this witness. He says he can't remember, and I can't cross-examine that stack of paper up there called a transcript."

Out of the hearing of the jury, Judge Keady then played a little trick on Judge Coleman, saying, "Mr. Coleman, if you were still *Judge* Coleman, how would you rule?" Judge Coleman said, "I know it's no use to object since I've written opinions myself approving the very thing Mr. Hailman proposes to do. But anyway, for my client's sake, we do object." Judge Keady wasted no time. "Overruled. Proceed, Counsel." We finished the case without further incident, and the jury quickly convicted both Little and his company on all counts. Little was sent to federal prison, where the warden, thinking he was being humane, gave Bobby

Little his brother, Thurston, as a cellmate. Within a week, however, they got in a brotherly fistfight and had to be reassigned.

Arguing a case at the Fifth Circuit in New Orleans against its former chief judge sounded like a challenging assignment, especially given some of the strange legal issues we had. To my surprise, the panel brushed them aside, and most of our "argument" was in fact reminiscences by Judge Coleman. The judges sort of took me under their wings as someone faced with the near-impossible task of opposing their former colleague. No way, they seemed to say, was I going to be put at a disadvantage.

Then came a final, unusual challenge. Our case being well known by then in legal circles for its legal questions and its famous defense attorney, the Fifth Circuit Bar Association chose the appeal hearing on our case as the centerpiece of its annual meeting. The large Fifth Circuit en banc courtroom in New Orleans was packed after our argument for a two-hour Q & A by the members of the bar. I feared that they would grill me about my sarcastic "concordance" or Bobby Little's conspiracy with himself or several other dicey points. I needn't have worried. Judge Coleman told funny war stories for two hours till our time was up, and I never had to open my mouth to answer a single question. So ended Operation Pretense.

One event several years later brought the case back vividly to mind, however. Long after I'd testified before the Judiciary Committee of the Mississippi Legislature about reforming our supervisor system by introducing a professional countywide administrator, an article appeared in the *Oxford Eagle* (known to its local foes as the *Daily Buzzard*). The article asked for bids to build a fancy new Chancery Court building. The winning bidder was a "new" outfit from Alcorn County named NMS. Checking with the Secretary of State's Office in Jackson, I learned that Bobby Little was its president and only stockholder. Having served his sentence, he had simply reopened his company under its initials, changing North Mississippi Supply to "NMS," and gone right back to doing business with counties, including ours, right under our noses.

News stories immediately claimed hundreds of thousands of dollars in kickbacks were offered to the owner of the land that was to be the site of the new building. The owner of the land, where the beloved Oxford landmark James Food Center and Deli used to stand, had allegedly refused an NMS bribe, but finally agreed to sell them the land legally anyway and would never admit to us any bribe was ever offered. Paul James was an old friend and very ill, and I didn't have the heart to lean on him. He died in 2010. The building, however, is quite handsome and a nice addition to the old street named after L. Q. C. Lamar, our local symbol of honorable lawyers, a former Ole Miss law professor and the only Mississippian ever to sit on the U.S. Supreme Court. Courses in ethics are now often taught in the building as part of our American Inns of Court programs. As always it seems, the more things change, the more they remain the same.

The Chicken House Caper[21]

Strange fads sometimes begin at Ole Miss football games and our legendary tailgate parties in the Grove. National sports broadcasters often say that their favorite place in the entire United States for a football game is Oxford, calling it the Little Easy, in favorable comparison to New Orleans's Big Easy. One beautiful fall afternoon was typical, but this time with a twist. The Ole Miss campus, although then legally dry under local law, nonetheless welcomed tailgaters openly lugging ice chests of beer and whiskey into the Grove. Stunningly dressed coeds in short dresses and high heels even carried large purses full of alcohol right into the stadium. Preppy frat boys and their well-dressed fathers carried leather-covered silver hip flasks filled with their favorite whiskey or mixed drink.

But there's always someone who lacks moderation and does something so outrageous that it gives hypocrisy a bad name. One of those, in Itawamba County east of Tupelo, a dry county, was such a man. He bore the colorful name Dorvin Gober. With his wife, Bertha, and some friends, and with protection from Itawamba sheriff Don Spradling, Gober converted a large, abandoned commercial chicken house half a football field long into a drive-through full-service bar. They might have gotten away with it if they hadn't overadvertised it, giving away hundreds of colorful T-shirts, with no names or writing on them, just a picture of a big, long chicken house.

As marketing it was brilliant. But for use in an illegal business, it was excessive. Word of the Chicken House spread far and wide. Students from Oxford drove to Itawamba County to load their car trunks with cases of beer and whiskey and, of course, to buy the fast-selling T-shirts. Local residents began to complain, not about the liquor but about the traffic jams. The real problem began when large numbers of Ole Miss and Mississippi State students began showing up at games wearing Chicken House T-shirts. Ole Miss Rebel-flag wavers and State cowbell ringers alike would bring back the T-shirts to their friends. Fraternities began wearing them en masse. The state ABC alcohol-control folks heard about it and launched an undercover investigation.

It is almost impossible to convict an elected sheriff in state court in Mississippi before a jury of his peers who did, after all, elect him. Sheriffs know how much law enforcement constituents want. Those who enforce alcohol or gambling laws too strictly are often not reelected. One told me once "John, I gave them more law enforcement than they wanted." For that reason, Itawamba DA John Young brought the case to us as a federal bribery case rather than prosecute it himself. The whole thing was a hoot. It was a piece of cake to get the evidence. The defendants sold to everyone. Catching the sheriff was almost as easy. ABC agent Frankie Daniels pretended to be corrupt and agreed to split payoffs from the Chicken House with Sheriff Spradling. Other local bootleggers also agreed to testify against Spradling once the case broke.

The sheriff hired Oxford attorney Grady Tollison to represent him. Spradling's main deputy, Charles Crayton, often picked up the payoffs for the sheriff, so we got him on tape and approached him about testifying against Spradling. He refused. His lawyer was Frank Russell, a colorful character given to practical jokes. Grady Tollison came forward on the Sunday night before the Monday trial and we made him a little better offer. It was a classic case of law in real time. "Gentlemen," Grady said, "my client thinks your offer is fair and wants to take it, but he can't sign until tomorrow morning." We immediately guessed the reason: "He hasn't told his wife yet, has he? He's told her he's innocent, and she's defended him against everyone and now he's going to catch unshirted hell." Grady nodded. "That's it. But we'll have a deal in the morning if she doesn't beat him to death overnight."

Spradling pled guilty the next morning, followed by the deputy. Grady and Crayton's lawyer, Frank Russell, stopped by our office on their way to interviews with probation officers. Frank said, "I'll bet you prosecutor boys have never seen a real attorney-client agreement, have you?" Not waiting for a reply, he pulled from his briefcase a formal-looking document with a blue back and a gold seal from a notary public. It read, as best I recall, "I, Charles Crayton do hereby solemnly agree to pay my attorney, Frank Russell, for his excellent services in my case by mowing his lawn as long as we both shall live."

"It's Hard to Tell the Truth When There's So Much Truth to Tell"[22]

In 1993, the aldermen of Holly Springs became concerned about drug trafficking in their city, especially the appearance that police officers were involved. Determined that outside help was needed, they directed Mayor Eddie Smith Jr. to seek help from the State Attorney General's office. Smith, a retired Rust College professor and the town's first black mayor in a century, had been in office just two years. The attorney general referred Smith to the Mississippi Bureau of Narcotics (MBN), a statewide organization. They referred him to the FBI because the matter involved not just drugs but police corruption.

Mayor Smith asked the FBI to investigate his police department, and furnished them all information they asked for, including names of all Holly Springs police officers. Mayor Smith asked the FBI not to keep him informed of the investigation or its undercover aspects. The next he heard of it was when four officers and a large number of drug dealers were arrested.

Mike Barker, the FBI agent assigned to run the investigation, was a former detective from North Carolina with fourteen years' experience and a B.A. in justice administration. Barker directed a joint federal-state task force of officers from MBN, FBI, IRS, U.S. Customs, ATF, and the U.S. Marshals Service. Undercover agents began buying drugs in "Crack Alley," the narrow street behind the police station, finding it so wide-open that dealers sold to total strangers in broad daylight. The agents had no success, however, approaching local police officers to buy protection. Only a known local person would be accepted, and given the demographics of the drug trade in Holly Springs, only a local black person could penetrate the obvious local police corruption. Stanley Woodson, a local man recently released after a year in federal prison for federal program fraud, agreed to work with the U.S. Attorney's Office as an undercover informant for the task force to catch the corrupt police officers he said he knew were protecting crack dealers.

Based upon predication, that is, reasonable suspicion that he was corrupt, the FBI first sent Woodson to Captain Willie Frank Jones to buy protection. Woodson claimed he dealt crack, the prevalent drug in the area. All drug buys made by the undercover agents were of crack, the drug a real dope dealer would be expected by corrupt police to be selling. Barker equipped Woodson with an expensive, Swiss-made Nagra tape recorder to record the exact words of Woodson and officers so there would be no dispute as to what was said about drugs and payoffs. Woodson also wore a transmitter, hidden inside what appeared to be a typical drug dealer's beeper, so that surveillance agents could hear him and assist him if necessary. As agent Barker explained, it is much harder to work undercover against officers than drug dealers because officers are trained in undercover and surveillance techniques.

Before each transaction, Barker placed a recorder on Woodson, started the tape, and announced the date, time, and place. He gave Woodson the amount of each payoff in cash, recording the serial numbers. After the payoffs, which took place in police cars, in courthouse bathrooms, and at defendants' homes, Woodson and Barker would rendezvous, often with us present, at Wall Doxey, a beautiful, isolated state park a few miles south of town. In all, there were thirty-four tapes of conversations, twenty-nine involving payoffs received by the four officers. We had a typed transcript made of each tape, which jurors could read at trial while each tape was played. Jurors had earphones to hear the tapes clearly over a sophisticated infrared system.

From January to June 1993, Woodson made ten payoffs of $150 each to Captain Jones; seven similar payoffs to Billy Ray Gray and deputy sheriff Sylvester Byers; and five $500 payoffs to Chief Anthony Marion, whom Woodson approached last, as suggested by Jones. A large computer-generated color chart of all the payoffs was used as a summary exhibit to assist the jury.

Woodson, a thirty-three-year-old truck driver, was well-known in Holly Springs. He first talked with Captain Jones, who agreed to protect Woodson's alleged operation selling crack cocaine (rock) and marijuana (weed). The meeting took place inside the police station, where Jones accepted $150 and instructed Woodson not to let his customers see all his dope, just the rocks they were buying, to avoid being ripped off. On February 5, Jones took another $150 and when Woodson said, "everybody is getting money" from dealers, Jones said, "I know." On February 16, Jones accepted $150 cash inside his police patrol car and told Woodson he had "partners," naming officer Billy Ray Gray and deputy sheriff Sylvester Byers, saying, "talk to Billy Ray." On February 19, Gray accepted $150 and confirmed that Jones had talked to Gray beforehand.

On February 24, Byers accepted $150 and said he expected to be paid $150 every Saturday unless Woodson was in Florida picking up cocaine. Jones took a $150 cash payoff that same day, saying Chief Marion would take payoffs later, but "right now is a bad time." Jones warned Woodson about "snitches," saying never to tell anyone when he was going to pick up a load of drugs. Jones said not to be seen wearing a pager, because drug dealers wore them, and told Woodson the police department's undercover technique of having officers hide their transmitters inside pagers. Ironically, that is precisely what Woodson was doing at that very moment. Jones told Woodson not to flash big rolls of money and that wearing gold chains and driving Cadillacs were bad ideas, likely to attract attention of the honest police officers. A major hitch that day was that a nearby police scanner broadcast part of Jones's words with Woodson over the airwaves, but fortunately for us, law enforcement had become so lax that no one seemed to be paying attention.

On February 27, Gray met with Woodson and Jones. Gray was nervous because he'd heard about the scanner picking up a conversation between Jones and Woodson somehow. He frisked Woodson but failed to find his recorder. Reassured, Gray proposed that whenever he or Jones arrested another drug dealer, they would give the seized dope to Woodson to resell and split the profits. Jones thought Lt. Gray's idea was too risky, so they never pursued it.

On March 4, Byers accepted another $150 at his residence and promised to protect Woodson from the police when he brought in two "keys" (kilograms) that Friday night. Jones met Woodson and told him Chief Marion was "ready to do business." Later that day, Marion met Woodson at a baseball field. In his squad car with Woodson standing outside, the chief agreed not to interfere with his drug operation "as long as we don't get too many complaints." Marion refused cash, however, saying ambiguously that he could not do that "now."

On March 16, Gray told Woodson he knew he had met with Chief Marion. Gray said he personally did not trust the chief, but "if you want to do business with him, I don't care." Gray warned Woodson about his pager, which might make some younger police officers, who were "straight," suspect Woodson was "fucking with dope." That same day, in an unexpected, unrecorded meeting on the road, Marion flagged Woodson down and told him he'd "had a dream" that Woodson was sent to help Marion with his financial problems.

On March 24, Lt. Gray took $150 and told Woodson that $7,000 would buy a quarter kilo of high-grade cocaine like "Peruvian flake," which Woodson could cut to make more money. That same day, Woodson decided to do a little freelance undercover work without contacting agent Barker. He called Marion, posing as a banker in Memphis and told Marion that Woodson had just deposited $94,000 in cash at the First Tennessee Bank. The "banker" said he was checking whether a bank might have been robbed. Taken in by Woodson's ruse and convinced that Woodson was a bigger drug dealer than he had thought, Marion met with Woodson later that day and accepted his first payoff, this time on tape, of $500. Marion warned Woodson about the call from the Memphis banker and the $94,000, saying Memphis was too close and that he should use a "Swiss bank account." Marion agreed to keep his officers away from a particular street so Woodson could "service" a customer there with a quarter kilo of crack that night.

On April 9, Lt. Gray followed up on the Marion conversation, telling Woodson, "Don't never put over $10,000 in the bank at one time. The IRS watches it. Get a safety deposit box in somebody else's name." The same day, Deputy Byers told Woodson he also knew about Woodson's money in the bank because "Willie Frank" had told him about it, thus completing the conspiracy between the officers about Woodson's unauthorized but successful ruse about the $94,000: The information had gone from Marion to Gray to Jones to Byers, demonstrating each had clear connections with the others.

On April 13, Jones took $150, noting, "You pleasing me." On April 15 and again six days later, Chief Marion took $500 from Woodson, promising, "If I hear some tips, you'll be the first to know," and "If you get fucked up, it won't be because of Anthony Marion, cause I do my part." Marion also confided that he had put in a good word for Woodson with Woodson's federal probation officer, Rusty Rasberry, which was true.

Having witnessed the success of Woodson's unauthorized pretext call, the FBI decided to make a pretext call of its own to show Marion would keep his promise to protect Woodson. Corbett Hart, chief of narcotics for the Shelby County Sheriff in Memphis, made the call. Hart, a twenty-two-year veteran of the FBI before he retired to take the sheriff's job, had served for a decade as head of the federal-state drug task force in Memphis. Tall and lean, Hart always wore a Stetson hat and strongly resembled a Texas Ranger. He was always one of our favorite officers. On May 3, Hart called Marion and told him there had been a drug raid in Memphis in which officers found the name "Stanley Woodson" in the dealer's address book with telephone and pager numbers, the same ones Woodson had given to Marion. Hart asked Marion if Woodson was a doper. Marion said, "Yes." Hart told Marion that if Woodson showed up in Memphis, Hart's men would arrest Woodson and asked Marion to let him know if Marion heard anything about Woodson. Marion agreed. At no time did Marion ever call Hart, nor did Marion tell him that Woodson was paying Marion $500 a week. Instead, that same day, Marion met with Woodson and warned him not to go to Memphis and to find a drug source elsewhere.

By June 7, the FBI had assembled agents to arrest all the drug dealers and corrupt police officers caught in the sting. They also made plans to catch Chief Marion in actual possession of payoff money. Woodson met Marion that day and paid him $500 in cash inside Woodson's vehicle, counting out on tape twenty-five twenties. Marion stuffed the money in the front of his pants and walked to his house, encountering his wife on the way, then got in his car. After his wife drove away, Marion was pulled over by task force agents. Officers seized $420 in $20 bills hidden inside Marion's pants. The serial numbers of the seized bills matched those given to Woodson for the payoff moments earlier.

FBI agent Mark Denham, leader of the arrest team, advised Marion of his rights. Marion first claimed he was investigating Woodson, but when Denham asked Marion where were any documents to prove it,

Marion dropped that story and began claiming he was trying to develop Woodson as an informant. When Denham told him all his talks with Woodson were on tape, Marion dropped that claim as well. On the ride from Holly Springs to the Marshal's office in Oxford, Marion told Denham he wanted to tell "the full story." He admitted accepting cash from Woodson, saying he knew it was wrong. Marion signed a statement admitting he had accepted cash four or five times, not counting the money on the day of his arrest. Marion never mentioned the call from Chief Hart of Memphis, nor the call from the "banker" about the $94,000 deposit.

At trial, all four defendants rested without testifying. Their attorney was veteran criminal defense counsel Joey Langston of Booneville. Langston tried to establish defenses entirely by vigorous cross-examinations, but utterly failed to shake Woodson, whose explanations flustered Langston. When asked if the case did not rest solely on the word of a convicted felon, Woodson replied, "It's not my word against they word. The tapes are the primary evidence." Listening to the judge's instructions, Woodson had become a lawyer overnight. Woodson noted that federal agents wearing badges could never, working alone, catch corrupt officers like these defendants who would only deal with someone with a shady reputation, saying: "If you want to shoot craps, you ain't going down to the church to find a game, are you?" When Langston questioned Woodson's unilateral decision to pose as a banker, Woodson explained, "Mr. Barker was an FBI federal agent, but Mr. Barker knowed nothing about the streets. I been out in the streets all my life. I been a pool hustler. I been around plenty of people selling drugs. I ain't no Johnny Lunchmeat/Sam Sausagehead son of a gun, you know. I didn't fall off no pumpkin wagon."

With a witness like Stanley Woodson you of course expect some problems. Even after reserving a separate room for him in a motel with FBI agents staying in rooms on each side of him for protection, he still insisted on driving to trial on his own. Little did we suspect he would travel not in his truck, but on a motorcycle. It poured down rain all day on the Sunday before the first trial began in Aberdeen on a Monday. Stanley was to arrive about 4:00 P.M. to go over his testimony. As we worried and tried unsuccessfully to call his family, he finally roared up at 8:00 P.M., soaking wet but happy. "That was a good ride. Settled my nerves. Now I'm ready to testify."

As we expected, Stanley Woodson made an outstanding witness. He was on the stand all day the first day. Joey Langston had hardly begun his cross-examination when the judge recessed for the day. Under court rules we were not allowed to talk to Woodson out of court while he was under cross-examination. We told him to just stay in his room and chill out. He said he was tired from all that thinking and remembering and was grateful for a chance to rest. He promised to stay in and be good.

In the morning, Barker awakened me early, knocking on my door. "Stanley's not in his room." Always the optimist, I said, "Maybe he went for a ride or an early breakfast." By the time I'd showered, Mike was back. "We found Stanley. He's in the local jail." I immediately jumped to the conclusion that the defendant officers had got some buddies to cook up a bogus arrest to ruin our case. Mike disabused me. "No way. He's in jail for attempted murder. We'll need a writ of habeas corpus to get him out." I got the judge's courtroom clerk to type the writ, and the sheriff brought Stanley to court in an orange jail jumpsuit just in time for court at 9:00 A.M. I had no time to speak to Stanley at all. He waved to me in the courthouse hallway and gave me a big, gold-toothed grin and a V sign.

I stopped by the judge's chambers and told his law clerk briefly what little I knew of what had happened and asked permission to re-call Woodson as our witness just to explain why he was in orange jail attire. I had no idea what his explanation would be, and our case was clearly on the line, but I somehow had an odd confidence that Stanley would pull it out. My first question was, "Mr. Woodson, you and I have not seen each other since court ended yesterday, have we?" He was deadly serious. "No, Sir," he said. "So you haven't told me why you're in custody, have you?" Again he said, "No, Sir." Turning to the jury I said, with a hint of frustration, "Then please inform the judge and the jury *and me* why you are wearing an orange jumpsuit from the jail." Woodson, just as the best-trained expert witness would have done, pivoted in the witness chair and faced the jury directly. "Ladies and gentlemen, Mr. Hailman told me last night to stay in my room where I'd be safe and get a good night's sleep. I tried to, but that attorney with all his questions had done made me so nervous I couldn't sleep, so I decided to go for a ride on my motorcycle. I came upon some old boys shooting dice in a little club. When I kept winning, they thought I was cheating. There was a loud argument, and being a stranger I was the one who ended up getting arrested. That's about it." With trepidation I submitted Stanley Woodson to Joey Langston for cross.

Joey jumped in with both feet: "Mr. Woodson, you forgot to tell the jury what you were arrested for, didn't you?" Stanley nodded. "Yes, Sir." Joey smiled at the jury and said, "It was for attempted murder, wasn't it?" Stanley shook his head and asked, "Can I explain?" Joey said smugly, "Please do." Stanley faced the jury. "Well, Sir, when they got to accusing me of cheating, I got mad. Words was exchanged. A knife was involved." Joey couldn't wait and broke in, "You tried to kill a man with that knife, didn't you?"

Stanley answered the question with a question: "Sir, you ever shoot marbles?" Hearing no answer, he pressed on: "Well, Sir, before the argument, we was playing another little game like boys do, like in Boy Scouts. It's a game where you throw a knife and stick it from different angles like over your back or between your legs and such. We'd been playing that game long before the argument. One time I stuck the knife in the wall behind the bar with a pretty neat throw over my shoulder. I hadn't seen the bartender coming up and it almost hit him. I felt real bad. He didn't mind at the time, but later when the fight broke out, he brought it back up to the sheriff's people."

Langston couldn't resist: "So you threw a knife at the bartender and nearly killed him, didn't you?" Stanley shook his head vigorously. "No, Sir, no, Sir. It was just a little game of mumblety-peg that got out of hand." When several men on the jury started smiling, I knew we were o.k. They had played the old boy scout game of mumblety-peg, throwing and sticking a knife, just like I had. All old scouts know mumblety-peg. Stanley's explanation made sense. The trial resumed.

Langston pointed out to Woodson how he had sometimes been wrong about the exact times and places of payoffs, which he admitted. "You were not telling the truth about those payoffs, were you?" Irked by the challenge to his memory and his veracity, which were remarkably good considering the large number of conversations, Woodson explained how difficult it is for an uneducated man to avoid being tripped up by a clever lawyer: "Sir, it's hard to tell the truth when there's so much truth to tell." Langston later joked that we had put those words in Woodson's mouth but had to agree that the remark was way too original for anyone but Woodson himself to have come up with. At least Stanley didn't do to

Joey what another of Tom Dawson's cooperating defendants once did to another defense attorney. When asked on cross if he was not selling out a friend, the witness replied: "Sir, he is not my friend. Jesus is my friend. He is just an associate."

When both sides had rested and the jury went out, Tom Dawson, Joey Langston, and I sat around and joked about what a character Stanley Woodson was. Tom and I felt the case was in the bag, but Joey seemed suspiciously confident. Sure enough, after several hours, the jury announced it was hopelessly deadlocked eleven to one for conviction. One woman flatly refused to discuss the case at all. The judge declared a mistrial. A few months later, we tried it again with the same result. Another woman had refused to deliberate. We told Joey we'd retry the four officers and convict them if it took us fifty trials.

The third trial went better. During voir dire, two ladies asked to speak to the judge privately. When he interviewed them, each told the same story. Defendant Billy Ray Gray had contacted them directly and tried to get them to find him not guilty. They had of course refused but were afraid to report the contacts until they got to court and were under oath. The judge excused the jurors and told us to have the FBI interview them before they left the courthouse. The trial went just as it had the first two times. This time, however, after being out less than an hour, the jury returned unanimous guilty verdicts on all defendants on all counts.

We got an indictment for jury tampering on Billy Ray Gray, who pled guilty to it, but claimed he acted on his own and refused to implicate anyone else. He got two years added to his sentence. At sentencing, I felt sorry for defendant Willie Frank Jones. We'd gotten friendly at recesses during all the trials, and to Tom and me, he was just a black version of a good ole boy. He was playing by the rules he'd learned while growing up in Marshall County. I felt even worse about Chief Anthony Marion. He came from an excellent family. His father was a respected preacher and local role model. Because of their good records, we'd offered them plea agreements with three years to serve, a tough sentence for police officers, who are always subject to abuse in prison by other prisoners. But Marion had listened to Langston and gambled and lost. As Tom Dawson had warned Marion, if he got convicted, under the mandatory sentencing guidelines, he would still be in prison when his small children were grown and would not be around to see them graduate from high school. Tom's prophecy came true.

The case had one final twist. After the second trial, our excellent FBI case agent Mike Barker got to missing his family so much that he resigned from the FBI and moved back to North Carolina. His replacement as case agent was Alan Tatum, who was himself, as explained elsewhere, later twice convicted of corruption for perjury and theft of evidence and went to prison. All in all, it was a case we'd never forget.

A Delta Lawyer[23]

When lawyers lose a case, their clients tend not to pay them, especially in divorce and criminal cases. The lawyers may then have to sue the client to recover their fee. Criminal clients often file bar complaints against their lawyers when they're convicted. Many file post-conviction complaints claiming their lawyer was incompetent. As the main expert witnesses to their competence, we prosecutors end up, in effect, defending the defense lawyers. That situation, ironically, has often helped relations between prosecutors and defense attorneys in our district to remain highly amicable. We may start as adversaries, but we know that in the end we may well be allies.

Prosecuting fellow lawyers is a touchy subject. For a variety of reasons, sometimes financial problems, sometimes alcohol or a midlife crisis of skirt-chasing, lawyers end up stealing from their clients to fund their bad habits. Some of my own law school classmates ended up this way. The most tempting trap for needy lawyers is client money. While representing clients, lawyers often end up as guardians of client funds, which are placed in what is called a trust account. Interest on the accounts, by some legal legerdemain of the state bar, goes to another trust fund used to pay for legal services for the poor, which is good. Unfortunately, some lawyers cannot be trusted with a trust and purloin the money. When lawyers are caught, the matter is usually handled by the state bar, and the guilty lawyer is disbarred for a period, but rarely prosecuted criminally.

In one memorable case from the Delta, a postal inspector brought us a client-fund embezzlement case to prosecute, probably because of the large amount of money involved. I don't single out Delta lawyers here. We've prosecuted lawyers from all corners of our district, most often for income tax fraud, but also for drug offenses and worse. But to lawyers from the Hills, Delta lawyers have always seemed to be a tad more flamboyant in their misconduct. Lawyers in the hills even say Dick Scruggs would never have been convicted if he'd stayed on the Gulf Coast instead of moving to Oxford, where morals are said to be more strict, but I wouldn't know about that.

One particular Delta lawyer needed money to finance a hot middle-aged romance. He found plenty of it in his trust fund belonging to a rich client of long standing who rarely needed the funds or checked on them. When caught, the lawyer hired some of the best lawyers in the state to defend him. In an unusual strategy, the lawyers asked us to allow the accused lawyer to testify in his own defense before the federal grand jury. That strategy is usually considered suicide by defense lawyers and prosecutors alike. Federal law prohibits defense attorneys from being in the grand jury room, so testifying defendants are pretty much at the mercy of prosecutors. But in this case, the attorney believed, rightly, that to save his reputation he had to testify and try to avoid indictment. He even persuaded the victim, an old friend as well as a client, to testify on his behalf in the grand jury as a defense witness to say that if the lawyer had just asked him, he would gladly have lent him all the money he needed without interest for as long as he needed it.

The guilty attorney made a splendid witness in his own defense. He basically confessed to what he did and tearfully begged forgiveness. Several jurors, men included, were openly weeping about what would happen to his children if he were convicted and lost his law license and income. Having the victim's support was also highly sympathetic. The prosecutor was Al Moreton, a fair-minded advocate who was visibly moved by the defendant's predicament and never tried to persuade the jury with cutting cross-examination or closing remarks; he just calmly presented the evidence as I watched. When we left the grand jury room for them to vote, Al and I guessed they would not indict. Through the door, down the hall where we waited, we could hear raised voices.

After nearly two hours, the foreman came out bearing the vote slip. How each federal grand juror personally votes is forever secret. No court reporter is present for their deliberations, unlike the testimony portion, which is typed up verbatim and filed under seal with the clerk.

The foreman handed Al the vote slip, which is handwritten and reflects only the number of grand jurors voting to indict. By law a federal grand jury consists of not less than sixteen nor more than twenty-three persons selected at random by computer from voter registration rolls. Twelve votes are required for an indictment, or "true bill," to be returned. In this case there were exactly twelve votes to indict, meaning that as many as eleven people could have voted not to indict.

By the time the case went to trial several months later, much debate had occurred among lawyers about the wisdom (or folly) of letting the lawyer testify unprotected in the grand jury. At trial, the victim again testified for the defendant. This time it seemed to me he created more sympathy for his own loyalty to his lawyer friend than he did for the friend himself. The trial jurors glowered at the lawyer-defendant. His attorneys, not knowing the grand jury vote, reasonably presumed that the grand jurors had not liked his testimony since they indicted him. The accused attorney probably felt the same, despite the grand jurors' tears. Faced with those facts, the defense made the decision not to put him on the stand. The trial jury convicted him in record time, and the judge sent him off to prison. He will never know how close he came to getting off.

A Little Bitta Justice[24]

My old Millsaps friend Lawson "Twinkie" Lawhon was the daughter of the former sheriff of Tupelo and used to regale us with her dad's law enforcement tales. He had special names for law enforcement officials. He called the highway patrol "roadmen." For those who were thorns in his side he had special names. Constables, who serve as process servers for Justice Court judges, he called "a little bitta law." The justices themselves he referred to as "a little bitta justice." Justice Court judges in Mississippi have evolved greatly since then, when we called them Justices of the Peace, as they still do in England. They once had virtually no educational requirements. After a long struggle in the Mississippi Legislature, a bill finally passed a few years ago requiring them to have a high school diploma.

It is a little-known fact that the first great English writer, Geoffrey Chaucer, was a Justice of the Peace for ten years. He is said to have gotten most of the characters for his famous Canterbury Tales from colorful litigants who appeared before him as a JP. But of course Chaucer was trained as a lawyer at the Inns of Court in London, and lawyers do not get elected to be JPs in Mississippi. I've known several who ran, but not one who ever won. It seems folks think lawyers have enough power and prefer to be judged in small cases by their peers, not some verbose barrister.

The money factor was definitely the prime mover in two of my more colorful prosecutions. In one, the highway patrol came to us with a case against JP James Mitchell Glenn of Columbus, who was said to be taking bribes to fix drunk driving tickets. The patrol already had some ideas about how to catch the guy but wanted our advice and input before they tried any investigative techniques that might not lead to evidence admissible in federal court. They feared they could not get a conviction in state court because JPs are, after all, elected in their local counties. Who knew but what a crooked JP had done a favor for a potential juror or their relatives? We'd already had the same problem with local jurors and county supervisors, who had graveled many a driveway and installed many a culvert pipe for constituents. They said the local DA shared their concerns and asked us to handle the case.

The patrol's investigative plan was to have an undercover agent pose as a drunk driver and have a cooperating patrolman pretend to arrest him, issue a DUI citation, and take him before Glenn. Luckily for us, none of the other local JPs and none of the MHP officers were suspected, nor were any local police or sheriff's deputies. The patrol brought with them the proposed undercover agent and the patrolman who was to "arrest" him. The UC was an unusual character named Albert Sidney Johnston IV. To any civil war buff, the question that immediately comes to mind is: You don't suppose he's a direct descendent of the Confederate general famed for his bold military tactics? He was indeed.

"Butch" Johnston, as they called him, was every bit as bold as his famous ancestor. At the time, he was working for the state auditor's office but was bored with accounting work and asked for any assignments offering more action. His supervisor told him MHP was looking for someone young who looked like a student and was from far enough away from Columbus that the suspect would not recognize him as a law officer. Butch fit the profile. In my life as a prosecutor, if I ever met anyone as gung-ho as our own ex-Marine AUSA Charlie Spillers, it was Butch

Johnston. We discussed how drunk drivers act so he could play the role effectively, just in case other drivers came by during the "arrest." His supervising patrolman seemed mature and responsible, so I sent them on their undercover way.

When they got to Lowndes County, things began to go wrong. Butch decided he needed to smell of alcohol so the JP would not spot him as sober and perhaps even as a UC officer, so they poured some bourbon on his shirt. Then Butch got to thinking too much. What if an honest policeman or deputy happened to be at the jail or the JP's office when they brought him in? What if they were suspicious that there was no liquor on his breath and wanted to do a breath test on him? I had told them not to present any false official documents to the court for its records. Federal courts had recently held that strategy improper in Chicago, so they planned for the patrolman just to tell the judge everything informally—on tape, of course.

Butch still kept worrying that someone would insist on giving him a breathalyzer to be sure they nailed him. Many officers did not like the way Judge Glenn let so many drunk drivers off. One thing led to another and soon Butch Johnston was having one drink of bourbon, then two. The officer was foolish enough to let Butch actually drive for a couple of miles after several drinks before arresting him. Butch even ran off the road a little but no harm was done. The patrolman took Butch straight to Judge Glenn, who agreed on tape to let Butch off for $500 in cash, but told him he was too drunk (he was) to drive home. While in the drunk tank, Butch threw up all over everything.

Later, after we'd arrested the judge, he seemed surprised that we'd used a real drunk driver to catch him. His attorney, my old friend Tom Royals of Jackson, was impressed: "John, you federal boys really go all out to achieve verisimilitude, I'll grant you that." Tom liked to use big words. After we caught Judge Glenn taking a bribe on tape, we had agents go through his records of every DUI ticket he'd dismissed in the last two years and subpoenaed every driver to the federal grand jury. Sixteen of them admitted to having paid off the judge.

After Judge Glenn pled guilty to two of the charges, we figured he'd get probation or perhaps a few months in a federal jail. Instead, Judge L. T. Senter threw the book at him, saying he'd heard for years of all the problems caused by JPs coddling drunk drivers for cash. The judge hit the judge with four long years in federal prison at Big Spring, Texas. He filed several motions to reduce his sentence but Judge Senter denied them all.

We uncovered a similar DUI bribery/extortion scam involving a lawyer in Tunica County while prosecuting two sheriffs there. It involved no judges, only the crooked lawyer and a bogus deputy sheriff. The lawyer, a former county prosecutor, had a deal with the deputy to bust gamblers from out of state (making the crime federal) who were driving away from casinos intoxicated. The deputy would threaten them with loss of their driver's licenses unless they hired the "right" defense attorney. The driver would pay a "fee" of $1,500, which the lawyer would split with the deputy. Since the JPs were honest and not involved, there were no court records for us to use as proof.

We discovered the case when we busted the deputy for another offense and he ratted out the lawyer. We subpoenaed several drivers whose names and addresses the deputy had foolishly kept, and they corroborated the deputy. The case was old when we got it, and two different AUSAs begged off because their kids were friends of the defendant lawyer's kids. Finally, one week before the statute of limitations would have run out, I asked Curtis Ivy, our toughest plea-bargainer, to take the case. We agreed to let the attorney have probation, figuring that revoking his law license would suffice as punishment under the circumstances. He took the deal, the judge accepted it, and the lawyer was convicted by guilty plea. To our shock, his pre-sentence report revealed he had over $1 million in a savings account made mostly as closing attorney on federal Farmers Home loans. The attorney transferred his probation to Gulfport and bought a run-down Holiday Inn. He insured it heavily, and months later, when Hurricane Katrina hit, he made a legal killing on the insurance. Some guys are just lucky.[25]

The Mississippi Beef Plant Fiasco: Slaughterhouse for Taxpayers[26]

Of all the corruption cases I handled, my last one was by far the most annoying, mainly because it involved so much corruption in an unhappy marriage of fraud and incompetence. The FBI, lead agency of the federal-state task force that investigated the case, named it Cattlegate like

Watergate. My own nickname for it came to me spontaneously in court one day when I blurted out that it was a "slaughterhouse" for taxpayers based partly on my visits to the plant and partly on my youthful experiences helping haul truckloads of cattle to the stockyards in Chicago, where the rats were often big as cats. The media, which were all over the case from day one, chose the name everyone now recognizes, Mississippi Beef, because that was the name of the state-financed plant that failed, costing the taxpayers over $55 million. The fiasco destroyed the jobs of several hundred hardworking Mississippians just before what is now called the Great Recession began.

The plan sounded promising at first, both economically and politically. The Farm Bureau and Mississippi Cattlemen's Association had been complaining to the legislature that "city folks" were getting all the state-supported projects and the jobs that went with them, especially the Nissan plant near Jackson. Years earlier, following the Great Depression, state leaders had come up with a solution to the opposite problem: Mississippi was then too agricultural; all the jobs and income were on the farms; cities had very few industrial jobs. The legislature, working with the governor, passed a bill called BAWI, or Balance Agriculture with Industry, creating a state agency, the A & I Board, to restore some equality. The program was a big success and helped balance the state's economy. Our current leaders were looking for a similar solution, but in the opposite direction, helping farmers catch up with factories.

As numerous witnesses testified, the idea for the plant came one day when two leading legislators, Billy McCoy and Steve Holland, were riding up the Natchez Trace toward home. At the time, the chicken industry in Mississippi was thriving, but Mississippi cattle farmers were not. Unlike chicken farmers, they had to haul their cattle out of state because there was no in-state processing plant. The state also seemed to offer a good market for processed beef. We Mississippians love our burgers, and the legislators figured that the state's schools would jump at the opportunity to buy locally produced beef for burgers, meat loaf, and other school lunch staples. Even the federal government would help, since it heavily subsidized school lunch programs, especially in the economically depressed Delta region. The state thus had both ample raw materials and a ready market; all it seemed to need was a local processing plant. The next day McCoy and Holland, both honest, well-meaning men, consulted other key legislators and agency heads, including Governor Ronnie Musgrove. Everybody liked their idea.

Like most plans that sound good, this one had problems. The biggest one was time. The legislature was about to go out of session for the year, and to make this project work, it had to move it along quickly and without much study. McCoy and Holland consulted knowledgeable employees and agency heads, who began looking for someone to build and run the plant. A well-regarded businessman named Richard Hall Sr. had once run beef plants at Grenada and in DeSoto County but had since retired and moved to Tennessee. A delegation flew to Tennessee on a state plane to meet with Hall, who said he was too old and enjoying retirement too much to undertake such an ambitious project. He suggested they talk to his son, Richard Jr., who had been his no. 2 man on his other beef plant projects. With very little thought, the state delegation offered Richard Jr. the deal, including some state financial support. The details are too excruciating to recount here, but interested readers can readily access them by Googling "Mississippi Beef Plant," usually followed by the phrase "fiasco."

Hall began seeking financing, but no bank would lend him the money. It appears in retrospect that the banks did the homework the state failed to do. Desperate to get the project going, the legislature then did something unique in Mississippi history: It agreed to guarantee 100 percent of all loans for the project. Cheap, centrally located land was found in Yalobusha County, south of Oxford, and the project was soon shovel-ready. A well-respected local contractor, Carrothers Construction of nearby Water Valley, which had built somewhat similar plants in the past and had important national contracts with the Defense Department, was hired to build the plant.

In their rush to judgment the state team had overlooked several critical facts: First, although he'd worked for his father at other plants, Richard Hall Jr. had no business experience. His main job had been driving a truck hauling cattle. Second, there were far fewer "cull" cows available in Mississippi for slaughter than had been assumed. Cull cows are inexpensive, older cattle suitable only for hamburger, not steak. Third, the market for hamburger meat was much smaller than anyone had figured, and profit margins were slim. The fourth factor was also critical: Richard Hall Sr. had retired from the beef business because his plants in Grenada and

DeSoto County were losing money. Beef plants in other nearby states were closing for similar reasons.

In hindsight, another obvious error was everyone's failure to consult the people in Mississippi who knew the most about the financial side of the cattle-rendering business: the experts at Mississippi State University. Just a couple of years earlier, they had written a comprehensive report on the subject of beef plants that came to a clear and stark conclusion: Any beef slaughtering plant built in Mississippi was almost certain to go bankrupt. Apparently no one bothered to read the report, or else did not mention it because the project was so politically popular and had so much momentum that no one could stop it.

So the building went forward. Sean Carrothers, president of the building company, constructed an excellent facility. The problem was Richard Hall. He had no idea how to write a budget for such a mammoth project and grossly underbid the job. Like the worst Pentagon nightmare, cost overruns began immediately. To cut costs, Hall began buying used and defective equipment. The state ended up with a clean, beautiful, efficient building filled with shoddy equipment that didn't work.

The plant opened on schedule, but when Hall could not find enough cattle to slaughter and not enough buyers to purchase what he did slaughter, the plant was broke, and within two months closed its gates and laid off all its employees except two security guards. The reaction among the public and the media was complete outrage. Over $55 million in public funds had been thrown away, and hundreds of hardworking Mississippians were put out of work. The media, citizens, and taxpayers were screaming for blood.

At that point, the case was dropped in our lap. The only good news was that we had one of the most outstanding white-collar investigative teams I had ever worked with. State auditor Phil Bryant had hired as his chief of investigations my old friend from MHP Jesse Bingham, the tough-looking, soft-spoken investigator who often worked undercover portraying a hired hit man. Jesse proved to be just as excellent as an administrator and organizer of agents. As chief of his auditing team, Jesse retained Earl Smith, the brilliant, dogged, recently retired head of IRS criminal investigations for Mississippi. Combined with the FBI and IRS, we had a great team. They went right to work and cooperated beautifully. That was the good news.

The bad news was that the public and the media had gone ballistic, assuming that crooked politicians were to blame and should be prosecuted—for something. That assumption proved wrong. The public servants as a group were guilty of sloppy research and negligence in failing to investigate properly such an important investment of public money, but they did nothing remotely resembling criminal wrongdoing. It bothered us from the start that our investigation was probably going to dirty up some innocent politicians, but we had no option but to pursue the case and hope the public would eventually understand.

False political rumors flew. Some asked why Attorney General Jim Hood did not prosecute the case in state court. Being himself an elected official, funded by the very legislators he would be investigating, there was no way any state attorney general anywhere could have done that job. Also without basis, veteran state representative Tommy Reynolds was accused of somehow having improperly influenced the deal because it ended up in his district. Others accused Steve Holland, who in private life has a funeral home in Tupelo, of having another one near the plant. Similar rumors made the rounds about numerous other politicos. None of them proved true.

From Day 1, my main doubt about criminal wrongdoing by public officials was that every one of them had a strong political interest in the project *succeeding*, not in helping it fail. Also, there was no sign that any official ever got any money. From the outset it was obvious Richard Hall was the problem. He simply did not know what he was doing. He lacked product; he lacked a market; and the equipment in his plant wouldn't work.

In a classic example of this fiasco, he bought huge vats to convert cow's blood into dog food, that dry red-looking kind that says "contains real beef." His employees then bought the wrong chemicals. Instead of flowing through big pipes for conversion to dog food, the giant vats of blood clotted, shutting down the whole system. Shoveling out barrels of dried cow blood by hand was vastly expensive and wasteful.

Richard Hall Jr. also had no reason to want the project to fail. The project was clearly not a bust-out scheme where a con man gets people to invest lots of money in a project and then runs off with it, having never intended for it to work in the first place. Hall was the exact opposite. He had invested every dime he owned in the project, including his retirement savings and that of his wife and his parents. He even invested his mother-in-law's retirement in the plant, a prospect any husband would shudder to contemplate. When it hit the fan, both families lost all their retirement savings.

But those mistakes were not all. With supreme confidence that the project would succeed, Hall failed to provide any salary for himself as president of the company. It was when Hall began to see that the project was failing that the crimes began. Hall began cooking the books by skimming money to pay back his family their life savings before it all collapsed. He persuaded a sympathetic Sean Carothers to add an illegal one-half percent to his contract and pay it over to Hall so Hall would have something to live on. Hall, a super salesman, also persuaded Carothers to hire Hall as a consultant for his own company. Carothers did not get a dime for helping Hall skim, his own legitimate profit being entirely guaranteed by the state. He went along with Hall only to try to save the project. I hated prosecuting Sean Carothers and told him so. Earl Smith, Jesse Bingham, and Bill Delaney, the FBI case agent from Jackson assigned to work full-time on this case to help the short-handed Oxford office, quickly uncovered Hall's schemes. Hall went to prison for eight years. Sean Carothers pled guilty and also went to prison briefly.

A good, bright man in a terrible spot, Carothers told us during our investigation that he had observed other things seriously amiss with the project which did not involve him or Richard Hall. When the state finally realized Hall was not competent to run the project, it had brought in, under somewhat suspicious circumstances, a big management firm from Atlanta called The Facility Group to audit and supervise Hall. When we asked their high-priced attorneys to help us gather the project records, the law firms stalled. At first we thought the lawyers might just be running their meters, i.e., billing the clients for all the hours they could bill in order to make more money from the case, a sad but common problem in corporate law practice.

As the records finally began to roll in, however, Earl Smith spotted a classic pattern. The Facility Group employees were billing the Mississippi Beef job for more hours than they could possibly have worked, sometimes for more hours than there were in a day. It was a classic corporate scam. The Facility Group was working simultaneously on other projects and billing both the other clients and the state of Mississippi for the same hours. I assigned that new part of the case with its new set of suspects to

AUSA Chad Lamar, who did a beautiful job of digging through row after row of boring file cabinets full of deceptive documents.

Attorneys for some of the company executives came over from Atlanta, confidently planning to steamroll us country boys with their money and political muscle. Their expensive power points had the opposite effect, convincing us that their clients were nothing but slick crooks bleeding the state. The key moment was when Facility Group's arrogant tasseled-loafer vice president, Nixon E. "Nick" Caywood patted Chad Lamar on the shoulder and told him as he went out our door, "Chad boy, next time you need to get yourself a *real* case." Chad knew he already had a real case, and I watched with real pleasure several months later when Caywood was sentenced to federal prison along with another vice president and the company president. As the U.S. Marshals took Caywood away, Chad patted the V.P. on the back and said, "Sorry, Nick. Guess this was a real case after all."

The case had other light moments. At Caywood's sentencing, he boldly asked to be given no prison time but instead to do community service by giving free financial advice to Mississippi's community colleges. Chief Judge Michael Mills pronounced himself "astonished" at such cheek and gave Caywood a prison sentence instead, saying, "I don't think we need to put you at Hinds Community College making decisions."

In contrast to the attorneys for the corporate president and other executives, the attorneys for the Facility Management company itself took a much more successful negotiating approach. Stressing the hundreds of people who would be put out of work if we indicted the company itself, which could be forfeited and put out of business, they offered instead to make restitution for some of what Mississippi lost. Richard "Rick" Dean, my old friend and former U.S. Attorney and U.S. magistrate for Atlanta, along with my old friend and colleague James Tucker of Butler Snow in Jackson, led this approach and it worked. For a prosecutor, having worthy opponents not only makes life easier, but it gives the job a sense of extra satisfaction when you can convict the guilty and avoid collateral damage to innocent bystanders at the same time.

The most troubling aspect of the case was its political campaign contribution angle. The Facility Group's executives had been required to make the maximum personal political contributions legally allowed to Governor Ronnie Musgrove's campaign, hoping to keep him happy.

Prosecutor graveyards are filled with the bodies of ambitious, idealistic young prosecutors who thought they would make a name for themselves by going after politicians over campaign contributions involving public sector contracts. Such cases are usually lost, especially on appeal, because so many deals that look and smell illegal are technically legal under our lax election financing laws. In this case we got lucky.

A cooperating employee told us how the deal worked from the inside. Top executives of the company had told the junior executives to contribute the maximum possible amount from their personal bank accounts in Georgia to the campaign of Governor Musgrove in Mississippi. That was legal. The deal became illegal, however, when the company kicked back, or reimbursed, the executives for those "personal" political contributions with corporate money falsely labeled "bonuses." Earl Smith made the computations and found the bogus bonuses were in the exact amount, to the dollar, of what the executives were required to give Governor Musgrove. They even added enough money to the "bonus" checks to cover the extra federal income taxes the executives had to pay on the bonus income they did not really receive.[27]

Understandably, there were probably very few Mississippi citizens who understood what happened. Some people reasonably questioned how the Georgia executives could be guilty of illegally *giving* Governor Musgrove the money while he was not guilty and not prosecuted for *receiving* it. The answer is simpler than it sounds. We grilled Musgrove hard, "reamed" him would be more like it, and were convinced he was innocent and did not know the company had kicked back to its employees their political contributions. They of course had every reason *not* to tell Musgrove what they did. Although totally innocent, Musgrove probably suffered politically when the guilty pleas came out regarding the illegal campaign contributions. We stressed in every legal pleading and press release that Musgrove was innocent, but the aroma of the deal probably hurt him in his run for the U.S. Senate against Roger Wicker, but we honestly felt we did all we could to treat him fairly.

The Mississippi media were apparently as conflicted as we were. Respected editorial writer Sid Salter did a humorous piece on the situation entitled "Musgrove Steps in a Cow Patty."[28] Having started down the slippery slope of mentioning the press, I find myself compelled to praise the calm and fair reports made over the years by beat reporter Arnold

Lindsay of the *Clarion-Ledger*, who was never shrill and always got each story right. The *Clarion-Ledger* even-handedly opined in an editorial that the real problems lay in the weak and confusing campaign finance laws themselves.[29]

In retrospect, probably the best thing to come out of the Mississippi Beef fiasco was the series of brilliant editorial cartoons by Marshall Ramsey in the *Clarion-Ledger*, some of which are reproduced here as illustrations. I never thought I'd see a cartoon as bitingly insightful as the Operation Pretense cartoons by Mark Bolton twenty years earlier, also reproduced here, but Ramsey equaled them. His cartoons alone were almost worth all the laborious hours we put in on Mississippi Beef. Almost.

It was during the Mississippi Beef case that the thought of retirement began to look attractive. I began wanting to get up later, take naps after lunch, and take weekends off instead of writing briefs and preparing witnesses for trial. It was time to hang it up. On August 31, 2007, I accepted the offer of a two-year fellowship at the Overby Center at Ole Miss for the main purpose of writing these memoirs of our trials. Chad Lamar took over the Mississippi Beef prosecution and did a superb job getting convictions of the Georgia executives and their companies. The beef plant building itself was later sold to another food company and is doing well, but the beef plant civil cases are ongoing and probably will be for years to come.[30]

Dickie Scruggs: The Dark Side of Robin Hood Is Revealed When His Merry Men Sue for a Bigger Share of the Loot[31]

One morning I was minding my own business and looking forward to lunch when I received an unexpected phone call from Judge Henry Lackey, an old friend of many years standing. I'd known Henry since he was a general practice attorney who represented most criminals of note in Calhoun County, some thirty miles south of Oxford. A dry county legally, it has such counties' typical problems: People like to drink but are compelled by loyalty to their preachers to vote dry. When I heard my caller was Henry, I assumed he was calling to discuss a nice little gift he'd sent me earlier: a box containing a fruit jar full of excellent wine whose label proclaimed in French that it was produced from *mures sauvages* (wild blackberries) raised on La Grande Riviere (Big Creek) by "cousin" Henry Lackey, "bon vivant" (one who knows how to live well). A formal letter had accompanied the wine:

> I am somewhat disappointed to find that in preparing your treatise on wines you failed to include at least a chapter on my Vin de la Grande Riviere, Vintage 2006. I am enclosing a sample for your cellar which I am certain you will wish to make the focal point of your next opulent dinner. It is made from the choicest berries, gathered only by young maidens trained from birth by the Monks of Banner [author's nota bene: a nearby hamlet not renowned for its cuisine].
>
> Yours truly,
>
> Henri Lafayette LaKey

It was actually an excellent, delicious dessert wine. Henry would never have given me a bad wine, even as a gag. It was not his style.

I'd learned Henry's style when I was prosecuting and he was defending some of Calhoun County's most colorful characters. One case involved his old client Wendell Blount, whose Uncle Eli I'd also prosecuted. Eli, a gun trafficker, kept his coffin open on his front porch ready for him to die, like a character out of Faulkner. Wendell, however, had another man's death more in mind. After a bitter dispute with his former friend and business partner, Jim Earl Aron, a wealthy timber merchant and car dealer, Wendell was indicted for hiring a hit man from Louisiana who had allegedly shot and tried to kill Aron but merely crippled his shoulder. In a famous state court murder trial, the jury acquitted the shooter. Wendell was not charged, but generally found guilty in the mind of his community. The jury foreman informed the local TV channel that the jury had invoked the time-honored Mississippi defense: Aron "needed killing."

My situation was a little more complicated. I was investigating Aron for conspiring to have Blount killed as revenge for the failed hit while secretly insuring Blount's life with several six-figure life insurance policies to sweeten the pleasure of Blount's death. If you're going to have your enemy killed, why not make a little on the side? To complicate matters further, I was simultaneously investigating Blount for drug smuggling and a variety of frauds. In the end, I could never prove the serious charges on either one, but convicted both of other felonies and called it a day. To reduce his sentence, Blount later became a valuable witness for U.S. Customs by testifying against some pretty dangerous fellow prisoners. Unfortunately, when he finally got out of prison, his car struck and killed a young Dutch tourist riding a bicycle on the Natchez Trace, and my office convicted him of vehicular homicide while impaired by narcotics prescribed to lessen the pain of cancer. Blount jumped bond, was caught, and will now spend the rest of his life in federal prison.

With that case as an example of Henry's experience with challenging clients, very little in life surprised Henry Lackey. A modest man and natural storyteller, Henry knew and got along with all kinds of people instinctively. When he was appointed and later elected circuit judge, Henry's life experience in Calhoun County was invaluable to him as a trial judge. He never sought higher office. He later served as head of the state bar ethics and disciplinary committee and was highly respected for his judgment in difficult and sensitive cases. Henry was, in short, an unusual and admirable character, and I always looked forward to spending time with him.

I'll never forget one day when I had a small group of prosecutors and judges from Tunisia visiting me in Oxford. I had been wonderfully entertained by them twice on teaching missions to exotic Tunisia and feared their reciprocal visit to Oxford could never be as interesting as the Kasbah in Tunis. Then Henry stepped in. I was supposed to take the Tunisians to a federal trial one day, but at the last moment the case settled. On a hunch I walked them down to the beautiful old state courthouse in the center of the Square, the one immortalized by William Faulkner.

A big civil trial was in progress. Billy "Dog" Brewer, the beloved Ole Miss football coach and former star player, was suing the university over his firing in the wake of an NCAA recruiting scandal. As I ushered the robed and turbaned Tunisians into the courtroom, I suddenly remembered which trial was going on. The atmosphere was electric. Coach Brewer's attorney, Jim Waide, was vigorously cross-examining Ole Miss chancellor Robert Khayat. The case was highly personal. Brewer and Khayat had been not only friends and teammates on Ole Miss's last national championship football team, but Brewer had been the holder for Khayat, the placekicker, about as close a relationship of trust as can be imagined. When Khayat acquiesced in Brewer's firing, a deep and lasting enmity had erupted. That was the scene I walked into with the Tunisians.

When Henry saw us, he waved to me and beckoned us forward. "Ladies and gentlemen, the Court believes we all need a break. We've been working hard, and I see a friend I need to talk with." Back in his chambers, Henry entertained the Tunisians with tales of colorful trials, as I translated, sprinkling them with folk insight highly appealing to the Tunisian love of anecdote. I had always enjoyed Henry's company but never realized till that moment the depth and subtlety of his humorous insights into human nature. He was a regular Balzac with his colorful stories.

We spent nearly forty-five minutes with him in chambers as he answered the Tunisians' every question about life as an American judge. They were reluctant to leave and later told me it was the most impressive thing they saw about the justice system in America, which they had already visited from New York to California. Henry was too modest to realize what a terrific impression he made on them. He was just being Henry and was wisely taking a little time to let his litigants cool down before continuing his trial.

Getting back to his phone call, Henry said he needed to come see me. I told him I'd be in all week. He said he was free right then and could be in my office right after lunch. I told him to come on. He did not say what he wanted to talk about, but indicated it was serious. I thought he was kidding and expected another wine gag. The receptionist told me shortly he was downstairs. In retrospect it's hard to believe it, but we spent the first ten minutes joking about old friends and old cases and his fine blackberry wine. Then he asked if he could close the door.

The visit turned serious and Henry got right to the point. "John, something terrible has happened. I don't know what to do or where to turn, but I thought of you and all those corruption cases you've had on lawyers and supervisors and sheriffs and all the rest." He proceeded to tell me what had happened. "You may not know this, but I'm very close to Tim Balducci. He has been like a son to me." I knew Balducci by sight but had never gone to trial against him. All his cases with me had pled guilty, and you don't really get to know a lawyer from such brief contacts. "When Tim and his first wife divorced, I was there to help and counsel him. Ever since then, he has come to me for advice. His new wife and children are like family to me." This deeply personal and emotional Henry was very different from the jovial, philosophical Henry I had known. But I still had no idea what had happened.

Henry continued: "Tim has come to me and said some things he shouldn't have. He just flat out asked me to decide a case in favor of a friend of his. He tried to use our friendship to influence me. Even worse, at the end of our talk, he offered me a job with his new law firm." Henry was visibly shaken, and it worried me. I knew he was over seventy, but his jovial demeanor had always made him seem younger and healthier and sort of invulnerable. Now I suddenly saw him as a victim and clearly suffering. To calm him, I asked him to tell me details. Instead he said this: "John, when Tim said those things to me, I first wanted to throw up. Then I wanted to take a shower." Henry became visibly angry, which seemed to improve his mood. He no longer looked despondent. He wanted to act. Again I asked him to tell me more.

"Tim says he's somehow working with Dickie Scruggs and that Scruggs and his firm have asked him to contact me about dismissing a lawsuit one of his former partners filed against him over some fees in one of their big tort cases." I had heard there were several million-dollar fee squabbles involving Scruggs but didn't know Henry had one in his court or just how big the money was. "A lawyer named Johnny Jones has sued Scruggs for allegedly shorting him $17 million on their fee arrangement. Grady Tollison represents Jones. The Daniel Coker firm represents Scruggs. They have moved to dismiss the case, and Tim wants me to grant their motion. But Tim is not even an attorney on the case. I'm sure the Daniel Coker people have no idea he's come to see me. It's a terrible situation."

My mind went into trial-prep mode. I asked Henry what he had told Tim. In every similar case I'd had, when an honest public official was offered a bribe, the official always got angry and threw the person out of his office, leaving us no opportunity to gather evidence. I had lost too many promising cases that way. What had Henry done? "Well, John, I'm embarrassed to say it, but I just kind of froze up. I couldn't say anything. I was speechless. I wanted to believe he hadn't said it. Inside, I was so angry my thoughts were scrambled. I wondered who was really behind Tim's approach to me. I just said nothing."

I was relieved. The case was not blown. "So where did you leave it with him, Henry?" I asked cautiously. "Well, he just kept talking and

I managed to kind of nod as he was leaving and told him I'd get back to him. I think he would talk to me about it again if we need to." I told Henry we definitely needed to and asked if he would "wear a wire," sounding like a TV show. He said, "I have my own pocket recorder I can use." What a pleasure dealing with a professional. I asked Henry to sit down right away and write out everything he remembered that Tim had said, *everything*. He said he'd already started.

I began to explain to Henry what we both already knew: The legal rules on entrapment. Let Tim do the talking, just react as normally as you can, don't push him, let him come to you. Don't initiate any corrupt ideas. Let Tim make all the offers. Henry had already thought of all that. It was my impression at the time that the offer had taken place that very morning, and only later did I learn that it had happened a week or so earlier. In the meantime, Henry had sought the counsel of his fellow judges and a local assistant DA. Judge Andy Howorth, my neighbor, had suggested Henry go to me at the U.S. Attorney's office. The case was too expensive for the county to handle and too political to take to the state attorney general, who would have been put in an impossible position with all the money and powerful players likely to be implicated if Dick Scruggs really was involved.

I told Henry we would contact the FBI, the federal agency with exclusive jurisdiction over corruption cases. Because of Henry's office and the suspect's position as a lawyer, we would have to coordinate closely our undercover investigation with the FBI and DOJ in Washington. Henry gave me his private cell phone number and home telephone. We agreed to stay in constant contact. We both knew it was going to be a long and tricky and highly publicized case, something neither of us looked forward to. Due its gravity, we decided to take this case straight to the supervising state FBI office in Jackson and its brand-new Special Agent in Charge, Frederick Brink, whom we had never met. Jim Greenlee, Tom Dawson, and I drove to Jackson for the encounter.

Fred Brink was a smooth, direct, sophisticated graduate of the U.S. Naval Academy. He seemed to accept us in good faith in all respects. Without our even asking, he assigned Bill Delaney, a classic old-style FBI agent, to the case. Bill was already working on the big $55 million public corruption case in our district involving the failed Mississippi Beef plant, a sensitive, politically tinged case, so his frequent appearances in our office would arouse no suspicions that he was also working on another case.

Based on what Henry had said, none of us knew if Dick Scruggs was really involved or whether Balducci was acting on his behalf. It could have been that Balducci was just freelancing and trying to get in good with Scruggs, hoping if he pulled it off by abusing his friendship with Henry that Scruggs would pay him for it and maybe associate him on other cases.

I began to contemplate Dick Scruggs. He had made hundreds of millions of dollars as a plaintiff's lawyer on the Gulf Coast, moving to Oxford before Hurricane Katrina hit, planning to slow his lifestyle and enjoy his money. He was becoming well known locally as a philanthropist with both public and private charitable gifts. Since most of his money came from suing tobacco companies, he was seen as a regular Robin Hood, suing the big guys and helping the little ones. He was the only billionaire I knew, unless John Grisham was one (some claim Scruggs was technically not *quite* a billionaire, but close enough for me). I saw Dick frequently on the street. He was always friendly, and we had some good chats, often several times a week.

Dick seemed intrigued by criminal law, which he'd never practiced, and was always asking me about my more colorful cases. I liked him instinctively. We also knew each other because I had taught federal trial practice to his son, Zach, at Ole Miss five years earlier. Out of over a thousand students I'd taught over twenty-five years, Zach was easy to remember: he was the only billionaire's son I'd taught. Zach was a clean-cut kid, popular with other students. In my class he prepared well but was low-key. In no way did he act like a spoiled billionaire's son. When he moved to Oxford with his father, I saw him weekly on the Square at lunchtime and always enjoyed our encounters.

Zach once called me to say that Osama bin Laden's sister-in-law Carmen had tried to retain his firm to represent her against Osama's brother in a divorce and property settlement dispute. Zach said he told her they didn't practice that kind of law. He joked at the time that he figured the Feds had her phone tapped and might have intercepted him and just wanted me to know they had nothing to do with such people. Later, when I read a fine book she wrote on her experiences, I wished I'd read it earlier and advised Zach to go ahead and take the case.

As I talked to Dick in our Oxford Square encounters, he asked me often about wine. My book, *Thomas Jefferson on Wine*, had appeared in November 2006 and was being positively talked about in Oxford. After all, not many small-town lawyers dabble in such esoteric subjects. Dick was getting ever more interested in wine. From John Grisham's interesting book *King of Torts* it was well-known that several plaintiffs' lawyers on the Mississippi Gulf Coast were deeply into wine, and Dick seemed to have caught the bug. He asked if I would consider flying with him to Bordeaux and Burgundy to pick out some wines to stock the wine cellar he was building in his new home on the site of the old Hovious family house, one of the rare private residences actually on the Ole Miss campus. I told him I'd love to do it after I retired, which I had already promised my wife I would do in August 2007. He said he'd "put me on the meter" or pay me by the hour, but I said no, the trip and a few choice bottles would be payment enough.

The undercover phase of the Scruggs case went well, but slowly. We could not afford to press Balducci; it might spook him. And Henry was still hoping Tim would back off. Henry was often in court and Tim was often traveling, so poor Bill Delaney was constantly driving from Jackson to Oxford and back as they missed meeting after meeting. Bill's equipment was great, however. The first recorded meeting produced one of the best undercover videos I'd ever seen. Bill stage-managed Henry's office, placing a briefcase holding the camera facing the only other chair he'd left in the room, so Tim had to face directly into the camera. As a veteran trial lawyer, Henry made a perfect undercover operative. He asked Tim lots of questions without seeming to. Yet it was a constant struggle with his conscience over what he was doing to someone he'd considered a friend and protégé.

Of course we had bobbles. One time, when Henry agreed to go to lunch with Balducci, Tim's partner, Steve Patterson, showed up with the firm's investigator, obviously checking to see if Henry was for real. The audiotape wasn't very good, with all the clinking of glasses and clatter of knives and forks on plates, but it was good enough, and we could tell the suspects had bought Henry's act.

The biggest problem for me was the delays. I had signed a written agreement with DOJ to retire on August 31, 2007, but every time there was to be a meeting, something happened to delay it. It was worse than an undercover drug case. We could never herd all the cats into one room at one time. We were becoming more convinced that Scruggs was actually involved to some extent but doubted we'd ever catch him. Our plan was to get Balducci cold on tape so that we could always convict him no matter what else happened but would not charge Scruggs unless we had a really solid case. If you try to kill the king of torts you had better succeed. Not only was Dick Scruggs a respected billionaire lawyer, but his brother-in-law was Trent Lott, one of the most powerful men in Washington, a United States senator, former Republican Majority Leader, and a high-profile, highly articulate regular on the Sunday talk show circuit. We couldn't afford to go bear hunting with a switch. It would also put U.S. Attorney Jim Greenlee, a Republican appointee, on a serious hot seat. But Jim never flinched and always told us to treat the case as much as possible like any other case.

I began to feel anxious about my role in the case. After all, I was the one primarily responsible for getting the office involved in it. How could I retire right in the middle of it? I was happy in my job and proud of my career but was more tired every morning. From time to time, I had chest pains. I was worn out from the constant stress of the endless Mississippi Beef investigation and the intense public interest in it. The media wanted blood and expected miracles. And several politicians, who were innocent, were having their reputations tarnished for no reason but understandable public cynicism about our political system. People had no idea how convoluted the evidence was, and we had no way to explain it to them.

Beside Mississippi Beef, the Scruggs case was actually simple, and except for the human cost, it was exciting. But it was taking too long. Finally my retirement day came and I went happily, leaving the Scruggs case to veteran prosecutor Tom Dawson with lots of consulting by U.S. Attorney Jim Greenlee and our team of assistants. Our aces Bob Norman and Chad Lamar, often partners in their cases, were working the evidence hard with brilliant AUSA Dave Sanders, another of my former students, doing the heavy lifting on legal issues. I felt bad but knew I was leaving the case and the office in good hands. Then we suddenly started losing players faster than a college football team. Dave Sanders was named U.S. magistrate judge. Jimmy Maxwell, another rising star advocate, was appointed to the Mississippi Court of Appeals.

At least I was able to help solve one big problem before I left. One Monday I walked into Tom Dawson's office. He had the longest face I'd ever seen. "It's over. Henry has recused himself and withdrawn from the case." Tom was depressed. Even the unflappable Bill Delaney looked concerned. I thought for a moment, and one simple thing came to mind: "I'll call Henry." When I asked him what happened, he said, "John, I have written a letter to the lawyers and the other judges and faxed it to them Friday saying I discovered I have a conflict of interest and have to withdraw." Hm. "What was the conflict?" I asked. "One of my former law clerks now works for Daniel Coker, the law firm representing Scruggs. I saw the law clerk at a reception late last week and realized it."

That didn't sound right. I had personally tried scores of cases before Judge Keady, the federal judge I clerked for. Wanting to reassure Henry but also be respectful of his feelings, I asked him: "Have you read any cases on these conflicts?" I had guessed right. "John, I read cases all weekend. I now believe I don't need to recuse myself after all. This is so embarrassing. I hope I didn't just lose my nerve and blow the case." I assured him he had not. The same keen sense of ethics that had caused him to pursue the investigation in the first place had made him think of recusal. Rather than just throwing Balducci out of his office, as most of us would have done, Henry had chosen the harder, better road. He had not taken the easy way out and would not do so this time either.

But I learned much later that I was mistaken as to his motives. The real reason Henry wanted out of the case was because the stress of his meetings with Tim had caused his heart defibrillator to go off during a meeting. Henry feared Tim would discover his wire. Henry's wife also feared he would die of a heart attack. I didn't learn till later that Henry had had bypass surgery and also wore a pacemaker, which he never told me. If I'd known he had such a bad heart, I probably would never have asked him to wear a wire. But the whole Scruggs case was full of twists like that.

Henry then volunteered, without my even asking, to simply "unrecuse" himself and fax the lawyers and his fellow judges another letter undoing the first one. When I went back and told Tom and Bill Delaney, they couldn't believe it. Bill, who knew I felt guilty about leaving the case, made me feel better when he said, "John, you've done a good day's work. This case was dead. Now you can retire with a clear conscience." I retired as scheduled and spent six weeks with my wife in a little village in southwest France that she and my daughter Lydia had picked out the year before. I put the Scruggs case out of my mind almost entirely, not even e-mailing or calling home for updates.

When I got back to Oxford, I got one good night's rest to sleep off the jet lag and headed for the office. Dawson had big news. "We've got it. Balducci just paid Henry in cash on videotape. He's paying him again tomorrow. Bill Delaney is going to brace up Balducci with a video player outside Henry's office and try to get him to cooperate."

The confrontation was as smooth and simple as a routine drug case flip. After seeing and hearing himself on tape, Balducci simply said, "What do you want me to do?" Bill Delaney wired him up and sent him straight to Dick Scruggs. Although a shameful example for young lawyers, Balducci was a wonderful undercover operative. He caught Scruggs on tape agreeing to pay him back for a bribe Balducci had given Henry Lackey out of his own "slush fund." Then things began to get complicated for me personally. Happily retired, I considered myself lucky to still be trusted to know about the case since I'd be a witness as to Henry's initial statements to me and our original planning of the case. Then I suddenly got drawn back into the vortex of the undercover investigation and what would certainly be a big-time trial.

One morning I got a phone call from recently retired state chancery judge and former U.S. magistrate Norman Gillespie. "John boy," Norman said. "We want you to join our new law firm." He was retiring, unfortunately, to the firm of Patterson and Balducci. In an amazingly bold stroke, Balducci and former state auditor Steve Patterson had formed a new law firm with offices on K Street in Washington, D.C., and in New Albany and Oxford as well. The whole thing was right out of John Grisham.

Patterson was not even a lawyer, but the former elected state auditor and chairman of the Mississippi Democratic Party. He and Tim Balducci had formed their new law firm in Washington, D.C., where non-lawyers can legally be partners with lawyers. He and Balducci, with very little visible financing, had convinced several respected retired judges to serve as "Of Counsel" to the new firm. Being "Of Counsel" used to involve only retired partners of the firm who retained an office and use of a secretary part-time and drew a small stipend from the firm. They would serve mainly as business-getters or "rainmakers" and also as business-*keepers*, persuading old clients not to leave for other firms after their retirement. It was a fairly recent idea for firms to retain retired judges and senior lawyers from other firms. In most cases it was a good arrangement for all parties. In my case it was a quandary. Poor Norman Gillespie, a totally innocent bystander, had been sucked into the Scruggs case orbit and was unwittingly trying to bring me in too. I called FBI agent Bill Delaney right away and told him the deal. He was not surprised. "These guys think they can walk on water, John. Go ahead and meet with them, just let us know what happens." When I told Tom Dawson he laughed out loud. "Hailman, you just can't seem to get this retirement thing right, can you?"

I went to the lunch, which took place at the City Grocery, Oxford's most prominent restaurant. Norman, Steve, and I sat at my preferred front table in the window looking out on the Square through tall French doors. It's the best table not only because it has the best view, but also is by far the quietest. The thought did cross my mind that if I had been wearing a wire, this table would have been the quietest place to record conversations. Since it was Steve's treat, I ordered a glass of expensive California Roussanne, glad to be retired and able to drink wine at lunch, which always made me too sleepy to concentrate on law afterward. Steve pitched the law firm to me, which, unfortunately, sounded great. They had fine offices near the White House in Washington and claimed partners in Zurich, Switzerland, and Caracas, Venezuela. I wouldn't have to do any real work if I didn't want to but would have a nice office above the old Duvall's boutique on the Square in Oxford. "We just want to use your name and reputation to attract business," Steve said.

In a way, it was a shame I couldn't accept. But declining was a problem too. If I did it too abruptly, they might get suspicious. Just then Dick Scruggs and his retinue of young attorneys walked in. They looked surprised to see me with Patterson. Instead of coming over to shake hands and chat as always, Dick waved sort of wanly and took a seat at a table far in the back. He looked a little nervous, I thought. No doubt the idea of a retired federal corruption prosecutor sitting in the middle of Balducci and Patterson's law firm in Oxford was a little unnerving. Patterson clearly had not run this idea past Dick Scruggs in advance. Then came the bigger surprise. After handing me a thick, impressive big-time law firm presentation folder with expensive individual pages on all the partners and their practices, Steve announced that Sara Biden, the wife of Senator Joseph Biden's brother Jimmy, was joining the firm as a partner in the Washington office. Would this thing never end?

To top off the weirdness of the occasion, when Steve Patterson had finished his presentation, which was actually very impressive, he announced he was only going to eat a bite or two of salad, which was unusual. Nicknamed "Big Daddy," Steve weighed 300 pounds and was no dieter. He explained that the week before he had undergone gastric bypass surgery and that his new stomach was no bigger than a tangerine and would accept very little food. On that bizarre note, it was time for me to explain myself.

I told Steve and Norman, truthfully, that the offer was attractive. It would be an ideal situation for me, and I would even have liked to practice a little (except for the illegal parts), but I'd already accepted an exclusive appointment as a Fellow at the brand-new Overby Center at Ole Miss. The Overby Center is the Mississippi branch of Washington's Freedom Forum and attached to the new Meek School of Journalism. Its CEO and namesake Charles Overby, also CEO of the famed Washington Newseum, the Smithsonian of journalism, established the Center to be a "forum for civilized discussion of issues of interest." The Overby Center was in essence Oxford's first think tank. I told Steve I'd already signed a contract with them and could not do outside work and thus could not accept the firm's attractive offer. To allay any suspicions, I asked if they would consider renewing the offer in a couple of years when my fellowship ended. He said they would, and we left on good terms. All seemed quiet.

Then came another twist. Less than a week before the FBI planned to raid the Scruggs law offices and arrest Scruggs, Balducci, and Patterson, I got a phone call from Jimbo Adams, an Oxford native who had done exceedingly well in real estate in Florida. Jim had asked me to speak on wine at fund-raisers before, but I was always busy in court. This time, the event was to celebrate the spectacular renovation of his beautiful condo in an exclusive gated area near Ole Miss called Van Buren Place. Lots of old friends would be there as guests and he had a fantastic wine list and wanted me to give a few toasts and remarks about the wines as we drank them. It sounded like another dream occasion. Then he gave me the punch line: "Your friend Dick Scruggs will be a guest of honor." Good grief. I could not decline but felt like a rat knowing what would happen the next week. But that was the deal. The dinner Friday night was great, the wines superb, the emotions expressed sincere. We all went home happy and full of wine Friday night. Then, on Tuesday, they busted Dick Scruggs and his partners.

The Scruggs story became radioactive worldwide. One day, surfing the Web, I found a front-page in-depth article analyzing the case in the English-language edition of *Pravda*, the leading Russian newspaper. When he pled guilty, a *Wall Street Journal* editorial treated him as a single-name celebrity, like Oprah or Madonna. The heading read simply: "Dickie's Plea." But the Scruggs case had one last personal twist for me. I had known Steve Patterson for years, ever since I was legal counsel to Senator Stennis in Washington and Steve was his student aide, operating Senate elevators. Steve was always an ambitious guy with a gift for telling funny stories. Politics was his love, and if things had gone differently he might have been governor. When the FBI arrested him and took him to the U.S. Attorney's Office, they put him on the line with Tim Balducci, who encouraged him to cooperate. Steve was not a lawyer but was always cautious and savvy. "I want to talk to John Hailman." The agents called me at home. "I'm retired," I protested. Bill Delaney sealed the deal: "John, if you'll come down, I think you can help us get Patterson to cooperate." I went to the interrogation room. Steve said, "John, I know you can't represent me and most of the big-name federal defense attorneys already represent other people and have conflicts, but can you recommend a lawyer who would not be too expensive and have my real interests at heart?"

Another ethical dilemma. I wanted to help Steve but also wanted to help our team get him to plead guilty and cooperate, which might or might not be in his best interest; at that point, I didn't know enough about his role in the case to know. So I gave Steve three names, as we used to do in my office. First was my old prosecutor counterpart James Tucker of Jackson, who had also just retired. "Too far away," Steve said. Then I suggested Bill Travis of Southaven, a savvy old paratrooper who was the best federal defense attorney no one knew about, loyal to his clients and highly effective. "Anybody here in Oxford?" Steve asked. "Yeah, Ken Coghlan, former star Ole Miss basketball player and a tough negotiator who has the trust of our office." Steve was decisive. "Please call him for me." The agents called Ken and I left. Ken's fee turned out to be too high, and Steve finally turned to his old friend Hiram Eastland, a cousin of the senator. I was glad to finally be out of the loop.

Most of the rest of the Dick Scruggs story, including his first and second guilty pleas, has already been told in two books: *Kings of Tort* by prosecutor Tom Dawson and blogger Alan Lange; and *Fall of the House of Zeus* by my friend and fellow Overby Fellow Curtis Wilkie, the veteran Boston Globe political reporter. *Zeus* received national attention and so far my greatest fear did not materialize: for once Mississippi was not made a national whipping boy. Most commentators have so far treated the Scruggs story of judicial bribery as a national problem, not a Mississippi one.

Zeus is a dark and funny piece reminiscent of a series of Vanity Fair articles dishing dirt on colorful characters from Steve "Big Daddy" Patterson to "Joey the Blade" Langston with lots of politics and typically incestuous Magnolia State backroom deals thrown in. From my own insider perspective, however, there is one point on which I must strongly disagree with my friend Curtis's book: his conclusion that the Scruggs case had no heroes. To me Judge Henry Lackey is definitely the hero, and I am in a large majority in that view. In 2008, the Mississippi Bar awarded Henry the coveted Chief Justice Award, the bar's highest honor. He was already serving as chairman of the Mississippi Commission on Judicial Performance when all this happened. As so many people who know him have said, it is beyond belief that anyone would be foolish enough to choose Judge Henry Lackey as someone who might take a bribe.

Yet human perceptions are incredibly varied. As shown above, Henry Lackey and I knew each other as friendly adversaries in some colorful criminal cases. I didn't even recall when Henry became a judge because as federal prosecutors we rarely appear in state court. If anyone had asked me what political party he belonged to, I'd have said the underdog party because that's who he always represented. If forced to guess, I'd have said he was a blue dog Democrat appointed by Governor Ronnie Musgrove instead of Republican Governor Haley Barbour. Shows how little I know. The idea that there were politics in his decision to help us investigate the bribe Tim offered him is absurd. In my mind Dick Scruggs always seemed more like a country club Republican than Henry ever was.

It even surprised me a little to hear that Henry was a Baptist. I would have guessed Methodist. But to treat him as some sort of back-country fundamentalist yahoo is equally absurd. His comments calling himself a "deepwater" Baptist are typical of Henry's tongue-in-cheek humor about himself. Henry is undoubtedly upright, but he was never uptight, otherwise he could never have represented all the Faulknerian characters he did. When I heard how his wife resented his characterization in *Zeus* as a sort of country cousin, I could not help but laugh. It was a case of the biter bit, as Shakespeare said. Henry played the "just a country lawyer" role so long that some people actually began to believe him.

My lasting image of Judge Henry Lackey came to me in a flash in a fancy ballroom at the Peabody Hotel in Memphis in October 2010. Henry was speaking to a Tennessee bar group, the first time I had ever heard him talk about the Scruggs case in public. His longish but well-trimmed head of thick white hair and his well-cut suit did not say "country." His demeanor was that of a courtly and thoughtful Southern judge. When I turned my head for a moment as he spoke, alternating stark seriousness about corruption with warm humor about the weaknesses of human nature, his voice suddenly gave me a powerful flashback to the early 1970s when I was legal counsel to Senator Stennis in Washington. One of my key assignments was to attend the Watergate hearings, in which a "third-rate burglary" by some of President Nixon's minions was being investigated by the U.S. Senate. As I listened to Henry speak, I realized I had heard that same wise and self-effacing tone, had seen that same subtle judicial demeanor before. Henry Lackey was Senator Sam Ervin of North Carolina reincarnated. Sam Ervin was the former North Carolina judge who presided with gentle humor and subtle literary wisdom over those hearings. A natural hero for his incredible ability to break tension with quotes from Shakespeare and the King James version, Senator Sam entitled his autobiography, as if anticipating Henry Lackey, *Just A Country Lawyer* (Indiana U. Press 1974).

I told a couple of people about my eureka moment, but no one seemed to know what I was talking about. Too young I suppose. Then one afternoon Curtis Wilkie was being interviewed before a full house at the Overby Center by Ole Miss journalism graduate Peter Boyer, a staff writer at the *New Yorker*. Curtis repeated his opinion that the Scruggs saga had no heroes. I had often told Curtis my opinion that he should at least admit, based on statements in his own book, that the Scruggs story at least has one Cassandra-like heroine, Dick's loyal wife Diane, who repeatedly warned him to stay away from Patterson, Langston, and P. L. Blake, the political fixer.

But Dick didn't listen. Just like he didn't listen when she tried to wean him from a cocktail of addictive prescription drugs, especially the powerful barbiturate Fioricet, to which he was admittedly addicted and which to my mind gave him the sense of bullet-proof euphoria that led him over the brink from merely paying off insider witnesses in lawsuits against big bad corporations, believing the ends justified the means, to outright bribery of judges. To me it was his drug-enhanced sense of invulnerability that combined with his sense of entitlement as a good-guy crusader to bring about his downfall. To me Dick Scruggs was not a fallen tragic hero as some said, but a regular human being who rose too fast, had his head turned by fame and fortune, and like Elvis was finished off by the euphoria of prescription drugs.

At the end of the program I approached Peter Boyer and told him my theory that Henry Lackey was the reincarnation of Sam Ervin. Peter pointed to a lady who had just walked up. "My wife told me the exact same thing two days ago when she first read Curtis's book. She said, 'That's Sam Ervin.' Y'all need to talk." We did talk, and I hope there will be others who share our view.

My other candidate for a Scruggs case hero was a critical player, but one whose name is almost totally unknown to the public: FBI case agent Bill Delaney. In an important sense Bill was the anti-Scruggs: modest and seeking neither money nor glory. When assigned the Scruggs case, he was already up to his neck as the case agent on Mississippi Beef, a thankless high-profile case of enormous complexity involving over $55 million in fraud against the state. A media frenzy followed Bill's every move in the case, but he wisely stayed below all radar. For my money, Bill is the kind of hero modern America needs.

A new paperback version of *Zeus* has now been released with a new epilogue which actually seems to attempt to exonerate Dick Scruggs. The new *Zeus* epilogue, which speaks at length through a quote from a letter written to supporters by Steve Patterson, actually alleges that Henry Lackey was the villain and Dick Scruggs the victim of extortion by Judge Lackey. I have to say that here the point of total absurdity has been reached. The epilogue, sadly, tries to turn the whole Scruggs fiasco on its head. On English TV there is a show called *Without Villains There Would Be No Heroes*. I'm afraid that, to raise up Dick Scruggs, *Zeus* had to try to pull down Judge Henry Lackey, a total travesty of justice.

In my view the neutral *Daily Journal* of Tupelo should have the last word because it got the Scruggs case exactly right in its editorial written just after Dick Scruggs's first sentencing for judicial bribery, even before the DeLaughter bribery case and his second guilty plea. The editorial is worth quoting in its entirety as the last, best word on the case:

JUSTICE TRUMPS ARROGANCE

The federal judiciary and its prosecutors delivered a humiliating blow on Friday to the enemies of integrity in the Mississippi state judiciary. The sentencing of famed plaintiffs' attorney Richard Scruggs and his former law firm associate, Sidney Backstrom, on charges of attempting to bribe a state circuit court judge, reverberates among all who think they can get away with anything because they are above the law.

Both pleaded guilty earlier in conspiring to bribe Circuit Judge Henry Lackey of Calhoun County. Lackey turned to the federal prosecutor's office in Oxford after being approached about a bribe by Timothy Balducci, a lawyer from New Albany who was in cahoots with Scruggs, Backstrom, and Scruggs' son, Zach Scruggs, also an attorney in the Oxford-based firm. Balducci has pleaded guilty and is cooperating with prosecutors. Zach Scruggs pleaded guilty to misprision of a felony— knowing about the planned bribery but failing to report it. He will be sentenced in early July.

Earlier, in a separate case but tied to the Scruggs firm, noted Boon-eville attorney Joey Langston pled guilty in a case involving attempting to illegally influence Circuit Judge Bobby DeLaughter of Jackson. That case also involves former District Attorney Ed Peters.

Former state Auditor Steve Patterson, who worked for the Balducci firm, has pleaded guilty in relation to the Scruggs conspiracy involving Judge Lackey. Langston and Patterson both are cooperating with federal investigators.

Langston pleaded guilty to trying to influence DeLaughter in an asbestos lawsuit fee case by promising that Scruggs could help DeLaughter get appointed to a federal judgeship with the help of Republican former U.S. Sen. Trent Lott, Scruggs' brother-in-law. . . .

This sordid web of deceit apparently is far from being fully untangled, but what's been revealed so far is enough to make Mississippians wonder why smart, successful people become consumed by greed and deluded by a sense of invincible power.

Scruggs, by consensus, was among the most famous trial lawyers in the world. He won a settlement from Big Tobacco for the state of Mississippi that made him, by all accounts and appearances, wealthy almost beyond belief. Dickie Scruggs, Zach Scruggs, Sid Backstrom, Steve Patterson, Joey Langston, and Tim Balducci failed themselves, their families, their communities, their friends, their innocent colleagues, and the legal profession.

But they got caught, the single possibility that apparently never entered their minds or touched their consciences.

(June 30, 2008)

3

CIVIL RIGHTS AND CIVIL WRONGS

Introduction

When I joined the U.S. Attorney's Office, because of my three years of civil rights experience with Legal Services during law school and my two years as law clerk for Judge William Keady during school and prison desegregation, U.S. Attorney H. M. Ray assigned me to do all the office's civil rights cases, both criminal and civil. For a few years, we had only civil class actions, handled by the Civil Rights Division in Washington with me helping. First there was *Gates*, a monster class-action suit to desegregate Parchman Prison; then came *Gipson*, another monster class-action with over five thousand plaintiffs claiming discrimination in hiring by the U.S. Department of Agriculture. Later came *Papasan*, a class action by school superintendents against Mississippi and the United States for frittering away during the Civil War all the lands set aside to support public schools.

Most difficult was the famed *Ayers* case to desegregate and equalize Mississippi's five white and three black state universities. The case lasted over three decades and outlived its plaintiff, its first trial judge, and numerous defendant governors and college presidents. When it was appealed to the U.S. Supreme Court, I ended up in Washington in the unique role of briefing U.S. Solicitor General Kenneth Starr as to its years of intricacies.

Eventually my criminal civil rights cases began and with a vengeance. Nearly all of them involved alleged use of excessive force by officers against citizens in custody, either inmates or persons just arrested. From Marks came the allegation that an intoxicated sheriff tried to fire a bullet between an inmate's ear and his head, fortunately missing both. The sheriff then cut the crotch out of his jeans with a sharp knife in an attempt to get him to confess. We won a victory of sorts in the first trial. The jury hung up 6–6, which was the first case in the history of our district where an all-white jury did not acquit a white officer for abusing a black defendant. Then we began to win. Several Delta cross burners pled guilty. A white jury convicted the chief deputy sheriff of Tippah County of beating a seventy-year-old black arrestee. The black chief deputy sheriff of Marshall County pled guilty to abusing a black inmate by accidentally shooting him while beating him with an illegal sawed-off shotgun. Even that victory was not wholly popular. When the deputy got back from federal prison, a large integrated crowd held a parade and threw a party for him. The sheriff hired him back. It was discouraging, but at least we had the races agreeing on something: They liked officers better than inmates. Next, a Justice Court judge pled guilty to sexually molesting several poor and defenseless female litigants who had cases in his court, boasting about his handy "pecker pump" paid for by his social security.

Then we got the big case. An anonymous informant from Parchman began reporting to us that guards had beaten an inmate almost to death. The warden and deputy warden were both allegedly present. It was our chance to put an end to the legend that beatings and killings of inmates at Parchman were commonplace and committed with impunity. With the help of master FBI interrogator and polygrapher Ed Lee of New Orleans, we got several guards to cooperate, resulting in several guilty pleas and jury convictions. We hoped it would help reduce the culture of brutality and silence that had so long ruled at Parchman. The legislature created a new, much more effective internal affairs unit headed by a retired FBI agent untainted by politics.

Then we lost another trial. A young businessman from Columbus, after drinking several shots of foul-tasting Jaegermeister in a local dance club, staggered next door and kicked in the plate glass window of a department store. When police arrived, the drunk tried to resist, and officers beat the stew out of him, breaking several ribs and collapsing a lung. One officer repeatedly practiced his karate on the victim, kicking him numerous times all the way across the large showroom. The whole incident was captured on the store's video surveillance tape. Our victim made a poor witness, however, and the defense experts on use of force and radiology were better than ours and the jury acquitted.[1] John Mott, my Ivy League–educated partner from the Civil Rights Division in the trial, now a D.C. judge, was a dead ringer for actor Pierce Brosnan, only several inches taller. Perhaps we were distracted because every night when we went out to dinner, good-looking women would stop by our table, chat for a moment, then slip John a piece of paper with their name and telephone number. A man of steel, he never followed up on any of the offers.

Not long after the karate kick case, John and I were assigned another beating case together. A minor local crack dealer, the grandson of a respected local civil rights leader, was caught after a hundred-mile-an-hour chase and beaten unmercifully by the chief deputy sheriff of DeSoto County.[2] The case had a problem or two. First, the victim was a drug dealer. Second, his grandmother was not a favorite of local whites. Third, the officer had an excellent reputation and had never before been accused of such an act. Fourth, which should have been (and was in the end) irrelevant, the defendant's best friend was my daughter's favorite teacher at Oxford High School.

Our case, however, was strong. An officer at the scene of the beating made a complaint to the FBI, saying it was the most sickening thing she ever saw. We subpoenaed every officer from the scene, most of them police officers from nearby towns serving on the county drug task force. Every officer testified that the chief, whom they all liked, had used grossly excessive force. He had just "lost it." But there was also a wild card in the case. Riding with the drug dealer during the incident was his sixteen-year-old date, a good student and star basketball player at nearby Byhalia High School. She had been asleep while he made a drug sale away from the car, which led to the chase and beating. When the officers forced his car off the road, they handcuffed the innocent girl, scared and unresisting, who calmly stretched out on the ground and went to sleep. After savagely beating the boyfriend, the deputy was walking around his car when he saw the girl handcuffed on the ground. As he walked by, he kicked her hard in the head and called her a vile name.

We argued the case passionately, knowing it would be tough to convict. We figured the jury might decide he got what he deserved and pardon the deputy with what they call a jury nullification. It had also come out in the evidence that the local DA had not prosecuted the drug case because of the beating. After several hours of debate, the jury came back with two verdicts: Not guilty of stomping the drug dealer but guilty of kicking the girl in the head. It was to us a reasonable, practical piece of frontier justice.

Then I saw Toni Everett, Judge Biggers's secretary, crooking her finger at me to come talk to her. "The judge wants to see you in chambers. And so do I." Following her in, I saw the judge smiling slyly: "That was a pretty slick move you made in your argument there, John." I asked what he meant. Toni answered, "Don't pretend you don't know what he means. You saw that movie last night, and you know some of those jurors must have seen it, too." I had no idea what she was talking about and protested, "I was at the office all evening, working on my argument and jury instructions. I didn't have time to be watching movies." Toni shot back, "We *know* you were working on your argument; it was certainly effective."

When I finally convinced them I had no idea what they were talking about, Toni explained it. "You know that tear-jerking argument you made about how that innocent little girl who got kicked in the head could have been your own daughter, who is a good student and plays basketball? You know how you said it could even have been the defense attorney's daughter and how everybody knows how hard it is to control who your children go out with?" Toni was right of course. I admitted I was proud of my argument, and that it was sincere.

"But not exactly original," the judge added. Again I was baffled. "John, are you telling us you did not know that last night on TV they ran that John Grisham movie *A Time to Kill* where the black father shoots and kills the white man who raped his daughter?" They had me. I had not seen the movie the night before but had read the book and seen the movie before and knew right away how seeing that movie could have affected jurors during my highly emotional argument. I needed an exit line to leave chambers gracefully. "Just shows why you shouldn't watch so much TV. If I'd seen Matthew McConaughey make that argument in the

movie, my keen sense of ethics might have deterred me from making it."
Toni said "Get out of here." It made the victory even sweeter.

After that case we went on to solve the highly charged national scandal of the arsons of black churches across the South, which turned out not to have a racial motive at all but an anti-Christian one. Then we reopened the fifty-year-old Emmett Till murder case. State Attorney General Jim Hood appointed me a special assistant DA for Leflore County for that case. The eighteen-month FBI investigation was well worth it because we exploded a lot of myths and answered a lot of questions about the case that started the civil rights revolution. I detail here some of lead FBI agent Dale Killinger's key findings, which were never adequately explained to the American public by the Justice Department, which seemed embarrassed because we found no one to prosecute. With the Till case over, it was beginning to sound like a good time to retire.

A High Sheriff Goes Wild[3]

Jack Harrison of Marks was the longtime sheriff of Quitman County. In the heat of the civil rights years, whites looked to him to keep black folks "in line." He cultivated a fairly ferocious image among both whites and blacks for doing what whites expected of him. In one case, he outdid even his own fearsome reputation.

A short, slight young black man was involved in stealing equipment from a wealthy plantation owner's shop. He was caught red-handed with some of the stolen goods and locked up in Harrison's jail. Harrison brought him to his office the next morning for questioning. Hoping to solve the case quickly and get the goods back and satisfy his powerful Delta constituent, Harrison tried without success all the normal techniques to get the young man to cooperate.

That night after dinner, Harrison returned to the jail liquored up and accompanied by a friend and a full bottle of whiskey. After several whiskies, Harrison went up and got the young man from the bullpen and brought him out in the hall. To soften him up and impress the other inmates, Harrison pulled out his revolver and said, "You lying SOB, I'm going to see if I can squeeze one in between your ear and your head," firing a bullet right past the inmate's ear. In his haste, the sheriff had forgotten where he was. The bullet ricocheted wildly off the brick walls before flying out the window. As the other inmates hid under their bunks, Harrison dragged the young man downstairs to his office for more questioning. According to the inmate, Harrison slapped, punched, and kicked him several times, but the inmate wouldn't talk, not wanting to implicate friends.

The intoxicated Harrison threw the inmate on the floor. In leg irons and handcuffed behind, the inmate was helpless as Harrison pulled out a sharp-bladed carpet knife and demanded the inmate tell him about the burglary or Harrison would castrate him. Harrison sliced away the crotch of the jeans but at the insistence of his friend gave up and had a jailer carry the inmate back to the bullpen where other inmates saw the blood on his face and the cutaway crotch of his jeans.

Word of the assault soon leaked out, and James Figgs, the head of the local NAACP, came to see us. FBI agent Wayne Tichenor was assigned to the case. He spent days trying to persuade fearful inmates to testify. The NAACP leader later told me how he admired Tichenor's investigation, saying he was "steady about his business." Having seen what happened to their fellow inmate, at first other inmates were not about to cross Harrison. They had pretty rough criminal records themselves, and convicted murderers and drug dealers would not make the best witnesses. In this case, however, racial solidarity began to come into play. Whatever the risks, several of them said they would not tolerate such vile abuse of a brother, and that if we would protect them, they would testify.

As luck would have it, one of our best friends in law enforcement, David Bryan, sheriff of the next county over, Panola, was a friend of Sheriff Harrison and agreed to keep inmate witnesses in the Panola County jail, as was customary in sensitive situations where certain inmates had to be separated from others. We later asked for about a half-dozen cooperating witnesses to be moved, along with a half-dozen non-cooperators, hoping to camouflage who was cooperating and that once out of Harrison's control they might all cooperate. As it happened, every inmate who agreed to cooperate was black. In the racially charged atmosphere of the time, we knew we would need at least one credible white witness to make the white members of what we knew would be a mostly white jury feel safe confronting the white community after convicting a white sheriff of abusing a black inmate.

The sheriff's friend, an insurance salesman, was at first the only white witness, and he of course sided totally with the Sheriff, saying absolutely nothing had happened. The other potential white witness was a skinny, long-haired, scared-to-death nineteen-year-old in jail on some minor charge. He was the only white person in the jail. When Wayne Tichenor interviewed him, he claimed he was asleep when the incident started and stayed in the back of the cell because he was afraid. Tichenor said the boy's mouth said he saw nothing, but his eyes said he had seen everything but was too scared to talk. Several black inmates said the white boy had seen it all, but they didn't blame him for looking out for himself.

One of my rules in trying cases was always to go to the scene of the crime to get a feel for it and to be able to question witnesses about where things were and how they happened, visually. When Tichenor and I got to the jail that day, there were no guards, just one radio dispatcher on duty. She was young, had no weapon, and weighed nearly 300 pounds. Wayne told her we were both "with" the FBI. He explained later that I was technically "with" him, and if he'd said I was with the Justice Department she probably would not have let us in. The girl waved her hand at the stairway and told us "help yourselves."

We immediately heard shouting from upstairs, where some twenty inmates were all in one mass bullpen lined with multiple bunk beds. We climbed the stairs, which were strewn with sharp pieces of broken glass from broken beer bottles. As we approached the cell, we saw the white inmate, standing alone facing us with his back to the others and a look of despair on his face. Four or five of the black inmates were trading punches and others were cheering. A couple of beer bottles hit the cell's bars. At first they didn't even notice us. When they saw our suits and ties, they abruptly stopped fighting.

Wayne asked where the sheriff was. "He and the deputies are at a trial at the courthouse across the street," one said. "Who are you?" They knew we were not there to sell them insurance. "FBI," Wayne said simply. "Hey, can you get us to Panola County?" Some were standing, some sitting on the floor, some on bunks. I thought how totally scary it would be to be locked in there. The white boy still stood alone at the front of the cell. Suddenly I noticed his lips moving. "Get me out," he mouthed silently. I tried not to signal a response to him in front of the others, but nodded.

Wayne chatted with them and asked who could pass a polygraph on his story. "Anyone who flunks it has to come back to Jack Harrison's hotel here." Several hands went down, but a few stayed up and Wayne took down their names. The white boy said nothing. Later we went across the street and talked to Larry Lewis, the straight, stand-up lawyer who was county prosecutor. He said he could help us by plea-bargaining the white boy's case so he would be released from jail without appearing to have cooperated. I thanked God for people like Larry Lewis.

At trial we picked what looked like a fair jury. New judge L. T. Senter, in his first federal trial, was calm and judicious and appeared totally in control of the case, a real relief given all the heat and threats of violence on both sides of the community. Our proof went well. The inmates' testimony was surprisingly believable, and the victim looked tiny and really vulnerable. Defense counsel Bill Liston did his best but never really laid a glove on any of our witnesses. Harrison, a real hothead, made a terrible witness. On cross I got him angry, his face turned bright red, and he talked and acted in court exactly as our witnesses had described him at the jail.

But we still had one big hill to climb: No white man had ever been convicted by a jury in the Northern District of Mississippi of abusing a black man, not in the entire twentieth century. So we waited. The jury stayed out for hours. Judge Senter recessed till morning, gave the jury an Allen instruction, the so-called "dynamite charge," which in those happier days basically told the minority of the jurors they should listen more closely to the majority. Nowadays the Allen charge is so diluted and politically correct that it often encourages jurors to think their difficulty in agreeing means they should give up and acquit if they don't reach unanimity quickly, defeating the whole purpose of having jury trials at all in difficult cases.

After many hours the jury finally came back and reported they were hopelessly deadlocked six-to-six. Judge Senter had no choice but to declare a mistrial based on a hung jury. U.S. Attorney H. M. Ray, who had lost several such cases in his twenty years as prosecutor, reassured me, "John, that's the most votes for guilty we've ever gotten. And this is the *only* hung jury we've ever gotten. All the others cases were acquittals." Mr. Ray got right up and announced we would retry the case as soon as the court and the defendant were ready.

Six months passed before we could go to bat again. By that time several things had changed. Our witnesses were much more fearful since we had failed to win the first time. Worst of all, our skinny, scared little victim had been sent to a rough camp at Parchman Prison where he got the usual education. Next time we saw him he had put on forty pounds lifting weights. He had corn-rowed his hair and adopted an inmate attitude. All was not perfect on the defense side either, however. Harrison, allegedly hearing his attractive wife was seeing another man, had gone home drunk one night from the jail and shot out every window in his own house. Word on the street was that his wife's secret boyfriend was none other than his star defense eyewitness. Following long tradition, we decided not to stir up domestic disputes. Whatever the truth was and whatever the defendant believed it was, his star witness testified, told the same story, and they still seemed to be friends. We didn't tell them any different. Besides, the story might well have been false and we wondered whether someone was just goading us into disrupting the defense. Still, I've always wondered what would have happened if we'd gotten word to Harrison that his wife's lover was his star witness.

My cross-examination of Harrison this time was quite a bit more aggressive. He finally admitted that he struck the inmate once but only to subdue him after the inmate assaulted Harrison first. "How," I asked, "could an inmate in leg irons and handcuffed behind his back have assaulted you?" Harrison demonstrated how the inmate had first tried to head butt him, then said the inmate barely missed him with a vicious kick. Excited and overconfident, I made the mistake of daring Harrison to show the jury how the inmate did it with handcuffs and leg irons on. Harrison agreed to reenact the scene. We had one of the U.S. Marshals in attendance handcuff the sheriff behind with his own handcuffs. Then they put the marshal's leg irons on him.

I asked the sheriff to stand with me in front of the jury in that pose and dared him to assault me. He did. I easily avoided his head butt, except that while his head was down, he suddenly swung around with his back to me and kicked up and back with his feet together like a mule would kick. I just barely backed out of his range, but I saw by the look on the jurors' faces that they thought it could well have happened just that way.

Then a funny thing happened. After the marshals took his leg irons off, the sheriff could not find his handcuff keys. Supposed to be on his belt, they were not there. I chuckled, but saw the jury staring at me in an unfriendly way. The marshals called his jail, but no one could find the keys. Harrison had to spend the rest of that day of the trial handcuffed behind his back at the defense table. I didn't think the jurors liked it. They looked hostile.

When we finally got to closing arguments, the feeling I got in front of the jury box was like a cold wind blowing in my face. They nodded with the defense and stared sullenly at me. My inmate witnesses were much weaker than the first time, my victim looked like a thug, and my supposedly clever experiment had backfired, making it look like maybe the victim did assault the sheriff. Nevertheless, we did have one of those unsatisfying moral victories. Apparently at least a few jurors believed in us, and the jury stayed out for several hours. In the end, however, they returned with a unanimous "not guilty" verdict. Our office had still never won a civil rights case. FBI agent George Barber, a retired Marine Corps colonel who really had his heart in the case and thought we would win, took our loss harder than anyone. Wayne Tichenor and I just chalked it up to experience.

Two weeks later I got another call from Tichenor. "You'll never believe it. George House, the serial bank robber, got out on parole and immediately robbed a couple of banks in the Delta and is hiding out in a swamp. Parchman has men on horseback and dogs out there tracking him, but we need a lawyer on the scene to answer legal questions about some things we're thinking of doing. Can you come?" Could I come? For George House, our district's most notorious bank robber and fugitive? "Why not?" I asked. "Well," Wayne replied, "the officer in charge of the case, because it's in his county and it was one of his banks that was robbed, is none other than Sheriff Jack Harrison." I went right over, we worked together fine, and we all later laughed about the whole thing.

Burning Crosses in the Night[4]

Over the next few years I prosecuted many more civil rights cases. With experience they became a kind of specialty. We began to handle them jointly with attorneys from the Civil Rights Division of the DOJ, often young, ambitious attorneys from Ivy League schools determined to change the world and make a name for themselves on their way to lucrative private practices. Most cases involved officers using excessive force on inmates or arrestees. Several, however, involved cross-burnings, an old-fashioned nineteenth-century offense outlawed by the Ku Klux Klan Act of the 1870s. It was in one of those cases that I first met Haley Barbour, soon to be head of the Republican National Committee and later governor of Mississippi. It was the only criminal case I ever remember him handling.

We met by phone late one evening when my wife, Regan, said, "There's a lawyer on the phone with the thickest Mississippi accent I've ever heard." Being from Rolling Fork in the deep Delta herself, she is an expert on Delta accents, so I was impressed. Haley Barbour had, as Oxford writer Jim Dees would say, "A mouth full of Mississippi." Haley said he represented six silly late-teen rednecks from Sunflower County who got drunk one night and burned a cross—for no particular reason—in a black neighborhood but not near any particular residence. No motive was apparent beyond general racism and drunkenness. I recall Barbour made a pretty good job of softening the racial impact of the incident by getting some prominent black citizens to give good character references on the white boys and say they thought the best thing for all concerned would be for them to be put on supervised probation so the incident would go away quietly. With Civil Rights Division approval, that's what happened. I should probably have been more impressed with Barbour's political skills, persuading the mighty Civil Rights Division to agree to probation in a cross-burning case, but he was so smooth in how he did it I hardly noticed at the time.

The most pathetic and slapstick cross-burning case I recall happened in DeSoto County, the fastest-growing, most urbanized county in the Northern District. Often thought of as mainly a bedroom community for Memphis, it still had some remote, old-time communities near the river, made famous by renowned legal-thriller writer John Grisham, who practiced law in DeSoto County and represented the county in the state legislature for several years.

One year a black woman and her two children moved into one of those all-white rural enclaves near Lake Cormorant, in the western part of the county. The first week she found a crude racial epithet spray-painted on the blacktop road in front of her house. The FBI sent agents

to investigate it as a Fair Housing Act violation. Their investigation identified likely suspects in the area, mostly teenagers who had conflicts with
the lady's children. The following month when the lady went to her mail
box, she saw a burned patch in her yard. Examining it, she saw a pair of
long two-by-fours, partially burned, with "KKK" painted on one. She
called the FBI again. "I hate to bother you, but these people are stupid
enough to be scary. The thing in my yard looks like a T, but I think it was
meant to be a cross."

The FBI opened a case and started interviewing suspects, many of
them minors. Piecing together information, we got a search warrant for
a house down the street and found some Klan literature but no hard evidence. A few days later, a lady called me and said, "My son and I need to
come talk with you while my husband's at work. It's about that cross." I
told her to come on. Fortunately a young woman from the Civil Rights
Division was already in Oxford working with us. She was originally from
Alabama and understood the nuances of the local culture. When the lady
arrived from DeSoto County, she asked to speak to me alone. "This FBI
agent fellow named 'Doc' Tichenor said you were a good man to deal
with. So here we are. My boy has something he needs to tell you. I may
be doing the wrong thing bringing him here, but I didn't raise him to do
things like this."

The lady left and came back with her son, a strapping eighteen-
year-old built like a tight end. He had long hair and wore rumpled work
clothes. I noticed a big bandage on one of his hands. The woman from
the Civil Rights Division joined me and the mother left. The boy said, "I
don't know what I'm doing here. I need to be at work." To get him talking, I asked about his work. "I used to think I was a pretty good shade tree
mechanic till a car slipped off its blocks and fell on my head last year. Now
I just do body work for this other guy." He wouldn't look me in the eye and
seemed nervous around the young woman. "I didn't know she would be
here. You mean she came all the way from Washington, D.C., over *this*?"

The word *this* triggered something in my head. I called the boy by
his name and talked to him like I was his football coach: "Now, you look
me in the eye. Your mama brought you down here to tell me something
important, and I can tell by how you're acting that you are ready to tell
me. Look me in the eye and tell me just what you did." For a moment
I thought how angry the FBI supervisors would probably be about two

mere lawyers getting a confession without an FBI agent present. I'd already called Wayne but he was out of town and told me to go ahead without him. I knew that could get him in hot water with the brass but figured we'd seen worse things happen. It was typical to have to worry about bureaucratic rules at such critical points in cases, but that was just part of the federal law enforcement game.

"Do I have to look at you while I tell it?" the boy asked. "Look anywhere you like, just get it over with." He got right to it. "Me and this other guy and his girlfriend got to drinking. After lots of beers, he said we didn't need no niggers on our street. They'd be stealing stuff and playing that god-awful music of theirs and making trouble and stuff. My dad can't stand niggers. I don't really mind them myself. I don't know why I went along, but I did." The boy said his friend got the bright idea of burning a cross in the black people's yard, thinking they would move away. They went out to the friend's garage where they found a gas can and a couple of long two-by-fours. They never thought about the fact that the KKK they wrote on one two-by-four would probably be burned up with the cross, but put it on there anyway. They walked down the road carrying the two-by-fours, a small can of gasoline, and a hammer and nails.

Not wanting to be seen carrying the cross, they didn't put it together until they got to the trailer. Hiding in a nearby thicket, they tried to make the cross. The boy told just how it happened: "Somehow, when we got there, we only had *one* nail left. I nailed the two-by-fours together while the girl stood lookout. When we held the cross up, the cross piece kept slipping sideways. It looked stupid, and the hammering was way too loud. Finally I just nailed one two-by-four real solid on top of the other like a T so it would stop wobbling."

I could not look at the woman from Civil Rights, afraid we'd both start laughing. The boy continued: "We took a hatchet we brought along and sharpened the bottom of one two-by-four and drove it in the ground. I poured gasoline on the two-by-fours, and the guy set it alight. But he rushed it. I started running, still holding the gas can, but the fire chased me and burned my hand pretty bad. We ran all the way to my friend's house and hid out." When his mother saw his hand burned, he told her how it all happened. She and his father argued about it for days until she took over while the father was at work and told her son he needed to "do the right thing."

I thanked the boy for doing the right thing and walked him out to the waiting room and left him with his mother. I told her he was a good young man who just needed to get better friends and stop drinking. She thanked me. I told her I'd talk to the woman from Washington and do all I could for her son. When I got back to my private office, I expected to have a good laugh with the woman. Instead, I found her crying. "That's the saddest thing I've ever seen," she said. Then we both started laughing. She called her supervisors in Washington and with her agreement we whipped up a plea agreement, got the magistrate to appoint the boy an attorney, and arranged for him to get probation for a misdemeanor so he would not have a felony record. The victim was well-satisfied and continued to live in the neighborhood. To my knowledge, the defendant has never been in trouble again.[5]

Stopping the Arsons of Black Churches[6]

Joey Hall, a former college football player from Alabama, was always one of my favorite investigators. Like most of us, his four-year B.A. degree had given him some knowledge of books and people, but when he graduated, he had no real idea how to make a living. Like many college athletes, he turned to law enforcement, where you had to be both physically fit and accustomed to competition and confrontation. As an ATF agent, Joey had worked with me on several bombing and firearm cases, plus an occasional arson or two. He was a natural good ole boy who dipped snuff and carried a little white Styrofoam spit cup, which helped him fit in with the good ole boys he was investigating. With his linebacker's build and Alabama accent, he had done several undercover jobs and fit in smoothly in honky-tonks where local criminals bought and sold their Saturday night specials and an occasional illegal machine gun. The worst weapon I ever saw was a modern steel version of the old English crossbow, which local Gangster Disciples used to employ to terrify their rivals by shooting big deadly metal arrows in the front doors and out the back of their rivals' clubhouses.

By nature calm and by appearance menacing, Joey could pose as just about anything he wanted to, his education and keen mind hidden under an "aw shucks" demeanor. Joey loved motorcycles and could ride with anyone. If you had seen him at home with his beautiful wife and happy children, you would have thought him an unlikely candidate for a member of an outlaw motorcycle gang, but the higher-ups at ATF were apparently good judges of character. The group known as the Bandidos were getting out of hand on the Mississippi Gulf Coast. They allegedly had a small affiliate clubhouse in Lafayette County, right under our noses, about fifteen miles from Oxford in a run-down hamlet called Tula. A century earlier, Tula was a thriving town with its own business college and several prominent families who were models for characters in Faulkner. Situated high on a hill where my wife and I used to go for drives on weekends to watch eagles fly, it was named for a province often mentioned in nineteenth-century Russian literature.

I once prosecuted the elderly postmistress of Tula for stealing mail. She usually sealed the mail back up and sent it on after reading it, without stealing anything. At her plea she admitted she'd done it for years. At sentencing the judge asked her why she did it. "Bored," she said. "Stone bored." That was modern Tula.

Seizing the chance for a little adventure, Joey joined a "class" for new Bandidos, a kind of trainee group on the Gulf Coast. When I heard what he'd done, I went to talk with him. "Joey, what are you doing? If you've got to play undercover, do another group. There is a nest related to these guys near Oxford. Some of them probably know you. If they find out, you know what they'll do to you. Informers die." Joey appreciated my concern but gave me a typical Joey answer. "John, it's my job. Besides, it's going great, I'm almost in. The coast is a six hour drive from here, and those guys at Tula are not really affiliated." He turned out to be right.

For months we went our separate ways and I didn't see Joey. Law enforcement rumors began to float back though. Other agents said the bikers liked Joey too much. If he would agree to become a full member, they would make him an officer. Of course Joey couldn't, because to be a full member you had to commit certain crimes, some involving drugs, others violence. You also had to participate in group orgies with the dirty women who ran with the bikers. Joey was already pretending to smoke weed (like Bill Clinton, without inhaling), but they wanted him to do harder drugs. But he did not want to pull out quite yet. The Bandidos were beginning to tell him their secrets about drug suppliers and wanted him as muscle on drug deals. He knew it was almost time to get out but begged his superiors to let him stay undercover just a little longer until he could get all the evidence they needed. He said he still felt perfectly safe.

More sinister rumors came back to me. Joey's wife was really worried about him. He had begun to like the biker life and sometimes referred to bikers as "friends." The agents were worried, too. Finally, fate intervened. The Oxford ATF office was understaffed by almost 50 percent. The agency, despite its agents' love of firearms and the gun culture, was under attack in Washington by lobbyists for the National Rifle Association (NRA) who wanted the agency abolished, or at least so reduced that it would no longer be perceived as a threat.

Then a new phenomenon occurred. Someone began torching rural black churches across the South. One day we woke up to find nearly forty had been burned from Kentucky to Georgia. The method was always the same: from tire tracks it appeared a car would pull in behind a small isolated church out of sight of the road and toss gasoline through a rear window and ignite it. The small wooden structures were quickly engulfed in flames, and by the time local volunteer fire departments could get there, they were burned beyond saving. The matter was becoming a national issue. Jesse Jackson began visiting burned churches, demanding justice. Church groups from Rhode Island and Massachusetts began sending buses of parishioners and truckloads of supplies to help black churches in the South rebuild.

Then the problem came home to us. One night a similar fire destroyed a church thirty minutes from Oxford at Como, home of bluesman Fred McDowell. This church was a little different, being a large solid brick structure near Interstate Highway 55 and of recent construction, but still hidden from view. We were devastated. Who would do this? Mississippi is said to be the most religious of all states and every year easily tops the list of all U.S. states for charitable giving, especially to churches. I knew from personal experience that members of small rural black churches in our district were most unlikely targets for white racists. Even they respected the conservative, nonconfrontational members of those tiny rural churches, bastions of religious conservatism of their own.

In the early days of civil rights, the large urban black churches had been centers of militancy, voting rights drives, marches, and demonstrations. But times had changed. The schools were now integrated. Marches and boycotts had largely ended. The Ku Klux Klan and Citizens Council were basically defunct. Although racism and prejudice were still strong, perhaps even predominant, these fires did not add up to me as southern. For one thing, not a single one of the burned churches had ever been involved in any civil rights activity. Most were tiny, with congregations of fewer than a hundred, often with most members belonging to one extended family. These were hardworking, God-fearing folk, the last people even the most prejudiced whites would think of harming. It was a time when people were seeking peace and ways to get along.

Another striking thing about the fires was that no one ever took credit for them. Hate groups would have boasted to the media or at least among themselves about what they did. Was there some crazy serial arsonist who did it for the thrill? Could it be teenage thieves and dope heads who stole gold crosses, sound systems, or whatever they could carry away? Likely not, since in every case the church members always said nothing was missing. A few blabbermouths on what I've always called "hate radio" began to suggest it was a conspiracy by black leaders to cause hatred of whites and reinvigorate the civil rights movement. But the facts did not fit that theory, despite the presence of the incendiary Jesse Jackson, and most whites I knew dismissed those ideas as wacko propaganda.

Then the problem came home. In the span of thirty minutes, two black churches burned in rural Alcorn County, previously known mostly for the Civil War battle at nearby Shiloh and for its famous sheriff, Buford Pusser, of the movie *Walking Tall*. The nice little town of Kossuth, named for the Polish patriot, was a peaceful place with no history of racial trouble, and Kossuth was about the least likely place ever to imagine a church arson, let alone two. The fires, captured in full color at the height of their burning, made national news, from *USA Today* to all the evening news shows. Something had to be done.[7]

Since arson investigations fall under ATF jurisdiction and civil rights cases fall under the FBI, we immediately formed a joint task force. Alcorn County gave us full use of their ample airport conference center and several interview rooms were made available to us full time. Top brass of both agencies flew in from Washington to staff a command center. Agents with arson experience were flown in from Detroit and L.A. on ninety-day tours. We met with the local black clergy. Touchingly, one of their leaders, whom I'd known for years, said this: "We know local white people would never do this, not the worst of them. We appreciate your sympathy, but we've got to catch these people and stop this nightmare—soon." It was one of the sorriest crimes I'd ever seen.

It was also the best cooperation I had ever witnessed between the FBI and ATF. The agents in charge bent over backward to give each other credit rather than taking it themselves. There were no squabbles over jurisdiction. Every interview was conducted jointly with one investigator from each agency. The big-city experts even deferred to the practical knowledge of the local deputy sheriffs and police officers. We scoured the area, shook down every informant. Some injustices were necessarily committed. Some people unfairly concluded that the amateur photographer who shot pictures of both fires somehow got from one church fire to the other too quickly. How could he know about one of them so quickly, let alone both? He had a good answer. He heard about both of them on his police scanner, and if you knew the back roads as well as he did, they were only minutes apart. He easily passed a polygraph on all questions.

Suspicion next fell on a white family who lived near one of the churches. Their son had been heard to use the "N" word and to complain about all the "hollering" during Wednesday night prayer meetings. But why would he burn a second church? And living where he did, with the transportation he had, how could he have gone to Kentucky or Georgia? He, too, passed a polygraph.

Next we got some more likely suspects: white teenage dropouts who hung out nearby drinking and using dope, often on bridges over rural roads in the county. One girl said she heard some of the boys talking about other church arsons and laughing and saying maybe it wasn't such a bad idea. "It was driving them niggers crazy," they allegedly said. Many of this loose gang of hardcore rednecks rode motorcycles and worshipped gangs. Some wore the traditional black jeans and jackets with cutoff muscle sleeves with hard-core patches on them and other wannabe paraphernalia. After a couple of preliminary interviews, I told the ATF agent in charge there was one thing I wanted him to do: Bring back Joey. If anyone could help with these guys, it was Joey. Besides being a master interrogator, his knowledge of cycle culture would impress them.

Being promised it was only a temporary detail, Joey came back. Most of our local agents had known him and had heard on the law enforcement grapevine that he was working undercover somewhere, yet even they were surprised at his forked beard and long, dirty hair. We kept

Joey away from the other agents and used him mostly to interview the teenagers. We soon learned that their name for themselves was "huffers," which referred to their habit of sucking in gasoline fumes siphoned from people's trucks. The more we tried to question them, the more we were puzzled. These people could not think straight. They could not remember things.

Most people who can't tell the same story the same way twice are usually lying. A classic interrogation technique is to have a suspect tell his version chronologically first, then tell the same story in reverse order. Liars usually can't do it. But these guys were not even sure they knew what backward was. The FBI profilers and psychologists we had on call at the lab back at Quantico, Virginia, said this was typical of huffers. Sniffing gasoline fumes had fried their brains. Already no candidates for a Rhodes Scholarship, these guys were felony stupid. No way they could coordinate two fires. Besides, even they seemed to feel bad about the church fires. I still remember one shaking his head and saying, "Them niggers didn't deserve that. They wasn't hurting nobody." Just to make sure, we gave some of them polygraphs, or tried to. The examiner came out each time after ten minutes or so and said, "This guy's brain is so fried he can't think straight. Any reaction I get will be useless. He's worse than a meth-head."

Several weeks went by with no progress. I got to spend a lot of time with Joey and one thing he said surprised me. "John, these Bandidos are not all that bad. They think a lot like I do. In some ways, they're pretty conservative (yeah right). Of course they break the law, but they're not nearly as bad as I thought, just fucked up by strong drugs and bad childhoods." This was not the Joey I knew. I asked him what he liked about them. "Well, for instance, a few weeks ago this one guy came up to me and wanted to trade punches. He was littler than me, so I told him I didn't want to hurt him. He insisted and went first and hit me on the side of the jaw. I felt a tooth come loose, and my mouth was bleeding." Joey went on. The guy said, "Take your time. Get you a drink before you get your lick in if you want to. Let your head clear." Joey said his head was already clear and his adrenaline flowing. "I cold-cocked that SOB as hard as I could. He went down with blood flowing everywhere. He was out cold. The other guys laughed themselves silly and began pouring water on him. When he came to, he put his arm around my shoulder and said something about brotherhood and led me off to drink beer out of a keg. It was a funny feeling I'd never really had before, but I liked the feeling."

Joey paused and gave me a long, searching look. "John, you and I are friends. I trust you. These bureaucrats are telling me I've been under too long and need to come out for my own good. What do you think?" I looked into Joey's light blue eyes and knew I had to answer his question carefully, without sounding preachy or bossy or like a virgin at a whorehouse. I finally said, "Joey, by the way you are asking me the question, I know you know the answer already. It's just a hard answer to accept." Joey grabbed my shoulder, then walked away without saying a word.

I didn't see Joey for a while after that and heard that he had gone back to the Gulf Coast and was "phasing out" of the Bandidos with as much evidence and as little chance of reprisals against him as possible. He had not told them much about where he was from and definitely wanted to go on living in Oxford where his wife and children were happy. A bad exit from the biker gang and somebody could get hurt. He might even have to relocate.

Early one Saturday morning, I got an urgent call that someone thought they had caught the church arsonist. He was picked up by an ambulance with third-degree burns over half of his body. While in the ambulance, in severe pain and loaded with morphine, he had babbled on about how he hated all churches and all religions. When asked how he got burned, he said he was burning a church when the fire blew back on him. He rambled on about being on a mission and said he couldn't recall how many churches he'd burned, but it was a lot. When they got him to the hospital, his girlfriend showed up to visit him, and she told the nurses about some of the fires. She then asked for a lawyer and one was appointed. Investigators and prosecutors from all over the country would be flying in soon.[8]

They had called us first because the girl, who had very little education, somehow seemed to remember the fires in Mississippi better than any of the others because she had seen them replayed on local T.V. She had grown up in a trailer park in a poor part of southern California and had never even learned to drive a car. Totally dependent on her boyfriend the arsonist, she rarely knew or cared what state they were in. She just did what he said. She remembered Mississippi because she had worked for a few weeks as a stripper at a joint near Corinth and people had been nice to her there. She also remembered it because that was the only time her boyfriend had burned two churches back to back like that. Her attorney said she had told him the whole story of their arson spree and was ready to testify if we'd make her a deal. She was in Indianapolis, Indiana. "We'll be there right after lunch," I told the agent who called me.

On a hunch, I called Joey's house. He answered. He was home for one day but getting ready to go back to Gulfport. "Joey, you're *the* man. I've got to have you with me to meet this girl. We can get a direct flight from Memphis to Indianapolis in a couple of hours." Joey said he'd really like to, but looked too bad. "I'll scare her to death, Hailman, looking like I do. I'm in full gang regalia, nasty and smelly. You won't know me." No matter. "I've got to have you, Joey. Come on over and pick me up." Joey was right about one thing. I hardly knew him. His hair was dirty and matted in all directions. His beard was even longer and still forked. He had on all black with grease on his black jeans. "You said to come in character," he said.

We were in Memphis in an hour, split up in the underground parking lot and went to the Delta counters separately. Me in my suit and tie with Joey in his get-up would have made an odd couple. We were on the flight to Indianapolis in an hour. On the way up to Memphis in the car, Joey filled me in on further details he'd gotten over the phone from other agents. The most amazing fact was the arsonist's thinking. A white man in his mid-twenties, he had been raised by ultrastrict holy-rolling Pentecostals in rural Indiana. For a variety of reasons, he had developed a fierce hatred for Christianity and all churches, but especially for small churches out in the country where he'd apparently had bad experiences growing up. The story the girl told her attorney had one most amazing twist: the young white man had nothing at all against blacks or black churches. In fact he had burned several rural white churches, more of them in the north than the south.

Racial tensions being what they were, everyone had jumped to the same conclusion: it had to be racial and southern. But it definitely was not. In fact, it was more of a "magic word" thing as the girlfriend explained it. Certain Biblical phrases and names like "Zion" or "Gilead" or "Pisgah" seemed to set him off. When he saw one of those magical names on a church sign, his eyes would sort of glaze over, and he would head straight for a filling station and fill the big gas can he kept in his trunk. He'd then drive around behind the church, open a window, pour in the gas, and light it with one of those long automatic lighters they use to fire up charcoal grills. That last night in Indiana he had accidently overlooked a burning heater under the window and set himself on fire. The girl apparently never participated in starting any fires but was always with him acting as lookout and was with him when they checked into motels afterward so he could watch his fires on the local T.V. news.[9]

Having been awakened from a sound sleep, I had planned to sleep on the plane ride, but it was not to be. I was seated by the window with the aisle seat occupied by a guy who had to weigh 350 pounds, much of it muscle. I asked him if he played pro football. He nodded. About that time a tiny hand started patting him on the shoulder from behind. A pretty, petite woman put her head between us and said to him, "Why don't you move back here. The seat beside me is empty." It sounded good to me and the football player never hesitated. The bright, perky woman moved up beside me. She was so energetic she literally bounced up and down on the seat. "Where are you going?" she asked. "Indianapolis." She told me she was a dancer and was dancing that night with a ballet troupe. I told her that was interesting, congratulations, and turned to take a nap.

"Why are you going to Indianapolis?" she asked. "Just business, nothing interesting like you." She peppered me with questions: where did I live, what was my business, did I enjoy it, how long was I staying. I told her it was totally routine and boring. Her reply was unusual. "I don't think it will be boring at all. I didn't move to help the football player. I wanted to sit by you." Now I am as egotistical as the next guy, but I am not used to attractive, totally unknown young women hitting on me on airplanes. "Why do you say that?" I asked. "Because I saw you in the parking lot. You were riding with that Hell's Angel guy up there, the scary-looking one everybody's been staring at. What are you, his lawyer?" This flaky bag of nerves would never keep the truth a secret, yet what could I tell her? For once, I was able to think quickly on my feet, or more accurately, on my bottom.

Starting off slowly, I told her that what I did was strictly confidential. "Oh, I won't tell a soul." Right. Fat chance. "I cannot tell you who I am or who the other gentleman is, but I can tell you what I do for a living. Maybe that will help. I am a psychiatrist." Having dealt in court with so many shrinks for so many years, I somehow figured I could pull it off. I knew how they talked and how they thought. "And that Hell's Angel guy is your patient?" she asked. "I am not allowed to talk about such things, so let's just say, in the abstract entirely, that some people, entirely harmless, have interesting fantasies." She was such an avid questioner that at some point she wormed out of me that we would give him the made-up name of "Joey."

I told her a few more things I've forgotten to lead her off the trail, then excused myself and actually went to sleep. When I woke up at the Indianapolis airport, she was already down the aisle toward the exit. At the baggage claim I met back up with Joey. "Hailman, who was that good-looking woman beside you? I could hear her talking six rows up. Who was she?" Before I could answer, a tiny hand patted Joey on the back. The woman sort of danced up on tip-toes beside her boyfriend who looked on suspiciously. She looked into Joey's eyes and said, "Don't worry about it, Joey. John is going to make everything all right," and danced away with her boyfriend in tow. "Hailman, you sorry SOB. What on earth did you tell that woman?" I had my reply readier than I expected: "I told her you were crazy, Joey." After dealing with her, our interview with the arsonist's girlfriend's lawyer was a piece of cake.

To make a long story short, the girlfriend testified and her boyfriend was indicted for arsons all over the South. She pled guilty to conspiracy in our three cases. The arsonist, facing the death penalty in Georgia because a responder to one of his fires had died, pled guilty to all charges from all districts and received life in federal prison without the possibility of parole. Joey left the Bandidos and went off to be an instructor at the ATF training academy. He is now a U.S. Marshal.

The Other Jake Gibbs[10]

Die-hard New York Yankee fans know Jake Gibbs as a catcher during the glory years, a buddy of Mickey Mantle and Whitey Ford. Die-hard Ole Miss football fans remember Jake Gibbs as the star quarterback in the glory years of Ole Miss football. Retired to Oxford where he is a fixture at athletic and social events, Jake Gibbs was well known to me. Then a tall, athletic, young FBI agent from Mississippi named Kevin Rust introduced me to another Jake Gibbs who represented a very different side of Mississippi and American life. The other Jake Gibbs was black and, although much smaller and not a famous athlete, he too had had an interesting life.

For nearly forty years, he had labored at building and repairing railroads, a John Henry–like life of long days swinging ten-pound hammers. A widower, Jake Gibbs was in his early seventies but still fancied himself a ladies' man. Agent Rust had visited his neat trailer home and seen numerous pairs of well-shined, fashionable shoes and boots neatly aligned under his bed with plenty of flashy Fred Sanford–like clothes in his little closet. Although no Redd Foxx in his talk, Jake Gibb's lifestyle reminded me of the popular actor and comedian. His hair was white, and he walked with a slight limp from his years of arthritis-producing labor. But he still liked the ladies—young ladies in particular.

One fine day that Jake Gibbs put a case of cold beer in a cooler in his car, which he kept neat and clean with his railroad retirement money. Although technically old, he had young ideas. He liked to flirt with the young girls who strolled around Walnut and Falkner, Mississippi, near where he lived. On that particular day, like most Saturdays, he invited young women for rides in his car to drink beer with him. How far he got with them no one knew, but the police never had a single complaint about him. That day, after many beers, Jake Gibbs ran his car into a ditch. No one was hurt, and if there was a woman in the car with him when it happened, she got away before anyone saw her. A passerby found Mr. Gibbs passed out behind the wheel and, seeing his age, called 911. Chief deputy sheriff Willard Butler, the only deputy on duty, came to the scene. He woke up Mr. Gibbs, called a tow truck, and carried him back to town. Butler knew Gibbs's reputation as a quiet, friendly man.

Although Gibbs was obviously drunk, Butler thought he was harmless and did not handcuff him when he put him in the back seat of his patrol car, where he figured Mr. Gibbs would soon fall back asleep. His patrol car had no protective screen between the front and back seats. Somewhere between the remote county road and Ripley, Mr. Gibbs got sick and threw up not only on Butler's car but on Butler, who then handcuffed him. When they got to the jail, just two people were present, the dispatcher and a local police officer, both white. They later told the FBI that Mr. Butler walked Mr. Gibbs into the booking area, took off the handcuffs, and began savagely beating the old man with a slapstick, a sort of blackjack used by old-time Mississippi officers to deal with arrestees without using deadlier force like a gun. A slapstick is made of flexible lengths of metal wrapped in leather. It leaves bruises but usually doesn't cut. It can stun and subdue a drunk without seriously hurting him, but if applied too hard to a bone, it can break an arm or leg. A blow to the head with a slapstick can kill a man.

The eyewitnesses told us Butler made no attempt to hide what he was doing. He beat Gibbs unmercifully, breaking several ribs, but did not hit him in the head. It was apparent to the witnesses he was punishing Gibbs for something, probably for throwing up on him and making a stinking mess of his patrol car, but Butler never told the eyewitnesses any reason for it. Nor did Butler ever say in our interviews that Gibbs did anything else wrong. I presented the case to the federal grand jury which at the time was predominantly white. They were outraged and eager to indict. Gibbs made a highly sympathetic witness. To me even more powerful were the dispatcher and the police officer, both of whom said they had received threats and open public criticism for siding with an old black drunk against a popular and respected deputy sheriff. Butler also had a good reputation, and what he had done seemed totally out of character. In a selfish way, I wished briefly there'd been more blacks on the grand jury to observe the courage of the white police officer and dispatcher who had told the truth and taken the heat for it and would probably continue to do so. One officer said he would probably have to resign and get out of law enforcement, which he did when the trial was over.

As the trial approached, Kevin Rust told me we had a problem with Mr. Gibbs. He was terrified, convinced a white mob would come and pull him from his trailer and lynch him. We told him, "Mr. Gibbs, those days are over. When all the facts come out, half the white people will be on your side." He didn't believe us. Kevin asked if we shouldn't get a material witness warrant for Mr. Gibbs and keep him in FBI custody at a motel until trial to assure him he was protected and to make sure he showed up. Kevin then withdrew his own request. "Don't worry, John, he'll come with me. It's not right to lock up the victim." To his credit, Butler had made no threats to Gibbs, personally or through intermediaries. He had excellent retained counsel in Steve Farese, who proclaimed his innocence. I wondered how, aside from raw racial solidarity if he got a mostly-white jury, he thought he could beat the case.

We compromised on getting Mr. Gibbs to court. Kevin visited him at his trailer a few days before trial and told him we would interview him the night before the trial, just like all witnesses, and because the trial was out of town at Oxford, he would stay at government expense at the Holiday Inn in his own room and agents would have rooms on either side of him. But when they knocked at his door there was no answer. His car was beside his trailer, but there were no lights on and the trailer was dark. Had some friends of Butler or white vigilantes gotten him? "No," Kevin said. "I was born and raised in McComb and I know that did not happen. He might have run off, though. He grew up in a different Mississippi than I did."

Kevin yelled: "Mr. Gibbs, Mr. Gibbs, it's Kevin with the FBI." No answer. Mr. Gibbs's hearing, after years on the railroads with their loud noises, was none too keen. Kevin thought of Gibbs's double-barreled shotgun and how he kept it loaded beside his bed. He decided to break the door, doing as little damage as possible, and knew the FBI would pay to repair it. Just in case, he hung a raid jacket over a rifle barrel in front of the window in the trailer door while he used a hammer to break the lock. No use getting shot in the gut by your own witness trying to get him to court. Once inside, Kevin went carefully to the bedroom where Mr. Gibbs's shoes were all neatly lined up under his bed. Slowly, carefully, he opened the closet door. Huddled on the floor and shivering with fright was Jake Gibbs.

That evening at my office Mr. Gibbs was calm and composed. I didn't ask him much. You can easily overprepare a witness, and I felt he was ready. The trial went really well. Although the jury was mostly white, I liked their looks. From their appearance they knew life. Whatever Gibbs's race and private proclivities, I didn't think they would tolerate what Butler did to him. The dispatcher and police officer both made absolutely untouchable witnesses. Mr. Gibbs was scared to death, totally unlike the night before. He was terrified to the point the judge allowed me to lead him a little. He admitted being drunk and even used some pretty salty language in describing what he wanted from the young women. When he came to the beating, he began to shake. The judge asked if he needed a glass of water, what you always do when a witness starts to break down. But this time the judge went further. "What about a couple of big aspirins?" Mr. Gibbs said he would appreciate that because his head hurt "pretty bad." He said he hadn't slept in a motel since he retired and didn't sleep much the night before.

The courtroom clerk handed Gibbs a big bottle of aspirins. As he held it, the jury saw for the first time that his left hand was crippled, the fingers curled up and stiff. He could not open the bottle. I went forward and took off the top for him and laid two big round white aspirins on the witness stand in front of him. He put one in his mouth with his right hand, then took up the glass in the same hand. His left hand lay shriveled and curled up in front of the jury. As he lifted the second large white pill to his mouth, it slipped from his fingers and rolled slowly across the carpet. We all watched as the round pill rolled some twenty feet, all the way to the end of the jury box. It was a dramatic moment, like in a movie. We all were mesmerized by how long it took to finally come to a stop. He relaxed and finished his testimony with no further problems.

On cross the able defense attorney was cautious and respectful, especially praising the victim's long years of hard work on the railroad. Then he surprised me. "Your Honor, may the witness approach the jury?" The judge wanted to know why. "It will soon be apparent during my case that our defense is self-defense and that Mr. Gibbs is a much stronger man than he looks despite his age." The judge let the attorney have Mr. Gibbs walk to the end of the jury box. He then asked if the jurors could feel the muscles in Mr. Gibbs's upper arms and shoulders. The judge denied the request, calling it "theatrics."

Virtually the only defense witness other than some character witnesses was the defendant Butler himself. He first told what we'd already heard, that he'd gotten a drunk call and put Mr. Gibbs in his backseat where he passed out. Then his version changed dramatically. According to Butler, at some point during an otherwise quiet drive to jail, Gibbs suddenly raised up on the backseat and put a knife to the front of Butler's throat from behind, and said, "I'll kill you, you sorry son of a bitch. I'll cut your damn head off." Butler said Gibbs was crazed and seemed to think he was being kidnapped. Butler testified he managed to hold Gibbs's arm with one hand and steer his patrol car to a quick stop with the other. "The man looks old, but his arms are like steel." Looking at the jury he said, "I wish you could feel them for yourselves."

Defense counsel then produced an old, rusty case knife with about a two-inch blade with the tip broken off. It had not been furnished to us in discovery, and we'd had no chance to show it to Mr. Gibbs. "Do you recognize that knife?" defense counsel asked. "That's the one he said he'd cut my head off with. I found it later under the seat of my car." Butler admitted he had "roughed up" Gibbs a little bit, but said not enough to break his ribs. "That must have happened when he ran his car in the ditch. He probably hit the steering wheel."

I had an easy time with Butler on cross. He was a tall man, easily a head taller than Mr. Gibbs and although sixty years old looked much younger. I led him fairly easily into boasting of his strength. The killer was when I asked him why he hadn't told us or the FBI or other officers about the alleged assault with the knife before. "Well, I couldn't find it till late, and I wasn't sure they'd believe me." I passed up the chance to say what they would say on TV, like, "I'm sure the jury won't either." The jury wasn't out long and came back with a guilty verdict. The judge gave Butler six months in federal prison. After his release, he was rehired at the sheriff's department and applied to go to the Mississippi Law Enforcement Training Academy, a new professionalism requirement to serve as a deputy. I wrote a letter objecting based on his conviction, and the academy expelled Butler, effectively ending his career in law enforcement.

As I thought about the case, one thing made me wonder. After the trial, out of curiosity, I tried an experiment I had thought about trying in court, but did not. I had thought about recalling Mr. Gibbs as a rebuttal witness and handing him the knife in a closed position and asking him to open it. But I knew from long experience never to try experiments in front of the jury for the first time. Always test them out of court first. You never know how they will turn out. Such dramatic experiments can win a case for you, but can also lose it, and I felt we had this one won. After the jury came back, however, I wanted to know.

Kevin Rust borrowed the knife from the court clerk and brought it to our witness room. I asked Mr. Gibbs if he'd ever had such a knife. "Yes, sir, something like it, but not all rusty like that and the tip was not broken." Wondering how a basically one-handed man could use such a knife, I handed it to him and said, "Take a closer look at the blade." Mr. Gibbs looked briefly at the pearl-colored handle, quickly put the knife to his mouth with his right hand, and deftly flicked open the blade with his teeth. He briefly held the knife, blade open, in my direction. "Not mine," he said. I wondered. I still wonder.

Lanny "Junior" Cummings, Mesomorph[11]

Strange things used to happen in Marshall County, especially when law enforcement was involved. With the election of Sheriff Kenny Dickerson, all that has changed. But its land is rich cotton country and has a majority of black citizens, as it has since before the Civil War. Its county seat, Holly Springs, has beautiful antebellum homes, spared, unlike Oxford, from being burned because Holly Springs was less hostile to Yankee troops during the War. Ulysses S. Grant had headquarters there during the Vicksburg campaign. Later, when L. Q. C. Lamar, the only Mississippi lawyer ever to serve on the U.S. Supreme Court, struck a U.S. Marshal and put his eye out in open court at Oxford in the course of a KKK trial during Reconstruction, the federal court itself was actually moved temporarily to Holly Springs, where the Ku Klux Klan had less sway.

Racial tensions and violence continued off and on well into the 1970s, when a black boycott of white businesses nearly closed Holly Springs. Slowly, things got better. Holly Springs became one of the first cities in the state to have a black mayor. Marshall County, notorious for corruption in law enforcement ever since the reign of sheriff and classic political boss J. M. "Flick" Ash, suddenly had two black sheriffs elected in a row. It sounds ironic to say now, but when we first heard a black inmate was complaining of abuse by a black deputy sheriff, and claimed white officers would support his claim, it was almost a relief, reflecting a surprising new harmony across racial lines.

The incident began harmlessly enough. Most inmates in the jail at Holly Springs were nonviolent, locked up for being drunk or awaiting trial. The hard-core, violent types were mostly sent straight to the state pen at Parchman. The jail was full of trusties, who were often let out to help work off short sentences on public improvement projects. There was also a tradition of inmates washing and polishing police and sheriff's patrol cars. Supervision was lax and the weather was hot, so the inmates got in the habit of going across the town square and buying beer or whiskey to cool them off. The system went along fine until one day a huge black inmate, a former athlete who weighed a good 300 pounds, had a couple of drinks too many. He was said to be a hard worker and strong as an ox and was nicknamed "Leadbelly" for his resemblance to the famous inmate blues singer Huddie Ledbetter.

One afternoon, after a particularly vigorous day of car-washing, Lead-belly decided it was too hot in the un-air-conditioned jail and refused to go back in. "I'll just sit here in the shade. I ain't going nowhere." He was well liked and none of the officers or jailers wanted to take him on because of his size and appearance. When chief deputy sheriff Lanny "Junior" Cummings came on duty, however, he asked, "What is he doing out there? He looks drunk." The officers explained the situation. Cummings, puffed up with the dignity of his position and concerned that the law was being flouted and the big man being given special treatment, ordered the other officers to help him bring the man back into the jail. Four officers stepped forward, two black and two white. Aroused, the big man got to his feet, less drunk than he appeared earlier and considerably less docile. He spread his legs, bent his knees, and raised both fists in a karate stance. One officer said "I heard he knew karate, but I didn't believe it." The four officers struggled to subdue the huge inmate. He pummeled them with kicks and punches. They finally got him to the ground but could not get their handcuffs around his huge wrists.

As they struggled, deputy Junior Cummings suddenly showed back up, this time with a double-barreled sawed-off shotgun in his hands. "Get that son of a bitch up," he yelled. "We ain't putting up with this." The other officers went on wrestling with the man to little effect. Cummings then stepped into the fray and tried to hit the inmate in the head with the butt of the shotgun, but instead hit the back of the hand of one of his fellow officers. "God dammit, Junior, you've broken my hand," he said. Later medical examination proved he was correct. The officer had three distal bones cracked in his hand. Cummings then changed tactics, for reasons he later admitted he did not really recall. He began hitting the man with the barrels of the gun instead. He later said he didn't know whether it was because he didn't want to hit the other officers again or, more likely, because the barrels were too oily to get a good grip on, so he held it by the stock.

Either way he hit the inmate ineffectually several times in the stomach with the barrels, then both barrels suddenly went off. The shotgun, kept in plain view at the jail allegedly for riot control, was loaded with buckshot. By some miracle, not one officer was hit. The inmate was not so lucky. In local terminology, he looked like he was "gut-shot," usually a fatal wound. Bleeding profusely, he was taken by the officers to the local hospital. The surgeon who operated on him later told the FBI with some amazement that "the whole load of buckshot seems to have gotten him at a sharp angle from the side. It shot the front of his stomach area off but missed his vital organs." Shaking his head, the doctor said, "Being fat saved him. His big stomach saved his life."

I prepared the case and presented it to the federal grand jury and got a two-count indictment, one for civil rights/police brutality and one for possessing an unlawful sawed-off shotgun. Shortly I received a visit from Jack Dunbar, president of the state bar and perhaps the finest lawyer in the state. "John boy, I'd love to have another joust with you in court, but this would not be a fair fight. I've talked to all the eyewitnesses, and there are just too many of them. You would kill us." The brutality count carried five years and the sawed-off count ten years, but that was before mandatory sentencing guidelines, so the judge did not have to give him any time at all, or could have given him fifteen years. Jack said, "To make you look tough, we'll plead to the ten-year count. Junior as a black man just doesn't want to admit he violated someone's civil rights." I knew where Jack was really going: "And you think the judge will be easier on him if he pleads guilty to doing something every law officer in the county was also responsible for, having an illegal sawed-off shotgun in plain view in the sheriff's office gun case." We didn't debate long, however. Even the Washington-based Civil Rights Division was so happy to get a conviction of a Mississippi law officer that they went along with the deal. They were usually hard-bargainers, but this time they weren't so sure what a jury, especially a predominantly black jury of Mississippians, might decide. The inmate had recovered quickly despite some bad-looking scars, and most of the community, black and white, favored Junior Cummings.

Judge Keady got the case. At that time he had a new local rule he was testing where the probation officers prepared the pre-sentence report before the guilty plea was entered. We hated the idea. For one thing, we weren't sure it was all that constitutional, but even worse, when the defendants read their pre-sentence reports, it sometimes persuaded them not to plead guilty after all and just go to trial. Better to take the risk than accept a harsh sentence without even fighting it. So instead of the standard two-step process in federal court where the defendant pleads guilty one day, then waits a couple of months till a thorough pre-sentence report is ready, in Cummings's case we did it all in one proceeding.

The day we showed up for the plea and sentence was a warm, humid one, not unusual for Oxford. Jack Dunbar and I and the two attorneys with us had all dressed, accidentally, in what we thought was appropriate attire for the weather. We had all four unknowingly chosen to wear identical bright-blue, lightweight "cord" suits, the next thing to seersucker but even brighter to the eye. Between us stood Junior Cummings, dressed like a normal person. Judge Keady ascended the bench and called us all forward. As we approached, I saw a bigger than customary twinkle in his eye. He addressed the defendant first, "Are you Lanny Cummings Jr.?" Cummings answered respectfully, "Yes, sir, Your Honor." Then Judge Keady unexpectedly diverged from the script, the litany of ritual questions about knowing the punishment, whether his lawyer did a good job, etc. Instead, Judge Keady asked him point-blank, "Mr. Cummings, from your attire I presume you do not plan to join in the singing with these other gentlemen, who all seem dressed for the occasion like a barbershop quartet?"

The judge enjoyed his little joke much more than we did, but somehow it told me that, knowing him as I did, and knowing his mindset and feelings, he was going to give Junior some prison time. Judge Keady always hated sentencing. Whenever he was going to give them probation, he always gave them a furious tongue-lashing first. If he was sending them off to prison, he always just asked them and their lawyer what they had to say and then with no further comment, said, "I hereby sentence you to the custody of the attorney general for imprisonment in a federal facility for umpty-ump years."

This time I had little idea before that moment what he might do. Black and white citizens alike had written strong, sincere letters recommending probation. These were not form letters, the usual seventy-five letters obviously written in identical words by the same lawyer but signed with seventy-five different names. The letters for Junior were all different. They spoke of the important role he'd played in restoring racial harmony in Marshall County and how he'd never been in trouble or been accused of abusing any other inmate, black or white. Junior Cummings also held a sort of unique position in law enforcement. For more than thirty years while I was a federal prosecutor, the highlight of our federal-state-local get-togethers was always a fish fry or a barbecue, two styles of public banquet that I discovered from reading the letters of Thomas Jefferson go back at least to the early eighteenth century. The cook for these affairs was always an officer. Being the cook was not only a sort of special service, but an honored position if that's not saying too much. And Junior Cummings held both positions. He not only made the best pork barbecue around but could fry fish and make great hush puppies. I'll never forget one letter to the probation officer from a black elected official who said, "I have often partaken of his cuisine, and to lose his services would be most unfortunate for law enforcement." That letter, I felt, explained the sentiments of many.

There was another letter, however, that gave a whole new level of meaning to the term *sui generis*. DOJ over the years sent me to many management conferences, at most of which we suffered through the latest fads in pop psychology. One year it was the four axes of personality structure: concrete, abstract, sequential, and random. Accountants are said to be both concrete and sequential. Artists and professors are said to be abstract and random. Another seminar tested our personalities on what was called the Graves Value Map, probing us with dozens of questions on how we would handle tricky situations. I recall one guy in our office, Al Moreton, scored as the most traditional person ever tested by Graves. He was the one who wore a black suit, black tie, black socks, and black wingtips every day of his life except for a gray sweater on special holidays. A prosecutor from another office once made an almost perfect score for the personality profile of a career criminal. I never heard what happened to him.

But my favorite psycho seminar of all involved the theory, somewhat popular at the time of Junior Cummings's case, which theorized that your body shape determined your personality. There were said to be three basic types, with various possible combinations of the three: the mesomorph, the large-boned, heavily muscled athletic type with caveman characteristics who tended toward fat around the middle with age; then there was the ectomorph, a small-boned, lean type with a large head and large eyes who was intellectual, quick, and agile and often lived a long life; and the endomorph, a soft, round easygoing person who tended to like dessert and lack ambition.

According to one letter-writer supporting Cummings's plea for probation, Junior was a complex person. Although his career as a gun-toting lawman suggested a mesomorph, he also had a concealed ectomorphic side reflected in his desire to restore order in the officer's attempts to subdue the inmate. But it was "obviously" the endomorphic side of Junior that was key to his personality and the most important element for the judge to consider in sentencing him. Junior's soft, easygoing body type predisposed him to seek the easy way out of situations. He was simply acting out his primordial urges, in combination, and in no way intended to hurt anyone. His love of eating, and even more so his love for feeding others, showed his endomorphic concerns predominated in his personality structure.

How all that entitled him to probation I couldn't figure, but after Judge Keady's crack about our barbershop quartet, I couldn't wait to hear his comments on how the defendant's endomorphic obsession with providing exquisite cuisine influenced his shooting a fat karate expert in the gut. Unfortunately, Judge Keady was very focused that day and ignored both subjects entirely. After a brief nod to his prior record of service, the judge said his conduct could not be tolerated and sentenced Junior Cummings to six months in federal prison. The fine folks in Marshall County had a going-away fish fry for Junior, where he insisted on doing the cooking himself. He even asked them to invite us, saying, "Those Oxford guys were just doing their job, and I'll be back soon anyway." Rather than turning him down, we asked the sheriff not to invite us and avoided any snub. When Junior was released a month early for good behavior, they held a big "Welcome Home Junior" parade for him in Holly Springs. Junior cooked the fish. We still didn't attend.

Getting the Blues on Parchman Farm[12]

For over a century, Mississippi had only one prison, a giant sixteen-thousand-acre cotton plantation in Sunflower County known as Parchman Farm after its previous owner. Everyone given a prison sentence in state court went there to serve it. Elvis Presley's father, Vernon, did several months there for changing the amount on a $4.00 check from his employer for the sale of a hog. Freedom riders, civil rights protesters, and juveniles once joined hard-core killers and rapists on prison work gangs. For many years, convicts raised and cooked their own food. For most of its history, Parchman was totally segregated into black and white camps, with separate camps for women. Over the years it developed a reputation as probably the toughest prison in the nation. As in the classic song "The Midnight Special," desperate inmates believed that if the rotating headlight from the midnight train from Chicago, the famed *City of New Orleans*, shone on an inmate, he would be released. The Illinois Central tracks ran right beside Parchman, as did the famed blues Highway 61, which also famously "ran right by my baby's door." Parchman is the classic heart of the Delta. To me the most enduring description of the Delta came from writer Willie Morris of Yazoo City:

> I recall the countless visitors I have taken through the Delta over the years. . . to the person, they were all struck by its brooding sadness, its physical power. . . To me the Delta is the Old Testament in its ageless rhythms and despairs—in the violence of its extremes, the excesses of its elements, the tension of its memory. The few who own this richest land in the world are among the wealthiest people in America, and the black laborers among the poorest. This land was in the words of one nineteenth-century traveler, "a jungle equal to any in Africa," a dark impenetrable forest of towering trees and thick undergrowth, [full of] panthers, bears, alligators, giant mosquitoes and spiders and blue-backed scorpions, rattlesnakes and cottonmouths.

Historian James Cobb calls it "the most Southern place on earth." Novelist Richard Ford calls it "the South's South."[13]

A good way to get a feel for what the Delta's Parchman Prison was like when I first visited it in the 1960s is to watch the movie *Cool Hand Luke* with Paul Newman as Luke. The actor who played the warden gave a very accurate picture of the prison atmosphere when he said with rich irony, "What we have here is a failure to communicate." Parchman was just like that but on a much larger scale.

While I worked at Legal Services, an inmate named Nazareth Gates sued the warden over the segregated and brutal conditions at the prison. When I clerked for Judge Keady in 1969, the Parchman case was already in full-throated litigation before him. Since it was essentially an equity case, with no jury, where the inmates sought not money but injunctions forbidding mistreatment, the judge had to make findings of fact, so he had me sit in and take notes on all the testimony. Another good way to get facts was to visit the place in person, which in law is called a *view*. We went to Parchman many times for views, visiting every camp from the intake building to death row. We ate what the inmates ate, watched guards on horseback direct their work in the fields, even saw a big sign on a door inside the black women's camp saying how many lashes with a black leather belt a woman would get for a particular infraction. By the time we got there they said the "strap" or "Black Annie" was no longer used on women, but they kept the threat of it posted.

We often had Sunday dinner with the warden and on other days ate at the canteen with the guards and trusties. I'm always amused when reporters spell the word "trustees" as if those inmates were some sort of board of distinguished citizens. As former governor Ross Barnett once famously said of one trusty who ran away while on release: "If you can't trust a trusty, who can you trust?"

The food was rich and southern and today would be called soul food because it was cooked almost exclusively by black women convicts who really knew how. Most of the cooks I talked to were in Parchman for having killed their "man," usually a cheating husband or boyfriend. The white women's camp seemed to be devoted mostly to sewing and was, in my experience, rather frilly and even cozy with curtains at the windows and little sense of the violence portrayed in kinky modern TV shows about "Women in Prison." Most of the women back then seemed to have been convicted for helping their men commit some fairly serious crime in which their role was secondary. I felt at the time that they were the people who least needed to be there. Nowadays the women there are much rougher and seem more deserving of their status as inmates.

Parchman had many unusual features, both real and imagined. It also had its own unique jargon. A "gunman" was not someone who carried a gun but the opposite, someone *under* the gun, that is an ordinary inmate. A trusty was called a "leg" because trusties had white stripes down the legs of their blue jeans. A "half leg" was a half trusty. One story that everyone believed was that a trusty guard could win parole, possibly even freedom, if he killed another inmate who was trying to escape. The rumor was that this unwritten rule resulted in many unfair revenge killings, but it certainly deterred escape attempts like those in "Cool Hand Luke." Escape itself was nearly impossible since the brick, inmate-built block-houses or camps were located deep within the prison grounds, which were surrounded by thousands of acres of flat cotton fields and swamps where you could be seen for miles and tracked by bloodhounds no matter which way you ran. Legend had it no one had ever escaped from Parchman for more than a few hours, which may well have been true.

Another unwritten rule was that anyone who tried to escape would be punished on the spot by having the living hell beaten out of him, the degree of the beating depending on the trouble it took to catch him and the whims of the guards administering the beating. The image of sadistic prison guards is a familiar one to most Americans, but when you get familiar with Parchman you realize it stands out for violence as much as Alcatraz or Attica. One legend inmates told me was that a guard over one camp followed a regular practice of having a dozen or so of his better inmates strip stark naked and stand in a row, then told them that the first one to get a full erection would get a weekend furlough. Many supposedly developed special fantasies just for those occasions.

Parchman was also allegedly the first prison in America to allow conjugal visits for prisoners and had special little one-room shacks furnished with only a mattress on the floor so they could have sex with their "wives." The practice was subject to much abuse and encouraged inmates to bribe guards with whatever they had to sleep with whatever woman they could persuade to come visit them. Women inmates were not given the same privilege. The conjugal visits allegedly started during segregation, it being believed then that black males were oversexed and were more manageable if given the hope of at least occasional sex. The white inmates complained long and loud about this practice and eventually gained equal treatment and access to their "wives."

There were other "good" sides to life at Parchman. Annual rodeos were highly popular, as were other regular forms of sport like basketball. But Parchman's best talent was musical. Some of Mississippi's best and least-known bluesmen and country singers went through Parchman but were largely unknown outside. Like everything else there, the bands were segregated by race with black bands and white bands, both of which were in big demand for "off-campus" concerts, which were rarely granted, but with Judge Keady we had the chance to hear some really talented inmate performers of both races.

Corruption and brutality were probably no worse at Parchman than at other prisons like Angola in Louisiana or Cummins in Arkansas. While a student attorney with CRLA (California Rural Legal Assistance) in the summer of 1967, I once represented an inmate at San Quentin. For my money I'd rather have served my time in Parchman than San Quentin as far as safety was concerned. Of course people say California trends become our trends twenty years later, and certainly Parchman is far more violent now and its criminals far worse people than were their parents' generation. Interested readers can get a full picture of life on Parchman Farm from Judge Keady's several published opinions about it as well as from his unusual little book *All Rise: Memoirs of a Mississippi Federal Judge.*

My own experience of Parchman was deepened when FBI agent Mike Beaver called me one day to report that an inmate had allegedly been beaten almost to death by a group of guards in the presence of both the warden and deputy warden. The inmate, Larry Floyd, the son of two Hattiesburg police officers, had been convicted ten years earlier, at age eighteen, of being an accomplice in a store robbery where the store owner was shot to death. His personal papers said he received two sentences, each for ten years, to be served concurrently, or "cc," meaning only ten years in all. Everyone agreed that Floyd, a skinny 6', 5" black kid, had been a model inmate. Not strong, he had submitted to the inmate code of violence and become effeminate, appearing homosexual. His job was a trusted one handling the money at a prison camp store or canteen where inmates could buy cigarettes and snacks and cold drinks, which were much in demand in the one-hundred-degree heat of Parchman.

One day after he'd served nearly all his ten years, Floyd got a message to go to the office of Christine Houston, the lady who handled the paperwork for inmate releases. Mrs. Houston, with whom I had many dealings over many years, was to me the soul of Parchman. Hard as nails on the outside to bad guys and bullies, she was polite to everyone and always totally cooperative with me, bending over backward to get us the paperwork we needed, usually certified copies of convictions and prison records for use either for federal sentencing or to prove our defendants were convicted felons for whom it was a federal crime to possess a firearm. Mrs. Houston was compassionate with good inmates who followed the rules and with those she believed could be salvaged as human beings and make it on the outside.

When Larry Floyd arrived at Mrs. Houston's office that morning, she congratulated him on his imminent release. She was sure his excellent conduct would get him paroled. One can only imagine how excited Larry Floyd was. To their horror, however, when she opened his file to look at the judge's actual sentencing order, she saw that Larry's two ten-year sentences were not concurrent or "cc," to be served side-by-side for just ten years, but were consecutive or "stacked," as inmates called it. Larry Floyd thus still had a *second* ten years to serve. Christine Houston cried along with Floyd when she told him.

Late that night the old broken-down car of a female prison guard left the farm. The male guard on duty was tired and indifferent and did not search the car as he should have, noting in his log only that the trunk lid bounced up and down, which should have caused a search, but the guard didn't bother. Equally suspicious was the "female" driver, who wore lots of bright red lipstick and had a big, bushy Afro (actually a wig) the guard thought looked funny. In his log he noted drily that the driver was "the ugliest woman I ever saw." It was Larry Floyd.

It later came to light that Larry Floyd, despite his appearance, still liked women and was having sex with the female guard who lent him her car keys for the escape. Surprised he made it out the gate, and expecting a quick pursuit, Larry Floyd drove as fast as he could in the midnight darkness along the curving gravel roads leading away from Parchman. He had not driven a car in nearly ten years and within two miles missed a sharp curve and flipped the car over several times. Although bleeding both from the wreck and from cutting himself using a blanket to crawl over a razor-wire fence to get to the car, Floyd was able to walk away from the wreck.

Knowing the guards would learn first thing in the morning that he was gone and would be out with horses and hounds looking for him, Floyd ran for hours in the cold, swam the narrow Sunflower River back and forth several times to throw off the dogs, and just before sunrise took shelter in an abandoned tenant shack which was in the process of being torn down. He hid under a pile of old boards, but it did not take the dogs long to find him.

Unfortunately for Floyd, his sudden decision to escape could not have come at a worse time. A committee of the state senate was visiting the prison that very morning to check on security conditions, and a rare escape was the last thing the wardens and guards needed. It was also the first day of dove hunting season, and they had planned to take the senators hunting later in the day. The pressure was thus great to capture Larry and to make an example of him. When the dogs had tracked Larry to his hiding place, the officers dragged him out, and in the presence of both the warden and deputy warden, began to kick and beat him fairly severely—in the usual way. After several minutes a voice, whom no witness ever agreed to identify, said, "That's enough." Floyd was handcuffed behind and thrown in the bed of a pickup on top of a roll of barbed wire. As he lay on the wire, one guard walked up to him and smashed him in the face with his walkie-talkie, gashing his lip and eye. Not to be outdone, a veteran supervising guard, Captain Terry Lynn Winters, pulled out his .357 Magnum revolver and slammed it into the back of Floyd's head, apparently with the metal sight at the end of the barrel hitting bone on the back of Floyd's head. The officers then drove Floyd back to Parchman with several riding on the back of the pickup. Halfway there, one officer told the driver, Col. Fred Childs, to stop, saying that Floyd was "spurting blood" from a gash on the back of his head. After briefly considering dropping him at the scene of the wreck to bleed to death, cooler heads among the guards prevailed and they drove Floyd to the prison hospital.

The prison doctor, John Dial, sewed up the gashes on Floyd's head and face and photographed the cuts covering his body. The officers told Dial he'd hurt himself wrecking the lady guard's car without a seat belt. This much of the story had come to FBI agent Mike Beaver who got it directly from a mysterious, secretive source inside the prison. At first we thought the CI might be an outraged officer, but soon learned it was an inmate who wanted us to move him to a safe jail and give him a sentence reduction in return for his information and testimony.

His written messages were literate and anonymous and it took us weeks to identify him. Finally Mike Beaver pieced together enough clues to figure out that our mysterious CI was none other than an inmate trusty working at the firehouse, with access both to a computer and to the best and most reliable prison gossip. His name was Bill, a former private detective who was in Parchman for killing, in a fit of rage, former veteran defense attorney Billy Jordan of Columbus. Jordan, an old and friendly former adversary of ours had been shot down dead by a shotgun blast in his own driveway after a dispute over a fee.

With these facts in hand, Mike and I contacted the Civil Rights Division in Washington. Until then we'd always had very positive experiences with them, contrary to what several other U.S. Attorney's Offices had said regarding ambitious, inexperienced "hairy-legged female militants out to get every police officer around." I'd had just the opposite experience, getting only highly competent professionals with lots of experience and good judgment and good supervision. Mississippi was, after all, considered the most challenging territory in the country for civil rights prosecutors, and they'd never sent us a rookie. Later that would change.

In this case, the prosecutor was highly unusual. Her clipped Yankee accent turned out to be not from the Northeast, as I first thought, but from San Diego, where her father was dean of the medical school. She sounded pretty tough, having spent a couple of years in the DA's office in Brooklyn prosecuting major, violent felons and sex crimes. She was no rookie. I called a couple of buddies at Civil Rights to check her out, then met her for lunch one day at Don and Wally Joe's Chinese restaurant in Cleveland, home of Delta State University and the most comfortable place to stay near Parchman. Small and voluptuous, Cynthia Alksne was true to her Scandinavian surname. Her face would have looked good on the body of a member of the Swedish bikini team. She had a sly, joking air about her, slightly flirtatious in a liberated seventies sort of way. I was wary, having been warned by friends at DOJ that she had been through a bitter divorce. That sort of thing can make you mistrust men. Still, she was beautiful and enjoyed it and sort of toyed with me. I was careful to be a perfect gentleman (as always), maybe even a little more so than usual.

As we discussed the case, I was pleasantly surprised at her cooperative attitude. "We're partners from here on out," she said. No Washington air of "just do what I tell you to do" from her. And we were both true to our word, right to the end. If I did one little thing slightly unpartnerlike, it was to ask her to handle the mysterious prisoner CI. Having dealt with so many of them, I didn't want this guy calling my house at all hours of the night with razzle dazzle cloak-and-dagger messages. My wife was thoroughly sick of all that. Cynthia, single and gung-ho for a Mississippi adventure, immediately agreed to handle "Bill." After all, she also lived far away in D.C. Later, after she'd endured months of being jerked around by the inmate, I felt a little bad about sticking her with him, but I honestly hadn't known at first just how much of a hassle he would be. Besides, Cynthia was way more than a match for him.

As the investigation progressed, with my being criminal chief who assigned and supervised all cases in the office while also handling my own full caseload, it became clear that I needed veteran help with the Floyd case. U.S. Attorney Al Moreton kindly gave me Tom Dawson as our third partner. A strong conservative who later worked gleefully for Ken Starr for nearly two years pursuing Bill and Hillary Clinton in the Lewinsky and other cases, Tom had never gotten near a civil rights case. Like me, he instinctively sided with officers. But when I briefed him on the Floyd case, he immediately liked the quirkiness of it. For several months, we worked with Cynthia and Mike Beaver, interviewing and squeezing officers who had seen the beatings but who had not participated. First one cracked, then another. Later several guards agreed to plead guilty to misdemeanors and testify. Civil rights crimes are not felonies unless physical injuries occur, and several of the guards had merely slapped Floyd and not injured him. I did manage to find and use one old civil case where a judge held that pain alone was a kind of injury, which we used to the hilt for the first time in a federal criminal civil rights case.

Easily the most interesting defendants were the wardens. Steve Puckett was a good man under immense pressure to back his officers. We suspected it was his voice that said, "That's enough" during the beating, but no one ever confirmed it. He was not even present when the guards hit Floyd in the face with weapons or when Winters bashed Floyd on the head with his pistol. The only legal theory we had to nail the warden was the old one called "failure to protect from harm." It sounded too much like something off the *Law & Order* show on TV, but it was all we had, and it was past time to send a message to stop the tradition of beating the hell out of everyone who tried to escape. The deputy warden, Chris Epps, was a young graduate of Mississippi Valley State and the only black officer on the scene as well as the only black administrator at Parchman. He had taken no part in the beating other than one alleged open-hand slap to Floyd's face, which Floyd didn't remember and probably never felt under the circumstances. One day, outside the grand jury, Epps called me aside to talk about Cynthia and her gung-ho ways: "Does she have any idea what it's like to be a black supervisor at Parchman? I'm not saying I slapped him, but you can see my situation. You live here, and I've checked you out. You will understand. Why is she torturing me? Am I just another notch on her belt?" I didn't tell Epps my real feeling, which was that Cynthia was gung-ho and over the top on *all* occasions, but tried to explain. "You know it's not racial." He agreed. "She's just young and inexperienced in the ways of the world, especially Mississippi." Epps nodded, seeming satisfied I was right.

Unbeknownst to either of us, Cynthia had quietly walked up behind us and heard my final comment. Later she confronted me: "What the hell was that about?" I told her Epps thought she was being too hard on him. "The SOB should have thought of that before he hit a handcuffed inmate." Their conflicts did not end there. Chris Epps would be back. He filed a motion to dismiss the indictment for "prosecutorial misconduct," claiming Cynthia came on to him to get him to confess, straightening his tie in a suggestive way and putting her attractive knee seductively between his legs. The tie part I believed, but never the knee part. Cynthia's enthusiastic ways had confused other people before. The judge agreed with me and rejected Epps's motion.

Meanwhile, after the grand jury had heard our last witness, I invited Tom Dawson and Cynthia to our house after dinner for a drink to celebrate. Cynthia brought her law clerk, a summer student from Berkeley who had volunteered for the case to see Mississippi, the scary, racist place that was also home of the blues and Elvis and all those other things she'd always loved. By this time we were on those funny, almost goofy terms you get in high-pressure, high-media-interest cases. I broke out from my cellar some really good old red Rioja wines from the 1950s. On our third bottle, as we sat on our back porch, the nicknames started flying. Dawson, who is from Meridian and always liked the TV series *M*A*S*H*, nicknamed Cynthia "Hot Lips," after the blond female character pursued by Hawkeye, whose character was based on a real-life army doctor originally from Meridian himself. Cynthia, never one to be outdone, coined a nickname for Dawson, whose hairline had receded a little since law school, calling him "Christophe" after Bill Clinton's hairdresser, who once held up traffic at the L.A. airport while cutting Clinton's hair. The nickname was triply appropriate because Dawson was also known to not much like the French, and he especially disliked Bill Clinton and his administration.

Those two nicknames were so good they forgot to give me one, which was good. Midway through our third bottle, Cynthia suddenly asked her law clerk, "So, what do you think of Mississippi now?" The young woman was unfazed. "It's even crazier than in the movies," she said. "And what about the U.S. Attorney's Office?" Cynthia continued. Without a minute's hesitation, the law clerk said with enthusiasm, "Those guys are the closest thing to a real MASH unit I ever want to see." In our own twisted way, we of course took it as a compliment.

So we went to trial. Al Moreton called my indictment "more of a press release than a legal document." It was colorful, detailing the most brutal elements of the beating, from the barbed wire to the blood-spurting head wound, and also included efforts by defendants to influence our witness, Bubba McKnight, to lie about what he saw. Still, we left out one of the most striking stories, of how one guard told Cynthia, with a smile, how he'd like to "grudge fuck" her. Somehow she did not feel threatened and laughed about it at the time, taking it as a bizarre compliment. And to have charged it would have disqualified her, as a witness, from trying the case. So we just let it go.

Our proof was going beautifully until one evening, just as we rested our case, I got a call at home from my friend Jim Silverwood, supervisor of the division of DOJ that oversees missions to train foreign prosecutors. Jim wanted me to go to Haiti, where dictator "Baby Doc" Duvalier had just been driven out and a new president, Bertrand Aristide, a former priest, had just been elected. It was a great opportunity and DOJ lacked French speakers to do it. I would be going as the lone DOJ attorney, assisted by two USAID employees, who handled the financial end of our assistance programs.

I told Tom and Cynthia of my dilemma. Cynthia was irate: "How can you possibly desert us during the case of our lives? You cannot do this." Dawson had the opposite reaction: "Hailman, if you're crazy enough to go to Haiti, how can we complain? Go ahead. I'll win this one for you." I explained to them that the Haiti trip was two months off, but the training began in two days. Cynthia insisted I stick with the trial till the last possible minute. After all, I'd put on some of the key witnesses, including our most important witness, Dr. John Dial, Parchman's on-site doctor.

Cynthia had a point. Dr. Dial had been a tricky witness. In our interviews, he had forthrightly warned me of his considerable baggage. The reason he worked at Parchman was because it was the only place he could get work. His license to practice medicine had been revoked twice, once for excessive intimacy (consensual) with female patients, and once for illegally running a "pill factory" practice where about all he did was prescribe feel-good drugs. He also had other little problems. His University of Mississippi medical degree was the last one granted under the old three-year program where Ole Miss accepted two years of credit from foreign med schools. Dr. Dial's was from Monterey, Mexico, and he didn't speak Spanish. Nevertheless, everyone agreed he was an outstanding emergency room physician, even though he had never before testified in court as an expert witness.

During one of our interviews, I asked John if he was board certified in emergency medicine. He said no, he'd never needed to be, but could recite from memory (which he proceeded to do) dozens of challenging operations in which he'd saved the lives of inmates grievously wounded in attacks by other inmates with everything from homemade prison shanks (scary-looking knives) to clubs, razors, stolen nightsticks, even pistols. Dr. John Dial knew his stuff.

He reached in his pocket and pulled from his wallet a time-worn piece of yellowed paper. "I did take a one-day course once in pathology, by correspondence, and passed some mail-order exam. They gave me this certificate." He unfolded it. It was all we had, so I got my secretary, the wonderful Joan Case, to make a clean, clear blown-up copy of it and then stuck a little gold official-looking sticker on it and put it in an expensive, official-looking black frame as if it had been there all along. No one ever questioned its origin. It seemed like a pretty mild, totally legal deception at the time.

Dr. Dial had also told me another critical fact: on Thursday nights he was part of a poker group with most of the defendants, and he didn't think they'd be too hard on him on cross. I reminded him that it would be the attorneys, not his friends the defendants, who'd be cross-examining him. "You'll see," was all he said. Later it occurred to me that he probably knew too many other things about them and that maybe they would not want to make him mad by roughing him up. He might just tell the jury (and us) all he knew.

At trial, I took Dr. Dial very quickly through his vast practical experience, never asked him about med school other than the Ole Miss name on his degree, which I figured was enough for a Mississippi jury. We also skipped his disciplinary problems and did not mention his never having testified before in any court. I just offered in evidence his "certification" as an emergency room physician and tendered him to the defendants for cross-examination on his qualifications. To my amazement, the defense attorneys all rose and said, "No questions." John Dial was suddenly not only our most critical witness as to Floyd's wounds but an expert on wounding.

Dr. Dial first described Larry Floyd's pitiable, near-death condition, and when I asked him if he had an opinion about what caused the artery on the back of Floyd's head to burst, while showing him Winters's .357 Magnum, Dr. Dial testified without hesitation that in his opinion the wound was entirely consistent with Floyd being hit with extreme force with the sight on the barrel of Winters's gun. The defense got nowhere with him on cross, and to me they seemed afraid to cross him very hard, just as Dr. Dial had predicted. I told Cynthia and Tom, honestly and not because it was in my interest to leave but because I believed it, that even if I left, the defense would never lay a glove on Dr. John Dial.

I then had to tell them one other small detail about the Haiti mission. The reason I had to leave right away was that the training was not in Washington, as it would be normally, but in Paris. Dawson fell out laughing. "Hailman, you've done it again. Why didn't you tell us that first—we'd have never had a problem." Even Cynthia agreed: "Ok, ok, you can go." The next morning, just before my flight, we announced to Judge Senter and opposing counsel that DOJ urgently asked that I be excused to prepare for a mission to Haiti. The judge was very gracious and I was flattered when the defense attorneys seemed glad to be rid of me. Tom and Cynthia waited till I was safely out of town to tell Judge Senter that the Haiti training was in Paris. They later reported he said, "That damn John Hailman. What an operator."

As we'd hoped, the defense was not strong. Our officer eyewitnesses, who had themselves pled guilty, were strong, especially when supported by the courageous Dr. Dial. Larry Floyd made a bad witness as we expected, doing all sorts of shifty inmate stuff on the stand. Later, when his attorney, Ron Lewis, asked me about filing a civil suit on his behalf against the state, I advised him against it. Ron went ahead anyway and invested a ton of time and money in the case. The civil jury came back with a verdict of zero dollars. They wanted the law upheld but did not want to reward a convicted murderer or put a financial burden on the families of the officers. Rumor has it this year they are about to make a movie about the Larry Floyd case.

In addition to the civil case, the Floyd case had one final chapter. The sentencing guidelines for civil rights violence cases were extremely tough, requiring Winters to serve a five-year mandatory minimum for using a firearm in a violent felony, plus not less than nine additional years for the beating itself. Defendant David Johns was to serve not less than three or more than four years under the guidelines. Johns was, after all, convicted not only of conspiracy in the beatings but of perjury before the grand jury and witness tampering. Judge Senter felt compassion for the isolation and violence the veteran officers would suffer as federal prisoners and departed drastically downward from the guidelines. Citing a "culture of violence" at Parchman, he gave Winters just one year and Johns only six months of home confinement, that is, no real time in jail at all.

The Civil Rights Division, which handles its own appeals without our participation, was outraged (we were not too happy either) and immediately appealed. The Fifth Circuit rejected Judge Senter's reasons and summarily reversed his judgment and sent the case back for resentencing. The judge then simply gave newer, more elaborate reasons and reimposed the same light sentences. The Court of Appeals reversed him a second time. At that time, the judge, suffering pain and disability from the effects of polio when he was a teenager, received a transfer to Gulfport in the Southern District of Mississippi where there were no more cold north Mississippi winters. He had a long and distinguished career there, although not doing exactly what he'd planned. After enjoying the warm, healthful Gulf Coast sun for a couple of years, he suffered serious personal losses in the infamous 2005 Hurricane Katrina and later became nationally famous for his landmark rulings in the lengthy and exhausting insurance litigation that followed in the wake of Hurricane Katrina.

A new judge, Allen Pepper of Greenville, was assigned to sentence Winters. He immediately took our original recommendation as to Winters, which Cynthia and Tom and I had struck with the defense attorneys. He gave Winters half the guideline sentence of nine and a half years, minus time already served. The Winters case was finally over. One night a year or so later, I was surfing TV channels when whose smiling face did I see but the still-beautiful but newly-blonde Cynthia Alksne. She had left DOJ and gone on to become one of Geraldo Rivera's expert legal commentators on criminal trials. Fiery and opinionated as ever, Cynthia was a great commentator. Tom and I called her and asked her what it was like. "Kind of like rasslin' on TV. They assign you a good guy or bad guy role and you play it to the hilt." She had not changed. After a few years, she had two daughters in quick succession and retired as TV gladiator but kept in touch with "Christophe" and me for several years. One night, on a training mission in Moscow, a group of us were at the Bolshoi Ballet. Walking out in a crush of mink-coated "new Russian" women and their machine-gun toting boyfriends, we walked past a high-end souvenir stand. Sitting there were two beautiful little pairs of ballet slippers. Catching up with my friends, I asked them to wait while I bought them for Cynthia's little girls. By the time I got back to the stand, however, someone else had already bought them. It was my only bad moment in the case, which for us had never ended, and in my memory, probably never will.

Most surprising was the fate of Chris Epps. At trial the jury was approximately half black and half white. Courthouse rumor later had it that the black jurors had refused to convict Epps, not wanting to make him a convict just because he might have lightly slapped an inmate who was already beaten up and didn't even remember the slap. Under the circumstances I understood Epps's situation. The white jurors were said by rumor to be ready to convict both Epps and white warden Steve Puckett, but were not willing to convict one without the other. After all, the warden had never touched Floyd. In the end the jurors allegedly compromised and found both men not guilty.

Republican Governor Kirk Fordice promoted warden Steve Puckett to Commissioner of Corrections. Epps continued to rise through the ranks and in 2002 was named Commissioner of Corrections by Democratic Governor Ronnie Musgrove. Impressed by the job he did, Republican Governor Haley Barbour kept him on, reappointing Epps to the job in 2004. I have followed his career closely ever since and feel he has made perhaps both the toughest and the most professional Corrections Commissioner in Mississippi history. Once again jurors apparently had a better feel for real justice than we did as attorneys, which is why I continue, after forty years, to be such a strong believer in our American jury system.

Coldest Case of All: Reopening the Murder
of Emmett Till and What We Learned

Any society that condones the killing of children does not deserve to survive,
and probably won't.
—William Faulkner, in a letter to the *Memphis Commercial Appeal* written
right after the killers of Emmett Till were acquitted[14]

For at least fifty years, the reputation of Mississippi, otherwise one of
the most beautiful and peaceful of states, has been stained by our history
of racial prejudice and violence. If one case symbolized for the nation
that dark part of our reputation, it was the murder of Emmett Till, a
fourteen-year-old boy from Chicago kidnapped from his bed while visiting his grandparents in Leflore County in 1955. The story, as generally
told, was that Till had whistled, or possibly touched and made inappro-
priate remarks to, a white woman in her store in Money, a small town
near Greenwood. Days later, when the woman's husband returned from
hauling shrimp to Texas, he and his brother-in-law took Emmett Till at
gunpoint from his grandfather's home in the middle of the night, beat
him, allegedly castrated him, and threw his body off a bridge into the
Tallahatchie River with a seventy-pound gin fan hung around his neck
to weigh him down.

Just five weeks later, an all-white jury in Tallahatchie County acquitted the two killers in less than an hour. The trial was a national sensation
in both the black and white presses. The murder of Emmett Till became
the civil rights case of the twentieth century. When Rosa Parks, a tired
black maid in Montgomery, refused to get up and move to the back of
the bus and thereby helped ignite the civil rights revolution, she said that
the image that motivated her was that of the broken body of Emmett Till.

From the early 1990s onward, a series of old, unresolved civil rights
murder cases were reopened and the defendants convicted, many years
after the events. First came Byron De La Beckwith of Greenwood, a
hate-filled Klansman who murdered NAACP leader Medgar Evers by
shooting him in the back in his own driveway in Jackson with a high-
powered rifle. Beckwith was tried twice for the murder by local state
DA Bill Waller, who was later elected governor, but those early all-white

juries deadlocked, or hung, and the case remained open and unresolved. Then, thanks largely to vigorous digging and reporting by Jerry Mitchell, a red-headed *Jackson Clarion-Ledger* reporter from Arkansas, new evidence and new witnesses were located and Jackson District Attorney Ed Peters and his assistant, Bobby DeLaughter, retried the case and convicted Beckwith, who was sentenced to life in prison. The Mississippi Supreme Court affirmed the conviction, in an eloquent opinion for the court by Michael Mills, now the chief federal judge in Oxford. When the case was retried, the Beckwith evidence was already nearly four decades old, but prosecutors DeLaughter and Peters succeeded in using the two old trial transcripts, the rifle with Beckwith's prints on it, plus the few witnesses still alive.

Later came the equally sensational retrial of Edgar Ray "Preacher" Killen for the infamous murders of the three civil rights workers who were buried under a dam near our largest Choctaw reservation. This case was almost as old, and the outcome hotly contested. One juror allegedly refused to convict a preacher of murder and the jury had to compromise on a lesser manslaughter verdict, barely avoiding another hung jury. But it was a conviction for the local DA and for attorney general Jim Hood, who tried the case personally. Local circuit judge Marcus Gordon gave Killen a sentence so stiff it guaranteed he would, as justice demanded, die in prison. Again, despite the age of the case and the deaths of key witnesses and the faded memories of others, the State Supreme Court affirmed. Many said the public outrage over a reversal on a technicality would have been too overwhelming.

The Civil Rights Division of DOJ continued reopening other old cases, which for some reason occurred mainly in the southern half of the state, outside our district. One day in January 2004, our turn came. Anita McGehee, secretary to U.S. Attorney Jim Greenlee, buzzed me and said Jim wanted me to take a call about reopening the Emmett Till case. It occurred to me how little I knew about such a historic case which had taken place in our district. The caller was Alvin Sykes from Kansas City, where my daughter was then attending medical school. Fortunately for me, Sykes had already done much of our work for us. "I met with the people at the Civil Rights Division last August, and I know that the federal statute of limitations on Emmett's case has run out, but they said your office had a good reputation in civil rights circles and that you might be willing to help persuade the state DA to reopen the case if the FBI will agree to investigate it."

Alvin Sykes was no screaming militant like many I'd dealt with. He was calm and low-key but persistent. And he knew what he was talking about. "We know there are only a handful of possible defendants still alive after fifty years, but we want peace of mind for Emmett's family. They say the woman who accused Emmett and pointed him out for killing is still around, as well as some black guys who supposedly helped transport him to his death." Sykes continued, "We also know the transcript of the trial has disappeared, and the two men who later bragged about doing the killing have died, but we still believe that a really thorough investigation might turn up enough evidence for a state prosecution for murder. If not, at least the family and the nation would finally know what really happened."

I certainly could not argue with Sykes's rationale. I told him I'd check into it further and call him back in a couple of days. He said he wanted a face-to-face meeting with the DA and the FBI at our office. He promised to bring with him Keith Beauchamp, a young filmmaker working on a documentary that featured on-camera interviews with several surviving witnesses. Then he said the thing that persuaded me: "I will also bring with me Simeon Wright, the boy who was sleeping in the bed with Emmett when he was taken and was also with him at the store in Money when he supposedly whistled and said things to the white woman. Simeon is now nearly seventy but smart as a whip and has a vivid memory of all that happened." From a different mindset I repeated to Mr. Sykes that I'd get back to him. The thought of hearing the story directly from Simeon Wright had convinced me to go ahead with the meeting.

First I called some old friends at the Civil Rights Division for counsel. They said the case sounded awfully old, a real long shot after nearly half a century but that Sykes and Beauchamp were serious people and worth a meeting. They too were intrigued by the idea of hearing from Simeon Wright, who had been thirteen years old at the time and would certainly be a powerful witness if there were any defendants left to prosecute. U.S. Attorney Jim Greenlee agreed. I called FBI supervisor Philip "Hal" Neilson, who shared similar doubts, but agreed that at least a preliminary meeting to evaluate our chances was a good idea.

Then I called District Attorney Joyce Chiles in Greenville, whom I had known for over twenty years, since she was a brand-new undercover agent for the Mississippi Bureau of Narcotics. In fact, I was the first prosecutor ever to use Joyce as a witness, long before she went on to law school. Joyce had just been elected DA. Tall and imposing in a calm way, she was the first black DA ever in the Delta counties of Sunflower, Washington, and Leflore, where Emmett Till was kidnapped. One key issue would be where Till was killed. The post-acquittal confessions of his killers to *Look* magazine reporter William Bradford Huie had raised more questions than they answered. Defendants claimed to Huie that they had gotten lost while driving Till around the Delta trying to decide whether to kill him and where to dispose of the body.

Joyce was her usual calm, firm self. "John, I will do what is right. If we have a case, I'll prosecute it, but I won't do it just to satisfy people's feelings. Reopening the case will reopen old racial wounds however it comes out. With our Delta juries and grand juries now predominantly black, I can easily get an indictment and probably a conviction, but it would be terrible for us to go forward without good evidence and try someone on prejudice alone. We've had enough of that. And what if we got a conviction and the state supreme court had to throw it out for lack of evidence? That would be a lot worse than doing the right thing now." I knew we would be in good hands with Joyce.

She continued, "There are two things I insist on. First, I need you to persuade the FBI to commit totally to a really in-depth investigation." I told her I'd do my best and thought they would. "My next request is personal: I want you to agree to work with me on the investigation as a specially appointed assistant DA and to try the jury case with us if we go to trial. I know Jim Hood has the authority to appoint you, and he will do it if I ask him." That put the case in a different light. From a theoretical problem for someone else, the Till case had suddenly become personal. It was as if someone had just draped a heavy winter coat over my shoulders. But I immediately agreed anyway, wondering what I was getting myself into.

My father used to kid me about how I handled problems. My first reaction, he said, was always to read a book about it if there was one. In this case, I walked straight to Square Books and asked owner Richard Howorth what he had on the Emmett Till case. In his usual calm, measured tone, Richard said, "There's a fairly new book out on the case written by Emmett's mother. I haven't read it, but reviewers liked it." The blurb from the *Washington Post* on the cover said it was "as eloquent as the diary of Anne Frank." That kind of hyperbole always puts me off. A highly emotional foreword by the Reverend Jesse Jackson did not help either. But the pictures on the cover of a pudgy, wide-eyed boy and his smiling, pretty mother persuaded me to try it. The title sounded right: *The Death of Innocence: The Story of the Hate Crime That Changed America.* Those words hit the right note. But it was the mother's words in the introduction that hooked me:

> For forty-seven years I wasn't quite ready to write this book. It took a
> long time for me to reach this kind of deep understanding. I have been
> approached oh so many times by people who wanted to tell my story
> or put words in my mouth to tell their version of my story. But I just
> couldn't do that. I owe Emmett more than that. I owe him the absolute
> understanding I have finally come to appreciate, this deep understanding
> of why he lived and died and why I was destined to live so long after his
> death. . . . Only now can I share the wisdom of my age. I am experienced
> but not cynical. It is only because I have finally understood the past,
> accepted it, embraced it, that I can fully live in the moment. And hardly a
> moment goes by when I don't think about Emmett, and the lessons a son
> can teach a mother. (p. xxiii)

That night and the next day, I could not put the book down. Its mature, philosophical tone was far more moving than any angry polemic could have been. The utter candor of Mamie Till-Mobley was stunning. Despite her deep love for Emmett, her only child, this daughter of the black bourgeoisie of South Chicago did not hesitate to tell things most people would have suppressed. She told of the infidelities and abuse of Emmett's father and of how she finally ran him off by pouring a pot of boiling water on him while he slept.

An educated, refined, and religious woman who became a teacher, Mrs. Till had to have suffered unbelievably from the death of her only child. Yet bitterness was not her tone. She told their story in an unforgettably stoical voice. Now I was really hooked. We had to do whatever we could for this worthy victim. When Alvin Sykes called back, I felt confident I understood much better what the Till case meant and why we should pursue it, and I told Mr. Sykes so. Then I revealed my ignorance again, asking if Mrs. Till Mobley might be able to come. "No, sadly, if we can obtain justice in this case, she will not be around to see it. Mamie died in January 2003, after her book was written, but before it was published. But Simeon Wright will be there."

As agreed, we all met in U.S. Attorney Jim Greenlee's conference room on February 6, 2004. After an hour of interesting discussions with Alvin Sykes and Keith Beauchamp about interviews with witnesses and the trial of the killers J. W. "Big" Milam and Roy Bryant, and their bragging to *Look* magazine after their acquittal, we felt the meeting was drifting. Alvin Sykes suggested we bring in Simeon Wright, who had been waiting downstairs.

A muscular, well-spoken man born the same year I was, Simeon Wright was one of those natural storyteller witnesses all trial lawyers look for. He needed no coaching or prompting but proceeded to lay out for us all the reasons we needed to reopen the case. After all, Simeon Wright was the only one who was with Emmett Till both at Bryant's store in Money and in bed with Emmett Till when Milam and Bryant kidnapped him. Simeon Wright had thought about the case for a half century and gave us several insights no one else could have. As soon as he left, we agreed unanimously, investigators and prosecutors alike, both federal and state, that we had to reopen the case and investigate it as thoroughly as humanly possible.

The next day I called Richard "Ricky" Roberts, assistant attorney general for the Civil Rights Division, whom I knew well from prior cases. He and the chief of his criminal division, my old friend Al Moscowitz, who'd been to our district on several earlier cases, said they wanted just one thing, but it was a big thing: a conclusive final report on the Till case, whether it led to a prosecution or merely closure of some kind. "Everyone in America," they said, "needs to know what really happened." We all knew that was a tall order, but I never expected the investigation to last until the year I retired.

Together we discussed several of the open questions: How did Emmett Till really die? Was he beaten to death, lynched, or thrown off a bridge and drowned? Was a hole drilled in his skull, as legend had it? Was he castrated or his body otherwise mutilated? Who else, black or white, was involved in his death? Was there any federal jurisdiction of any kind under which we could prosecute? What state jurisdiction, if any, was not barred by a statute of limitations? In which of at least three counties could a state prosecution be pursued: Leflore County where he was kidnapped, Tallahatchie where his body was supposedly found, or perhaps Sunflower or even Bolivar County, where he was actually killed? Rumor supported all of these choices. What did Emmett Till actually do to provoke such a horrifically violent murder? Did he just whistle, as witnesses said? Or did he "do some talking" as Milam and Bryant claimed? Or did he go so far as to grab Carolyn Bryant by the waist, as she had claimed?

When we finished talking, I had several pages of questions. Could anyone ever sort them all out? What would the FBI agree to do? How far would they go to answer all the questions? We soon had our answer. The new FBI agent in charge for Mississippi, Bob Garrity, after consulting both with FBI Director Robert Mueller, a former U.S. Attorney, and his Mississippi agents, decided on a full-court press. Garrity assigned Oxford agent Dale Killinger, a native of Pennsylvania relatively new to the area, to work on nothing else but the Till case for as long as it took.

Dale was given extraordinary freedom, especially to travel for witness interviews. In routine FBI investigations, such as bank robberies, the case agent never leaves his district but sends out "leads." If an eyewitness to a crime in Mississippi is located in Ohio, the Mississippi agent will send a written request to the FBI office in Ohio nearest the witness. An Ohio agent will then go ask the witness the relevant questions. That procedure, fast and economical in routine cases, would never work in the Till case. There were too many detailed questions, which only a totally informed case agent could probe into and follow up on and fully understand the responses. Dale Killinger was therefore given full authority to go everywhere and do everything necessary to produce a final, conclusive report answering all open questions. He received this plenary authority in May 2004.

In August 2004, we had a thorough meeting in the courthouse at Greenwood with Joyce Chiles and her chief assistant, Hallie Gail Bridges, a tough-talking veteran prosecutor, who grew up near the scene of the crime and lived near Midnight, for which this book is named. H.G., as Joyce called her, was as tough and pragmatic a state prosecutor as I could possibly have wished for. We had a good team. Leflore County sheriff Ricky Banks, an old friend from a variety of tough cases over the years, guaranteed—and delivered—full cooperation. Another valuable ally was

Lent Rice, a retired FBI agent who grew up at Sumner in Tallahatchie County, where the trial was held, and had known the Till case and its players since childhood.

The investigation started off well. While the national media from CBS to the *New York Times* stoked the emotional fires demanding an investigation, Dale and his partners quietly carried it out in relative anonymity. To our surprise, Dale persuaded Carolyn Bryant Donham (since remarried) to talk with him several times both in person and on the phone. While in some ways unreconstructed in her idea that Till brought his troubles on himself, she also insisted that she never wanted him killed and had not at first told her husband what happened, only admitting it when he confronted her after someone else told him. She said she had feared what he would do.

Evidence began to roll in. Civil rights reporter Jerry Mitchell had always said that none of these cold cases could ever be retried without a transcript of the evidence from the original trial. With a transcript, the trial testimony of witnesses who had since died would be admissible if they were cross-examined at the previous trial. The last copy of the Till transcript that anyone knew of had been in the possession of Florida graduate student Hugh Whitaker who quoted from it extensively in his unpublished master's thesis way back in 1962. Out of the blue, one of the team's contacts produced an ancient, fragile, faded copy that witnesses who knew the handwriting of the deceased court reporter authenticated by his signature. Other witnesses who'd been at the trial verified that it seemed correct and complete. Two FBI clerks spent several weeks retyping it, page by page and word for word. It was a gold mine of detail.

Somewhat to our surprise, the trial, for its time, was very professionally conducted. Circuit judge Curtis Swango excluded the testimony of Carolyn Bryant from the hearing of the jury as not relevant enough and not probative enough to overcome the extreme racial prejudice it would have injected into the trial. Unfortunately, the local jurors had already heard all about it on the street and from informal visits to their homes by members of the White Citizens Council as verified by the files of the State Sovereignty Commission.

Dale Killinger plugged away, disproving the rumors that all sorts of shadowy white men had participated. Some of them did not even exist. He established that there was no Ku Klux Klan involvement. Especially tricky was the obvious involvement of certain black males who allegedly pointed out to Bryant and Milam the house of Preacher Moses Wright where Till was staying, as well as riding with the killers while they transported Till from place to place, helped dispose of Till's clothing, and washed Till's blood out of Milam's truck after it was over. Most of them turned out to be deceased, and a couple had severe mental problems from age and the stress of living with those terrible memories.

From our own office came my biggest surprise. One day, AUSA John Marshall Alexander came to my office, as he often did. I assumed he wanted to talk about a case we'd been working on together. John Marshall always had a dry sense of humor. A native of Cleveland, a graduate of Delta State, and the son of respected state senator William Alexander, John Marshall had a keen appreciation for the subtleties of reopening a case like Emmett Till. He started off slowly: "Well, John, I know you've got to be under a lot of pressure about this Till matter. I'm glad we've got Joyce Chiles as DA. She has a lot of credibility with blacks and whites alike." I agreed. "And even if you can't find anyone alive to prosecute, at least we can say we convicted Roy Bryant and sent him to the pen."

I didn't understand. "Convicted Bryant? What are you talking about?" He chuckled. "Well, you assigned me the food stamp fraud cases back in the 1980s, and one of them was on Roy Bryant, who was buying food stamps at his store for fifty cents on the dollar." I didn't remember that. "We handled it just like any other case. Judge Keady gave him probation the first time." "The *first* time?" I asked. "Yeah, then we caught him again. Judge Davidson gave him two years in the federal pen. That outstanding Department of Agriculture undercover agent Dave Thomas caught him cold on tape. But the press never picked up on who Bryant was." I had my secretary pull the files and there he was, Roy Bryant, convicted, first in 1984 and again in 1988. He pled guilty both times. When sentenced, he asked Judge Davidson for extra time to report. Denied. He asked the judge to reconsider his sentence. Denied. He asked two more times for his sentence to be reduced. Denied. Denied. Bryant eventually died of cancer in 1994. That was our first surprise.

The new investigation kept moving forward. In October 2004, we had a long conference call on our progress with the new head of the Civil Rights Division, Wan Kim, a gung-ho Korean American ex-soldier with degrees from Johns Hopkins and the University of Chicago Law

School. We discussed all our new facts, from where the body was thrown into the Tallahatchie (near Swan Lake, where Milam squirrel-hunted) to whether and why Carolyn Bryant had sworn that her sister-in-law, Juanita Milam, was present in the store in Money at the time of the incident that provoked the murder. Juanita swore she was not. We discussed most of all how cruelly ironic it would be to prosecute one or more of the elderly black men who, even if they were still alive, had helped Bryant and Milam only under severe duress. Everyone agreed the investigation was going well by staying out of the press, which might have caused witnesses and informants to clam up. My friend Charles Overby of the Freedom Forum and First Amendment Center would probably be appalled, but that's how it was.

The next time we discussed the case in detail with Washington was in August 2005. We met in the Main Justice Building, across the street from the FBI, in the very office occupied for many years by J. Edgar Hoover himself. Later it was the office of Mark Felt, the FBI agent who as "Deep Throat" had broken the Watergate story to the *Washington Post*. The agents regaled us with war stories about how Hoover had allowed only one chair in the office—his own—which forced visitors to stand at all times in his presence. It no doubt helped keep visits short.

Dale Killinger had made lots of progress. We now knew that the state trial had been held in the wrong county. The point in the Tallahatchie River where the body was found was actually in Leflore County, not Tallahatchie. The white teenager who found it, somewhat eerily, still fishes there because it is such a good, deep fishing hole. The gin fan that had hung from Emmett Till's neck was missing, but Dale had somehow retrieved Big Milam's military .45 revolver. We also learned exactly how Till died: Milam shot him in the head from point-blank range using a pellet-filled shotgun shell rather than a bullet. Called by some an "emergency load," these shells were issued in World War II to pilots flying over enemy territory to use in escaping capture by spraying their pursuers with steel pellets rather than single bullets. The modern equivalent is still around. Called "rat shot" it is used in barns and stockyards on the same theory. Shells are easy to find since a .410 shotgun shell will fit in a .45. We also learned for certain where the killing took place, in a barn on the old Shurden Plantation, which was managed back then by Leslie Milam, brother of J. W. "Big" Milam. According to believable witnesses, J. W.

asked Leslie to participate, but he refused, saying they needed to "take that boy back where you got him." Leslie Milam, like J. W. and Roy Bryant, was long since deceased.

We met again in Washington in December 2005, this time for three days of detailed discussions of the evidence and all remaining factual and legal issues. Dale and his team had done a marvelously thorough job. Finally, in December 2006, our local team met in Joyce Chiles's office at the courthouse in Greenwood. Assistant state attorney general Charlie Maris joined us. An experienced appellate prosecutor, Charlie knew state law better than anyone. He resolved for us most outstanding Mississippi law questions now that Dale had all the facts we were going to get. First of all, the best state charge we would have on Carolyn Bryant was that she aided the kidnapping by personally identifying Emmett Till as the one who wolf-whistled or did the talking at the store in Money. But that charge would not stick. In 1955, the Mississippi statute of limitations on kidnapping was an unbelievably short two years. Even worse, under Mississippi law in 1955 there was no felony-murder law, meaning that we could not even prosecute her for helping cause Till's murder by aiding in the kidnapping that resulted in his death.

The trial transcript itself even went against us on the kidnap and felony/murder points. It showed that Moses Wright did *not* say *at trial* that the voice out in the truck who identified Emmett Till was a woman's voice, but just a "light" voice. Simeon Wright confirmed this in his fine recent book *Simeon's Story* (Chicago, 2010), saying Medgar Evers, who was helping Mr. Wright prepare, told him not to say that the person in the truck was Carolyn Bryant, but only what he knew for sure. Mr. Wright thought it was her, but could not be totally positive even that the voice was that of a woman. And she was not on trial even though Leflore County sheriff George Smith had had a warrant issued for her arrest for kidnapping. For one reason or another the warrant was never served. Otherwise, the woman known in the national press as the "Crossroads Marilyn Monroe," might have faced trial, but probably with the same result given the attitudes of the times. Today I wonder: If Moses Wright had testified that the voice was that of Carolyn Bryant, whom he knew from weekly visits to her store, I feel we would have prosecuted.

On Wednesday, February 21, 2007, Joyce Chiles and Hallie Gail Bridges presented the new Till case to a Leflore County grand jury composed of thirteen black and seven white citizens of Leflore County. The state grand jury secrecy rule prevented discussion of it for six months, but after a long February 27 conference call between our team and FBI Director Bob Mueller and Civil Rights Division Chief Wan Kim, U.S. attorney general Alberto Gonzales announced the end of the Till case at a press conference that day. Mr. Gonzales first announced several indictments that had been returned in other cold cases, then noted briefly that "not every case can be resolved."[15] At that time all he could say was that the official public records of the Leflore County grand jury report showed no indictments for cases from 1955, and thereupon Gonzales quietly pronounced the end of our Emmett Till investigation.

We were sorely disappointed. The closure we'd hoped for did not come for the American public. The failure of the grand jury to indict was reported on the front page of the *Jackson Clarion-Ledger* but only on inner pages of the *New York Times* and *USA Today*.[16] We were certainly not looking for publicity for what would be seen as our "loss," but we wanted resolution. In another lengthy telephone conference call with Director Mueller and AAG Kim, they had strongly supported us in our insistence that the Till family be told first, before the public. Joyce Chiles and Dale Killinger flew to Chicago and personally explained the case to Emmett Till's closest living relatives, including Simeon Wright and Wheeler Parker Jr., both of whom were at the store and in Moses Wright's house when Till was kidnapped.

In response to a FOIA request from the Associated Press, a 135-page summary of the twenty-eight-volume, 8,000+-page case report was released. Sadly, by the time the FOIA units finished deleting "sensitive" materials like names, "redacting it like crazy," Dale's outstanding report was a mere shadow of its robust former self but still has interesting details of many kinds.[17] It may be found online in a somewhat longer 464-page summary at the FBI website, which does include at least a complete copy of the trial transcript.

In 2010 the new Meek School of Journalism at Ole Miss, led by new Journalism Dean Will Norton, completed its own project on the case, bringing principals like Wheeler Parker and Simeon Wright to the university and to the crime scenes in the case. Funds are now being raised for various Till memorials in the Delta, including the remains of the ruined Bryant store in Money. The Moses Wright home, a nice four-bedroom house with screened porch which was occupied by whites both before and after the Wrights lived there, has since unfortunately been totally destroyed by a tornado, perhaps fittingly not unlike the storm that swept away the system of segregation that Emmett Till helped destroy by refusing, even on pain of death, to admit to Milam and Bryant that he was inferior to them because of his race.

What We Learned That Made the Case Worth Reopening

We learned new insights into the players. From old file pictures, Carolyn Bryant was indeed as beautiful as they said back then and had won two beauty contests, (not easy in Mississippi), before dropping out of school to marry Roy Bryant. We were reminded of the propensity of Mississippians to give colorful names to their towns, such as Money, Swan Lake, Sidon, Quito, Inverness, Pentecost, Sunnyside, and Schlater (pronounced "slaughter"). Other towns in the circle of the Till case are now known, thankfully, for their more distinguished former residents, such as Morgan Freeman of Charleston, B.B. King of Indianola, and Archie Manning from Drew.

We also learned, to our surprise, that in 1955 the first reaction to the killing of Emmett Till by whites across the state was outrage. Governor Hugh White and the state's leading newspapers strongly denounced it, and even the white segregationist Citizens Council, a far more powerful force in the state than the Klan ever was, said it was "deplorable," facts Dale Killinger turned up in his investigation and which I recall reading but which are no longer available to me. With the always-correct benefit of hindsight, some can now call those reactions mere paternalism, but to me they were both human and humane.

Even more surprising to me was that Leflore County sheriff George Smith immediately arrested Roy Bryant and J. W. Milam and obtained confessions from both men to the kidnapping of Emmett Till, even though they denied killing him. Sheriff Smith also obtained an arrest warrant for Carolyn Bryant for aiding Milam and Bryant by identifying Emmett Till as "The one who did the talking at Money." Somewhere in the vast FBI files that I read weekly for months at a special office in Oxford dedicated to the Till case is a picture of Bryant and Milam chained to a tree in front of a courthouse. Given the mood of whites at the time, it is possible they might have been convicted, at least of kidnapping, if the case had been tried in Leflore County instead of Tallahatchie.

In my forty years of traveling the three hours from Oxford to Greenville for court, my favorite route was always down old Mississippi Highway 35. If you cross the high railroad bridge at Batesville and take a hard left on 35, it takes you straight through Tallahatchie County, where the wooded bluffs of Appalachia on the left meet the flat and treeless Delta on the right as far as the eye can see. That unique part of the Delta is strangely like one of California's central valleys. The population of the hills to the left is mostly white; the Delta flatlands on the right are overwhelmingly black. The jury for Emmett Till's killers was chosen, purposely, from the "hill people," as Faulkner called them. Leflore County would have been different; it is virtually all Delta. The FBI report notes that every juror received a personal visit before trial by at least one member of the White Citizens Council. Jury tampering was and still is an active part of our culture, as I can attest from personal experience.

According to people who were there, the change of heart—or rather, the loss of heart by the majority of white people—came with national media attention. The *Brown* school desegregation decision had come the previous year in 1954. White Mississippians, always highly sensitive to pressure from people they still saw as Yankees who had plundered their lands and forests for nearly a century after the Civil War, hated outside interference. Led by the worst among us, within a month white sentiment in the Till murder changed from demanding punishment for Bryant and Milam as "white trash peckerwoods" who embarrassed the state to circling the wagons against "outside agitators." Rather than Sheriff Smith and other whites like William Faulkner who wanted to punish the cowardly killers of a fourteen-year-old visitor, the focus shifted to hostility to out-of-state civil rights leaders and in-state NAACP leaders like Medgar Evers, who played a crucial role in the trial by producing witnesses like Willie "Chicken" Reed, the eighteen-year-old who testified at trial he saw J. W. Milam at the barn where Till was murdered. Writer Willie Morris feelingly recounted that whole matter in his excellent but little-known book *The Ghosts of Medgar Evers*.

Upon closer examination both Roy Bryant and J. W. Milam come off a bit differently. Roy Bryant had a twin brother named Ray. Naming twins Roy and Ray gives outsiders some image of their backgrounds. Roy

Bryant was a veteran U.S. Army paratrooper with the 82nd Airborne, serving from 1950 until honorably discharged in 1953. He stood 6' tall and weighed 190 pounds. To Mississippians, who send a larger percentage of their citizens to military careers than any other state, military service is an important factor, and John William "Big" Milam had an outstanding career. Standing 6', 2" and weighing 220 pounds, Milam not only fought combat missions in World War II from 1941 to 1945 but received both a Purple Heart and a battlefield commission to lieutenant, signs of some trust and respect. He was a racist and a bully, but his military record gives a little different perspective on his propensity for violence.

To those who followed the reopened Till case, the most important part of the investigation was our decision to have Emmett Till's body exhumed. At the 1955 trial the entire defense (other than prejudice, intimidation, and jury tampering) was that the body discovered in the Tallahatchie was not that of Emmett Till. No autopsy was ever performed. The face was too decomposed from being in the river several days at the mercy of fish and turtles for even his own mother to recognize him. Till was first identified by Moses Wright only by the silver ring inscribed "L.T." (for Louis Till) which Emmett Till had lent to Simeon Wright to wear. The ring disappeared after the trial and we never found it, but it clearly appears in pictures from the trial. The gin fan has also disappeared.

The findings of the recent autopsy begin at page ninety-nine of the FBI report and are necessarily gruesome. Other than the damaged face, however, the body was remarkably well preserved. Emmett Till was definitely not castrated or sexually mutilated as rumored. His left leg and both wrists were fractured, the latter possibly during physical abuse, but possibly from being thrown off a Tallahatchie bridge. Given the seventy-pound gin fan tied around his neck with barbed wire, it is surprising the body managed to float nine miles downstream, a testament to the power of the river currents in that area. The autopsy, performed fifty years after the death, revealed numerous head wounds inflicted prior to death. The brain was missing. Most surprising of all was the presence of several small lead fragments inside the skull. They proved to be #7.5 chilled lead shot made for use in a shell fired from the Remington .45 caliber pistol of J. W. Milam. Eyewitnesses said they'd often seen Milam shoot it and that he would "shoot bumblebees out of the air with it," meaning he probably used shotgun-type shells in the .45 on a regular basis, it being extremely difficult to hit a flying bumblebee with a single bullet.

Comparison of dental records confirmed the body buried in Emmett Till's grave was indeed that of Emmett Till. Mouth swabs of mitochondrial DNA from his cousin Simeon Wright correlated to that of intact muscle fiber taken from Emmett Till's exhumed body, but only to a "42% upper bound." We wanted more conclusive DNA proof, but there was only one way to obtain it and that meant major embarrassment to the surviving Till family members. The best DNA could only be obtained from the male line, and this would have involved exhuming the body of his father Louis Till, and when we began our investigation no one knew where his body was buried.

Mamie Till Mobley had already revealed in her memoir the shocking fact that Louis Till, Emmett's father, was one of a handful of U.S. GIs executed for serious crimes against civilians committed in World War II. Louis Till was convicted by court martial near the end of the war of raping two Italian women and murdering a third. Through his military contacts, Dale Killinger, himself a decorated paratrooper and sniper (and cancer survivor) who'd fought in the U.S. invasion of the island of Granada, persuaded the army to find Till's body, which was located in an army cemetery outside Paris. After consulting with the family, we decided not to have Louis Till's body exhumed until after the grand jury met. If they indicted anyone, we would no doubt have obtained a more conclusive DNA result for use at trial. In the end, the exhumation proved unnecessary and we avoided further embarrassment to the Till family.

We deeply regretted that the public, and especially Mamie Till Mobley, never knew all we learned from reopening the Emmett Till case. But not one of us ever regretted for a moment reopening the case to pursue the truth and make it known. Perhaps the present brief recounting will make it a little better known and help close this chapter of U.S. and Mississippi history.

4

KILLERS AND WANNABES

Introduction

Most murders are not federal crimes. State DAs handle most homicides unless they are committed on federal lands like national parks. Fortunately for prosecutors in our office who get satisfaction from putting killers behind bars for life (like me) north Mississippi is rich in federal enclaves and interstate highways. The Natchez Trace Parkway seems to be the crime scene of choice for federal killings in Faulkner country. Most emotional and unforgettable for me was the locally famous Natchez Trace sniper killing where a paroled rapist used a high-powered rifle to murder a nine-year-old boy returning home from Christmas with his grandparents. That episode is recounted here at length as the final story of this chapter. Such seemingly senseless killings are well explained in a recent book *Why They Kill* by Richard Rhodes, who covers in depth killers and other violent criminals from Lee Harvey Oswald to Jack Ruby to Mike Tyson in an unusually persuasive way for those, like me, who try to understand such people.

The other major source of federal jurisdiction in murder cases is when the murder affects interstate commerce and is done for money. In a sad commentary on our society, many of those cases involve husbands or wives wanting their spouses killed. In our district, an amateur local hit man will usually do the job for less than $5,000, often for less than $1,000. One positive thing I learned while prosecuting so many of these cases is just how many informants our investigators have. Bartenders, prostitutes, and jilted lovers usually make great informants. After a few drinks, angry spouses tend to ask bartenders to recommend a cheap, reliable hit man to knock off their erstwhile life partner. Over my career, we averted several hired killings by inserting undercover officers to pose as hit men and tape-record the spouse asking for the killing and handing the officer a down payment. We always had to act quickly, before the spouse found someone else to do the job faster or cheaper. There are way too many shooters out there who need money. One of our most successful such cases was where a local judge, outraged at a young lawyer with the famous Farese law firm, tried to hire a hit man to blow up their entire office with them in it. Our key informant refused to testify, but we persuaded the judge not to run again, and nobody was blown up.

One particularly troubling case happened at remote, idyllic Puskus Lake near Oxford where a meth-crazed drifter killed an Ole Miss honor student because the student's lively black lab had disturbed his fishing. Another sicko beat a gay architect to death with a piece of heavy metal at a rest stop on the Natchez Trace for threatening his manhood by propositioning him, or so he thought. But not all of our cases have been so depressing. Several included here involve laughably incompetent wannabe killers.

My favorite venue for a failed murder-for-hire was a seedy concrete-block bar atop a hill near Mayhew Junction appropriately named the Bloody Bucket Lounge. Jesse Bingham, my good friend and an ace undercover capable of playing multiple personalities, solved that one. Others were solved by an itinerant CI frequently used by FBI agent Wayne Tichenor. The CI, who always refused to tell us his real name, was a former Hell's Angel with great acting skills. We got him jobs as a maître d' in a fine restaurant, as a clerk in an expensive men's store, as a bouncer in a strip club, and as a bartender for several gigs. Our deal with him was that he would only gather information and would never have to testify or be identified in any paperwork such as search warrants. Wayne may have known how to find him, but I never did. We knew him only as "California Jim." His unique MO was that he took his young son, aged eight through twelve when we knew him, wherever he went. I wonder how that boy turned out.

This chapter begins with two of the most vivid almost-murder cases. The first is the attempted murder of Senator John Stennis by a group of robbers who shot him in front of his Washington, D.C., home while I was working as his legal counsel. Fortunately that case had a happy ending legally. The second case involved Ku Klux Klan leader Dale Walton, who had traveled to Fayette, in the Southern District, and tried to kill civil rights leader Charles Evers, brother of the assassinated NAACP leader Medgar Evers. That plot failed, and we prosecuted Walton in the Northern District for possession of the machine gun he planned to use to kill Evers. Just as prosecutors once got Al Capone using the tax laws, we used the firearms laws to go after Walton.

I have known several serial killers. The worst was Marion Albert "Mad Dog" Pruett, a former protected witness and the killer of another protected witness and several others, whose deposition I took at Parchman one cold day while he was on death row. My worst personal encounter with a killer was with one of the Lampkin brothers from near Starkville. While cross-examining him in a judge's chambers, the pudgy, fiftyish Cleveland Lampkin, not liking my questions, leapt like a cat across the judge's conference table and tried to choke me. The marshals easily pulled him off. He was on trial for a minor firearm charge. The rest of that killer's chilling life history is also recounted here.

My most colorful "lady" killer was Linda Leedom of DeSoto County. She killed her best friend after the friend unwisely made Linda the beneficiary of several life insurance policies. It was a really challenging case, as told in this chapter. Another "lady" killer, Teresa Hutchison, wanted her husband dead both for his life insurance money and so she could "have a better life." Her case was so colorful it ended up on the Sally Jessy Raphael show, whose proceeds went to help raise her children while she was doing her prison time.

Another incompetent wannabe killer was Bobby "Riverboat" Gaines, who unwittingly hired ace undercover agent Randall Corban to kill an Oxford bootlegger who refused to pay a gambling debt. The most laughably incompetent killers were the Tohill clan of Beaumont, Texas, whose bumbling attempts at professional murder made the Keystone Cops look like pros. My "favorite" unsuccessful killers, if there are such things, were

Harold Shaw and his uncle William Shaw, a Parchman inmate already serving life for killing his wife and her lover. William was a cousin of some of the killers of the three young civil rights workers buried under the earthen dam near Philadelphia. His attempt to have his sentencing judge killed, recounted here, featured classic undercover work to save innocent life. It is no doubt impossible to stop all the killing, but as shown here, good investigators can keep it under control.

The Shooting of Senator John Stennis[1]

Although I had been a lawyer for three years, my first real in-depth experience with a big-time criminal case came, ironically, while I was working as legal counsel and speechwriter to U.S. senator John Stennis. On the evening of January 30, 1973, the senator asked me to drive him from his Senate office to a 6:30 National Guard reception. After an hour, he told me to go home and "have dinner with your young wife," that he would get someone else to drive him back to the Senate. Little did I imagine what a big impact that simple decision would have on my life.

As Regan and I sat on our screened back porch having dinner, the phone rang. It was Mildred Ward, the senator's trusted personal secretary, who lived just three blocks from us. Aunt of actress Sela Ward, Mildred was a lovely, dark-haired woman in her 50s, single and fiercely loyal to the senator, who was the center of her life. After twenty years in a high-stress job, few things bothered Mildred. She could tell presidents to hold the line without batting an eye. But that evening she was sobbing. "John, please come right away and drive me to Walter Reed Hospital. The senator has been shot and is not expected to live. I'm too upset to drive."

As I drove, Mildred gave me details from Miss Coy, the senator's wife, and Eph Cresswell, his trusted chief of staff. The senator had driven himself home in the brand-new white Buick he'd just bought Miss Coy as a birthday present. After he parked in front of his house, two young men had robbed him and shot him twice, once in the leg and once in the stomach, meaning to kill him.

As the night wore on at Walter Reed, a dozen or more senators came to check on Senator Stennis, who was not only powerful and respected but also greatly loved by senators of both parties. Lloyd Bentsen of Texas

"Snakeman," a Satanist priest prosecuted by the author for kidnapping a fifteen-year-old victim in our district and forcing her into prostitution. Bank robber Paddy Mitchell tried to call the Snakeman as a defense witness in Mitchell's trial for attempted escape from the Lafayette County jail. He failed.

Convicted bank robber and self-proclaimed Native American shaman Thunder Eagle Ghost Dancer, whose request to appear in court in "a ritual cloud of smoke" was denied, with his appointed attorneys Johnny Gough and Kent Smith.

Tony and Man Craft caught in the act of robbing the federally-insured Bank of Lula, Mississippi.

Tony Craft pulling the trigger (unsuccessfully) on a bank teller.

09-30-2003 TUE
21:58:32

Suspect enters thru N.E. door

presents package to cashier as "bomb"

Placing money in purse.

The attractive blonde stripper known as the "Honey Bun Bandit" robbing the Grand Casino in Tunica, presenting a box of Honey Buns to a cashier with the box disguised as a bomb.

DeSoto County Sheriff Harvey Hamilton before a jury convicted him of racketeering, the first RICO conviction ever in the state of Mississippi. (Courtesy of Memphis *Commercial Appeal*)

"TAKE MY WORD FOR IT
DAMN YOU, OR STEP
OUTSIDE !   "

The author as portrayed after a brief courtroom scuffle in the trial of Sheriff Harvey Hamilton. Pen and ink drawing by FBI undercover agent Les Davis while posing as a mafia enforcer.

YE OLDE
SYCAMORE
TREE.

MR. TICHENOR, HONEST! YA'LL CAN HAVE
ALL THE CAKE AND ICE CREAM, YOU WANT!

Drawing by FBI undercover agent Les Davis of Sheriff Harvey Hamilton depicting one of his colorful quotes caught on tape by Davis: "You can nail my nuts to a sycamore tree and I'll never squeal, but any SOB who does won't be out there eating cake and ice cream. He'll be dead."

A series of brilliant editorial cartoons by Mark Bolton satirizing county supervisors during "Operation Pretense," a statewide FBI undercover investigation into corruption. (Courtesy of *The Clarion-Ledger*, Mark Bolton, cartoonist)

Editorial cartoon likening the self-inflicted fall of Dickie Scruggs to that of Saddam Hussein. (Courtesy of *The Clarion-Ledger*, Marshall Ramsey, cartoonist)

In the saddest development in the case, Zach Scruggs, son of Dickie Scruggs and a former student of the author, leaves the Oxford federal courthouse after pleading guilty to conspiracy. (*The Oxford Eagle*, Bruce Newman)

Dickie Scruggs in the custody of U.S. Marshals Neil Cruse and Scotty Peters after pleading guilty to bribery the second time. (*The Oxford Eagle*, Bruce Newman)

Former State Auditor and Democratic Party chairman Steve "Big Daddy" Patterson, aka "Kingfish," leaves the U.S. Courthouse after being indicted for bribery in the Dickie Scruggs case. (Courtesy of *The Clarion-Ledger*, Ryan Moore, photographer)

Judge Henry Lackey testifying in the Scruggs case.

Truck driver Richard Hall, Jr., CEO of the ill-fated Mississippi Beef Plant.

A series of brilliant editorial cartoons by Marshall Ramsey of the *Clarion-Ledger* satirizing state officials during the Mississippi Beef Plant investigation.

Jay Scott Ballinger, the so-called "black-church arsonist," and his girl friend and accomplice from California. They burned scores of rural churches across the South. As it turned out, Ballinger, a native of Indiana, did not target black churches at all, but all rural churches based allegedly on abuse he suffered during a harsh fundamentalist childhood. He is serving life without parole. (Courtesy of *The Daily Corinthian*)

The Ku Klux Klan in north Mississippi is greatly weakened, but not yet totally dead, as reflected in this November 2009 photo accompanying the story by *Daily Journal* writer Melanie Addington of a Klan meeting in a double-wide trailer near Tupelo in Robert E. Lee County. The author took a special interest in the Klan because two of his ancestors were members.

Emmett Louis Till Jr., a fourteen-year-old visitor from Chicago, was kidnapped from his grandparents' home in Money, Mississippi, in 1955. He allegedly whistled at or touched a white woman and was murdered for doing it, igniting the civil rights revolution. Mississippi Attorney General Jim Hood appointed the author a special assistant district attorney to assist D. A. Joyce Chiles of Greenville and the FBI in reopening the nation's coldest case, which finally resolved many open questions surrounding Till's murder trial of his killers. (Courtesy of the Tallahatchie County Visitors' Bureau)

Prosecutor Charlie Spillers in his former life as an undercover narc for the Baton Rouge P.D. and the Mississippi Bureau of Narcotics, posing very believably as a hired hitman. Charlie is now writing a colorful memoir entitled "Confessions of an Undercover Agent."

Ronald Glen Shaw, known as the "Natchez Trace Sniper," was convicted of using a high-powered rifle in the Christmas-night murder in 1980 of a nine-year-old boy who was riding home on the historic Natchez Trace Parkway after visiting his grandparents. Shaw will be eligible for release in the year 2024. (Courtesy *The Commercial Appeal*, Sabrina Long)

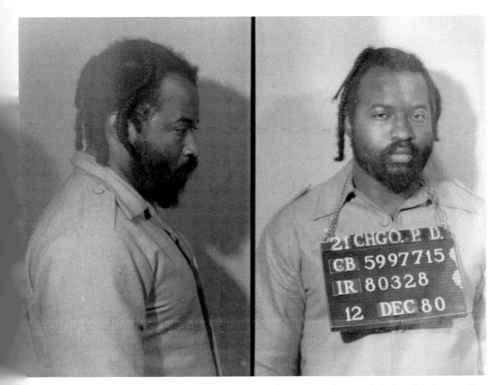

he infamous Jeff Fort, an Aberdeen, Mississippi, native who became the dreaded "Angel of Fear," leader the El Rukn and Blackstone Nation street gangs in Chicago. (U.S. Marshal's booking photo)

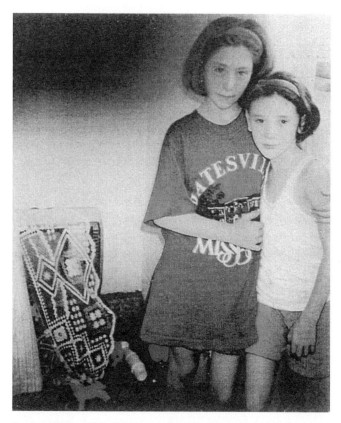

Sara and Megan El-Sarji, kidnapped and held captive in Lebanon for ten years until their mother rescued them in a story eerily reminiscent of the movie *Not Without My Daughter*, starring Sally Field.

Dr. Abdel Ashqar, Ole Miss graduate student and international secretary of the Palestinian terrorist organization HAMAS, convicted in Chicago and sentenced to eleven years' confinement for criminal contempt of court.

Terrorist turned protected witness Adnan "Captain Joe" Awad on a U.S. Navy ship near Athens, Greece. He sued the Federal Witness Protection Program in Mississippi and lost, but he later gained a reward and U.S. citizenship for his courageous and helpful testimony against Iraqi terrorists. He and the author became friends during the trial.

إلى أنسان اتخذ موقف
ضدي في المحكمة
رغم ذلك لي الشرف
أن أكون صديقاً له
عدنان عواد

To a man, I consider a friend,
even when he fights against me
Enshallah! Adnan Awad

TERRORIST

The Inside Story of the
Highest-Ranking Iraqi Terrorist
Ever to Defect to the West

Steven A. Emerson
and Cristina Del Sesto

VILLARD BOOKS
New York
1991

came straight from a fancy party wearing an elegant tuxedo. Henry "Scoop" Jackson of Washington, always energetic and talkative, paced the floor for hours as we waited. The TV reporters were less respectful. All of them wanted details, the more gruesome the better. Several were updating the prepared obituaries they already had on film, primed to run when the senator died. They always referred to him as the "powerful" chairman of the armed services committee; as if powerful were his first name. Sam Donaldson, eyebrows twitching frantically as always, asked every three minutes, "Is he still alive? What are his chances? Have they caught the shooters?" It was a spectacle I'll never forget, and it created in me a disdain for some broadcast media I've never really shaken. The print reporters, however, were both somber and respectful, and despite their deadlines, exhibited an attitude of seriousness and sorrow more fitting the occasion.

After midnight, Eph Cresswell came out with lead military surgeon Robert Muir. Dr. Muir said there was good news and bad news. The good news was that the senator had arrived at the perfect time. The top surgeons, all with extensive battlefield experience in Vietnam treating grievous gunshot wounds, were still on duty. Thirty minutes later and most would have been off duty, having their first drink of the evening and thus could not have operated. The team which did the surgery was perhaps more qualified than any team anywhere in the world.

All the other news was bad. The first wound, to the senator's left leg, had struck the bone, but rather than breaking the bone had itself broken in several pieces. They got the larger ones out but did not get every piece, which would later cause infection. The second bullet, from a .22 caliber pistol, had done extensive damage. A hollow-point "police round" with a copper jacket, it had been manufactured to cause maximum destruction and it had done so. Muir said that if the senator had been a healthy twenty-year-old with that wound found on a battlefield in Vietnam, they would have considered him beyond saving and given him plenty of morphine to decrease the suffering from being gutshot and medivac'd him out to die comfortably in a hospital.

The bullet had passed through the Senator's stomach and cut completely in two his portal vein, the major vein that brings blood back to the heart from the lower half of the body. Because he was such a public figure and crucial to the military, they had gone to extraordinary lengths to save him, despite his extremely limited chance of survival. With the best equipment in the world, they performed experimental surgery on his portal vein, splicing it with a cow's vein, which they expected his body would reject. There was no other vein in his own body large enough to use. Despite the odds, Dr. Muir said that because the senator had been in excellent physical condition, there was a chance the experiment might work.

The likely fatal wound, however, was to the senator's pancreas, a thin, flat organ that produces vital enzymes. His pancreas, freakishly, had been cut cleanly in two pieces by the copper-jacketed hollow-point bullet. The pancreas could not be sewn back together and was secreting enzymes that would inevitably lead to massive internal infections which would inevitably lead within a few days to an agonizing death. In short, Dr. Muir felt that there was virtually no chance that the senator would live.

I drove Mildred home just before sunrise in a somber and depressed mood. It seemed so unfair. A man who had done so much for so many, who had not an enemy in the world that we knew of, was going to die for no good reason. After an hour or two of sleep, I picked up the *Washington Post* from my doorstep. The front page was all reports and speculation about the shooting of the respected senator. No one speculated that politics were involved, but everyone wondered if the shooters knew their victim was a prominent senator. If so, they certainly found a way to bring down the full weight of the U.S. government on their heads. The shooters would surely be caught and severely punished.

According to the scant details the senator gave his wife and the ambulance driver, he had had no money on his person but had offered them his expensive Swiss gold pocket watch on a gold chain that also held his Phi Beta Kappa key from the University of Virginia Law School. The FBI debated that night whether to keep that detail secret but decided there were so few leads that the watch was the one item that might be sold or pawned and thus lead them back to the shooters.

The veteran agents assigned to the case were eager to interview the senator, show him photographs of known robbers, and ask him to help a police artist make a sketch of the robbers, of whom the Senator had told the police there were two. They also knew that if they did not interview him soon that they might never have the chance since the doctors told them his death was imminent. On the occasions the surgeons let them speak to him, it was apparent that between the pain and the painkillers the senator was in no condition to give a coherent statement. He himself had the presence of mind to tell them he couldn't think straight enough to help them. Later, the attempts they did make to persuade him to describe his assailants were used against him at trial to impeach his testimony.

Meanwhile we waited. After two or three days, Dr. Muir told us, "He is the toughest old man I've ever seen. For some reason, his immune system has resisted all infection. It's remarkable." The cow's vein implant also seemed to be working. In terrible pain, the senator clung to life. After a week had passed, Dr. Muir's attitude began to change: "It defies medical science, but it appears possible he might make it. For anyone it would be a long shot, but for a man of seventy-two, it will be a miracle."

The miracle happened. Once it appeared he would make it, a temporary office was set up at the Walter Reed Hospital with several phones to answer all the sympathy calls. It was overwhelming how much good this one old man had done for so many people in his life and how grateful they were to him. The caller who touched me most was Dizzy Dean, the old St. Louis Cardinal pitcher from Wiggins, Mississippi whom I'd watched broadcast every Saturday of my childhood on the *Game of the Week*. During the seventh-inning stretch, Ole Diz would sing his version of "Wabash Cannonball," an unforgettable piece of the old America I grew up in. Dizzy Dean would call two or three times a week and never failed to break down and cry during our talks.

After several weeks, the senator was strong enough for the staff to visit him briefly, one at a time. When my moment came, he wasted no time on sympathy or office work: "The men that did this to me, I want them caught and punished—severely. From here on out, your sole and exclusive job will be to work with the police and the FBI and the prosecutors and make sure what they did to me does not go unpunished. I've told them all that you're to have access to everything and everyone. Make sure to contact me with anything you learn that you think I need to know. Don't try to 'protect me' from bad news or problems."

It was a heavy responsibility because so far there seemed to be no leads at all. But what surprised me most was the vigor of the senator's desire for revenge. It was deep and primordial, almost Shakespearean. I don't believe I'd ever seen anyone so furious or determined to get someone.

Perhaps it was the secret of his success in politics. He played hard, and he played for keeps. To this day, after over thirty years as a prosecutor, I have yet to see any victim quite as angry as the senator was.

For weeks, the investigation led nowhere. A whole team of the FBI's best agents worked tirelessly with D.C. detectives. Every informant was questioned, every pawn shop owner was leaned on. The U.S. Senate raised a large reward for information leading to an arrest. Nothing. Then one day, about six weeks after the shooting, while the senator lay in severe pain and the rest of us worked the phones, a break came. An off-duty D.C. sanitation worker called the police and said he had something. John Thomas was a big man, tall and broad and black, with a long black beard squared-off at the bottom. Twenty-eight years old and a devout Jehovah's Witness, Thomas called the police not to seek the reward (which he later got anyway) but just as a good citizen. His story had the ring of truth.

The day before, while he was driving near his home on 13th Street NE, a young fair-skinned black woman with orange hair dodged into the street in front of him from between two parked cars. She was bleeding from the head. Having barely avoided hitting her, Thomas made the block and went back to check on her. As he got there, an athletic young man who looked to be in his early twenties hit the woman hard on the head with a stick of wood. Thomas asked her if she was alright. The man interrupted, telling Thomas the woman was his wife and to butt out. To emphasize his point, the man hit the woman on the head again. When Thomas objected, the man angrily told him to go away, then asked him sarcastically, "You ain't the police, are you?" Thomas replied, "I could be," thinking it might cool the man down. Instead, it encouraged the woman: "You so damn smart, why don't you tell him how you shot that senator?" Thomas, who said he was just two or three feet from her when she said the words, asked her to repeat what she said.

Looking at her husband, the orange-haired women repeated it, louder than before: "Why don't you tell him how you and the other boys were in the Stennis shooting?" This time she actually used the senator's name. Thomas later insisted he asked her three or four times in all, and each time she said the same thing. The husband dropped his stick but said nothing, then finally yelled at her, "Are you crazy? He might be the police." As some young people walked by, the husband said to them, "This girl told him I was involved in the senator shooting." Then he again asked Thomas if he was the police. Thomas drove away without replying and flagged down the first police car he saw.

The northeast Washington area was then a nice old neighborhood of neat middle-class homes, formerly all white, but by 1973 mostly black. A good friend of mine lived on the street. The FBI quickly joined D.C. police in canvassing the neighborhood, focusing on social gathering spots. There was considerable hostility toward the police there, but because the FBI were federal and enforced the civil rights laws, they were somewhat better received by local residents. At a local record shop called the Psychedelic Haven (it was the age of LSD), the officers hit pay dirt. Several young men told the FBI and police both on and off the record what had happened. The robbers had bragged a lot about the shooting. The young men knew considerable detail concerning the robbery, including the fact that the senator had no money on him, that he had given the robbers a gold pocket watch which the witnesses had also seen, even the number of times the Senator was shot, and where the robbers had obtained the gun.

They all said the robbers were local residents John Marshall, known as "J. B." and his brother, Tyrone. The getaway driver was their friend, Derrick Holloway, who also furnished the gun. While John Marshall held the senator down, Tyrone was the shooter. He was also the leader and did all the talking during the robbery. It was Tyrone's orange-haired wife, Debra, who denounced him to witness John Thomas after Tyrone beat her on the head with a stick. The Stennis case was finally on its way.

There was still a lot of work to be done, and the agents and officers went after it with a fury. They knew who did it, now they had to persuade the witnesses to testify. Because most had criminal records, their statements had to be corroborated. The officers also hoped to find the gun and the watch. An intensive neighborhood investigation began. The police obtained a search warrant for the Marshall house but found nothing, not even news articles about the shooting. With the gun they had better luck. Through an amazing series of handoffs, the rusty old revolver, its chamber held in place by an improvised bolt, was located and seized. Confronted, Derrick Holloway confessed, implicating the others in detail.

Veteran assistant U.S. Attorney Roger Adelman, who later prosecuted John Hinckley Jr. for shooting President Ronald Reagan, was assigned to lead the prosecution team. His key assistant was Steve Grafman, a resourceful and vigorous young prosecutor. Adelman was tall, calm and imposing, and looked and sounded more like a senior judge than a prosecutor. Grafman brought a whiff of feisty southern enthusiasm to the team. U.S. Attorneys changed as the case went along, with Harold Titus being replaced by the famed Earl Silbert, long known as one of the nation's preeminent trial lawyers with the nickname "Earl the Pearl."

On March 12, 1973, a criminal complaint against Holloway and the Marshall brothers was served on them, and their arrests were made public less than two months after the shooting, showing some really good police work. But from that point on I began to see a dark side of the U.S. criminal justice system I'd somehow missed, despite what seemed to be my substantial experience as law clerk and attorney. The first problem concerned bail for the defendants. Despite numerous threats to the witnesses, in the nation's capital pretty much every defendant was released on bond and free to intimidate the witnesses against him. Prosecutors requested a $100,000 bond on Tyrone Marshall, but a federal magistrate quickly reduced it to $25,000. Another magistrate reduced it to just $10,000, with only a 10 percent or $1,000 security deposit required. It meant that if anyone would deposit $1,000 with the court clerk (which they would get back after the trial), the shooter would be a free man, despite the fact that he was already on probation from another case and faced indictment in two more street robberies. Washington began to look like a jungle and the legal system a joke. The $1,000 bond was appealed, but fortunately the judge who got the case was Chief Judge John Sirica, of Watergate fame, a former boxer and law and order Eisenhower appointee. He refused to reduce the already ridiculously low bond any further.

Tyrone Marshall still could find no one to go his bond. His parents refused, as did his friends, who apparently felt safer with him locked up, because he didn't know which ones had told on him and which ones hadn't. The FBI and D.C. police did their part by letting it be known that numerous neighborhood witnesses had implicated the robbers, thus giving some anonymity to the handful of real witnesses. The Marshalls did not know who to intimidate.

Then out of the blue came a weird phone call. A worker at the home office of the Church of Scientology near the Hilton Hotel called to say she believed that the three men arrested for the shooting of the senator, whose pictures she'd seen in the *Washington Post*, had been at services at the Scientology Church that same night. If so, they would have been required to show an ID and sign in, and the time they arrived would have been noted. These rules existed not just to discourage the frequent robberies in the area, but to help the Scientologists proselytize and make new converts. When we heard, we collectively groaned. We all knew the wacko reputation of the Scientologists and doubted that the conservative Christian black women who made up the majority of D.C. juries would be likely to take them seriously.

My own experiences with Scientologists were probably typical. They trolled the streets in front of the Wine & Cheese Shop where I worked part-time during law school and on weekends. Their beliefs were, to put it mildly, not mainstream. And if they were presented with a Bible to take an oath as a witness, we hated to think what their responses might be. My personal low moment with them had happened a few months earlier, after a trip to Montana with Senator Stennis when I'd caught a late night cab from Capitol Hill to Georgetown. As I got into the cab, I noticed on the seat a stack of books by L. Ron Hubbard, founder of the cult, whose name sounded more like a lawyer than a high priest of a new religion. The cabbie unfortunately saw me look at his books and launched into a spiel on the marvels of Scientology. It was surreal, farther out than most science fiction. To be polite I asked what he got from practicing Scientology. He'd only been practicing a couple of years but was totally committed. His ultimate goal was to get a "clear." He explained in Zen-like terms that a "clear" was a state of the soul where your every feeling is at one with the rhythm of the universe, a sort of nirvana which he said he'd obtained briefly on a couple of occasions. His problem was he couldn't remember what the conditions were that allowed him to reach that state, but said he would just keep hoping and studying L. Ron Hubbard. Maybe L. Ron's people could give us some corroboration about Tyrone and his buddies, maybe give me a "clear."

A whole team of investigators spent days questioning the Scientologists who had been at their temple on the night of the shooting. They found all three defendants' signatures on the sign-in sheet, showing the three young men were together not long after the shooting. Police figured defendants had foolishly thought they would show they were somewhere else that evening, but it in fact not only put them together but seemed suspiciously like an attempt to do just what they intended: establish an alibi. Investigators timed the potential routes from the senator's home to the Scientology church and proved that the robbers could easily have done the crime and still have had plenty of time to check in at the time noted on the Scientologists' records.

Prosecutors Adelman and Grafman were busy. Realizing the testimony of the neighborhood street dudes might not stand up and facing a motion from Tyrone Marshall's attorney to exclude his wife's statement as out-of-court hearsay, they got a court order compelling Derrick Holloway to testify. The order was for what is called "use" immunity, meaning the witness must testify against his codefendants, but his testimony could not be used against him in his own trial. The court had already ordered a separate trial for Holloway from the Marshalls so his confession could not be used against him in his own trial but would have been introduced against the Marshall brothers only. This court-created rule is called the *Bruton* rule and is a reasonable safeguard for the accused.

When ordered to testify under use immunity at a pretrial hearing, Holloway refused, and the trial judge ordered him jailed for civil contempt. Holloway ignored the order. What was a little jail time to him when he faced possible life imprisonment as a principal in the notorious shooting of a U.S. Senator? The prosecutors had a weak case and the defendants knew it.

Tyrone's wife was so fearful she would be killed to prevent her testimony that the FBI hid her out with relatives until trial. Derrick Holloway, in return for his eyewitness testimony, demanded absolute immunity or "a walk" as detectives say, that is, that all charges against him be dismissed and that he be allowed to walk off scot-free. Even then we were not sure he would ever tell the truth. With the judicial system as weak as it was, what would keep him from lying? It was a quandary.

The wheels of justice began to turn, however slowly. Co-defendant John Marshall, the older of the brothers at age twenty-one, decided to plead guilty. His motives were entirely manipulative. Under a federal law at the time (since mercifully repealed) defendants under age twenty-two on the date of sentencing were entitled to plead guilty conditionally, to serve a much shorter term, then have their record expunged or canceled if they behaved. John Marshall's eligibility for such favorable treatment would expire on his twenty-second birthday. He therefore pled guilty, sort of. His lawyer helped him beat the system, however. Under *Alford*, which was then a recent decision of the U.S. Supreme Court,[2] defendants were allowed to plead guilty and still claim they were innocent. The hare-brained basis for this decision was the anti-death penalty movement. Defendants, usually those facing the death penalty, could plead guilty and receive life imprisonment, often with the possibility of being paroled.

In that context the *Alford* decision had at least some logic behind it, but courts immediately expanded the *Alford* precedent well beyond its original purpose, especially courts like the D.C. Circuit. In the case of John Marshall, he claimed he was innocent while technically pleading guilty. He also refused to testify against his brother Tyrone and codefendant Derrick Holloway. Over the strong objections of the prosecution, the trial judge permitted this maneuver.

With John Marshall's case disposed of and Derrick Holloway set for a separate trial, the prosecutors were able to focus on the shooter, Tyrone Marshall. Trial was set for June 1973, but Senator Stennis developed complications from the second bullet, the one that devastated his internal organs and settled near his spine. The bullet had begun to move and Dr. Muir decided it was finally safe, in fact necessary, to remove it. The operation was again long and recovery painful, but successful. The trial was reset for October 1973. Preparations for the trial were probably the most tense and interesting thing I'd experienced in my young life as a lawyer. Handling the witnesses was a nightmare. Holloway, the key witness, still refused to testify, as did John Marshall, who was not very believable anyway. The flaky crew at Scientology tried to help but could really prove nothing except that the three defendants were all together in one car around two hours after the Stennis shooting, possibly trying to establish an alibi. That left just two major sources of evidence: Tyrone's wife and his friends, to whom he had confessed and who could trace custody of the gun. But the friends were naturally reluctant and possibly unreliable witnesses. And Tyrone's wife Debra could testify only to Tyrone's failure to deny her accusation to John Thomas that Tyrone had participated in the robbery and shooting. Any confessions made to her by her husband in private would usually have been barred by the time-honored marital privilege. Since medieval England, that rule of evidence has treated statements between spouses as confidential and never admissible in court, the theory being to encourage trust within the bonds of matrimony. There are, however, exceptions to the marital privilege. One exception is when a statement between spouses is made in the presence of a third party, in this case the garbage collector who courageously intervened when Tyrone was beating his wife and then called the police and reported her statements. A different legal problem arose from that statement. It was not a statement by Tyrone, but by his wife, and as such was normally inadmissible as hearsay, another curious technicality of Anglo-Saxon law, which courts have spent centuries dealing with. Never let a lawyer tell you hearsay is easy. It is not. In non-English-speaking countries, the concept does not even exist. In all other countries statements by one witness about what someone said to him out of court is simply treated as secondary evidence—that is, not as reliable as if you heard the witness say it himself, but admissible for what it's worth.

In the Stennis case, however, there was a classic exception to the exception: admission by silence. This old rule says that when someone is accused, in the presence of a third party, of wrongdoing that an innocent person would normally deny, the accused will be assumed to have admitted the accusation unless he denies it. On that slender reed rested what was perhaps the most convincing part of the prosecution's case.

Ken Mundy, the able attorney appointed to represent Tyrone Marshall, made every argument he could to keep Debra's statement out, citing every known case where respected judges had excluded such evidence. He even had some support for his argument that Tyrone had implicitly denied the accusation, stressing Tyrone's statement his wife was "crazy" to say that. But that statement was ambiguous because it could be interpreted to mean that Tyrone just meant she was crazy to reveal his boast about shooting the senator to a man who might be with the police.

In the end the decision came down to a purely discretionary judgment call by the trial judge, Joseph Waddy, a serious and dignified black man known as a solid judge even if he had something of a soft spot for young black defendants and had to answer to the then-radically liberal D.C. Circuit Court of Appeals, led by judicial activist judges J. Skelly Wright and David Bazelon. Judge Waddy carefully considered this difficult question and decided the statement was worthy of consideration by the jury. To those who heard the statements directly from the witnesses, in context, they were powerfully credible. As authority for his decision, Judge Waddy cited a persuasive source, Warren Burger, recently named chief justice of the U.S. Supreme Court by President Richard Nixon. While serving as a judge on the D.C. Circuit, then-Judge Burger had approved admission-by-silence evidence under circumstances similar to the Stennis case. With that ruling, the prosecution at least had a chance of winning the trial, even though they knew a black D.C. jury would not think highly of a prominent segregationist senator from Mississippi. They did have a theoretically winnable case, but more than once approached the senator about giving absolute immunity to Holloway who, after all, "only" drove the getaway car and never personally attacked the senator. But the senator was adamant. "That man gave them the gun that nearly killed me and changed my life forever. I will never consent to his getting off scot-free."

As jury selection began, things immediately began to go wrong. U.S. Marshals reported improper contacts with jurors in the courthouse cafeteria by a man "with a peculiar-shaped head." Jurors said he told them his son was on trial and reminded the jurors of when they were all in junior high school together. A retired teacher said he reminded her of when he was a janitor at her school. The man was accompanied by an "orange-haired woman parading up and down" with a small child in tow, said to be the defendant's child. The marshals said the jurors would identify the jury tamperer by name if asked.

Judge Waddy cut right to the heart of the matter: "It's clearly Joseph Marshall, the father of the defendant, who has just what the jurors recognized, an unusual contour of his head." Out in the courtroom Joseph Marshall sat with a hat on, but the judge was not fooled. He asked the prosecutors and defense attorneys if they thought this would "poison the jury" either way. They conferred and decided the same thing might happen with any jury in that venue. Washington, D.C., has some surprising attributes of a small town where everyone from certain social circles knows everyone else.

The jury selection did have its light moments. In D.C., as in many federal jurisdictions, the *voir dire* or questioning of potential jurors was conducted mainly by the judge, not the attorneys. When one elderly man said he didn't know if he could be away from his wife for two weeks because she had a serious heart condition, the following colloquy occurred:

Judge Waddy: "Is she ambulatory?"

Juror: "No, sir, she's not."

Judge Waddy: "How does she get around?"

Juror: "Well, walking seems to help her some."

Within several hours a jury was selected, all black citizens with two black alternates. The prosecutors had helped strike some of the tiny handful of whites on the panel based on their answers expressing hostility to law enforcement and reluctance to convict based on objections to what they considered overly harsh punishments of blacks. They were D.C. liberals and didn't want to look prejudiced.

One critical issue remained to be resolved. It had never been finally decided whether the senator would endeavor to identify in open court Tyrone Marshall as the man who shot him. While in the hospital, over his objections, he was repeatedly asked to describe the man who shot him. There were conflicts between interviewing officers, some saying the senator said the man was as short as 5', 8" and as old as forty, while others said he said he was as young as sixteen and the same height and weight as the senator, which he was. Fearing the conflicts would give the jury an excuse to doubt the whole case, the prosecutors promised the judge and the defense attorney they would not attempt an in-court identification by the senator, and there was therefore no hearing on the reliability of any ID.

The senator, however, was adamant about identifying Marshall in court: "I was nose-to-nose with that man for a considerable time. I looked into his eyes. I believe now that I'm well, I can identify him. How can a victim be prohibited from identifying his attacker? Where is the justice in that?" After considerable discussion, we arrived at a solution. If the senator honestly believed he could ID the man in court, he would signal us by putting both elbows on the ledge in front of the witness stand and locking his fingers together. We did not tell the judge or defense counsel this was our signal. It nearly blew the case.

The trial began with Senator Stennis as the first witness. He was led into the courtroom by a black Deputy Marshal past the fourteen black jurors, the black court reporter, court clerk, and probation officers. He and Judge Waddy nodded respectfully to each other. The courtroom was filled mainly with supporters of the defendant and his large family. I know there must have been reporters there, but media attention had decreased concerning the trial itself, no doubt due to the many delays. I honestly now don't recall which reporters were there. For a man of the senator's background and experience of white supremacy, the courtroom scene had to be surreal. The only white faces I recall were the prosecutors and Eph Cresswell and me behind them. At the first recess, I spoke with the senator knowing we could not talk about his testimony, but asked him how, as a former trial judge himself, he felt about the courtroom scene. "Well, I just thought for a moment there I'd died and woke up in hell."

It is impossible to give a flavor of the trial and the senator's old-style demeanor and diction without quoting directly from the transcript of his trial testimony. His voice, since his recovery, had returned to its former vibrant, ringing sonority. Of all 100 members of the Senate, he had perhaps the strongest voice. He had a seriousness and a dignity, without bombast or pomposity, which were reminiscent of the nineteenth century. If you've never heard it, it's hard to re-create. Not one member of the current Senate, north or south, retains it.

Roger Adelman asked the senator, as is normally done, what he did for a living. When he said he was chairman of the Senate Armed Services Committee, the defense objected that was irrelevant. Remarkably, they were sustained. Turning to the night of January 23, the senator told of the National Guard reception and his ride home. He said he drove a brand-new white Buick, "they call them Electras now," and how he parked his car in his usual space right in front of his house, which his neighbors never parked in "as a courtesy." He said he left the Senate office building at around 7:30 P.M. and took his accustomed route home: down Constitution Avenue, up Virginia through Rock Creek Park, turning onto Massachusetts at the big Muslim mosque, across 34th Street to his own quiet street, Cumberland, which is only two blocks long in Chevy Chase, D.C. As he pulled in, "a car shot by me, gunning the motor." As the senator reached back into his car to get his dry cleaning, he saw two men coming toward him "at a sort of lope. The one on the street bumped me and said, 'This means money. We want money and we're going to have it.' By his expression I knew he meant business. I reached for my money, which I always keep in my pocket in a simple paperclip and realized I had trouble. I had given all my cash to Miss Coy that morning to buy groceries. The only money I had was three thin dimes and a nickel."

The senator tried to make a run for his house, but the second man blocked him, pushing him up against his car. One of them struck him a hard blow to the head with something, bloodying him. The senator continued his account: "I knew what his demand meant, but I wasn't in any way to cope with it, so I undertook to outtalk him. I tried to keep the matter subdued and quiet, to negotiate a settlement. I pulled out of my pocket an old-style gold pocket watch given to me several years before in Europe. It had a gold chain and my Phi Beta Kappa key. I told him it was appraised recently for $800. I always wear a wristwatch, but it was in the shop for repairs. All I had was this antique one." The defense counsel objected that what an appraiser told the senator was hearsay. Judge Waddy overruled, saying simply, "The man can value his own watch." The point was important because to be a felony under D.C. law, the property stolen in a robbery had to be valued at over $500.

The senator continued:

> The men pushed me into the car, and the second man tried to crush me to the ground. I came out and broke his tackle, which surprised me. He was muscled up pretty good, but so was I from years of gymnasium work. I seemed stronger than him, which really surprised me. Things were moving mighty fast by then. The mean expression on his face became more pronounced. Then for the first time I saw the gun. I saw only the barrel. The second man was still blocking my flight, trying to push me down. I visualized if I went to the ground the first one would shoot me in the head. I began shouting to give the alarm. Talking was over. Then I saw smoke from the gun barrel. One bullet had hit me just below the heart area. I don't recall the other.

The senator recalled the shooter saying, "I'm going to kill you anyway," then watched as "they withdrew, making sounds of jubilation or triumph." The senator said he walked up the steps and into his house and told his wife what happened and to "call Walter Reed Hospital. I feel faint and must be going into shock. I knew I was seriously wounded and in great pain." He testified a man soon said, "We are the ambulance," to which, amazingly, an objection was sustained to hearsay again. Another voice said, "Take him to the nearest hospital, George Washington." The senator had just enough strength to order them, "No, no, take me to Walter Reed. They have the surgeons I will need."

When asked to describe his main assailant, the senator said, "He was about my height, 5', 11", and weight, I weigh 171 pounds today. I weighed at the Senate. I could see him well, up real close. Now, I see a gentleman over there at the table—" The senator was clearly about to make a forbidden in-court eyewitness identification. Roger Adelman stopped him.

Defense Counsel Ken Mundy moved for a mistrial because the prosecution had breached its promise to allow an out-of-court hearing before an in-court identification was attempted. I felt terrible. My only job was to watch for the senator's signal, but I'd never seen it during the hour or so he testified. I had blown it. Judge Waddy excused the jury and had the senator continue his testimony: "I've been noticing this gentleman since I sat here. He's in a green jacket, turtle top. I had a good chance to look at him while the Bible was being obtained for the oath. After that he's kept his eyes mostly closed and averted. But I'd like to be closer to him. I believe that's the man that had the pistol."

After lengthy arguments, Judge Waddy ruled that the senator would be prohibited from making an in-court ID, but that his statement before the jury was ambiguous: "He could have been about to say Mr. Marshall was *not* the man." The crucial motion for mistrial was denied. The judge personally addressed the senator on the stand, knowing he was used to having his own way and difficult to control. The senator was still reluctant: "I will gladly obey, Your Honor, but based on my observations, and the attorneys know nothing about this . . ." Judge Waddy then raised his hand, and the senator said, "Very well . . . all right . . . I will obey the court." Defense Attorney Mundy perceptively said, "I'm afraid to cross-examine him now. Who knows how I might open the door for him to make an ID?" Judge Waddy told him to do the best he could.

After lunch, Mundy tried to cross-examine the senator, asking him details, suggesting that if his client had stolen the watch, it should have been found. The senator described it: "The watch was a work of art, trim and nice-looking, about the size of a silver dollar." When asked whether the senator himself fought robbers, he replied firmly, "No, there was communication between us, but it was totally ineffective because of his demands." When asked if he did not misidentify his attacker at the hospital the senator denied it, "It was against my judgment to talk at the hospital at all with all the drugs and pain. They wanted me to make a sketch, but I could not. I was not conscious but a moment." He flatly denied any misidentification: "I was talking all out of my head. My first real conscious moment was several days later." When Judge Waddy agreed the senator could stand down, their mutual courtesy was a tribute to the legal system given the intense racial animosity in the country, especially in Washington and in that case.

The prosecution next called Derrick Holloway, in chambers, after agents had searched for hours for his lawyer, who was habitually absent. The lawyer promptly moved to have Holloway dismissed as a witness, claiming the prosecutors had committed misconduct by leaning on him too hard to testify: "Their relations with my client have been so tainted they should have no right to harass him further." At that point I thought to myself that my father had been right. Lawyers are lying parasites and our legal system is a joke. Judge Waddy restored my faith: "Motion denied. The witness will testify now or remain in jail." Tyrone Marshall's attorney then demanded a copy of the written confession Holloway had signed. Judge Waddy denied that too: "Since he refuses to testify, you don't need it to cross-examine him."

The prosecution then called John Thomas, the key to the case. Tall and calm with a firm voice, he readily identified Tyrone Marshall as the man who was beating his wife Debra's head bloody with a stick when she blurted out that "he and some other guys did the Stennis shooting." Thomas insisted she said it three or four times, even as other men walked by during the beating. These men were never located. Thomas told how Tyrone said, "You crazy girl, he might be the police." To the passersby, he also said, "This girl told them I was involved in the Stennis shooting," before hitting her again. On cross-examination, as good witnesses will often do, Thomas got even stronger. "The man was in a rage. He said what he did was none of my business. No way did he deny doing it."

The next three witnesses, all teenage neighbors of the defendant, turned out to be surprisingly strong. The first, eighteen, had known Tyrone Marshall since junior high. He testified he saw Marshall the day after the shooting at the Psychedelic Haven record shop and Tyrone bragged, "I shot the dude twice. He wouldn't quit hollering. All we got was a quarter or so and an old watch. Derrick was driving. We robbed another old dude later on our way home. I didn't know he was a senator till we heard it on the radio." Defense counsel got nowhere on cross and quickly quit.

The next witness, age nineteen, said he didn't see Tyrone Marshall till the following weekend, walking home from the record shop. Marshall told him he shot the senator while robbing him. When asked why he did it, Marshall "just laughed. He tried to sell me the man's watch, but

I didn't want it." On cross he also got stronger. When asked if he hadn't first told the police Marshall only said he was "involved," the witness looked defense counsel in the eye and calmly said, "When I had more time to think, more of it came back to me." He was totally believable.

The next witness, also nineteen, knew all three defendants well. One day in early February he was riding around with Holloway, who showed him the gun used in the shooting. Holloway drove him to the Marshall house and called out Tyrone, who said, "Yeah, that's the gun. I shot the dude twice with it and gave it to P. W." According to the witness, P. W. had used the same gun to shoot someone else in another robbery. When confronted, apparently in the witness's presence, P. W. gave the gun to the FBI. On cross the witness was asked if he knew there was a reward and how much it was. "Yeah. $60,000." Asked if that was his motive for testifying, he admitted he wanted the reward but said he had told the truth to the FBI before he read about any reward.

At this point Juror #3 asked aloud if he could question the witness. As is customary, the judge refused. We never found out what the questions were but wished the judge had let him submit the questions in writing for the judge to ask if they were proper. But that sort of thing can of course quickly get out of hand. Everyone might have wanted to play Perry Mason so the judge was probably right.

The next witness was Dr. Muir. He testified as an expert in gunshot wounds, noting that he had performed over ten thousand surgeries on such wounds during Vietnam from 1967 to 1970, mostly at hospitals in Japan. He had been a career surgeon with the U.S. Army for thirteen years. Dr. Muir testified he first saw Senator Stennis at 8:05 p.m. at Walter Reed Hospital. The Senator was cold and clammy and in extreme pain. The jurors looked surprisingly indifferent, several even looking away, which was unusual and an extremely bad sign for us. Muir told how he had retrieved the main portion of the bullet from the Senator's leg and had initialed it with an "M." He confirmed saying following the first surgery that the senator "would not survive." The jury looked as indifferent as ever. Muir said the senator was on heavy narcotics through April. In all, the senator spent six months in Walter Reed Hospital. On cross, the defense attorney, probably sensing the jurors' apparent lack of sympathy, belittled the injuries, asking if the senator wasn't allowed to go home on weekends and even fly to Mississippi in April for two days.

Tracing the would-be murder weapon was challenging. T. B. Hester, a federally licensed firearm dealer from Georgia, testified he sold the pistol, a classic Saturday night special, to a Tommy Thornton. Thornton then testified that he, a resident of Georgia, bought the gun illegally for his cousin, who lived on 13th Street in NE Washington near the Marshalls. The cousin wanted the gun but could not buy it legally because of Washington, D.C., gun-control laws. He testified he sold the gun in January 1973, just before Senator Stennis was shot, along with a half-box of hollow-point "copperhead" bullets for $40. Several other witnesses testified how, after the shooting, the gun had passed from hand to hand and was finally pawned for $15. One testified when he got the gun he dropped it and the pin that held the chamber in place fell out and he wired the gun together with a piece of coat hanger. By such threads hang human life.

An FBI firearms expert with twenty years' experience testified he examined and test-fired the gun. He testified he had not only a Ph.D. but was the one who examined for the Warren Commission the rifle Lee Harvey Oswald used to assassinate President John F. Kennedy. He said the RG22 had eight grooves with a right-hand twist and, as the friends of Marshall had said, was wired together with a coat hanger because the cylinder pin was missing. He said it still fired with deadly effect. He said in conclusion only that the gun *could* have fired the bullet extracted from the senator.

On cross the defense attorney made full use of this weakness. He showed the FBI expert eleven other RG22s with eight grooves and two right-hand twists. The expert said the bullets could not be matched because the gun was so old the grooves in the barrel were full of lead from the hundreds of slugs fired through it and there were not enough "micromarks" to ID the bullet. Defense attorney Mundy asked if it were not a fact that at least a thousand other RG22s could have fired that bullet. The expert, surprisingly, volunteered it could be a hundred thousand. Later, in argument, the prosecutor tried to explain to the jury that they put the expert on to show they had left no stone unturned in investigating the case. They claimed they wanted to show nothing was hidden. The jury did not look convinced.

At this low moment, with Holloway still refusing to testify without complete immunity, the prosecutors had no one else to call but the Scientologists. The first, ironically named Duke Snyder like the famed Dodger centerfielder, identified church records showing Tyrone Marshall signed in to receive instruction on Scientology on the night Senator Stennis was shot. Other church staff indicated Marshall came in around 9:15, their records being "loosely done," but they all clearly remembered the Marshalls and Holloway because Scientologist recruits were almost invariably white and those three were "strange" in their attitudes and dress, with bright-colored clothes and cornrowed hair, a fashion then fairly new. Our informal conclusion on the prosecution side was that if you looked strange to a Scientologist, you must be pretty strange.

Irby Todd, a questioned document examiner or handwriting expert with a Ph.D. and twenty-three years' experience with U.S. Treasury, who had testified in over 15,000 cases and taught for seventeen years at the Secret Service School, testified that he interviewed Tyrone Marshall and took handwriting samples from him. Todd said Marshall had a unique handwriting style easily distinguishable from all others, and it was easy to conclude defendant wrote the signature "Tyrone Marshall" on the Scientology sign-in sheet. Interestingly, Todd said it was equally easy to see that Marshall had attempted to disguise his writing on the samples he gave, but that he didn't know what to change and that his attempts to deceive just made it clearer that he was the writer of his signature.

Defense Attorney Mundy announced "I don't plan to cross." Judge Waddy said he didn't see "how this is relevant" to the shooting, but let the testimony stand just to show the three defendants were together that same night.

Finally, on Thursday, October 4, prosecutor Adelman announced to Judge Waddy that Holloway had at last given them a full and believable account of the robbery and shooting the night before, but still refused to testify. They had decided to give Holloway full and absolute immunity and dismiss all charges against him. Defense attorney Ken Mundy asked for access to Holloway to interview him more fully to reevaluate his position on whether to go forward with the trial or enter a plea.

The Wednesday night before that announcement was one of the most difficult of my personal and professional life. The whole prosecution team had worked for months to persuade Senator Stennis to agree to immunity for Holloway. He had always adamantly refused, and they had honored his wishes. Now we were down to the ultimate decision. None of us liked the look or feel of the jury. The senator had not been in the courtroom for two weeks like we had. Finally Roger Adelman approached me. "John, the senator trusts you like a son. He trusts your judgment. You've got to convince him. Otherwise we've lost the case. The jury is against us."

With that flattering statement in my ears, I called the senator and asked to meet with him at the office that evening. I was sure he knew what it was about. Because of the rule on witnesses that says no one can tell a witness what other witnesses have said until the trial is over, I could not tell him what had happened. We sat at the long mahogany table in his senate office. He asked me how the trial was going. I apologized for the mix-up on the eyewitness ID, and he brushed it off. I told him the jury did not look good. Any fair jury would convict. The FBI and police and prosecutors had done a magnificent job, but with this jury we were simply going to lose the case. "What do you propose, then?" He knew full well what I would say, but we had to play it out. "Holloway has finally given us everything. He is smart and articulate. Ken Mundy is hinting he'll plead Tyrone guilty if Holloway testifies."

As I expected, the senator bristled. "You propose to let that man off entirely? The other one already got a light sentence, might even get it expunged. What's the use?" The senator was pale and drawn, many pounds lighter than when we had dove-hunted together in Virginia that fall and fly-fished together in Montana. I could not hurt the man but absolutely had to get him over this hump. I remained silent because I didn't know what to say, something my father always advised me to do. "Are you all unanimous?" His resistance was breaking. "Yes sir, all of us." He shook his head sadly. "I never thought I would see the day." He looked me deep in the eyes and said something that chilled me: "I trust your motives, and I have to trust your judgment. I don't know enough myself. I will never approve it, but I will not object to whatever you do. Make the best decision you can." When I told the others later that evening, we all had the same reaction: What a responsibility we had to that man. We had to make the right decision. We hoped we had.

When court opened the next morning, Roger Adelman stood up in the presence of the jury and stated: "We call as our next witness the codefendant, Derrick Holloway." The jurors finally looked interested. Ken Mundy asked to approach the bench. "We are ready to plead, Your Honor." The jury was dismissed, Tyrone Marshall pled guilty, speaking disrespectfully to Judge Waddy, saying "Yeah" to most of his questions and often ignoring the judge altogether. Once again over government objection, Marshall asked to plead under *Alford*, insisting he was not guilty but claiming through his lawyer that as a tactical matter they could not overcome the government's evidence.

Judge Waddy accepted the *Alford* plea and called the fourteen jurors back into the courtroom and told them only this: "Ladies and gentlemen, this case has been disposed of. Your services will no longer be necessary. With the thanks of the court, you are finally discharged." I stood there wanting to jump and shout but held myself in check. As Roger and Steve and I quietly shook hands with Eph Cresswell and the FBI agents, the second alternate juror came out of the jury box right up to me. We had made quite a bit of eye contact during the trial. He had a fully shaved head, not yet then a fashion, and had rings on all eight of his fingers. He asked, fairly enough I thought, "Say, man, what happened?" I told him Tyrone Marshall had pled guilty, and the judge would sentence him later. He said, "No way, man. We already talked. That dude didn't do nothing. It was all made up. We were going to cut him aloose." I looked at the rings on the alternate's fingers and wondered if our jury system could survive.

On March 22, 1974, just days before sentencing, defense attorney Ken Mundy moved the court to allow Tyrone Marshall to withdraw his guilty plea entered in October 1973. He claimed prosecutors had tricked him and committed misconduct by first saying they would never give any defendant immunity, then doing so. He also said that since the plea was entered, Holloway had been convicted of a separate street robbery and sent to prison. If a new trial was ordered, that conviction could be used to damage his credibility and the government's case would be weakened. And, after all, Tyrone Marshall still insisted he was innocent.

The prosecutor's reply was succinct. Tyrone Marshall did not deserve to get away with such a game. Since his plea, he had been convicted of two other robberies in D.C. Superior Court. His real motive for wanting to withdraw his plea was Judge Waddy's recent ruling that he would not be allowed to benefit from being sentenced as a youthful offender. He was too hard-core. He would be sentenced as an adult. Again the prosecutors relied on Justice Burger as their support, citing another recent U.S. Supreme Court case, ironically named *Brady v. U.S.*,[3] which held that a defendant was not entitled to withdraw his plea merely because he discovered after the plea was accepted that "his calculus misapprehended the quality of the state's case or the penalties attached to alternative courses of action." Judge Waddy agreed. Tyrone Marshall had finally lost.

Months later, after many hearings and much analysis of Tyrone Marshall's possibilities of rehabilitation, Judge Waddy finally ruled he was not worthy of treatment as a youthful offender and sentenced him as an adult to not less than ten nor more than thirty years in federal prison on all counts. A few months later, he was also convicted in D.C. Superior Court of yet another armed street robbery, and given more years consecutive. Derrick Holloway was also convicted of a separate robbery and sent to federal prison as an adult as well. It took a herculean and, to my mind, an unnecessary effort, but Senator Stennis's assailants finally got at least part of what they deserved. To me personally, the case had a powerful and lasting influence: It made me think for the first time that I might want to be a prosecutor one day. It was prosecutors, not defense attorneys as I'd previously thought, who were most needed to see justice was done.

The Ku Klux Klan Tries to Murder Charles Evers, Brother of Medgar[4]

One morning during my first month in the office, U.S. Attorney H. M. Ray laid a thick file on my desk: "Here's one you may want to decline prosecution on. This guy has been in Whitfield for years." Intrigued and not burdened by other cases, I began carefully reading the file. The contents startled me. Dale Walton had for many years operated a convenience store in Tupelo. It was the heyday of civil rights and racial confrontation, and Walton had been at the center of several controversies, including his arrest in Fayette for possessing an arsenal of guns, including a machine gun, and conspiring to assassinate Mayor Charles Evers, brother of slain civil rights leader Medgar Evers. On another recent occasion Walton had gotten into a dispute with a black customer over two cents in sales tax on a pair of dice and had pulled out a shotgun and killed the customer on the spot. His lawyer had him declared mentally unbalanced and committed to the State Mental Hospital at Whitfield, where he had remained for nearly three years.

Another controversial incident soon occurred involving Walton. After being released from Whitfield heavily medicated, he painted a broad yellow stripe on the sidewalk in front of his store which said, "No Niggers beyond This Point." A citizen called FBI agent Don Greene, who called ATF agent Billy Pace in Aberdeen and told him that in addition to the painted sign, Walton had hung on the front door of his store a loaded 45-caliber machine gun of the World War II variety known as a "grease gun." Pace, who knew Walton well from previous encounters, drove straight to the store. When he saw the weapon, which was cocked and loaded, Pace approached it to seize it. Walton came running from inside the store and offered to "make it safe." Pace declined, uncocking and unloading the weapon himself.

Pace was a most unusual agent. Calm and politely southern on the outside, he was cool and steely on the inside, as I witnessed in several cases. On this occasion, as usual, Billy did not follow the standard ATF procedure requiring agents to go armed at all times. The unarmed Pace invited Walton back into his store where they stood at the counter by the cash register. The two had the sort of cordial relationship that sometimes develops between an officer and a frequent suspect, a sort of respect between professionals. "Dale, I'm sorry, but this time I'm going to have to arrest you," Pace said. Walton quickly reached under his belt and pulled out a 45-caliber pistol and raised it high in the air. Billy told me later his knees had buckled slightly at that moment, but he could not afford to show fear. Walton calmly laid the pistol on the counter, saying, "I guess you'll want this one, too." Before Pace could say anything, Walton produced a .38 from his jacket pocket and another pistol from an ankle holster, both of which he placed peacefully on the counter. At this point, Pace told me later, his head was starting to swim.

Gathering up the guns, Pace told Walton, "Dale, it's time to go." Walton reached behind him and opened the door of a cooler and said, "Billy, I will only go with you if I can take a cold six-pack with me." Pace replied, "Dale, I can't let you do that." Walton had a wild look of rage on his face until Billy calmly raised three fingers and said, "You can only bring three." The remainder of the arrest and incarceration went peacefully.

After reading the file, including the psychiatric reports, I doubted whether Walton met the legal test for insanity. It seemed authorities might have just gone along with committing him to a mental hospital rather than taking the risk that a racially inflamed state jury might let him go. The federal charge also seemed to have good jury appeal since Walton clearly knew he was possessing a machine gun and that it was illegal, regardless of some obvious mental instability. The worst fact from our standpoint was that earlier in the case Walton had been examined by a federal prison psychiatrist, who declared him incompetent to stand trial. Nevertheless, it just appeared to me that Walton was too dangerous to be let loose on the community without a serious effort to convict him.

We obtained an indictment from the grand jury, whose enthusiasm for the case was encouraging. I subpoenaed the witnesses, including the psychiatrist, Dr. Harry Fain. Shortly thereafter, I received a confidential phone call from the director of the psychiatric unit at the Springfield prison hospital, who told me, in only slightly veiled terms, that Dr. Fain was a cantankerous and difficult witness and that I would want to spend some quality time with him to get control of him before I put him in front of a jury. Dr. Fain's trial schedule was so packed, however, that I only had the Sunday before the Monday trial to spend with him.

I met Dr. Fain at around 9:00 A.M. at the door of his room at the Holiday Inn in Oxford. He was a sight. Approximately seventy years old, he had an interesting mixture of red and gray hair. Bald on top, he had plaited his long hair around the fringes and then circled the plaits into a sort of knot on top of his head and fastened the ends together with rubber bands of various colors. I seem to recall that he had a trimmed white beard like so many psychiatrists, and he definitely looked the part.

As we began to discuss the case, I noticed that Dr. Fain spoke almost entirely in abstruse psychiatric jargon, rarely using ordinary language. When I tried to persuade him to speak plain English, he would repeatedly say, "Who is the shrink here? I know how to communicate. Stop trying to control me. I may have to psychoanalyze you if you continue to be so anal." After a couple of hours, Dr. Fain asked if it was possible to "get anything to drink in this town." Oxford at that time had some strange laws. Liquor was illegal on all occasions. Beer could be sold, but only warm and never on Sundays. Therefore, most of us kept coolers in our trunks for such occasions. We got some ice from the hotel and iced down several of my beers. After drinking them, we began to communicate better—so much better that I decided it was advisable for me to walk home rather than drive. As I left Dr. Fain's motel, he grabbed me by the shoulder, shook my hand vigorously, and declared in true psychiatric fashion, "I really have enjoyed interacting with you."

Convinced I had him under control, we were ready for trial. The next morning, I saw Dale Walton for the first time. He really did appear seriously mentally impaired. Heavily sedated, the pupils of his eyes were huge. His court-appointed attorney, Tommy Gardner, later a respected state circuit judge, asked me if I wasn't ashamed to be prosecuting anyone this obviously crazy. I brushed it off but later noticed that if I stared hard at Walton at counsel table, his feet would both rise up off the floor and visibly tremble. I had never seen that before.

The trial lasted several days, longer than I had expected. One evening, I invited Billy Pace and Dr. Fain over to my house for a bottle of wine. My wife was out of town. Late in the evening, after several glasses of wine, the three of us were sitting in the den. My wife came home unexpectedly and heard us carrying on. She peeked in the door without our knowing it and somehow jumped to the conclusion from his strange appearance that Dr. Harry Fain was the defendant Walton. She started to call the police but decided not to and we all had a good laugh, especially Harry.

The next morning I put Harry on the stand. At first, things seemed to go well. He was explaining everything in nice plain language, making it sound perfectly reasonable that he could say Walton was crazy one day and then, years later, decide upon reflection that the same Walton was sane enough to stand trial. I do not recall all of the details of his various psychiatric opinions, but one is hard to forget. After administering the MMPI, or Minnesota Multi-Phasic Personality Inventory, a test to determine whether a subject is faking or "malingering," Dr. Fain described Walton's interpretations of some Rorschach inkblot tests, which he said were "unusual and somewhat troubling." To get a better grasp of Walton's view of reality, Harry asked him to give a self-assessment in the form of a freehand pencil drawing. Although I would not have wanted the jury to see it, under the Court's rules of discovery, the defense already had all of our materials and if I hadn't shown it to the jury, the defense would have anyway, so I went ahead.

At the top of the sheet of paper Walton had spelled out his name, printing D-a-l-e vertically and W-a-l-t-o-n horizontally, with the two words meeting and sharing the letter *a*, which gave a definitely less than adult picture of the person doing the writing. Worse, but according to Dr. Fain fairly typical, was Walton's drawing of himself. His head was just a circle, his arms two sticks with smaller sticks for fingers. His legs were two straight sticks protruding down from a circle which was his torso. Dominating the entire picture, however, and about twice the size of his entire body, was an enormous oblong penis, which was longer than his legs. According to the rules, all exhibits are handed to jurors for them to examine. I had no idea what the jurors would think. I hoped they would see Walton for the joker and faker I thought he was, but I was concerned. Harry, of course, was totally unfazed.

At this point I asked Harry to explain away his former diagnosis of Walton as a paranoid schizophrenic. Following our usual pattern, I had him use the term, then explain it in everyday English. Harry started off just fine. A very professional witness despite his bizarre hair style, which one juror later told me he thought was perfectly normal for a psychiatrist, he would turn and look directly at the jurors as he spoke, like a kindly doctor. "Schizophrenia is a kind of break with reality where a person sees one thing but thinks it is another. People often misperceive not only other people but especially themselves as something other than what they really are. They also totally misinterpret events in the same way."

He continued, "Paranoia, on the other hand, is somewhat different, although many people are both schizophrenic and paranoid at the same time. Let me explain paranoia to you further with an example." Something about the way Harry said that gave me a little thrill of anxiety. He looked directly over at me and gave me a menacing smile. "Paranoia is an irrational anxiety. It often exists at the same time with schizophrenia, and each one can trigger the other." He then smiled maliciously at me and looked directly at an elderly white-haired lady sitting closest to him in the jury box and said, "Now, take this sweet little lady here. Suppose she thought that the Russians were dangerous to our country and might drop nuclear bombs on us. That would be a normal, reasonable fear." He continued, "But suppose she thought that the Russians. . . . . (he started lengthy, repeated pauses) had secretly planted . . . . . a listening device . . . . . in her rectum? Now that would be paranoia."

At that point, unable to crawl totally under the table as I felt like doing, I covered my face with my hands. When I finally glanced up, to my utter surprise Harry and the old lady were staring at each other, and she was smiling from ear to ear. When Tommy Gardner finished trying to cross examine Harry, the court took a break. I confronted Harry in the hall. "What do you mean saying something like that to that old lady?" Harry replied calmly, "Did you see the look on her face? She loved the attention, especially that kind of attention. Like I keep telling you, I am the shrink here. Just follow my lead."

Then we caught a break. Hubert Jones, the big old gap-toothed deputy marshal guarding the courtroom door, stepped up to me in the hall. "John boy, I didn't want to get up in this, but there is something you need to know. When I picked up Walton the other day from his cell, he asked me for a favor. He wanted me to let him show out in front of the other inmates and the sheriff. He threw himself on the floor and flopped around all crazy-like. When I told him it was time to go, he hopped right up and did what I told him. As soon as we were down the hall out of sight, he winked at me and thanked me."

As soon as the recess was over, I called Hubert straight to the stand. When he told the jurors about Walton playing crazy, several nodded and smiled. I felt we were home free. They wanted to convict, and now they had a good reason. Walton may have been crazy in a sense, but he also knew what he was doing. Sure enough, the jury convicted, and like nearly all juries that convict, they came in looking very grave and staring at the floor. Experienced trial lawyers know that when a criminal jury comes in smiling or looks at the defendant that they have probably acquitted. This jury had definitely convicted. The old lady repeatedly smiled in our direction, no doubt looking for Harry.

Judge Orma "Hack" Smith startled us totally by sentencing Walton to probation on supervised medication. While preparing this book I found one of the jurors from the case and asked him what he thought about that. "Outrageous. We wanted him locked up forever. That was never reported in the paper. That man was really dangerous, and we needed some racial peace." Of course we should have known better than to doubt the judgment of Judge Smith. Walton stayed on his meds and out of trouble for several years, with no further Klan or racial incidents. He died violently in a suspicious farm equipment accident, but apparently no one ever seriously followed up on it.

The Lampkin Brothers: I'm Assaulted in Chambers[5]

Our office had a considerable history with a family named Lampkin and had every reason to know the family's propensity for violence. Our acquaintance began when the FBI, the Highway Patrol, and the Oktibbeha County sheriff executed a search warrant on the forty-five-acre farm of the father, John Sharp Williams Lampkin, named for the former congressman of that name. Officers knew the father as "JSW." He and his sons ran the largest stolen-car chop shop in the district. On September 9, 1976, a federal-state-local team of agents served a search warrant and began collecting stolen engines and transmissions, over sixty of them, not to mention all the stolen vehicles themselves. At first, no one appeared to be home, and brand-new Sheriff Dolph Bryan, who had taken office just one week earlier, placed a copy of the warrant on JSW's porch as required by law and began searching. Then all hell broke loose. JSW appeared and ordered the officers off his property. Sheriff Bryan tried to explain about the warrant and that the judge said they had to serve it.

Highway patrolman Virgil Luke, a stolen-car specialist, had gone inside the house to search for ownership documents. From outside, officer Dan Davis saw a young Lampkin pointing a rifle at Luke and yelled, "Virgil is in there." Another brother had just blocked the only exit with a pulpwood truck. JSW had twelve sons, several of whom lived nearby. Sheriff Bryan entered the house followed by other officers. He told the gunman to drop his weapon, but the man kept it pointed at Luke. Bryan boldly grabbed the barrel of the rifle. Leroy Lampkin, who was holding it, stood 6', 2" tall and weighed 220 pounds to Sheriff Bryan's 160. Leroy Lampkin pulled up on his rifle, leaving Bryan's feet dancing in the air while he clung to the rifle barrel with both hands. Lampkin, who had a bandillero of shotgun shells across his shoulders and an ammunition belt of rifle shells around his waist, began swinging Bryan around in a circle, trying to break his grip on the barrel.

Highway patrolman Donald Wood stepped up to Lampkin and put his .357 Magnum revolver to Lampkin's head and said, "Drop the Sheriff," three separate times. Bryan then heard a huge explosion right beside him. When he looked around, he saw that half of Leroy Lampkin's face was blown away. JSW yelled to his wife to "Get my machine gun out of the back, and I'll slaughter these blood-thirsty SOBs." When she didn't move, JSW told them again, "Get off my property," and yelled at his wife to "Get my shotgun." She did not, and the officers placed JSW Lampkin and his several sons under arrest, including Cleveland Lampkin.

The case soon reached my desk in two forms: first as a federal stolen car case against the Lampkins and second as a potential criminal civil rights case against Wood and other officers for use of excessive force. There were over a dozen law officer witnesses and nearly that many Lampkins. I sent the stolen car case to the state DA at Sheriff Bryan's request. I declined prosecution of the officers, finding the force used, while extreme, was reasonable under the circumstances. The Lampkins then filed suit in federal court under the wrongful death statute. The suit was dismissed, but only years later.

In the process of studying all the reports, I discovered that several of the armed Lampkin brothers, including Cleveland, were convicted felons for whom it was a federal crime to possess a firearm. After months of investigation and a study of sketchy records in several states, a report on Cleveland's case came in from the ATF, and I obtained an indictment on him for possessing firearms illegally in Mississippi and transporting them to Chicago to resell, along with stolen cars and parts.

People have always asked if I was ever afraid of the defendants I sent to prison. I've usually said, "No," because the hushed, church-like atmosphere of a federal courtroom seems to civilize all of us, prosecutors and defendants alike. Winston Churchill once said great public architecture improves people's behavior, and I believe he was right. The solemnity of federal courtrooms, the black robes, the high benches, the fine leather chairs, and long shining wooden tables seem to put most people on their best behavior. It also doesn't hurt that there are U.S. Marshals there, who, while formally dressed in blazers and ties, also carry loaded handguns. Under federal security rules, most defendants have always worn not only handcuffs but leg chains. Yet in my experience, the most important element in keeping down the hostility that leads to violence is simple courtesy. Not only the U.S. Marshals but all our court personnel have always referred to defendants as "Mr." and defendants usually react accordingly. There are, of course, exceptions. The most memorable one was Cleveland Lampkin.

One day in 1979, I was finally prosecuting his gun case, which appeared routine. As explained earlier, Lampkin was buying guns illegally and transporting them back to Chicago to resell, falsely claiming to be a resident of Mississippi. He would deny under oath on federal firearm purchase forms that he was a convicted felon. His conviction was a non-violent one for possessing stolen autos (the family business), but it was still a federal crime, and in those days we prosecuted them all. When I rested my case, Cleveland Lampkin took the stand. His defense was that he didn't know he was a convicted felon, thinking he had pled guilty to a misdemeanor. It was not an unbelievable defense, and I cross-examined him on it pretty hard. I had convinced myself that he was not violent. After all, he had not actually used his weapon in the incident where his brother, Leroy, was killed. Besides, we were in federal court. What could go wrong?

My questioning involved Lampkin's knowledge of firearms laws from several of his brothers also being convicted felons, as was his father. My questions were pretty vigorous, trying to appeal to jurors, who tend to dislike convicted felons, especially entire families of them. To make sure my questions didn't go too far, Judge Smith ordered us all back to his chambers for a sort of trial run on whether my questioning was too preju-dicial. As Mr. Lampkin sat beside the judge in a big dark leather chair, I stood at the conference table about ten feet from him. His attorney, Cornelius Toole of Chicago, the family's retained counsel in all their mul-titude of conflicts with the law, objected vehemently to my questions, probably emboldening Mr. Lampkin to be more combative.

Then I asked the famous "one question too many." Partly from irrita-tion with Toole's objections, I asked Lampkin rudely, "By the way, other than your brother the preacher, is there even *one* of your brothers who is *not* a convicted criminal?" That set him off. Without saying a word, the 5', 7", 190-pound Lampkin leaped from his chair like a cat and was upon me like a linebacker before I could move. He grabbed my jacket with both hands, but before he could choke me or pull me down, two burly U.S. Marshals had him on the floor. Neither one struck him. Lampkin let go of his grip and sat back down into his chair. No one hit anyone. No one said anything that I can recall.

Judge Smith, a former defensive tackle for the Ole Miss football team, said sternly to Lampkin, "Now let's not have any more of that. Mr. Hail-man, you may continue your questioning." I did and nothing else dra-matic happened. The jury convicted Lampkin. Despite the incident and his criminal record, federal law at that time pretty much required Judge Smith to set him free on bond pending his appeal. Back in my office, there was no talk of prosecuting Lampkin for the assault. It all happened so fast, it seemed as if it never happened. We figured Judge Smith would take it into account at sentencing on the firearm convictions.

Months later, a news flash came on TV: "Five men killed in bloody Illinois shootout." Two highway patrolmen and a relative had been shot dead by two gunmen on Interstate 57 near the University of Illinois. Two of the shooters, who had been stopped for speeding while driving in a four-vehicle convoy, had panicked because they were hauling trunks full of illegal guns in their stolen cars. The shooters were dead, both shot by officers responding to radio calls for help. When the announcer gave the names of the shooters who were dead on the scene, it sent a chill through me: Cleveland Lampkin and his brother David. I called Dolph Bryan. He asked me why I was so surprised.

A story in the *Starkville Daily News* the next day told the events. When an Illinois trooper blue-lighted the four carloads of Lampkins for speeding around 11:30 P.M. on April 9, 1979, three stopped, but Cleveland Lampkin sped off in a stolen 1978 silver Mustang. When the trooper forced him over a few miles down the road, Cleveland came out shooting and was killed by the trooper. His passenger, David Lampkin, then shot and killed the trooper. A second trooper arrived and killed David. A local police officer who arrived to help the troopers was shot and killed by Monroe Lampkin, as was the brother-in-law of a trooper who was riding with him. The local DA tried and convicted Monroe Lampkin twice for the murders, but both convictions were overturned on appeal by the Illinois Supreme Court on technical grounds. Undeterred, the Illinois DA tried Monroe a third time, finally obtaining a third conviction and life sentence which were upheld on appeal.

While researching this book, I Googled "Cleveland Lampkin." A lengthy, dramatic article by reporter Will Brumlee appeared in the Paxton, Illinois, *News Gazette* for April 6, 2009. Entitled "30th Anniversary of 1979 Shootout Still Haunts Former Officer," it recounts in gruesome detail the shootout between the Lampkins and the officers, calling it a "bloodbath." Little did I know when Cleveland Lampkin assaulted me in Judge Smith's chambers how easily I could have been one of those victims. Looking back, sometimes it's better not to know.

"Riverboat" Gaines[6]

One of the most effective undercover agents I've known is Randy Corban, the son of C. B. Corban, the ATF agent who covered Marshall County back when it was notorious for corruption. Randy later became chief of police at Ole Miss and still later my office's law enforcement coordinator, but he first worked for MBN and helped federal agencies in his UC role as an all-around thug which made him welcome in every kind of criminal circle. Randy was lean and athletic and spoke in low tones in a Gary Cooper sort of way that got bad guys' attention. In this case, he was working undercover from Guntown in Lee County through Pontotoc and down to Chickasaw, hanging out in illegal beer joints and gambling dens, of which there were plenty. At the Corral Club on the Lee-Pontotoc County line, Randy met Bobby Gene "Perk" Gaines, better known to gamblers as "Riverboat" because his main job was repairing diesel engines on towboats.

Having heard of Randy's reputation as a man who would kill people, Riverboat approached him one night at a game about a "little job." A man named Ben Prude owed Riverboat $10,000 on an unpaid gambling debt, and people were beginning to laugh at Riverboat because he couldn't collect. He had already approached local thugs about the job, but they all said it was too high-profile. At the time, Prude ran the famous honky-tonk in Marshall County just across the Tallahatchie River bridge from Oxford where Ole Miss students went for their illegal beer and whiskey. The joint has catered to Ole Miss students ever since William Faulkner's day and later when it was known as Johnny Zanola's. In addition to underage Ole Miss students buying beer, backroom dice games attracted colorful characters. Randy recalled one guy who had a special tube in his obstructed esophagus to funnel Budweiser straight in without him swallowing. If anything happened to the owner of Johnny's, the shooter would be in a heap of trouble. The place still operates today, legally, as Betty Davis's BBQ and has excellent fat and spicy ribs.

Riverboat had not been very discreet in his boasts about having Ben killed, and heard Ben had gotten wind of it and had his son, Todd, standing guard at the joint with a rifle, making a hit on Ben much riskier. Riverboat needed a pro, and Randy sounded like his man. Not knowing Randy was wired for sound, Riverboat handed him a .30 caliber carbine with a big scope and the serial number ground off, saying the gun was "safe" and had already been used in two successful murders. Randy got Riverboat to take him to a site uphill from Ben's joint and show him the best angle facing the back door. Randy was to shoot Ben late that night when he came out for a smoke.

When caught, Riverboat cried and confessed. He hired former federal prosecutor Will Ford of New Albany to defend him. Will was a bold and confident trial lawyer. The indictment was tricky. At first I had a hard time finding a federal offense to fit the facts. I was, after all, still pretty new. Finally, I found the "extortionate collection of credit" law, which made it a federal crime to threaten someone to collect a debt, even an illegal gambling debt. That was count 1. It was of course also an offense for anyone to use a firearm in any other federal offense, so we had a second count there. The first count carried a penalty of twenty years and the second count ten years consecutive, "stacking" the penalties as federal inmates call it. Count 1 colorfully depicted the violent means Riverboat used to intimidate Ben Prude to collect his illegal gambling debt:

> In February defendant telephoned Ben Prude demanding payment of a $10,000 gambling debt, stating if the debt was not paid defendant would have Ben tended to and that defendant "had the boys to do it." Gaines made similar threatening calls on ten different occasions through June. On one occasion defendant telephoned the minor son of Ben Prude and threatened to kidnap him and blow up his trailer and the adjacent business and kill everyone inside.On July 8 defendant handed undercover agent Randall Corban a rifle and eight rounds of ammunition plus $30 for expenses and directed Corban to take the said rifle and shoot up the trailer, place of business and motor vehicles of Ben Prude, promising Corban that if as a result of the shooting, Ben Prude repaid the $10,000 gambling debt, Gaines would pay Corban $3000 for the shooting. If Prude still failed to pay after the shooting, Gaines agreed to pay Corban another $3,000 to kill Prude.

Will Ford pled Gaines guilty and with the help of several prominent citizens of Union County as character witnesses somehow persuaded the probation officer and the judge that Riverboat was not really serious, and he received a sentence of just a couple of years. Perhaps the judge was right. We never had any more trouble with Riverboat Gaines.

Jerry and Terry, the Hit Man Twins[7]

FBI agent Newson Summerlin brought us a murder-for-hire case in 1994 that was unlike anything I'd ever heard. The first part was not unusual: A wife tried to hire a hit man to kill her husband and accidentally asked an informant to do the job. She claimed she had tried other people, but her husband seemed to be hard to kill. The wife, Teresa Hutcheson, first offered to pay Terry Wilbanks $30,000 to take her husband, Jimmy Dean Hutcheson, hunting and kill him and make it look like an accident. Although not a bad price, Terry reported the offer to his friend, Jimmy Dean, the husband, who thought the whole thing was a joke. Teresa then decided to do it herself, but her husband wisely declined to go hunting with her.

The plot thickened. On May 24, Teresa told her husband the electricity had been off all day while he was at work. Like a good husband he crawled under the house and found a main electric wire had been cut. He told Teresa to turn off the current. While Jimmy Dean was splicing the wire back together, Teresa turned the juice back on full force. Jimmy Dean screamed and writhed in pain but finally managed to pull his hands off the live wires. Terry Wilbanks visited Jimmy Dean at the hospital and commiserated with him over his badly burned hands.

In early November, Teresa again tried to persuade Terry Wilbanks to kill her husband, this time on the first day of deer season. This time he'd heard enough and went to the sheriff, who went to the FBI. As they pondered whether to believe it, Teresa's grandfather, William Hinson, approached Jerry Wilbanks, twin brother of Terry, about killing his granddaughter Teresa's husband, Jimmy Dean. Jerry was noncommittal. In early December 1994, the grandfather bought a .30-.30 deer rifle and a box of ammunition and took them to Jerry Wilbanks and again asked him to kill Jimmy Dean. This time Hinson offered Jerry $25,000 from the life insurance of Jimmy Dean, saying he and Teresa both wanted it done. He didn't say why.

This time Jerry Wilbanks went to authorities and agreed to help them catch Hinson and his granddaughter. He taped a phone call that same day and agreed to meet Hinson and discuss the killing. They met at a Wal-Mart, where Hinson gave Jerry a measly $40 to seal the deal, promising he and Teresa would have plenty of money for him once the insurance company paid off for Jimmy Dean's accidental death in a "hunting accident."

A week later, Jerry arranged to meet jointly with Teresa and her grandfather to finalize the details, again wearing a hidden tape recorder and transmitter for agents to listen in. Teresa told Jerry it would be about two weeks before the insurance check arrived and that she had just remembered they also had a second life policy through the bank on which she could immediately collect $1,000 while waiting for the rest. She said she would pick up Jimmy Dean from work and have him in the woods the next day by 4:30 P.M. After discussing where in the woods she wanted her husband shot so Jerry could get away before Teresa "discovered" the body, the cold-hearted woman made her intentions perfectly clear: "Shoot him in the head or heart. I don't want to have to look after a cripple."

Jerry asked why she wanted him killed. "For a different life," she said. She told Jerry if anyone asked about the thousand dollars, he should say it was payment for a new transmission for her truck. She said she'd give the money to "gramps" to give to Jerry. At the conclusion of the conversation, federal and state agents emerged from hiding and arrested Teresa Hutcheson. Other agents then arrested her grandfather William Hinson.

Up to this point, the case was depressingly familiar to the agents, but nothing unusual. One spouse having another killed is not just a staple of modern life and country songs, but has a long and undistinguished history back to Henry VIII and before. Teresa and her grandfather were indicted by the federal grand jury on attempted murder-for-hire charges. Their attorneys agreed for them both to plead guilty. During pre-sentence interviews, Teresa and gramps finally confessed the real reason for the murder: Jimmy Dean Hutcheson was "in the way." He had married Teresa after she had already given birth to three children by another unnamed man while still in her teens. Jimmy Dean was helping raise those children. But Teresa wanted to be with their father, not Jimmy Dean Hutcheson.

At sentencing, veteran U.S. district judge Neal Biggers, who had been both a state district attorney and a state circuit judge before his appointment to the federal bench, expressed astonishment at certain statements in the probation officer's pre-sentence report: "I thought I'd seen everything, but this is the most shocking and disgusting case I've ever witnessed." The father of Teresa's children, the lover she wanted to be with so badly she would kill her husband to achieve it, was none other than her own grandfather, William Hinson. Talk about keeping it in the family.

When the case hit the local media it was first greeted by groans of "Oh no, another black eye for Mississippi," followed quickly by questions as to which counties were most subject to inbreeding and incest (the Northeast Appalachian region won). *U.S. News & World Report* ran a tongue-in-cheek story about the case that led to an invitation to Teresa to appear on the *Sally Jessy Raphael* show in New York. We were a little surprised Jerry Springer did not have the grandfather and the husband on his show for a bout of choreographed fisticuffs.

The show was ostensibly to discuss how to prevent or stop sexual abuse of young women by family members, although public interest in the more prurient aspects no doubt played a bigger role. At the request of her attorney, Andy Howorth of Oxford (now circuit judge Andrew Howorth), Judge Biggers reluctantly allowed Teresa Hutcheson to travel to New York *only* so she could earn the hefty fee Ms. Raphael was paying to help with the care of her children while she and her grandfather were off serving their federal time. I suppose that was a plus. When released they moved together to another state, far away from Mississippi. Cases like that one could give incest a bad name.

Mississippian Jeff Fort Becomes the Angel of Fear, Leader of the El Rukns, Chicago's Most Dangerous Gang since Al Capone[8]

Eddie "Cowboy" McNairy was a most unusual man. A tall, lean black man with a dignified manner, he made his living as a professional gambler in large games with wealthy white bankers and planters. He lived in a family compound of several houses filled with brothers and cousins and their families in the hamlet of Egypt, a few miles north of Aberdeen, the beautiful antebellum city where one of our federal courthouses was located. You first noticed Cowboy by his unique mode of dress: He always wore starched, sharply creased blue jeans with an expensive western shirt and bolo tie. He wore the best-looking, most expensive leather cowboy boots I ever saw. None of your snakeskin for Cowboy. His boots were plain dark-brown cow's leather with no fancy stitching or metal trim. His boots looked like something you might have had made for yourself by hand in London and could have worn to a dinner party of U.S. Senators in Washington and outshone the boots of even the richest western senator. How Cowboy survived as a black gambler taking rich white men's money was a mystery to us at first, but after we got to know him better, he explained it to us as a combination of moxie and subtle, bold-faced cheating.

One afternoon Cowboy was sitting with some friends in Aberdeen at a local service station, waiting for a big dice game that night. Across the street was the biggest black church in town. As he watched, an unusual procession pulled up at the church. Five matched maroon Lincoln Continental Mark VIs pulled up and parked, all in a row. Large black men in suits wearing Muslim-style caps got out of the first and last cars. They gathered around the middle car in a protective circle until a short, thick man emerged wearing quite a costume. On his head was a multicolored, sloped-down leather hat of the kind worn in East Africa. He had lots of rings on his fingers and below his burly neck was a full-length deep-brown mink coat, the kind only big-time drug dealers can wear and look natural. On his face was a mean, cold expression. No one that day recalled ever seeing him smile. Cowboy McNairy had one immediate thought, which he expressed to his pals: "This man means money for Cowboy."

His pals said the man was the most important gang leader in Chicago and perhaps the entire United States. He was the kingpin of a coalition of smaller groups who controlled drug dealing and other crimes on the South Side of Chicago. The bodyguards around him were the leaders of the smaller gangs he had brought together. He called them his "generals." His gang was first called the Blackstone Rangers and later renamed the El Rukns. His name was Jeff Fort, and he was a killer.

Cowboy's friends told him Fort was born in Aberdeen but moved to Chicago when he was nine. A skinny kid with one of those fade hairdos that gets bigger at the top, he was a charismatic speaker who developed a following as a preacher of Black Power while still a teenager. In his twenties he was invited to Washington by the Nixon administration to lead an antigang initiative as part of the War on Poverty left over from the Johnson administration. Fort was given a large budget to get the program going. Over the first year he stole over a million dollars and used it to build up his gang. When Congress realized what had happened, they subpoenaed him to testify about how he spent the money. When Fort brazenly took the Fifth, Congress held him in criminal contempt and he went to federal prison for a year. He came out a different man, muscled up from weightlifting and with no further smile on his face. Certain blogs now say it was sexual abuse in prison that turned him from a smooth con man into a vicious killer, but whatever the reason, Fort came out with a powerful will to rule over others and no longer just by verbal persuasion.

In prison, he converted to Islam and sought to join Elijah Muhammad's Nation of Islam, but they rejected him as an insincere opportunist. Always the entrepreneur, Fort set up his own ersatz form of pseudo-Islam, giving his followers Arabic names and a Muslim facade to support his main goal: tax-free status as a religious sect for his gang's many businesses. To look more Islamic, Fort and his generals required their women to wear Islamic gear, from long gowns to head coverings and even a few veils. He called his restructured group the El Rukns and himself Malik, Arabic for prince or "angel." When he changed the name of his group from the Blackstone Rangers to the El Rukns, no one was fooled: it was still Jeff Fort's gang and he still ran it like a medieval prince.

The El Rukns that Cowboy McNairy saw were all males, all from Chicago. After learning who Fort was, Cowboy began to look for a way to become an informant and profit from the occasion. He found a cousin of Fort's among his acquaintances and paid the cousin for Fort's direct private phone number. When Fort returned to Chicago, Cowboy called him and got right through. Fort answered his own phone, saying in his whispery voice, "This is Angel." Cowboy told him who he was, bantered a little, and then came to the point: It was too bad Fort had lost touch with his Mississippi roots. The law enforcement was not as tough in Mississippi, and if Fort was interested, they could make some serious money together distributing drugs in Mississippi if Fort would supply them. Fort said he was interested. Cowboy said he'd have one of his people call Fort back with specifics and asked if it was all right to use that same number. Surprisingly, Fort said O.K.

Cowboy immediately talked to a friend in law enforcement who gave him the number of the Mississippi Bureau of Narcotics (MBN) in Jackson. The agent who answered the phone told Cowboy he'd check it out and see if they were interested. The agent called a Chicago narcotics officer, who said he'd never heard of Jeff "Ford," but would check. A few minutes later Chicago gang unit officer Rich Kolovitz called back. The only agent at the MBN office at the time was Bill "Tank" Marshall, a white former Ole Miss football player. When Kolovitz heard that the Chicago guy in question answered to "Angel," he realized the guy was Jeff "Fort" and not "Ford." Kolovitz could not believe it. He had been working murders, welfare fraud, extortion, gun trafficking and several drug cases against Fort and the El Rukns for years and had convicted some subordinates but could never get near Fort himself. Now some white Mississippi rookie had Fort's private line.

To break Marshall in a little, Kolovitz told him how Fort ran his marijuana operation. He would find a source, buy a few pounds at first, then hundreds of pounds. Fort would next have his men rip off the dealer, killing him if necessary. The violence had gotten so bad that Fort's sources for marijuana had mostly dried up. Fort was too protected at his headquarters, a fortified brick building also called "the Fort," for retaliation by his drug suppliers, so most dealers just avoided him. His Fort was located in a desolate neighborhood of vacant lots, burned-out shells of buildings, and blocks of welfare hotels, where Fort made the tenants give his gang their government checks and other income and then doled out to them what he thought they deserved.

Kolovitz's description of Fort's operation gave Marshall an idea. What if he proposed to Fort that Marshall would swap him all the marijuana he needed in exchange for cocaine, which allegedly was in short supply in Mississippi? Kolovitz said he'd fly to Mississippi, but Marshall told him to let them handle it with Cowboy to start with, and they would be glad to have Kolovitz's help later on if the case went anywhere.

Marshall touched base with his boss, Captain Charlie Spillers, who was in charge of the north half of the state for MBN. Spillers, a bold and innovative agent, said he wished he had a black undercover agent handy to make the call, but liked Marshall's style and told him to go ahead with his plan. Marshall called Fort. To everyone's surprise, Fort was willing to deal with a white Mississippi "drug dealer." Speaking a kind of El Rukn code that reminded Marshall of pig latin, Fort agreed to send a couple of his generals to Tupelo, where Marshall told him people would be less wary of outsiders, but which Marshall figured had the large group of narcotics officers they would need to arrest the Chicago gangsters. Detective Bart Aguirre of the Tupelo P.D. worked closely with Spillers, Marshall, and the others. They managed to engage Fort in several taped phone calls planning the deal. Fort sent two trusted generals, Henry Timothy and Sundown Doyle, to a Tupelo motel to do the deal.

The Mississippi agents were astonished that such supposedly big-time gangsters were falling for such an old and seemingly obvious undercover ploy. When Timothy and Doyle arrived and insisted that one of their group hold their marijuana and cash in one motel room while others looked at the cocaine in another motel room, the agents were again surprised. Such rudimentary security might help protect against rip-offs by other drug dealers, but blundering into an undercover narcotic sting like this gave a whole new level of meaning to the word "amateurs." Teams of Mississippi agents simply burst into both rooms at the same time and busted everybody.

The officers brought me the case and held the defendants in custody while we got a quick indictment before his underlings could get word to Fort that the deal had gone sour. Rich Kolovitz and his partner, Dan Brannigan, loved arresting Jeff Fort in Chicago. They used a battering ram to break the front door of his Fort, and Brannigan came to Oxford with a cast on his hand from breaking it while breaking the door, but said it was well worth it.

Unfortunately, Fort was allowed bond by a magistrate, but in those days just about everyone made bond. Preparation for trial was unlike anything we'd expected. Glen Davidson, an experienced former state district attorney, was our brand-new U.S. Attorney. His style was that the head man should try the big cases himself, which was great with me. When I asked him how he wanted to split the witnesses, he said, "50–50." When I showed him a witness list with outlines of testimony and asked him which 50 percent he wanted to take, he said, "Just give me your sorriest ones." I took him at his word. Davidson was great at witness prep, especially with drug dealer witnesses. He'd lean back in his big leather chair, stuff a cigar in his mouth like Senator "Big Jim" Eastland, and say, "Now let me tell you how it's going to be." And that was it. In the Fort case, he wanted to take Cowboy: "John, this guy is fascinating, a real piece of work. I've never met anyone like him before. How does he survive?"

Rich Kolovitz and Charlie Spillers felt the same way. Kolovitz insisted Fort's defense would be to have Cowboy killed. While I did the paperwork to get him in the federal Witness Protection Program, Charlie

Spillers had a team of agents live 24/7 in a motor home in front of Cowboy's house in the McNairy family compound. His brothers and cousins were all armed and experienced. Cowboy and his wife and children became so personally close to the agents guarding them that every night she made them big dinners and brought them out to the motor home. Sometimes they ate together inside.

In the meantime I flew to Chicago to interview every witness we could find, including witnesses to all the other drug conspiracy deals he'd been in. The Chicago P.D. gang unit, which included federal ATF agents because of the El Rukns' heavy trafficking in firearms, was terrific. They introduced me to former El Rukns and former wives of El Rukns, who explained to me the code words they used and the different aliases Fort used. Several were in a local Witness Protection Program run by the city. Two witnesses in particular stood out. One was a nurse who'd made the mistake of marrying an El Rukn general. Her eyewitness descriptions of Fort's lifestyle, mannerisms, use of code words, and brutally violent character gave me ideas on how to cross-examine him, which Glen Davidson had offered to let me do.

Another witness who really impressed me was a retired Chicago police captain who had worked for years against Fort, who called the detective an Uncle Tom and ridiculed him until one night when Fort and his men shot and wounded the captain so badly he had to retire. While he was in the hospital, Fort sent him flowers. As soon as he was released, the captain walked, using a cane, up to the front door of the Fort compound and nailed Fort's note and his flowers to the door. No one was going to intimidate him.

The trial was a strange one. Unlike most defendants, Fort and his associates did not stall or delay. His Chicago lawyer hired our best local attorney, Jack Dunbar, and said he was ready to go. That was unusual. There was of course considerable media attention. In the courtroom were a handful of Fort's most presentable associates in coats and ties who kept giving each other the hand and head signals that the nurse had explained to me. Fort looked exactly like what he was—a menacing, scowling thug who communicated mostly by grunts and hand signals.

The case against his codefendants was clear-cut. They were caught red-handed with the dope in their possession. Our only concern about them was that our jurors, especially the black ones, might be threatened privately without our knowing it, and be afraid to convict the fearsome-looking Chicago gangster. The case against Fort himself was not as strong. All we had were Cowboy, the handful of cryptic tape-recorded phone calls, and Marshall, who knew little about Fort except what he'd been told, plus a series of witnesses from Chicago who would positively identify Fort's unmistakably whispery voice from the tapes setting up the deal. Our key witness was Cowboy. Unfortunately for us, his time to testify came late one afternoon. Normally you like to get key witnesses on and off the same day, so the defense has no time to prepare their cross-examination overnight.

As Cowboy walked into the courtroom and took the oath, I watched Fort's reaction. So did case agent Charlie Spillers, who sat at counsel table beside me. Apparently everyone else was watching Cowboy, who was a striking figure. As Cowboy approached the clerk, Fort turned to his chief lieutenant out in the crowd. He first leaned his head way back, then lowered it with his eyes closed, then turned and nodded his head three times at Cowboy. The general Fort was looking at repeated the gesture.

Glen Davidson began questioning Cowboy, but Fort's Chicago lawyer kept objecting and making belated oral motions to suppress and exclude the tapes. At one point I became sure he was stalling for some reason. By the time 5:00 P.M. arrived, Cowboy had hardly gotten through the first taped phone call. Judge Senter turned to the jury and apologized for the trial going so slowly but that certain legal questions had come up and he was going to let them go home so they could hear the rest of this witness's testimony in one day. When the jury was gone we went straight to the witness room and told Kolovitz and Brannigan about the signal Fort had given. They responded unanimously "That's the El Rukn death sign. They're going to try to kill Cowboy tonight. That is their defense." We redoubled the protection on Cowboy, using a bulletproof van to transport him home.

Around midnight a tragedy nearly happened. Cowboy's daughter, a college student at Jackson State University, decided at the last minute to come home that night without calling ahead. As she drove up Highway 45 in Cowboy's black Cadillac, just before the turnoff for Egypt, one shot from a high-powered rifle hit her windshield right in front of her face. By some miracle, or perhaps a particularly well-made windshield, the slug bounced off. The windshield shattered. Cowboy's daughter was terrified but unharmed. When officers later found the slug nearby it was too badly damaged to identify and we didn't have the rifle to match it with anyway.

Having put several people in the Witness Protection Program before, and having represented its director, Gerry Shur, when he was sued, I knew what to do. I called the DOJ Operations Center, and they placed me straight through to him at home. I told him who the defendant was and what had almost happened to his daughter. I asked Gerry when they could be put in the program. Like most witnesses, they did not want to relocate and move far away from family and friends, but with the El Rukns after them, they agreed they had no other choice. Gerry Shur said, as he had said in an earlier case, "Upon my authority, they are in the Witness Program this minute." I thanked him. Then he asked, "Are there any special problems with this family?" I told him there were. Not only did Cowboy earn his living illegally, but he and his wife had nine children, one of whom, a fifteen-year-old student, was on kidney dialysis three times a week. "Okay," Gerry said. "They're in, but we will have a devil of a time finding a place to put them. Can your agents help the marshals guard them a little longer?" I told him we would do it. We had to do it.

The next morning, when court opened, we got another surprise. The defense attorneys announced their clients were all ready to plead guilty, including Fort, without hearing any more of Cowboy's testimony. They had already heard the tapes and knew what was coming. Fort's only defense apparently had been to kill Cowboy before the jury could hear him. The pleas went down smoothly. Fort was again let out on bond. The pre-sentence report on Fort read like Al Capone's, only worse. It would be hard to imagine a worse criminal, yet he had only once ever been convicted of anything, and that was the bizarre offense of contempt of Congress for refusing to tell how he stole poverty program funds. The judge gave Fort a sentence of eight years, then threw us a curve. Despite his attempt to kill our main witness, Fort would remain out on bond "on his honor," if that can be imagined, to turn himself in when ordered to do so.

When turn-in day came, of course Fort was nowhere to be found. He called in from a Caribbean island that had no extradition treaty with the United States. Our jubilation and relief turned to anger and disgust. Then, within months, came a bigger surprise: Fort had ordered his generals to send him plenty of money each month for him to live in style. After a couple of months the money stopped coming. The previously subservient generals had started infighting to take over Fort's position as prince, figuring he'd never be back. El Rukn discipline collapsed. Their illegal businesses didn't do well without Fort to keep people in line. Then Fort called again and made us an offer: If he would turn himself in, would we keep him safe from physical retaliation by the Chicago P.D.? We agreed, and what we thought was a much-chastened Fort came back and was locked up in the maximum security prison at Terre Haute, Indiana. Again we thought we were home free.

The U.S. Attorney's Office in Chicago began preparing cases on Fort using the RICO statute, which allowed them to lump together not only all the federal crimes he'd committed but numerous state murders and other offenses as well. Charlie Spillers and I both received subpoenas to testify about seeing the death sign put out by Fort on Cowboy. The Chicago investigation dragged on. It had become apparent to Kolovitz and Brannigan that maybe Fort wasn't so stupid in returning. In prison, he developed quite a following and appeared to be running the El Rukns again, so he was moved to the supermax federal prison in Colorado.

Within months another revelation came from his new prison. Apparently unaware that his phone conversations were all taped, Fort was caught red-handed offering to sell U.S.-made missiles to the mad dictator of Libya, Muammar Gaddafi. Jeff Fort had become not only the most notorious gangster since Al Capone; now he was the first U.S.-born Islamic terrorist, all while serving our Mississippi sentence.

Since then much has happened to Jeff Fort. After several missteps and a couple of reversals, the Chicago U.S. Attorney's Office finally got him sent off for life without parole. The federal prosecutor handling the case subpoenaed Charlie Spillers and me to testify, then himself got in considerable hot water with some Chicago judges about how the Fort trial was handled. Those complex incidents are ably explained at great length in a fine *New Yorker* piece by Jeffrey Toobin noted in the bibliography.

Today, like many hard-core inmates, Jeff Fort is for some reason still allowed to e-mail and blog from his twenty-three-hour per day confinement at the supermax federal prison in Colorado. But blogs and e-mails are two-way streets. While reading a selection of Fort's communications on-line a few months ago, I began to notice regular messages to Fort from two of the people who have known him the longest and best, detectives Kolovitz and Brannigan. One message summarized it all: "Dear Jeff,

We're still out here and you're still in there. And you always will be. Love, Dan and Rich."

The Shaw Boys Contract to Have a Judge Killed[9]

William Shaw was doing time in Parchman for murdering his wife and her lover. His family was no stranger to trouble, relatives having been defendants in the famous case where the three civil rights workers were murdered and buried under an earthen damn near Philadelphia as portrayed in the movie *Mississippi Burning*, which made our state look about as bad as a place can look. But there is always some upside to every story. The clever, resourceful FBI agent played in the movie by Gene Hackman was closely modeled on real-life agent John Proctor, who trained FBI agent Wayne Tichenor, to whom this book is dedicated. The scene where Proctor drops by the local beauty parlor and schmoozes the girls into telling him everything going on in town is classic Tichenor. If every federal district in this country had just one FBI agent with that kind of moxie, our conviction rate would go up 50 percent.

But in William Shaw's case, the clever agent was not with the FBI but the U.S. Postal inspectors, a little-known but highly professional outfit whose best agents are among the best federal investigators of all. I'm thinking here of retired Inspector Harold Stuart especially, who is mentioned in other cases of mine. The Postal Inspector in Shaw's case was named Gary Eager. He was assigned the thankless task of breaking up the infamous Parchman prison money order scam, later immortalized by John Grisham in one of his best lawyer-thriller novels, later a popular movie. Called *The Brethren*, the book is about a federal judge and a state J.P. who run a similar scam from prison, ripping off gullible correspondents by getting them to buy low-dollar money orders and mail them to inmates who then forge them into high-dollar amounts and smuggle them back out and get the victims to cash them and return the cash to the inmates. The elderly and lovelorn widows and homosexuals were the most frequent victims of these prison scams. Both Angola in the Grisham book and Parchman in real life were hotbeds of the scheme. In our case Inspector Eager was paying an inmate to inform him about the scheme. To his surprise, one day his inmate CI reported to him not about money orders but about an offer he'd received from an inmate named William Shaw to kill the circuit judge who sentenced him plus the two lawyers who represented him.

Shaw's proposal itself was right out of the movies. He explained to the CI that he was indeed guilty of murder. He and his wife were estranged. During a cooling-off period, Shaw had agreed to live in a house he owned across the street from the marital home. One day when he was supposed to be out of town, Shaw unexpectedly came home to find his wife entertaining another man in their home, even feeding him lunch post-sex. Shaw got his pistol, walked into the dining room, and shot his wife's lover dead as he ate the dinner she'd cooked for him. He then chased his wife furiously around the house until he caught her and shot her dead too. He then turned himself in to the sheriff and confessed. If he'd lived in France, he would have gotten off scot-free for justifiable homicide. As it was, Shaw decided he'd rely on the local common-law tradition: "They needed killing."

Shaw claimed to Eager's CI that he had met privately with the circuit judge, Marcus Gordon, who had sympathy for the wronged husband and allegedly told Shaw he'd have to plead guilty to satisfy his wife's family, but that when things quieted down, the judge could reduce Shaw's sentence if he'd move out of state when released. Shaw said that when he asked the judge how much money he wanted to reduce the sentence, the judge cut him off, saying, "Don't ever communicate with me again. Handle it through your attorneys." Shaw totally misinterpreted the judge's empathy for a wronged husband for corruption.

Shaw put his nephew Harold on his visitor's list and told Harold where to find $35,000 in cash he'd buried in a coffee can in his backyard as a nest egg after he split with his wife. Shaw told the CI he had told Harold to dig up the money and take part of it to his lawyers to give to the judge. Shaw claimed his nephew said he had done it, and Shaw had then waited for over a year to be released but nothing happened. His lawyers claimed they were filing motions to reduce his sentence and for a further fee would ask the governor for a pardon. Shaw did not believe them and finally decided to resort to self-help. He asked the CI if he knew a reliable hit man who would kill both the judge and his lawyers. The CI said he would check with some "friends," instead alerting Inspector Eager.

When Eager learned of it, he arranged a meeting with Jesse Bingham of the Highway Patrol, a clever, burly man with a low voice and thick beard who often played hit men in our cases. Bingham agreed to play "Pat O'Brien," a professional killer. Bingham spoke several times with nephew Harold, who confirmed that William Shaw wanted the judge killed and his lawyers too. "One of them cheated him, maybe all of them, he don't know, so you might as well just kill all three of them."

Bingham asked how much money Harold had and told him $15,000 would be enough. He would charge $5,000 for each murder, starting with the judge. Following real hit-men scenarios, Bingham told Harold he had to have half of the first $5,000 up front. When the job was done, they would meet, and Harold would pay him the rest. Jesse said he'd take pictures of the judge dead so Harold would know he got his money's worth. He also asked Harold, "Do you want him to know before he dies who got him killed?" Harold agreed and looked pleased. "I'll tell him you and William had him done," Jesse said. He also warned Harold not to double-cross him: "You'd better be there to pay me when and where I tell you, or *you* become the problem. Don't make me do another one for free." When I heard that comment, I worried a little that a good defense attorney might plausibly argue that by threatening Shaw, Jesse could have entrapped him by intimidating him out of any chance he had to back out.

To save travel and keep jurisdiction local, Jesse told Harold to meet him in the parking lot of the Holiday Inn in Oxford. That way we could arrest Harold and take him straight before a magistrate, even on a weekend. That's just how it worked out. Jesse showed Harold a picture of the judge lying down pretending to be dead. We decided pouring ketchup on the judge to look like blood might be too risky since seeing the blood-splatters on the judge's "body," might provoke Harold to blurt out something sympathetic on the tape. The plan worked perfectly. Harold jumped headlong into our trap and confessed the whole thing when Jesse told him he was a highway patrolman working undercover.

Harold was ready to plead guilty, but his father refused to let him: "That boy don't know what he's doing. William and those federal boys could talk him into anything." That idea was of course negated by the tapes showing Harold's obvious glee at the idea the judge was dead. Harold's lawyer, Bill Liston of Winona, announced ready for trial, and we were ready to give him one. The judge also thought Harold should plead guilty considering our powerful evidence, but Harold's father wouldn't stand for it. So we went to trial. William had pled guilty with no resistance, seeming almost proud of his maneuver. When Harold called him as a defense witness, William basically testified for us and was a powerful witness. The case was overwhelming. Then Harold's lawyer declared to the judge that Harold's father insisted Harold take the stand. Judge Biggers, trying to be reasonable in face of the father's foolish intransigence, allowed Harold's father to come inside the bar with the lawyers and to sit in a special chair right below Harold's witness chair. It was unique to say the least. Harold basically admitted everything on the stand but claimed he had tried to back out of the hit—not because it was wrong but because he thought too many people knew about it and they would get caught. When I asked Harold on cross if he knew why William didn't want the DA killed too, he showed his criminal knowledge: "William told me it was the judge and his own lawyers who screwed him. He hadn't paid the DA nothing. He said the DA was just doing his job." That response showed way too much understanding for the jury to let Harold off.

After the jury found Harold guilty, it came out in the pre-sentence investigation that William Shaw had passed a postal polygraph exam as to whether he'd given his lawyers money intending to bribe the judge. He clearly did not understand that the judge was just being sympathetic and that the lawyers were just doing what they were supposed to do in being paid to try to get his sentence reduced. William simply misunderstood the judge's and lawyers' intentions. He could pass the polygraph because he really did believe the judge would take a bribe, although he definitely never would have. And his lawyers had no idea he was sending them bribe money and not legal fees. But there was some consolation. William was happy with us and one year thereafter, convicted murderer William Shaw sent me a Christmas card from Parchman.

Protected Witnesses: Marion Albert "Mad Dog" Pruett[10]

The federal Witness Protection Program has been one of the Justice Department's greatest success stories, not only in fighting traditional organized crime, for which it was designed, but in many other cases as well, recently including terrorism. From its inception, the program has kept our witnesses alive. People often ask me if we federal prosecutors are not afraid for our personal safety. When I say "no," it usually surprises them, but there is a good reason. There are plenty of prosecutors, and defendants know it. If something happens to one of us, two more prosecutors will step in to take our place.

The same thing goes for federal judges, only more so. Killing a judge or prosecutor is as bad as killing a police officer: Whole squads of police come after the killer. We have always known, but do not like to talk about it, that the people who are in most danger are our witnesses. They cannot be replaced. If they die, the case often dies with them. That's why police officers are in more danger than prosecutors or judges. Officers are often irreplaceable key witnesses. Organized crime bosses and most other "professional" defendants have always known that, and one of our hardest jobs and biggest concerns is protecting our witnesses from intimidation and death.

Department of Justice prosecutor Gerald Shur came up with the original idea for protecting especially important witnesses: move them out of their zones of immediate danger to a place where no one knows them. In extreme cases, we could even change their identity, which is costly and time-consuming and extremely hard on the witnesses' families, who must either move with them and change their own identities or stay behind and perhaps never see the family-member witness again. I served as our office's witness security officer, handling our initial offers to join the program with the AUSA handling the case until the case was over and long thereafter. The job requires intense and very thoughtful consideration. Most witnesses, when they hear what is involved, opt not to join. Of those who do, many only stay in the program for a few years. When they cannot stand the separation from their families, and the heat is off them once the defendant is in prison and all appeals are over, there is much less reason for the witness to fear living as himself again. They then simply move back home and resume their old identities.

During my years as witness protection officer, this phenomenon happened many times. My office typically put one or two witnesses in the program each year. As discussed in the Corruption and Terrorism chapters, some witnesses quit the program and some have been kicked out, but a few, like Cowboy McNairy, actually stay in for life. Most of our protected witnesses have been honest people who happened to be in the wrong place at the wrong time and witnessed events that put them in danger. Nationwide, however, the majority of protected witnesses became witnesses because they were criminals themselves and had intimate knowledge of crimes because they helped commit them. Problems with this part of the program were documented by former CBS TV reporter Fred Graham, whose book, *The Alias Program*, was the first to shine light on the program and its problems.

One case Graham cited was that of serial bank robber and killer Marion Albert "Mad Dog" Pruett. A vicious criminal, Pruett began his ties to the program in a most unusual way: by killing a protected witness. While Pruett was serving a long federal sentence in the federal penitentiary in Atlanta, a colossal paperwork error caused a protected witness, who was just passing through Atlanta en route to another location, to end up as Pruett's cellmate for one night. Through the prison jungle drums, an inmate learned the witness was in Atlanta for one overnight stay.

When prison guards found the witness slashed to death by a homemade prison knife the next morning, the first person they questioned was Pruett, who told them quite a story. Pruett's version was that while he was sleeping another inmate somehow got into the cell and by the time Pruett awoke, his new cellmate was already bleeding to death. His story was so convincing that the AUSA assigned to the murder case decided Pruett himself was in danger and needed witness protection. Incredibly, the killer became a protected federal witness. Later, after he had testified, his sentence was cut to time served, and Pruett was released. He promptly began a nationwide crime spree, robbing and killing across the country. Finally caught, he was sent to Parchman for shooting a Jackson bank teller and leaving her paralyzed for life. While in Parchman, both Arkansas and Colorado sought his extradition to try him and give him the death penalty.

Since Pruett's Mississippi crime happened in the Southern District, we originally had no contact with him or jurisdiction over him. Then, one cold winter afternoon, my phone rang. It was a DOJ attorney saying that private lawyers were taking Pruett's deposition at Parchman the next morning. The DOJ attorney handling the case was tied up in court and could not be there. Could I handle the depo on such short notice? Better believe I could. What prosecutor would miss the chance to question one of the worst serial killers of our time?

The DOJ attorney quickly explained the case to me. In a typical Pruett scam, he had agreed to testify against the witness program and its officers, including Director Gerry Shur, who had been so helpful to me in earlier cases. In a magnificently brazen move, Pruett had offered to be a witness for the families of the people he had killed. In return for their support in asking courts not to give him the death penalty, Pruett would testify that DOJ and it officers were grossly negligent for believing him, a known killer, and setting him loose on an unsuspecting public with disastrous results they should have foreseen. Pruett's maneuver gave a whole new level of meaning to the word "audacious."

Sadly, as my father always said, you can always find a lawyer who will do anything for the money. For this case the lawyer represented the families of victims murdered by Pruett. He hoped to hit a jackpot fee as a percentage of what his clients got, with Pruett's help, from the taxpayers and public servants trying to protect witnesses. We were introduced outdoors in the freezing cold. Pruett was even worse than I had expected. He had reddish hair, a scruffy beard and spoke in a loud, shouting sort of voice. He looked and sounded totally crazy. He wore the usual leg irons with a heavy chain around his waist holding his hand-cuffed hands tightly in front of him. He was shouting as several guards looked on, scowling. Looking at us, he volunteered to no one in particular, "I'm Marion Albert Pruett but I'm *not* a mad dog killer. If you roll up my sleeve, you will see a tattoo I got a long time ago. It will show you the name came from my drinking Mad Dog 20-20 wine. It had nothing to do with that stuff I did later. Reporters just made up all that 'Mad Dog Killer' story to sell papers."

The lawyer introduced himself to Pruett and shook his manacled hand. When he turned to ask if I represented the DOJ and I said I did, he started introducing me to Pruett. My reaction to the introduction surprised me. The guards later thanked me for it, but I did not do it to show off. I just suddenly got really furious at the whole scene. When Pruett wiggled his fingers at his waist, asking me to shake his hand, I surprised myself and the others by blurting out, "I don't shake hands with scum like you." Pruett went crazy, screaming that the deposition was over and demanding the guards take him back to his cell in maximum security. The guards were smiling broadly. The plaintiffs' lawyer then debased himself even further, "Oh Marion, please Marion, you are such a good man to help these poor people. Please don't let this government lawyer trick you. You're doing just what he wants you to do." Pruett looked at me with his crazy, wild smile and giddily changed his tone. "Ok," was all he said.

The guards put us in a small, unheated room. The plaintiffs' lawyer began to question Pruett. I had been instructed to object where needed but not to ask any questions of my own. As it turned out, that was unnecessary. Pruett needed no coaching. He boastfully told the story of how easily he had fooled the government lawyers. He told which inmates had asked him and helped him kill the witness. As he began to describe the actual stabbing itself, his eyes widened, his voice got louder, and spittle spewed from his mouth as he boasted of all the times he had stabbed the witness and how he bled and pleaded for his life.

In the middle of the deposition, we took an eerie sort of recess. The in-house Parchman lawyer invited the lawyers and the court reporter to lunch at the nearest restaurant, which proved to be at the country club in an old antebellum house at Sumner. I still remember vividly how delicious the plate lunch was because of the implausible contrast between the white tablecloths, ceiling fans, and delicious food and the dingy, freezing shed we had just been locked up in with a raving madman. The courteous service was so calming that even the plaintiff's attorney talked about everything in the world but Pruett and his case. After an hour in this peaceful haven, we went back to Pruett and the freezing room and finished the deposition. True to form, Pruett ranted wildly for hours.

Gerry Shur and my other clients were eventually all cleared individually, but it was obvious there had been negligence somewhere, so whatever amount of money the victim families received from the Justice Department as a settlement they certainly deserved. I owed an apology to their attorney. Getting the madman Pruett to help his victims' families was a master stroke.

And the case did have a happy ending. On April 12, 1999, the state of Arkansas put Marion Albert Pruett to death by lethal injection, ending one of the saddest sagas in the history of the American criminal justice system. I never saw Pruett again, but would gladly have helped with his execution if requested.

Linda Leedom and the Chinese Wall[11]

Linda Leedom and Lula Young had been best friends for years. Linda had money problems, but otherwise the two friends were doing well. In 1990 Lula developed breast cancer. After a radical mastectomy and many painful treatments, the doctors told Lula her cancer had metastasized and she had only a few months to live. Lula thought of what useful thing she could do with the rest of her life. A devious and not exactly legal idea came to her: take out big life insurance policies on her life with her best friend Linda as beneficiary.

But there was an obvious problem. Insurance companies required medical exams before issuing life policies, and with her cancer, Lula could never pass such an exam. So she suggested to Linda a nice, simple solution. "You take the exams in my place." Since they were the same age and lived near each other the switch was simple. With Lula's agreement and connivance, Linda Leedom took out several life insurance policies in Lula's name with Linda as beneficiary: One was with Met Life for $75,000; another was with Met Life for $200,000; one was with Nationwide for $500,000; and there was a Credit Life policy for $38,000.

Linda took the medical exams for Lula, passing with flying colors. She signed the applications "Lula Young." No one is immortal, so despite her own good health Linda made her daughter Jennifer Leedom Dotson the second beneficiary just in case Linda somehow died before Lula. Both friends were satisfied with the arrangement for several months. Then the unexpected happened. Lula Young failed to die. The doctors could not say she was in remission, but for some reason she just kept on living.

Linda's financial problems worsened. Finally, she decided she could not wait any longer. Linda hired a local hit man to kill Lula by opening a propane gas tank in her house and setting fire to it with an electric heater to blow up the evidence and create the impression of an accident. The hit man convinced Linda the explosion would kill Lula instantly, and her friend would not suffer. Unfortunately, as in most criminal schemes, nothing went according to plan, and Linda's friend Lula apparently suffered a slow and painful death by fire. The arsonist's plan for destruction of the evidence did not go too well either. The fire marshals immediately suspected arson. Linda Leedom did not delay in claiming the insurance proceeds, however, mailing and wiring proofs of claim to insurance companies in Florida, Ohio, and Rhode Island. One of the Met Life offices was ironically located on "Boy Scout" Drive in Tampa. Insurance checks began to roll in, then were halted as suspicion focused on Linda.

Local District Attorney John Champion, son of the respected law professor Bill Champion and a former student of mine in federal trial practice at the Ole Miss law school, began a murder and arson investigation. He ran into some problems, however, and asked us to help apply pressure to the defendants by doing a parallel federal investigation for fraud by wire and mail against the victim insurance companies. John had problems with the admissibility of some of his evidence, which was illegally seized beyond the scope of his state search warrants. His undercover tape recordings of the hit man also looked inadmissible, so John asked if we could prosecute Linda first on federal fraud charges while he sorted out the legalities on his murder case. We all worried about how we could keep his tainted evidence from tainting our case.

Fortunately I had first attended and then taught seminars dealing with tainted evidence. The approved way to keep our case clean was to erect what is called a "Chinese wall," after the famed Great Wall built to keep out barbarian invaders. The way a legal Chinese wall works is that "taint teams" act as "cut-out" men who examine possibly tainted materials before giving only the admissible items to the trial prosecutors. In *Leedom*, I assigned a separate prosecutor, Paul Roberts, to handle the case. I received all of John Champion's evidence and reviewed and screened it, giving Paul only what I judged was clearly untainted and admissible.

Former U.S. Attorney Bob Whitwell had joined the best-known local criminal defense firm, Farese, Farese & Farese, to handle only civil litigation. Bob swore on leaving he would never handle a criminal case against us. But Bob was a very religious and kind-hearted man, and when Linda Leedom came to him with a sob story about how John Champion was persecuting her while she was still mourning the death of her best friend, Bob agreed to handle her case in state court for nothing. When we joined the case, it put Bob in the box of having committed himself in writing to defending her, even against us.

As always, Bob was a perfect gentleman. He challenged the admissibility of our evidence, and when that failed, he asked for and received a federal mental exam for Linda. Unfortunately for her, the psychiatrists found nothing wrong with her mentally other than a disorder associated with unusual levels of cold-hearted, self-centered greed. Seeing no chance of acquittal on the fraud charges, the insurance agents having testified they recognized Linda as the person who had posed as Lula during the insurance exams, Bob pled both Linda and Jennifer guilty to mail fraud, hoping to avoid much more serious state murder charges. Each received a two-year sentence, typical for fraud cases. Judge Glen Davidson also ordered Linda to make restitution to insurance companies of the $250,000 they had already paid her, a debt which would follow her and punish her for the rest of her life since debts incurred in frauds are not dischargeable in bankruptcy.

John Champion had not been idle. As he had told us, federal prosecutions can scare new witnesses into testifying, and this one did. His investigators also uncovered a second insurance fraud/murder scheme, this time against a retarded ward of Linda's innocent parents, who were his guardians. The ward, unlike Lula Young, had no knowledge of the plot against his life. Using the same modus operandi as in Lula Young's case, Linda had forged the signature of the ward on a life policy for $250,000, another for $200,000, and a third for $200,000. Linda was a beneficiary on the first two with her husband secondary beneficiary on the second policy and her daughter beneficiary on the third policy. It was a true family insurance plan.

Unfortunately for Linda, her daughter's boyfriend lost his nerve about killing the ward and confessed and agreed to testify against Linda and her whole family in both cases. DA John Champion obtained an indictment on Linda for capital murder, using the federal fraud conviction to make her a habitual offender. The jury convicted, and Linda was sentenced to life without parole plus twenty years. On appeal, Justice Fred Banks delivered an eloquent opinion detailing the intricate web of Linda's cruel and devious murder schemes. The opinion is well worth reading as an example of our Mississippi justice system at its best. The case was also an example of federal-state cooperation at its best. And no one breached our Chinese wall.

Killing the Killer of Sheriff Harold Ray Presley[12]

Nicky Hall was for several years our LEC, or law enforcement coordinator, serving as liaison with state and local investigators. It was a critical job and Nicky, former chief deputy sheriff in Tupelo, did it to perfection. Shot twice in the line of duty, Nicky still had the slugs in his leg and back, joking he "had more lead in me than most pencils." He was also a great storyteller.

One of his favorites concerned Harold Ray Presley, a local butcher and young cousin of Elvis. One night, Nicky got a call from a bartender saying Harold Ray had had too much to drink and someone needed to get him home. The bartender knew he could never handle him and figured the diplomatic 240-pound Nicky, an old friend of Presley's, was the man for the job. Nicky drove over to the bar and walked up to joke with Presley, who immediately said, "Now, Nicky, I know they called you to drive me home, but I'm not ready to go. I'll let you know when I'm ready." Nicky hung around and waited.

Presley soon began to get really rowdy but stared at Nicky as if to say "Not yet." Finally Presley punched a couple of guys and offered to fight everyone in the bar. No one took him up on it. He went back to the bar and ordered another drink. The bartender refused to serve him. Presley objected. Nicky made up his mind. He couldn't whip Presley, but he had to do something. It was what they paid him to do. He discreetly pulled out his nightstick and slipped up behind Presley. As he told me later, "John, I drew back and hit him as hard as I could on the very top of his head, but he didn't go down. He just turned around and looked me right in the eye and said, 'Nicky, that hurt. Don't do that again.'" Nicky stood around while Presley got another drink. After about ten minutes, Presley came over to him and said, "Nicky, can you take me home? I've got a headache."

Nicky and Harold Ray remained good friends when Harold Ray was elected sheriff several years later. Although rough around the edges, Presley was making a pretty good sheriff. Then one night I got a call from Nicky at home. He told me someone had killed Harold Ray, and Nicky wanted my approval to join the investigation. I told him to go straight over there. By the time he got there, not only had the local deputies caught Presley's killer, they had killed him too, stomping him to death. According to Nicky, his head "looked like a busted watermelon."

The story, as it unfolded in subsequent trials, was like a TV detective story. A convicted felon fleeing the law had kidnapped a young black woman and was driving up the highway north of Tupelo when he ran upon a police DUI roadblock. Knowing he was drunk and had kidnapped a woman and had a gun illegally while on parole, he ran right through the roadblock. Sheriff's deputies and highway patrolmen gave chase. During the pursuit, he pushed the woman out of his truck, her hands bound with duct tape. The officers accidentally ran her over, killing her.

The man eventually stopped the car and fled on foot. Sheriff Presley, always a man of action, responded to the call. He led a group of officers behind a house where witnesses saw the man flee. As Presley opened a door, he was suddenly face-to-face with the fleeing felon, who shot him several times in the chest before Presley could reach his gun. Other officers quickly subdued the shooter and took him outside and handcuffed him face down. First one deputy then another walked by and kicked him and stomped him and hit him with nightsticks. By the time paramedics arrived to help Sheriff Presley, the shooter's face was unrecognizable. Deputies drove the sheriff to the hospital, but left the shooter lying in his own blood for a good hour before carrying him to the hospital. Ironically, medical witnesses later testified that if Sheriff Presley had been flown by helicopter immediately to the hospital, his life would likely have been saved. By spending their time beating the shooter to death, his officers probably cost Presley his life.

State DA John Young believed there was no way a Lee County jury would convict law enforcement officers of murdering the murderer of Sheriff Presley. We agreed with the FBI, however, that as a civil rights brutality matter, the evidence looked strong, and we might well get a conviction. We had EMTs, highway patrolmen, nurses, even other deputies giving statements that they saw the beatings, that they were totally unnecessary, and they named the officers who did the killing. Even though the shooter deserved what he got, he deserved to get it from the legal system, not law enforcement vigilantes.

Then the Civil Rights Division insisted on stepping in. For years we'd had excellent relations, but this time a flammable mixture of bureaucratic arrogance and rookie zeal combined to screw up our case. I started the case, and after a dozen or so excellent preliminary interviews, I stepped out to handle other cases, leaving the Presley case to Bob Norman and Chad Lamar, two outstanding veteran AUSAs I felt sure would have our best chance of winning the case at trial. But the Civil Rights Division continued to interfere. They called our witnesses liars if each witness didn't make his or her testimony match perfectly with every other witness's story. The officers were not just offended, they stopped cooperating. The Washington prosecutors repeatedly impeached our own witnesses before the grand jury, not only alienating the witnesses but creating damaging statements for use on cross-examination by defense counsel at trial.

By the time trial was scheduled, Bob and Chad had gone from angry to despondent. They said the case was wrecked. I tried to encourage them, saying that jurors in predominantly black Greenville, where the case was transferred to be tried, did not usually take kindly to officers abusing people, whether black or white. But Bob rightly pointed out that our victim, a hardened criminal who had just murdered a sheriff, was white and had also caused the death of an innocent black woman he had kidnapped. The crime was thus in a sense white-on-white, but with a black victim thrown into the mix.

When the defense attorney was announced, we were not surprised. Joey Langston of Booneville had joined Steve and Tony Farese to take up the mantle of "Big John" Farese after his death by volunteering to represent for free any officer sued for use of excessive force. By this means they hoped to earn the officers' goodwill and business, as in auto accident cases where they are often the first witnesses on the scene. Langston's partner was none other than young Zach Scruggs, sent there by his father to be trained by Joey in how to handle cases. After several excruciating days and many unhappy witnesses, came the verdict on all defendants: not guilty. The widow and children of Sheriff Presley promptly brought a civil wrongful death suit against the county for what its employees did and won a good financial settlement. Another Elvis Presley cousin named Larry Presley was promptly elected sheriff, continuing the Lee County Presley dynasty.

The Tohills of Beaumont[13]

Charles Wiley Spillers deserves his middle name, however you spell it. A born-and-bred Cajun and former Marine Corps sergeant with a purple heart from Vietnam, he came home to south Louisiana to become an undercover narcotics officer in Baton Rouge, then moved on to the same job with the MBN and on to the Ole Miss law school and a job as a federal prosecutor in Oxford. Charlie was never an ordinary prosecutor. I never knew him to have an ordinary case. Whatever case Charlie tackled always had some kind of twist.

If there is ever a Spillers Defendants Hall of Fame—and there should be—among its first honorees should be the infamous Tohill clan of Beaumont, Texas. In Mississippi, we normally think of Cajuns as fun-loving party people, the only Americans who write nearly as many country songs about food as they do about broken hearts. But the Tohill clan was different. They must have taken a wrong turn somewhere in Sicily because if there was ever a mob family, it was the Tohills.

Undisputed leader of the clan was Jessie Tohill Sr., who would be called a warlord if he lived in Afghanistan. With his sons, Jessie Jr., Freddie, and John Paul, he ran a drug distribution network from Beaumont through Louisiana, Mississippi, Kentucky, Indiana, Ohio, New Jersey, and New York. After months of dogged investigative work, Charlie Spillers built a powerful drug conspiracy case against the family. In the first Tohill indictment, which charged Jessie Sr. as kingpin and godfather, the ten named defendants attracted such attorneys as Mississippi bar president Jack Dunbar and future U.S. senator Roger Wicker, not to mention veteran Oxford criminal defense attorneys Dave Bell, Grady Tollison, Will Ford, Bill Duke, Sonny Mason, David Calder, and Peggy Jones. Attorney Paul Buchanan of Beaumont was the only outlier.

With his usual thoroughness, Charlie Spillers began contacting attorneys for lesser defendants in the indictment as well as Tohill cronies not yet indicted. Charlie had most of them served with federal grand jury subpoenas. When Jessie Tohill heard the Feds were making offers to people to testify against him, he decided some folks needed to get killed to slow down Charlie's momentum. To get the ball rolling, Tohill told Michael Haskett to find and kill two potential witnesses. Jessie Sr. told Haskett his codefendant Maye Haney, an older lady known to the group as "Aunt Maye," would go with Haskett to Mississippi and help them locate the witnesses for killing. Before they left, however, Jessie Sr. learned that Aunt Maye herself had received a subpoena. She had refused to testify, but Jessie Sr. did not know that. He therefore told Haskett and his son Freddie to kill Aunt Maye herself after she'd led them to the other witnesses. They were then to kill Aunt Maye's son and codefendant,

Kevin Larue Haney and his wife Wanda and their two children, just to be sure everybody got the message.

The Tohills first planned to kill the Haneys by injecting them with massive overdoses of cocaine. That plan sounded too complicated, so in June 1989, Jessie Sr. told Haskett to just go ahead and shoot Aunt Maye instead, using his .38 revolver to do it. On June 9, Jessie Jr. and Freddie and Haskett went target shooting in front of witnesses so they would have an explanation if police found gunpowder residue on their hands. After midnight Freddie Tohill took Haskett to an after-hours bar where Haskett would be seen by people and supposedly have an alibi. At around 4:30 A.M. on June 10, Freddie gave Haskett his dad's old .38 and told him to "make sure no one saw him" kill Aunt Maye.

Later that morning, Haskett reported to Jessie Sr. that he had shot and killed Aunt Maye. Little did they suspect the mistakes Haskett had made. Satisfied with his work, Jessie Sr. drove Haskett to Lake Charles and gave him $150 and a bus ticket to Indianapolis and told him to stay there for a while. It was a pretty low-budget operation. Jessie Sr. later wired Haskett money for a bus ticket to return to Beaumont. Upon his return, Haskett showed Jessie Sr. and John Paul where he had tossed the murder weapon into a drainage ditch. They discussed whether they should try to retrieve it, but decided not to, since no one had seen Haskett and the police would never know where to look for the gun.

Then out of the blue their whole world came down on them. Jessie Sr. and Michael Haskett were arrested in Texas on a federal indictment from Oxford, Mississippi, for the murder of Maye Haney, a subpoenaed witness in their drug case. Jessie Sr. wondered how in the world the Feds had figured it out. It seemed like such a perfectly executed crime. Jessie Sr. should have questioned Haskett better. At first, things had gone well. Haskett drove to Aunt Maye's trailer and when she locked the front door against him, he kicked it in. He heard her hiding in the bathroom begging for mercy, swearing she was not a witness, which was true. But Haskett had his orders. He shot Aunt Maye through the door, then pushed her body back using the door and finished her off with a shot to the head. Feeling proud of himself, Haskett drove back toward the bar where they would pretend he'd been all evening.

Then their perfect plan began to unravel. En route, Haskett ran out of gas. Luckily, he thought, he rolled up to a gas station just as his car stalled out. Reaching in his pocket, he realized he'd forgotten to bring any money to buy gas. No problem. He at least had thought to bring the number of the bar with him. With the only money he had on him, one quarter, Haskett tried to call the bar from a pay phone. Unfortunately for him, he misdialed the number. His last quarter gone, there was nothing left to do but hitchhike to the bar. Leaving his car at the station, Haskett began thumbing a ride. Again he felt himself lucky. Streams of cars came out of nearby factories whose shifts had just changed. Scores of drivers passed Haskett before one kind-hearted soul stopped and picked him up. Haskett was surprised that the driver was black because few blacks lived in that area or worked at those factories, but was grateful and didn't think about it further. The guys at the service station saw him being picked up. The driver dropped Haskett at the bar. Everything once again seemed copacetic. The next morning, the Tohills took Haskett back to the station to pick up his car.

When Charlie Spillers heard of the shooting of Maye Haney, he immediately suspected the Tohill clan. He also felt remorseful, wondering if his subpoena had triggered them to suspect she was a witness when she wasn't. Taking Tom Dawson with him, Spillers headed for Texas. At the Orange County Sheriff's office, they told the detectives of their suspicions about who had killed Aunt Maye. The detectives began regaling them with Tohill stories. One involved a local guy who once went to Jessie Sr.'s back door to pick up some dope. On the porch was a dead body. Jessie said not to worry, they were going to move him later. The customer left quickly without the dope and never came back.

As Spillers and Dawson looked at Tohill files, a local detective came by with an interesting find he had made that morning. While driving to work near Maye Haney's house, he had spotted something that looked like a gun barrel sticking up out of the mud on the far side of the ditch along the road. The detective jumped the ditch, retrieved the gun, and brought it to the office. Everyone was looking at it because of its unusual appearance. It was a .38 revolver, but instead of the usual round barrel, someone had replaced it with the square-shaped barrel of an automatic. They test-fired it and, somewhat surprisingly, it fired perfectly.

In the kind of coincidence that only happens to Charlie Spillers, just at that moment one of the detectives who had worked on Charlie's Tohill case walked in. He had been on the team that searched Jessie

Sr.'s residence when he was arrested. He said, "Hey, I know that gun. That's Jessie Tohill's. There's not another weird gun like that anywhere." An intense series of neighborhood interviews began in the area between where Maye was killed and where the gun was found. It turned up service station employees who remembered the guy who ran out of gas and started hitchhiking after trying to call the bar, which the detectives knew as the bar where the Tohills usually hung out. The detectives got a list of the workers whose shift had ended when Haskett was hitchhiking. Officers soon found the Good Samaritan who'd given Haskett a ride. They showed him a photo spread of Tohill associates. Without hesitating, he positively identified a photo of Haskett as the man he picked up and dropped off at the Tohill "alibi bar." All their clever planning had been for naught.

Ballistics matched Tohill's gun to the slugs in Maye Haney's body. Confronted, Haskett confessed and agreed to testify against the others. As Charlie was preparing Haskett to testify before the grand jury, I was sickened at how cold-blooded Haskett was. His sense of humor, if he had one, was macabre. He laughed at how, when he shot her, the elderly lady's false teeth flew out of her mouth and landed in the bathtub. In an effort to humanize him a little before he faced the grand jury, I thought I'd shame him by asking him a question that would allow him to say how sorry he was about killing the old lady. I naively asked him if there was anything he'd do differently. As he thought, he slowly began to look even dumber, then suddenly seemed to brighten up as if he'd just understood the question. "Oh yeah. Next time I'd plan it better." So much for provoking him to remorse.

The wording of the murder indictment sent a chill of fear through the defendants' camp, even if it created no remorse. Every Tohill pled guilty to everything, and no one had to testify. A few months later Charlie received a phone call from the mother of one of the witnesses he hadn't needed. She said Charlie had promised her son that in return for his testimony Charlie would help her son if he ever needed it. Charlie said he remembered it. As the mother talked, Charlie typed in the name on an inmate locator on his laptop.

Charlie asked the mother if her son had ever been convicted in connection with his dealings with the Tohills. He had been. Charlie then asked if he was doing a sentence for drugs. "Oh, no, sir, it was for a murder," she said in a heavy Cajun accent. "Who did he kill?" Charlie asked. "A witness," she said. "Why did he do that? Did the Tohills put him up to it?" She responded indirectly. "Well, you might say that. He didn't want to do it, but Jessie made him. He did it out of scaredness and afraidness of Jessie."

Charlie wanted to laugh, but the mother put an end to that, explaining that her son was so scared of the Tohills that after he shot the guy he ran away. Then he remembered that Jessie had told him to get rid of the body and he decided to go back. Charlie asked one final question: "So did they find the body?" Her answer guaranteed her son would get no help. "Well, sir, that boy of mine was so scared of Jessie and them that he went back to the guy's trailer and took a butcher knife and cut the body in pieces and threw them all in the bayou. But they still found a few pieces. Can you help him?" Charlie said with finality, "No ma'am, I'm very sorry. You see, the help I promised him was strictly limited to drug charges." And that was true.

Murder by Moonlight: The Natchez Trace Sniper[14]

Of all the hundreds of cases I've tried, one stands out in my memory most starkly: a nine-year-old boy killed by a high-powered rifle on Christmas Night on the Natchez Trace Parkway while returning home from visiting his grandparents. The case came to me via telephone from FBI agent Jerry Marsh. I was playing with my daughter under our Christmas tree when my wife said grumpily, "It's the FBI calling. Got to talk to you. Don't they know it's Christmas?"

Jerry apologized at once and said he knew I'd understand once I heard what happened. A little boy had been shot the previous night and had just died of his wounds. Since it was on the Natchez Trace, the case was federal. Jerry said he had at least waited till morning to call me. His own Christmas had been ruined by a call to his home from the first park ranger on the scene, Jerry's own cousin, who had the unusual name of Urbane Breeland. His cousin told Jerry the basic facts. Just after midnight, Kenneth Brinkley was driving south on the Trace from Tupelo toward Jackson with his fiancée, Linda Johnson, beside him. Her two children were asleep on the backseat. Kenneth was telling Linda about an accident he'd had a year earlier when he slid off the narrow two-lane road during heavy rain and hit a tree near the Ballard Creek rest stop. They were paying close attention, looking for "his tree" as he called it.

It was a clear night with a bright nearly full moon, making the trees look particularly beautiful as they arched over the highway, sometimes forming almost a tunnel. It was as peaceful as the previous century when the Trace had been the major south-to-north road for returning travelers who'd floated by boat down the Mississippi. Abe Lincoln's father once took the Trace back home to Kentucky. Andrew Jackson rode it back north to Nashville from the Battle of New Orleans. As they passed the Ballard Creek rest stop, Linda and Kenneth saw a maroon Ford pickup parked there with no driver in sight. Seconds later, there was a huge explosion inside the car. Brinkley knew it was too loud for a blown tire. The children immediately started screaming. Linda's twelve year-old daughter, Lachelle, who was sitting in the middle, said her leg hurt, and they saw blood on her hip. Her nine-year-old brother, Terrell, who was sitting on her right, was wide-eyed and shaking violently. Blood was spurting from both his legs.

Realizing they had been shot, Kenneth sped up to get away from the shooter and head for the nearest hospital. Linda climbed over the seat and pressed on Terrell's wounds to stop the bleeding. Kenneth took the exit for the nearby town of Mathiston and stopped at the police station to report the shooting and get directions to the hospital. Terrell's teeth were chattering and his face was already pale from the loss of blood. His wounds were the size of golf balls. He still hadn't spoken. Police officer Roger Miller directed them to the hospital and headed for Ballard Creek with two other officers. He also called county sheriff Hays Mills. The officers looked around the Ballard Creek area for clues, trying not to disturb the scene.

Sheriff Mills, an experienced hunter, found a suspicious area behind a pair of twin-oak trees. He described it to me later as a "wallowed-out place," four inches deep, where the thick carpet of dead leaves had been deliberately scraped back. There were four deep indentations in the soft earth which looked to Mills like what he and other hunters would make when prone while lying in wait for a deer. The indentations were consistent with where a hunter's elbows and knees would have been, but that was of course speculation.

The other officers looked for spent shells and other evidence but found only a freshly broken whiskey bottle. As they searched, a two-tone maroon pickup slowly approached at thirty miles an hour. As it passed, Miller recognized the driver as Ronald Glen Shaw, a convict just paroled from Parchman following his second rape conviction. Both rapes had been committed the same way. Shaw had entered a women's restroom at a strip club and raped a stripper using a carpet-cutting knife as a weapon.

The officers pulled out and turned on their blue lights to question Shaw, who took off with the officers in pursuit, reaching speeds in excess of 110 miles per hour. When they finally forced him off the road, Shaw got out with his hands up. They arrested him for speeding and, after smelling him, for DUI. He asked them, "What have I done?" Through the open door of his pickup, officers saw in plain view five live rifle rounds on the driver's side floor. One officer pulled the driver's seat forward and shone his flashlight into the backseat, where he saw a .35-caliber lever-action deer rifle, which he seized.

The officers read Shaw his Miranda rights but did not ask him for a statement, and he volunteered none. They drove him to the sheriff's office at Ackerman and read him his rights again. This time he said he'd like to tell them what happened. He said he'd been driving around drinking and stopped at a "pull-off place" to throw up. He claimed he had not fired his deer rifle since early that afternoon. Sheriff Mills knew Miller and Breeland had felt and smelled the rifle when they seized it and said it was "fresh fired." The next morning, December 26, FBI agents Jerry Marsh and Don Greene went to the jail and again advised Shaw of his rights. He repeated his story that he had not fired his rifle since early afternoon. The agents told Shaw that Terrell Johnson had just died of his wounds.

That night, a hospital janitor, while mopping out the operating room, found among Lachelle's discarded clothes the bloody slug that killed Terrell. The agents returned to the jail the next afternoon, December 27, and readvised and requestioned Shaw about his story. Marsh showed Shaw the slug and told him it would be flown that day to the FBI lab and Marsh thought it would match Shaw's rifle. At that point, Shaw said he would answer no further questions without an attorney present. The agents told his parents, who were present for the interview even though Shaw was already twenty-nine years old and intelligent, that they expected a ballistics report by Monday morning December 29, an unusually short turnaround for any crime lab.

A Mississippi FBI agent personally flew the slug to the FBI crime lab in Washington. The Jackson agent in charge personally called the FBI director to get the ballistics exam expedited. The case was assigned to the same expert who had examined the bullets taken from President Ronald Reagan when he was shot by John Hinckley. The .35 slug was in good condition with plenty of identifiable riflings. It matched perfectly Shaw's rifle, which the Mississippi agent had also carried with him to the FBI lab, where it was test-fired.

At 10:30 A.M. on Monday, Shaw's parents called the FBI agents, saying their son had changed his mind and now wanted to talk to them without an attorney. The agents declined, saying FBI rules would not allow it since he had asked for an attorney. The parents insisted. An agent called me and asked for legal advice. I told them to go ahead but only after getting a written waiver and to tape record both the waiver and the interview and their talks with the parents. Otherwise he'd claim later he tried to tell us the truth, but we wouldn't listen. The agents said FBI regulations did not allow taped interviews because they created too much paperwork. I told them to go ahead without the tape, even though I knew their stupid policy would later cause us credibility problems if we went to court.

Shaw dramatically changed his story. This time he said that because he was on parole he had not wanted to admit he possessed a gun and was headlighting deer on the Trace at the Pigeon Roost rest stop. This time he claimed that while walking in the woods along the Trace with his truck lights on to blind any deer that might come along, he slipped and fell, causing his gun to discharge accidentally toward the Trace. He claimed to have seen a car go by just then and at first he feared he'd hit it, but when the car did not brake or slow down, he figured he'd missed it. He said he sat in his truck for several minutes, then drove on toward Ballard Creek, where the officers stopped him.

The next day, December 30, Sheriff Mills filed a state complaint charging Shaw with first-degree murder under Mississippi law, his county having overlapping jurisdiction over crimes on the Trace. Sheriff Mills and the local DA asked me to prosecute, however, because the case would be very expensive and difficult for the county to prosecute. We agreed and began looking for a motive. Why would anyone do such a horrible thing? At the jail, the agents had seen Shaw's girlfriend, who was named Janet. She was a strange-looking girl, but about right for someone like Shaw: tall and skinny with long black hair which contrasted sharply with her milk-white complexion. She walked awkwardly, having one leg shorter than the other. Her strong resemblance to the witch-like girl in a popular TV beer commercial of the time caused the agents to nickname her "Mortitia." Local informants said it was rumored she'd been seeing another man while Shaw was off in the pen, a man who drove a car almost identical to the one driven on the fatal night by Kenneth Brinkley.

We filed a federal criminal complaint, and the FBI arrested Shaw and took him into federal custody. On January 12, 1981, we gave Shaw a preliminary hearing before U.S. magistrate Charles "Mo" Powers, who bound him over to the federal grand jury. Our theory of the motive at the hearing was that Shaw had thought he was shooting a rival for the affections of Janet.

At this point, veteran democratic U.S. Attorney H. M. Ray, who had been in office since John Kennedy appointed him in 1961, was replaced by republican Glen Davidson, a former Tupelo district attorney and Ole Miss basketball player. Glen had prosecuted numerous murder cases, and Al Moreton and I looked to him for guidance. Al and I had neither one ever prosecuted a murder case. And our proof seemed to be getting weaker. FBI ballistics experts had just completed a bullet-trajectory study using dowel rods to show angles of entry. They concluded that Shaw had shot the car from the front, long before he could have seen whose car it was or what color it was. There was no reason to believe he would have thought his rival for the affections of Janet would be on the Trace at that time and place. An interview of that man revealed he never drove on the Trace, finding it too isolated and scary.

Al and I had a long meeting with Glen Davidson where we explained the proof we had and what the defenses would be. He said, "You boys are good. I've seen you in action. Whatever you decide to do, I'll back you to the hilt. But if it were my case, I'd be happy with a plea to involuntary manslaughter. No matter what kind of sorry bastard the defendant is—and he is totally sorry and the jury will hate him—it sounds like a drunken hunting accident to me, and I think that's what the jury will decide." In our minds Al and I agreed, but in our hearts we could not let the case go. We decided we'd rather lose the case than give it away, and Glen agreed for us to go ahead.

We first studied the legal issues. Under the "assimilated crimes" law, we could charge Shaw with violating the Mississippi murder statute within federal jurisdiction. I read that law for the first time since law school. Then I read the federal murder statute for the first time. One phrase caught my eye: "Every murder perpetrated by poison, lying in wait, or any other kind of willful, deliberate, malicious, and premeditated killing . . . or perpetrated from a premeditated design . . . to effect the death of any human being other than him who is killed, is murder in the first degree." We liked the part lawyers call "transferred intent," that is, if you shoot intending to kill one person and accidentally kill another, you're still just as guilty. We liked even more the part about "lying in wait," which fit perfectly Sheriff Mills's description of the "wallowed-out" place behind the twin oaks.

Shaw had first lied about doing any shooting, then lied about where he did it, moving the site from Ballard Creek to Pigeon Roost for some reason. Still, we had no credible motive. Then Al said, "You know, John, proving motive is important in the movies, but the law doesn't require it. The judge will instruct the jury that proof of motive isn't required. That's what the standard jury instruction says." Al loved a challenge and always had a plan.

The FBI investigation continued on apace. Our whole office offered to help us with legal research, but that was the easy part. What we needed was evidence, not law. I finally drafted an indictment in five counts. The first count was for possession of a firearm by a convicted felon and carried five years in prison. That count was a cinch. Count 2 was for the murder of Terrell Johnson and carried life without parole or the death penalty if we asked for it. Count 3 charged Shaw with using a firearm in that murder and carried another ten years. Counts 4 and 5 charged assault with intent to kill Terrell's sister Lachelle and using a firearm in that assault, again carrying life plus ten years. Legally we felt good.

Al and I drove down to the scene one freezing night in January to see what it looked like under similar conditions. We felt like it was a bad omen when the heater on my decade-old Mercedes went out. Our fingers got so cold we could hardly feel them as we surveyed the scenes with flashlights and I tried to take notes. We found the twin oaks, but the wallowed-out place had been destroyed by officers trampling over it searching for spent shells. No one had photographed it.

On January 29, 1981, the grand jury enthusiastically voted an indictment and strongly encouraged us to go all the way with the case. They wanted the death penalty. We were less confident. At that time, the Ole Miss Law school had its own federal defender program, established by Judge Keady to train students and to save money on court-appointed counsel. It was staffed by one professor and as many law student researchers as he could handle. There were plenty of inexperienced volunteers. We knew that appointment meant we'd be flooded with legal motions but also knew the professor, Robert Doyel, had little practical experience in criminal law and none in murder cases. We were even a little concerned that if Shaw were convicted, an experienced appellate attorney might convince the appeals court that such a tricky case with a man's life at stake should not have been entrusted to such inexperienced counsel. That fear turned out to be unfounded.

The case went as we'd figured. The students did a fine job on the legal issues, bombarding us with motions, the most important of which were to exclude the rifle as illegally seized without a warrant and Shaw's statements as illegally obtained in the absence of an attorney after Shaw had specifically asked for one. The case was assigned to veteran Judge Orma Smith, who made short work of the motions. When Professor Doyel argued in chambers that the murder counts should be reduced to manslaughter because there was no proof of deliberation by Shaw, Judge Smith, who had defended murder cases himself, asked Doyel point-blank, "Mr. Doyel, what if I reached in my drawer here and pulled out a pistol and without saying a word just shot you dead right here in chambers? Is that not murder? Your motion is denied along with all the others."

As trial approached, we got one big break. FBI agent Don Greene, who will always be in my personal law enforcement hall of fame, somehow found us two new witnesses who became crucial. Leigh and Ann Avery, a teenage brother and sister who were students at Mississippi State University, not far south of the crime scene, regularly drove home up the Natchez Trace. They told Greene that early on Christmas Night, after dark, they'd been driving down the Trace near a dumpster by the Mt. Pisgah church when they passed a truck looking just like Shaw's with a lean-faced man on the driver's side who closely resembled Shaw. Just after they passed him, curious about why he was there, they looked back. To their shock, Shaw was leaning out the window of his truck, sighting over his rifle at them. Leigh took off, telling Ann he recognized the rifle as a lever-action .35 Marlin deer rifle, the exact one Leigh himself had. We decided to hold the Averys back for rebuttal since their evidence was really damning. We feared if we offered it in our own case-in-chief, the judge might exclude it as too unrelated and prejudicial, but if we waited till after the defense, they might inadvertently make it relevant and open the door for us to get it in.

Then we received some critical help from inside our own office. AUSA Tom Dawson, an avid hunter who regularly traveled to the Yukon and Canada's north woods to hunt elk and caribou, also had a .35 Marlin lever-action rifle identical to Shaw's. Dawson badly wanted to try the case with us and kibitzed constantly with Al and me. One day, reading the FBI reports of the seizures and Shaw's various statements, he had a eureka moment: "I may have this wrong, John, but I know my rifle, and maybe you can use this on cross-examination if they're stupid enough to put this fool on the witness stand." In his final version, Shaw had told the FBI that he'd stopped at the "pull-off place" because he'd seen deer there as he was driving. He said he'd stuck his rifle out the window and fired a single shot and hit one deer and followed it unsuccessfully into the woods.

Dawson was emphatic: "The key thing is the number of shells. These Marlin .35s hold just seven shells. The officers recovered five shells from the floor of the truck, right where Shaw said he ejected them when he saw the officers following him. A sixth shell was found jammed in the tube that feeds the shells into the chamber. Shaw didn't know that. If you count the one shell he used to kill the boy with, that makes the full seven. It proves his story about shooting a deer is bogus. That would have been an eighth shell, and the Marlin only holds seven. His own story hangs him." Dawson smiled broadly. "You boys need some hunters on the jury."

Al and I wondered how we could use this theory. The best way, if we could keep it straight, would be in cross-examining Shaw, but he might not take the stand. Otherwise, we'd have to have a firearms expert testify to it, and our period for informing the defense of our expert witnesses had passed. Plus, we had not yet decided which of us would cross-examine Shaw if he did take the stand. Al had never hunted, and I hadn't hunted much since high school. But the issue of which nonhunter would cross-examine would be resolved shortly.

Interviewing witnesses and preparing them for trial was always one of my favorite parts of trying cases. You get to size them up as narrators, focus them, calm them down, and generally make them better witnesses. I also enjoy preparing them for cross, usually acting myself as a cross-examiner. My witnesses often told me after trial that I was harder on them in pretrial prep than opposing counsel was in court. And that's how it should be.

We'd already prepared Kenneth Brinkley, an intelligent and articulate witness. But we'd avoided talking to Linda Johnson, knowing how painful it would be for her to relive the suffering and death of her son. But one night a couple of weeks before trial, we scheduled a meeting with them at their motel in Oxford, where we felt she'd be more comfortable than in an office. As we approached the door, Al, a veteran Navy enlisted man who was always fearless and hard as nails, put his hand on my arm and stopped me: "John, I just can't do this. Tell you what, if you'll interview Mrs. Johnson and put her on the stand in court, you can cross-examine Shaw. I just can't do it." I've never known a more courageous man than Al Moreton. He's one of the rare stoics I've ever met. Al ignores pain, physical and moral. It made me feel cold and heartless that I could do this without a problem, but to me it was just something we had to do.

When Linda opened the door, Al was gone. I told them he'd been called away. The interview went fine. I assured her that no attorney in his right mind would dare be ugly with her at trial. She seemed reassured. It made me feel dirty to be so cynical, but I was doing it for her as a victim when I told her, "We'll make this quick tonight. I don't want to cause you pain or make you cry, but if you break down and cry in front of the jury it will help our case, and it's your right to let the jury see what pain this monster caused you." She said she'd lived with it and could handle it and she still had her daughter, Lachelle. She was pretty and articulate and looked just right that night barefoot and wearing jeans. I wished she could have testified that night and gotten it over with. But she was even better on the stand at trial.

Judge Smith having swept away the blizzard of motions by the law students, Al and I turned to the order of witnesses and who would question each one. That was no problem. We would just alternate. Al asked if

I would question the prospective jurors on voir dire, my favorite part of the trial. "If you don't mind, I want you to do the first part of the closing arguments and summarize our evidence. You're good at that. Then I'll do the final part. You tend to get pretty wound up, and I'm afraid you might get too emotional and commit error." I knew Al was right. "And if you want to make the opening statement after I do voir dire, that's fine too. You're better at that," I said.

Al looked concerned. "I've been meaning to talk to you about that, John. I know you'll disagree, but hear me out. I want to waive opening—not even make an opening." I erupted, as he knew I would. "Not open!" I yelled "Let them box us in? Speak for us? Are you crazy?" Al made his point calmly. "John, I like opening almost as much as you do. But this is a shaky case. We don't know exactly what we're going to prove, so it's better we don't limit ourselves." It was true that our key witness, Sheriff Hays Mills, had gone missing for a week. After an argument with his wife, he'd left town, and no one could find him. I figured he was too committed to the case to let the victims down, but who knows what humans will do? Trial was less than a week away, and no one had heard from him or seen him in at least a week. Reluctantly, I went along with Al. He was right a lot more often than I was.

Later that week, Bob Doyel came to us and offered to plead his man guilty to the firearm count and ask the court for a five-year sentence if we'd dismiss the murder counts. Hays Mills was still missing. He could be dead for all we knew. But we still had the proof of defendant's different versions. We could prove he lied. And just like in a mystery novel, he had returned to the scene of the crime, then run away when he saw the police. We told Doyel no. We'd still rather lose the case than give it away. The day before trial, Sheriff Hays Mills called from Vicksburg. He was on his way back. We could count on him. The next time I saw him, he was smooching with his wife outside the courtroom.

Al's strategy of waiving opening worked far better than even he had imagined. When Judge Smith asked, "Who will open for the government?" Al said quietly, as if it was perfectly normal, "We'll waive, Your Honor." Al had told the judge's clerk what he would do ahead of time, so the judge acted as if waivers were routine. "You may now open for the defense, Mr. Doyel." Caught whispering to a law student, Doyel had not heard him. The judge repeated himself, this time considerably louder.

Doyel lost his cool and sounded nothing like an attorney. "What?" he said. "You may open for the defense," the judge intoned. Doyel stuttered, "But what about the government?" Judge Smith smiled slightly. "They've waived. It's your turn, Mr. Doyel." "I—I—I'm not ready," he stammered. Recovering himself a little, he added, "Can we reserve our opening till we start our own case? That's what they do in most courts." Judge Smith did not like the implication. "This is *my* court, Mr. Doyel, and I've found it is unwise to let the defense hear the prosecutor's evidence before they say what their proof will be."

Coming from Judge Smith, usually so mild-mannered and even-handed, that was pretty strong and subtly damaging to Doyel, suggesting fabricated testimony. I wondered if it would be error on appeal. The jurors looked puzzled. After several speechless seconds, Doyel asked for a recess. Judge Smith said, "I'm reluctant to start a trial with a recess, but if you feel you really need it to get organized the court will grant it. Everyone be back in your places in fifteen minutes." Judge Smith whacked his gavel hard on the bench, also unusual for him.

After the recess Doyel made one of the most nervous, evasive, slippery sounding openings I'd ever heard. Our proof then went beautifully. Every witness was better than they'd been in interviews. The cross-examinations went nowhere, often making the witnesses stronger and more determined by challenging them. We put on only Shaw's first two statements, where he denied firing his gun. Then we put on the agents who said they smelled the odor of fresh-burned gunpowder when they seized his gun. We ended with our expert from the Reagan case saying Shaw's gun absolutely fired the fatal bullet that killed Terrell and lodged in Lachelle's hip.

Doyel had opened for the defense by admitting Shaw was guilty of Count One and asked the jury to find him guilty of that. He followed up with a little trick. He called Jerry Marsh to testify to Shaw's last interview, the one where he finally admitted he had fired the bullet that hit the car and the children. We objected that under the circumstances Shaw's exculpatory out-of-court statement to the FBI was hearsay. If they wanted the jury to hear that story, they would have to put Shaw on the stand and let him tell the jury that himself. Judge Smith agreed, sustaining our hearsay objection. Doyel was boxed in. No way he wanted the sinister-looking Shaw testifying. To stall, he then put on some people who'd been with

Shaw that night to testify that he was not violent when they were with him. But they still had to admit he was very drunk.

His female cousin and a friend had asked him to take them home after visiting several clubs. Those witnesses also admitted that although he was a convicted felon forbidden to have a gun, he carried a rifle and hunted illegally all the time with the very gun that killed Terrell Johnson. The girls also had to admit Shaw was angry when they left him because his cousin's girl friend would not go drinking with him any further that night. In the middle of trial, it suddenly occurred to Al and me that the volatile Shaw might well have been so drunk and angry about being rejected that he just shot the first car that came along.

After exploring every other option and calling several witnesses who clearly had little to offer, Doyel finally bit the bullet and reluctantly called his client to the stand. Shaw had a lean, haunted look. His shoulder-length hair was dirty and uncombed. His clothes hung loose on his lanky body. He had a vacant stare and never looked the jurors in the eye. Doyel made the mistake of asking him first about his two prior rape convictions, stressing that they were not for murder and did not involve firearms, which opened the door for me to ask on cross what weapons he had used and to make Shaw speak the words "carpet knives." Doyel got through his direct very quickly as if to avoid his client slipping up on anything.

When I rose to cross-examine Ronald Glen Shaw, I was as nervous with pent up adrenaline as I'd ever been in my life. I took him back through his various "revisions" to his story. Then I surprised him when I asked if he'd stopped by a dumpster at the Mt. Pisgah church that same evening. The key to a good cross-examination is the element of surprise, coming at a witness from an oblique angle he doesn't expect. Shaw looked worried, as if he was wondering how we knew about Mt. Pisgah, since no witness had mentioned it. He looked over to Doyel for help, but there was none coming. We had kept Doyel as in the dark as his client. Finally he said, "Yeah, I stopped there to take a leak," smirking as he said it, showing the jury for the first and only time his sinister smile.

As Al had feared, I got pretty vigorous during cross, treating Shaw with the contempt I thought he deserved and the jury expected, bringing up numerous times—just to question his credibility of course—his two prior rape convictions. I was actually afraid I'd screw up the potentially deadly cross-exam question about the number of shells and was hesitating before starting into it. I looked back at Dawson, who was sitting inside the bar right behind counsel table. He nodded encouragingly and I started in.

Glancing repeatedly at the jurors that we knew from voir dire were deer hunters, I asked Shaw about the rifle. He said it was his father's, but he used it all the time and knew it well. I asked him how many times he'd fired it that night at the deer. "Once," he said. "Can you give the jury a reason why the officers never found an empty shell casing at the scene?" He could not. "Do you know how many rounds you jacked out of the rifle when you saw the officers chasing you?" I asked. "They said it was five," he replied. "No reason to doubt their word on that, is there?" He agreed. "Did you know they found one round jammed in the feeder tube to the chamber?" I was afraid by now he'd start counting, but he didn't. "Yeah, I had one jammed in there and hadn't had time to get it out." Shaw was had. He just didn't know it yet. I proceeded to show him, bullet by bullet.

"All right," I continued a little nervously. "Now, Mr. Shaw, I don't have a gun like yours. Can you tell us how many rounds it holds?" He suddenly looked confident. This was *his* turf. "It holds seven." He still didn't see it coming, even as I began counting it out for him. "So, let's see now. Five on the floor, one jammed in the gun, and one to shoot Terrell Johnson." I held up seven fingers. "That makes the seven. But you said you shot a deer first. That would make eight. But you know your rifle only holds seven." There were gasps from the jury box. Shaw looked blank. From somewhere in my subconscious came the old English phrase for confronting a witness: "I put it up to you, Mr. Shaw, that there was no eighth shot because there was no deer. You made that story up to cover your tracks. This was not a shooting accident. The only thing you shot was those children." Shaw was speechless. The jurors were muttering audibly. It was not my best cross-examination ever, but it is still my favorite. At least I didn't get the numbers confused and screw it up.

After a devastating rebuttal by the Averys about seeing Shaw pointing and sighting the same rifle at them, total strangers, the same night, we rested. I argued first and went about as crazy as Al had feared, vilifying Shaw as a serial liar and "double-convicted rapist." The defense's closing was as weak as their opening. Doyel was well prepared and articulate, but the proof had just broken totally against him. I was curious to see how Al, known for his devastatingly calm and logical arguments, would handle this one.

Al walked to the podium and began, "Ladies and gentlemen of the jury . . . " Then his voice broke. The manliest of men first teared up, then quietly sobbed for several seconds. After a marshal brought him a glass of water, Al made a low-key, pro forma argument totally devoid of emotion. Tears come to my eyes today as I recall it thirty years later. Al wrapped up quickly, and the jury got the case. We agreed that the verdict would be swift. After two hours, however, we knew it would not. After three hours, we were worried. Perhaps our initial fears were right. Finally, a note arrived from the jury foreman, a hunter from the Delta.

Amazingly, the jurors had found Shaw guilty of both murders and using the gun in both murders almost immediately. They were hung up only on count one, the firearm possession count, which we had never mentioned because Doyel had told them in opening to find him guilty on that count. For that reason we'd never mentioned it and the jury apparently had forgotten it or perhaps never even heard it. Judge Smith repeated to them his instructions on that count and that the defense had stipulated Shaw was guilty of it. They went back out and returned in five minutes with a guilty verdict on that count as well. It was the strangest of my many experiences with the reasoning of American juries. Later we heard from a spectator who was out in the hall that some jurors didn't much like some of the federal firearm laws. They also said they weren't sure what "stipulate" meant.

But their hesitation to convict actually helped us on appeal. It showed they were not carried away by emotion and hell-bent to hang Shaw but were carefully considering all evidence on every charge. As in most cases, jury disagreements, especially acquittals on some counts, tend to show the court of appeals that the jury was fair and unbiased and their verdicts were based on reason and evidence and not on emotion or prejudice. And on this appeal, we felt we would need that support.

While the pre-sentence report was being prepared, great sadness came to the court. Judge Orma Smith, after undergoing multiple bypass surgery, suffered a series of strokes, leading to his retirement and death. After more than a year in limbo, new district judge L. T. Senter, a veteran state trial judge, succeeded Judge Smith and took over the Shaw case. He got off to a strong start, sentencing Shaw in March 1982 to life imprisonment for the murder of Terrell, five years' imprisonment for shooting Lachelle, two more mandatory ten-year sentences for using the rifle in the shootings and another three years just for possessing the weapon, all consecutive, none concurrent, meaning a total sentence of life plus twenty-eight years. Shaw was ordered confined to the rough maximum security prison at Terre Haute, Indiana, which I've visited and would not want to see again.

On appeal, Professor Doyel and his law students outdid themselves, accusing me of committing no fewer than sixty-nine reversible errors. In response I managed to lump them under seven broad categories in a seventy-one-page brief. We were disappointed when Chief Judge Charles Clark set the case for argument in his home courthouse in Jackson rather than New Orleans. Traveling to that wonderful city and its great restaurants was one of our most prized perks as prosecutors. It was probably just as well in this case, however, because the week before the argument I ruptured another disk in my lower back and could barely manage to walk the block up Capitol Street from the old Walthall Hotel to the elegant old courthouse. I'd called ahead and gotten permission to argue the case sitting down. When he learned of it, Doyel objected, implying I was faking and seeking sympathy, which the judges rejected out of hand. Doyel began his argument with a rehearsed, melodramatic, and amateurish statement. Referring to the trial date, he said, "From April 20 to April 23, 1981, justice in the Northern District of Mississippi took a vacation." Before he could continue, Judge Clark cut him off sharply: "Please spare us the theatrics, Mr. Doyel. I drive the Trace every month to visit my grandchildren. Just stick to the legal issues."

It was surprising how personal this case was to everyone who came in contact with it. The arguments were spirited, with abundant questions from all three judges on the panel, which included veteran wisemen Alvin Rubin of Louisiana and Jerre Williams of Texas. In their unanimous opinion, written by Judge Williams and delivered March 15, 1983, the court rejected every last defense contention in an opinion that occupied over thirty printed pages. When I got to work on March 18, my birthday, I found a copy of the court's opinion in a big gold frame, with a congratulatory note from Glen Davidson, which meant a lot. He was going to be a fine man to work for.

Doyel, undeterred, moved for a rehearing, which was denied in another published opinion on September 15. The U.S. Supreme Court refused to hear the case. The Shaw case was finally over. In the years since that trial, one thing has always stood out in my mind. Unlike almost every other inmate, Ronald Glen Shaw has never made one complaint to us or the courts—not one motion, not one letter. Looking back at his demeanor at trial, I now feel I know how Shaw felt at trial. At the time he fired the fatal bullet, he was mad at the world and drunk and didn't care who he killed, but since then I've always felt that he had remorse that an innocent little boy was killed by his action. And he's had the rest of his life to regret it from a prison cell. His release is now scheduled for the year 2024.

5

FARAWAY PLACES WITH STRANGE-SOUNDING NAMES

The Age of Terror

Introduction

We have entered your country for years living quietly, becoming employed in your auto plants, your business, your stores, your gas station your motels. All the while we prepare for the jihad. You think this not so. You will be destroyed from within. You will see. The 911 attack came from outside but the true jihad will come from within your own borders. You will see, stupid amerikkan.

—Islamist Internet Posting

When I joined the U.S. Attorney's Office in 1974, it never occurred to me that I would ever know a terrorist beyond the Ku Klux Klan nor have any use for the fluent French I acquired during my two years as an undergraduate at the Sorbonne in Paris. Oxford did not sound like a launching pad for terrorism or for using my French to get free trips to exotic foreign cities. For five years, the only time I used my French at all was for a couple of interesting interviews with the French-Canadian wife of a Montreal drug dealer passing through our district. Then the ever-inventive Thomas W. Dawson, the sage of Lauderdale County, got hold of a fraud case in which an American con man based in Tupelo bilked several businesses and a Swiss bank out of hundreds of thousands of dollars. The Swiss bankers, having heard our judicial system was hard on bankers, refused to testify in the United States, insisting we go there under a brand-new U.S.-Swiss treaty and take their depositions instead. Dawson was tied up in another trial, so U.S. Attorney H. M. Ray dispatched me to Geneva in his place. The details of that trip will be included in the follow-up to this volume.

Another decade passed before Washington, checking its computers, found in 1989 that its "special skills" section listed only two fluent French-speakers in the entire Justice Department nationwide who could handle a French-speaking case, and the other French speaker had already declined. She claimed she did not want to meet Yasser Arafat or his PLO, then headquartered in Tunis, formerly Carthage, on the north African coast facing Italy. Tunisians speak French as well as Arabic from decades of occupation by France. That mission to Tunis and the trials I observed there resulted in reciprocal visits to Oxford by Tunisian prosecutors and kick-started a series of twelve more foreign missions from Russia to Indonesia before and after the terror attacks of September 11, 2001.

In the early 1990s, when the Soviet Union broke up, DOJ needed to lend someone to the American Bar Association to do training and reconnaissance in Chişinău, capital of the former Soviet Republic of Moldavia. I told them I didn't feel qualified. The DOJ international people said, "Oh, they all speak French there as well as Romanian. It's an old tradition." The tradition turned out to have been true but had ended back in the 1920s when the Russians occupied Moldova and renamed it Moldavia. Since then Moldovans had been required to speak Russian.

The Moldovan mission got me firmly on the DOJ foreign circuit. Attorney general Richard Thornburgh formed a special new training unit called OPDAT (Office of Overseas Prosecutorial Development and Training) to work with foreign prosecutors on international criminal networks using all the new treaties we had signed with emerging countries around the world. Before I knew it, I was part of the first group of U.S. prosecutors ever to attend the annual Russian National Prosecutors

Conference in Moscow. There I witnessed three Russian murder trials where they used their new American-inspired jury system. The Russians then made return visits to Oxford.

DOJ sent me to magistrate school in Paris, back to Tunis and onward multiple times to Rabat in the Kingdom of Morocco, Tbilisi in the new Republic of Georgia, to Interpol headquarters in Lyon, France, to Muscat, the beautiful capital of the Sultanate of Oman, next door to volatile Yemen, and which guards the entrance to the Persian Gulf across from Iran (into which you could shoot a rifle if so inclined). From there it was on to Jakarta and Bali in exotic Indonesia. Those missions will be the backbone of what my editors see as the third in a trilogy of books on my criminal trials.

A few foreign terrorism stories made the cut for this first volume. The first began in Oxford when an Ole Miss coed married a Lebanese Shiite student and ended up reliving the agony of an international parental kidnapping eerily reminiscent of Sally Field in the movie *Not without My Daughter*. Another concerned the investigation and prosecution of Dr. Abdel Ashqar, international secretary of Hamas, the Palestinian terrorist group, who spent seven years as a graduate student in Oxford where he got his Ph.D. while raising millions of dollars for Hamas through Oxford banks. My last civil trial involved a suit by Adnan Awad, a Palestinian veteran of the PLO hired by terrorists in Iraq to blow up the Hilton Hotel in Geneva. Terrorism expert Steve Emerson wrote his biography, *Terrorist: The Inside Story of the Highest-Ranking Iraqi Terrorist Ever to Defect to the West* (1991). Awad, or "Captain Joe" as I called him, was in the federal Witness Protection Program but had to be relocated numerous times for talking too much about his real-life exploits. His final relocation was to Tupelo where he married the pretty blonde daughter of a dentist, then talked too much and was kicked out of the witness program. Frustrated by our bureaucracy, he sued the FBI, U.S. Marshals, and several federal officers including one U.S. Attorney. I was assigned to defend them. The case was so secret that its title was *Sealed Plaintiffs v. Sealed Defendants*. Captain Joe's story is the last in the book. It is a fitting end, perhaps, since my first case involved our own local terrorists from the Ku Klux Klan and my last a reluctant terrorist who finally rejected militant Islam. It was quite a ride.

Alice El-Sarji: "Not without My Daughters,"
an International Parental Kidnapping[1]

Alice Livingston had it made. Her father was a successful contractor who owned a big farm near Sardis, less than an hour from Oxford. The farm had chickens, ducks, and all the other farm animals that can make a child's life so enjoyable. But Alice was no simple farm girl. Her uncle was a psychiatrist in Seattle, her family was educated. But of all the attributes with which nature had blessed her, the most important was her beauty. When I first met her at my office as a victim of crime, she was already in her mid-30s and resembled the English actress Dana Wynter, with refined and delicate features, an educated way of speaking and a charming smile. Her story, however, was less pretty.

At eighteen, Alice had gone off to Ole Miss as a happy, carefree coed. She enjoyed the parties and did not study very hard, but was doing well enough. Then she met a handsome business major from Lebanon. A real charmer who sang and danced well, he swept Alice off her feet. Hassan El-Sarji had adapted well to American life. Funny and enthusiastic, he fit in well with the culture, taking the good ole boy nickname "Sonny." Being Lebanese was not that exotic at Ole Miss. The state has long been rich in Lebanese Christians, natural businessmen who thrived in the deep south climate. When Alice and Sonny married, it presented several problems. First, she needed to finish her education. Second, Sonny had no intention of becoming American. He was a Shiite Muslim and insisted on living in a Muslim country and that Alice become a strict Muslim wife. Alice married him anyway.

As long as they stayed in the U.S., things went fairly well. Sonny had a habit of chasing women, which wounded Alice deeply, but she kept taking him back. Finally, seeking to make more money more quickly, Sonny moved them to the United Arab Emirates. Although places like Dubai can look as free as Las Vegas in external ways, behind closed doors and off the main streets the UAE is a very conservative patriarchy. The couple had two children with good American names, Sarah and Megan, but Alice had to learn to wear the veil and keep her body covered from head to toe. And Sonny was disappointed that he was not becoming rich. There was too much competition. The Emirates were crawling with talented young men seeking their fortune. Sonny was frustrated. With

Alice's whole-hearted agreement, they returned to the U.S. Again things got steadily worse. Sonny could not find as much income in the U.S. as he had in the UAE, even with lots of help from Alice's father. His womanizing got completely out of control. The little girls were the only ones who were happy, loving their grandparents and life on their farm. In 1989 Alice filed for divorce and got "paramount" custody of the girls with Sonny having visitation rights.

Sonny had many relatives in Southern California and began traveling between California, Lebanon, and Mississippi on business. During vacations Alice let the girls spend a month each summer in California with their father and his brothers and cousins. The divorce was fairly amicable as those things go. But Sonny wanted more. He wanted the girls to visit their grandparents in Lebanon, where his family had not only a multistory apartment complex in Sidon but a fine old stone house with swimming pool, high in the beautiful Lebanese mountains. The girls had always enjoyed the warm, loving family of their father and had a hard time understanding the divorce.

In July of 1991, Alice let the girls go with Sonny to California to be with their father and his family for the summer. In August, Alice agreed to let them travel on to Montreal to spend five days with their cousins. On August 18, Sonny and the girls called and said they were fine and the girls would fly back to Memphis on August 23. When they did not arrive, Alice called Sonny's sister-in-law in Montreal. She claimed their family had not seen either Sonny or the girls, but had "heard" they had all flown to Lebanon to visit the girls' grandparents. Alice called Lebanon. Sonny laughed and gloated over his clever plan, "If you ever see them again, it will be here in my country and only as I say." He sent Alice a videotape of the girls playing happily in his courtyard with their cousins. For Alice, a long nightmare had begun. She begged Sonny to bring the girls back, to let her visit them, anything. He laughed as he refused. Finally, when the girls realized they were being held there and could not go home, they persuaded their father to let them at least speak to their mother on the phone. At the time, Sarah was nine. Megan was just four years old.

Alice went to Sheriff David Bryan of Panola County, where she had her custody decree. He took her to court and got an arrest warrant for Sonny for kidnapping children under the age of ten. They took the state arrest warrant to veteran FBI agent John Lavoie, who prepared a federal warrant for unlawful flight to avoid prosecution (UFAP), a device by which the FBI can help state prosecutors catch fleeing felons. It rarely succeeds outside the United States. Lebanon does not extradite its own citizens, so the chances of Alice getting her daughters back looked remote. But she was not about to give up. Alice first tried every possible means to persuade Sonny to let her visit her daughters. Sonny's father finally made him agree. Alice began to visit the girls in Sidon, sometimes twice a year. They exchanged letters and photos.

Once Alice saw her daughters in person, she realized what their futures would be. They were virtual prisoners in the El-Sarji compound. They could not go out alone, even to the corner candy store. The girls, especially Sarah, also began to realize their predicament. They developed secret code words to use in their letters and phone calls. But nothing worked. Alice tried the State Department, which basically said they had thousands of such cases and if Lebanon would not help, there was nothing they could do. Alice hired a Lebanese lawyer and paid her well, but she also failed. She tried, but as she said, "Women, especially Muslim women, have few rights here."

Alice took a job as a secretary in the Ole Miss Admissions Office. Through her Ole Miss contacts Alice met Dr. Chester Quarles, chairman of the Legal Studies Department. Former head of the Mississippi Bureau of Narcotics, Quarles had written over a dozen books on law enforcement issues, including terrorism. He also had a creative personality, and Alice persuaded him to pull out all the stops. They decided to seduce Sonny into coming back. Whatever his other faults, Sonny had once loved Alice and probably still did. He had remarried and started another family, but his brothers said he was lonely and miserable, a foul-tempered middle-aged man who little resembled the carefree student she had married a dozen years earlier. With Quarles's help, Alice wrote a series of passionate love letters to Sonny which were some of the hottest I'd ever read in my life. If published, they would have ranked high on the erotic best-seller list. For a moment, it looked as if Sonny might weaken and try to return to her. He really wanted Alice back, but only in Lebanon, and only on his terms. After eight years of mental torture, Alice cracked and became severely depressed. Psychiatrists prescribed the strongest anti-depressants, but they did not solve her problem: her separation from her daughters.

She stopped eating and grew emaciated. Her broken-hearted parents finally had her admitted to a hospital for treatment for her depression.

One day, FBI agent John Lavoie was visiting the Panola County Jail where David Bryan was Sheriff. As he walked through the cells to visit a witness, Lavoie saw a gaunt woman who looked like a meth addict. Lavoie was eating an apple his wife Helen had given him that morning. As he munched on it, the woman, who was wild-eyed and only weighed about 80 pounds on a 5', 6" frame, put her hands through the bars. "Please," she said pointing to the apple. John felt sorry for her. "David, could I let her have a bite? She looks like she needs it." The sheriff agreed. "Go ahead. She's on her way to Whitfield on a Chancery Court civil commitment. She's been trying to starve herself to death."

John Lavoie handed the woman the apple. She turned it over in her hands slowly, then began to eat it. The sheriff said, "Don't go too fast, Alice. You'll make yourself sick. Your stomach is totally empty." When John heard the name "Alice" he looked back at the woman. "Who is that?" he asked. Sheriff Bryan told him, "I thought she was your case? You know, the woman whose girls were kidnapped to Lebanon by their father? That's Alice Livingston." John Lavoie later told me it was like someone had kicked him in the stomach. He went over and talked to Alice. She didn't seem crazy to him at all, just totally devastated by the loss of her daughters. There was little he could do then, but he made up his mind to make another run at the case.

The next day I got a phone call from John, who told me about the case and said he'd like me to meet Bill Livingston, Alice's father. Al Moreton, who had the case, had been named U.S. Attorney by the judges and was not able to handle cases anymore. As the office's international security officer, I was a logical choice to take over. Besides, John and I had worked a lot together, and he knew I loved kidnapping cases, and as Criminal Chief would probably assign the case to myself anyway. When I got to work the next morning at 7:30, Bill Livingston was already there, not at the front door where the public comes in, but at the back gate to the parking lot where the prosecutors enter. "I didn't want to take any chance of missing you," he said. A tall, lean man with a resemblance to Gary Cooper in both his looks and demeanor, Bill told me the story from the top. His daughter Alice was doing much better with medication and was coming home the next weekend. He asked if we would try again on the case. I told him frankly it looked next to impossible, but we'd pull out all the stops.

Bill Livingston had spent his savings and the girls' college funds flying Alice and her mother to Lebanon. Alice had also, at weak moments, fallen for con artists who promised dramatic rescues of the girls. Bill said he thought there was an outside chance Sonny was weakening some. The girls were miserable and wanted to come home. Much as they loved the little cousins they lived with, they knew they were little more than prisoners and had begun to dread what would happen to them when they reached the age to be married off. Alice, having watched the film *Not without My Daughter* with Sally Field, had been talking about getting the girls back herself. Bill feared she would try that if all else failed.

John Lavoie joined us. We came up with a scheme to persuade Sonny. I prepared an official-looking legal document with a gold seal, red ribbons, and a blue back, signed personally by me and the state DA, guaranteeing Sonny El-Sarji that if he let the girls come back to the United States to visit, perhaps go to school, he would not be prosecuted for kidnapping nor would any other legal action be taken against him. We communicated the offer by phone to his father and brothers. Sonny called Alice and told her he was seriously considering it. Would making love with her still be part of the visits? Of course. We heard nothing more from Sonny for several weeks, then came a letter saying he wished he could accept our offer, but he had talked to lawyers, and they thought it was a trick, that once the girls were in the United States, we would never let them go back to Lebanon and would probably put him in prison for years. He was half right. We would never have let the girls go back to Lebanon. But we would probably not have put him in prison because we had legal problems.

The sheriff had gotten only a Justice Court arrest warrant for kidnapping, not an indictment, and the state statute of limitations for kidnapping had run out. Worse, at the time Sonny took the girls, parental kidnapping was not yet a federal crime: Only recently had Congress made it a federal crime to kidnap your own child in violation of a U.S. custody order, and that law did not apply retroactively to Alice's case. Under the Ex Post Facto Clause of the U.S. Constitution, you cannot be prosecuted for acts that were not crimes when they were committed.

When we met with Alice, she reacted more quietly and stoically than I expected. She'd been deceived so many times. "I never thought he'd go for it anyway," she said, thanking me for our efforts and leaving my office. Two weeks later, I got another early morning visit from Bill Livingston. "Alice has disappeared. We think she's gone to Lebanon to get the girls. They've been talking a lot on the phone, sometimes using strange words that don't make sense to me. What can we do?" I called the State Department office responsible for international parental kidnapping cases. They were not encouraging. Inside their honeyed words, the message was basically, "Forget it. We can't help you." I did not tell Bill at that time that Alice had called me a week earlier and asked me if we could have a little secret between us without telling anyone, especially not her parents. I knew what it had to be, and figured knowing her plans and keeping her trust was worth it, even if it meant deceiving her parents by my silence. Alice was severely distraught, and my job was to look out for her as my crime victim, whatever it took. "John, I'm going to get my girls. It's all planned. We've talked about it. I just need you as backup in case anything goes wrong." Knowing it was useless to argue with her, I went over the risks with her again. She had strong answers for all of them. "Sonny has just contracted to marry off Sarah, who is turning eighteen, to a hideous old rich man next month. Sarah plans to run off with her school bus driver unless I can get her out. Without Sarah's support—she is so smart and tough—I don't think Megan can survive alone. She is much worse off than Sarah. I'm afraid she might take her own life." I stressed to Alice what could happen to her. She didn't care: "My life here is a prison already. If I get caught, they can rape me, torture me, kill me, it doesn't matter, but I've got to try to get them out. And I don't think they will treat the girls any worse if I fail." I told Alice goodbye for what I feared was the last time.

A couple of days after Bill's visit, the receptionist called, "Mr. Hailman, this call has to be for you. It's some foreigner. I think they're trying to speak English, but I can't understand her." A Lebanese operator came on, ascertained my identity in French, then Alice came on the line. "John, I've got the girls. I'm well hidden in a cave in some mountains in Syria. Christians here are bringing us food and water, and I've paid a man to get us out. I've got a cell phone, but every telephone call here is intercepted, so I don't dare tell you any more. I didn't have the heart to talk to my parents. Please call them and tell them we're ok, and to tell the El-Sarjis when they call that I went away on vacation."

Unbelievably, that story worked. The El-Sarjis thought the girls had run away on their own. They called the Lebanese police, but never put out any wanted posters or missing children alerts like we would have, which was a great break for us. And they never suspected Alice or reported her to the police. For a couple of weeks, Alice called me every day on her cell phone. The man she'd paid to take her out of Beirut harbor by boat after dark had taken her money and never showed up. Another who took a payment to drive them out by car via Turkey did the same. All along, I'd been talking to John Lavoie, dreaming up schemes to get her out. Alice somehow made it to the American embassy in Beirut to ask for asylum. They refused to take her. They said that under Lebanese law, she had kidnapped the girls. One embassy officer, however, was courageous and sympathetic. "Washington leans on us hard not to get involved in these cases. There are so many of them and our relations with the Lebanese are at a very sensitive stage so we really can't afford to destabilize things. But my heart goes out to this lady. If you *really* need something, call me at home. Here's my private number." We made up some code words to use, and I thanked him.

Alice made it back to her cave. She later told me that she and the girls had slipped into Syria and back without incident. Their worst problem happened when they tried to enter Israel, thinking it would be a safe haven. But with her foreign accent and the girls with their native Arab accents, all of them veiled and covered in Islamic robes but unaccompanied by a male relative, the Israelis were suspicious. With Lebanese border guards watching and listening, she could not tell the Israelis her real situation, and dared not speak English or say much even in Arabic for fear there were warrants out for their arrest. She finally gave up on Israel as her escape route. Her latest call was not as clear as the earlier ones. "My batteries are going, John, and I'm losing my grip. We're totally broke, and I don't know what to do." I didn't either, but we had to do something.

First we scratched up a little cash, went to Walmart and got the right cell-phone batteries. With John Lavoie, I went to the local mental health center in Oxford and talked to the sympathetic psychiatrist on duty. After showing him our IDs and making him swear that what we told him would be privileged doctor-patient information, we told him Alice's history and in vague terms her current predicament. He gave me without further question 3 large anti-anxiety prescriptions for Alice, which she had run out of. My own pharmacist quietly filled them. I called the helpful Embassy employee in Beirut and he agreed to receive the money, batteries, and medicines by diplomatic pouch and somehow get them to Alice. John Lavoie got the package out and, as if by miracle, within three days Alice called back from her cave on a strong cell phone in a much more hopeful mood. Now we just had to get her out.

John Lavoie asked me, "Have you ever heard of Kroll Associates?" I had heard of them. Kroll was a private company made up of retired FBI agents and former CIA case officers. People in the Arab countries and especially in France thought they did "black bag" jobs outside of U.S. law. French prosecutors with whom I had worked on terrorism cases called them "assassins." Lavoie was outraged. "That's bullshit. Several friends of mine work for them. They're the good guys." Thinking ahead to retirement, I asked John what their legal department was like. He laughed, "That's one of the best things about them. No lawyers are allowed at Kroll. If they get sued, they hire private lawyers. They are pure investigators. No lawyers are invited to their party." John got me a guy on the Kroll desk for the Middle East, and I told him our problem. He was remarkably sympathetic, not at all the kind of soldier of fortune the French had led me to believe. He said he regretted it, but he doubted they could risk any of their "assets" in the region, but said he'd check into it. The very next day he called back.

"There are no warrants for your lady, just a missing persons report on the girls as runaways. If you don't mind giving me her cell phone number, we just might be able to help them." I gave him the number, but felt I needed to add: "This is a very strange deal. This lady is broke, the State Department won't touch it, and I doubt that Justice or the FBI will agree to pay you, and I know you guys are expensive." His answer was simple: "There will be no charge. This woman needs help. Consider it what you lawyers call professional courtesy."

The operation went smoothly. I will never tell how, but local people helped Alice and the girls to an airport in the Middle East in the middle of the night, and they flew right out straight to Memphis. "Daddy Billy" Livingston and his wife and a crowd of friends were all there with John Lavoie and me to meet them. Alice looked radiant. The girls were a sight. Megan, at fourteen, was tall, dark, and beautiful and looked about twenty-five. Sarah, at nineteen, was blonde, round-faced, and a full head shorter than Megan, barely five feet tall. Most amazing were their clothes. They had somehow gotten full western dress: no head scarves, no long dresses. Around each one's neck hung huge Christian crosses, almost down to their waists. Each was holding a tiny American flag. But their ordeal was not over.

The girls' adjustment to American life was as difficult as we'd been warned. They missed their cousins, their only friends during their captivity. Without Alice's knowledge, they called their cousins and even talked to their father and grandfather. Alice was convinced Sonny and his brothers would come back to the United States, using their fluent English and considerable financial resources, and re-kidnap the girls and drug them and somehow get them back to Lebanon via Mexico. She especially feared Sonny's contacts in California. She and the girls were living on an isolated farm where someone could conceivably slip in and snatch them.

Mostly to reassure Alice, I carefully reread the law to see what we could do. Hidden in the gobbledygook of the international parental kidnapping statute was a provision I'd overlooked. Not only was it now a crime to take children out of the United States in violation of a U.S. custody order, it was also an offense to "retain them outside the United States with intent to obstruct lawful parental rights." Retaining was a continuing offense not barred by the five-year statute of limitations. It was a crime they were still committing. A gleeful John Lavoie joined me in reinterviewing the girls about their treatment in Lebanon. I drafted an indictment charging not only the father, Hassan "Sonny" El-Sarji, but also his father (who came to California twice a year for free medical treatment as a dependent relative of a U.S. citizen) and various brothers and sisters-in-law who were actively assisting in holding the girls in bondage. The girls were careful to describe which relatives were kind and encouraging to them and those people were not charged. During the testimony of Alice and the girls, grand jurors wept openly, men as well as women. They wanted the kidnappers and their accomplices to experience an American prison—all of them. We had the indictment sealed but put it into the National Crime Information Computer (NCIC) system so if any El-Sarji tried to enter the United States anywhere they would be arrested and in custody before they could get to the girls. The Memphis

International Airport is, after all, only thirty minutes from where the girls were living with Alice and their grandparents.

Alice was still worried that Sonny would send paid accomplices to snatch his daughters. She was sure he was not courageous enough to do it himself. His brothers had told her numerous times that he was the "black sheep" of the family, to use their own phrase, a bully and a coward. After some discussion, she gave us permission to call Sonny and tell him that there was a federal warrant for his arrest for kidnapping. I told him personally and got a warm feeling of pleasure from the moment. He wanted to see the indictment, but we refused, deciding to let him sweat. This time we made no offers of leniency, no offers of any kind really except to lock him up for life. We also gave him no hint that anyone else had been indicted. Unfortunately, two of the relatives who had helped in the kidnapping ten years earlier were living in the northern U.S., and we could not charge them since they had done nothing since the new federal law was passed to restrain the girls from leaving Lebanon. We waited for the others to arrive in the U.S. and looked forward to seeing the handcuffs and leg irons on them.

A few months later, a U.S. Marshal called from Los Angeles. They had Mohamed El-Sarji, one of the brothers, and shipped him back to Oxford in custody. Our local U.S. magistrate set the case for a bond hearing. I put Sarah on the stand first. She testified eloquently how the family had kept her under constant surveillance. They were both definitely retained against their will. She had to admit that Mohamed was more encouraging and less openly hostile to them than the others but still had always kept an eye on her and Megan and told them not to try to leave. Under Islamic law, they could go nowhere without a male relative and were basically prisoners. Sarah also translated an audiotape of her father and one of her uncles discussing how they produced bogus American passports and visas and sold them to anyone who had the money. Fortunately for Mohamed, the bail hearing was held before September 11, 2001, and he was not a party to the discussions of bogus passports and visas. Since he was the brother who came to America most often, we felt he was involved, but could not solidly prove it.

When Mohamed El-Sarji took the stand, he was quite an actor. A smooth talker with excellent English, he soon had the Magistrate hanging on every word. He told of how he had been a diving instructor in

Southern California. He produced a news article describing his underwater archeological explorations off the coast of Sidon, calling him the "Jacques Cousteau of Lebanon." A local Lebanese businessman offered to put up a large cash bond for Mohamed. He later turned out to be a person of interest in the terrorism trial of Sami Al-Arian in Tampa. The most touching of Mohamed's stories was of how he missed his wife. Seeing him kissing his long-time American girlfriend outside the courthouse that day made me considerably less sympathetic toward him, but I had to admit he had charm. If Sonny was anything like Mohamed, no wonder Alice was taken in by him.

At the end of the hearing, we decided to agree to dismissal of the charges against Mohammed without prejudice so we could rearrest him if he ever came back. In the meantime, he would be more useful to us in putting the family back in Lebanon on alert as to what American jails were like and what would happen to them if any of them ever tried to enter the United States and take the girls. To date we have never heard from him or any other El-Sarji again.

Sarah soon learned to drive, started dating, graduated from college, got married, and had two fine children. She tried to join a U.S. law enforcement or intelligence agency, but it would have required being away from her family and moving to a large city. She now teaches in a public school while her husband is in graduate school at Chapel Hill. Megan had a little more trouble adjusting, having left the United States when she was only four. But she and Sarah had kept up their American English, and Megan quickly became a popular actress in local dramatic productions. She came to visit me several times to ask about her father. She said she felt like half her life was missing. She wanted to understand her past. After Alice, I believe Megan suffered the most but also believe she will follow through on her plans to get a college degree. She now has a good job managing a restaurant and is returning to college. Her excellent intelligence and stunning beauty will take her a long way.

Alice retired from her job at Ole Miss, married a retired Coast Guard officer and lives near her parents. I see her sometimes on the Square in Oxford where we have warm little conversations, having shared a truly unique life experience. She is of course still wounded by her experience, but is doing well, as are her wonderful parents, who are so happy to see their family back together. The coda to the story was blurted out to us one day when I took Alice to the office of Bobbie Vance, an old friend and experienced Chancery Court attorney. She offered to help us get the girl's names changed for free. We had not noticed that her son, a student at Ole Miss, was working in the library beside us with the door open. After Alice stepped out, I heard Bobbie say to her son: "Can you believe that? What an adventure story." Her son, with the wisdom of youth, summed it all up for us. "It's simple, Mom. It's like my sociology professor told us: Never marry outside your culture."

An Honorable Terrorist:
Abdel Ashqar Finances Hamas through Oxford Banks[2]

Abdelhaleem Ashqar began life, as he recalls it, as the serious son of the mayor of a small Palestinian village. When the United States and its European allies created a homeland for the remaining Jews not murdered by the Nazis, however, Ashqar's peaceful life was gone forever. Palestine became Israel, and Ashqar and his family became foreigners in their own country. His father, a member of the Sufi sect of Sunni Islam, bore their displacement with philosophic calm. Abdel did not. He eventually joined the violent anti-Zionist group Hamas, an outgrowth of the Muslim Brotherhood, founded in Egypt to drive out its British occupiers.

Ashqar moved quickly up through the Hamas ranks, becoming the primary spokesman for the Islamic University of Gaza, a hotbed of the movement to oust Israel from Gaza and the West Bank of the Jordan River. Ashqar became the chief lieutenant of Mousa Abu Marzook, the best-known leader of Hamas. Quiet and literate and fluent in English, if left to his own devices, Abdel Ashqar would probably have become a happy professor of history or an accountant. Because of his accounting and P.R. skills, Ashqar was chosen to be Marzook's chief treasurer and fund-raiser for the "Outside," the term Hamas followers use to refer to the world beyond Palestine, which they called the "Inside." A study of international financial patterns persuaded Marzook and other Hamas leaders that America was where the money was. Despite its long and steady support of Israel, both in money and arms, the United States also had large Arab and Muslim populations, many of whom had become affluent in the political and economic freedom of America. To harvest this financial crop, Hamas began sending fund-raisers to America to seek money for the Palestinian cause. Marzook chose as his chief fund-raiser the serious and studious Abdel Ashqar. Although he insists he be called the full "Abdelhaleem," I've always shortened it American-style.

Like many Palestinian refugees, Ashqar had a passport from Jordan, the primary country to give asylum to Palestinians who did not wish to submit to Israeli authority. Because Islam forbids the charging of interest, considering it usury, Ashqar would have been out of place studying U.S. banking. Nor could he sign up as a student of political science, his preferred subject, because his militant anti-Israeli views and preference for violence would have gotten him ejected from any American university he chose. So he chose business administration, a vague and neutral subject close to money but far enough from politics that he could glide with relative anonymity through graduate school to his ultimate goal, an American Ph.D. He hoped to return to a new Palestinian state as a full professor.

Ashqar's preferred university was Iowa State. Cold in the winter, Iowa seemed a strange choice. But Ashqar had friends there, important to an Arab living in a foreign land. He also had friends in Louisiana and Texas and applied there as well. In all, Ashqar applied to seventeen U.S. universities and was rejected by all but one: the University of Mississippi at Oxford. Ole Miss, with its history of racial troubles, was recruiting minorities to comply with court orders in the famed *Ayers* anti-discrimination case. To help Ole Miss comply with those orders, the federal government was showering the university with cash grants for minority students. Foreign graduate students in pharmacy and engineering were pouring into Ole Miss, rapidly changing its culture and the appearance of its student body.

From his paymaster Abu Marzook, who taught at Louisiana Tech in Ruston, Ashqar knew Oxford had a thriving mosque with two active congregations composed of Palestinians, Saudis, Lebanese, and Muslim students from a score of Islamic nations. The two congregations, interestingly, were not divided into Sunni and Shiite, as might be expected. One group was composed primarily of professors and their families, the other group primarily of students, although the line was informal.

Based on his good academic record, USAID gave Ashqar a full academic scholarship and a living stipend as well. With his wife Asmaa, a pale-skinned young woman who was even more militantly Islamist than Abdel (nearly all her course work had been in *Fiq*, or Islamic religious studies), they moved into a nice brick duplex on Harris Drive in west Oxford near the Ole Miss campus. Ashqar did well in his studies, which were supervised very lightly by a respected Ole Miss professor who was dying a lingering death from cancer caused by frequent sprayings of Agent Orange while serving in combat in Vietnam.

At first all went well. Classes were easy and the childless couple had lots of time to enjoy an active university-town social life, avoiding only the famed pep rallies in the Grove on football Saturdays because alcohol was such a prominent feature there. By pure chance, the Ashqars rented a duplex just one block behind the offices of the FBI and IRS. Despite that proximity, the Ashqar duplex faced away from FBI's windows so no one noticed at first all the cars carrying robed, bearded figures who visited the Ashqar home.

After a couple of years, things began to go wrong. Ashqar could not contain his militancy and began haranguing students at the mosque, encouraging them to join the armed struggle to expel by violence the "Zionist occupiers of our Arab lands." The leaders of the mosque quietly expelled him. They also told the university and the FBI of his statements favoring violence. At the time, my older daughter was spending a year "abroad" in Oxford living in the home of her best friend, the daughter of a Saudi professor who taught at Ole Miss. His wife kept telling me that all her Arab friends thought their phones were tapped because whenever they used their phones all sorts of clicks and buzzes were heard. I told her they were paranoid. If their phone was tapped, I would know.

Then one day I got a call from an Oxford banker. In small towns like Oxford, where everyone knows everyone and informality prevails, it is hard to stay anonymous for long. "John, there is something weird happening here. This Arab graduate student is receiving and sending tens of thousands of dollars every week by wire transfers. I know their system is different, but this doesn't look right." The banker told me he didn't want to violate any laws, but that he'd talked to other bankers in town and they had noticed the same thing. I told him we couldn't just subpoena records to the grand jury with no basis, but I'd get back to him. I called the local IRS. A quick check revealed Ashqar not mentioning anything about possessing such sums on his tax returns.

The idea of a terrorist connection did not occur to me at first. Although I had been the office's international security officer since the program was founded in the 1970s, most of our international cases involved drugs or financial scams, never terrorism. Then I got a call from a detective at the Oxford P.D. At the request of a local Arab professor, they had run a wiretap check on the professor's phone and got a hit suggesting Ashqar's phone was tapped, but it was professional and untraceable, causing them to suspect it was ours. I called Rich Calcagno, the FBI agent supervising the Northern District. He said, "John, I want to work with you. You know I do. But I'll have to get back to you on this one."

The next day Rich called back and apologized, saying Washington said they should have gotten in touch with our office earlier. He asked if I had a top-secret security clearance. I told him I did, but was the only one in the office who did, although I had never needed it. "Well you're going to need it now." We met at his office that afternoon. Agent Steve Taylor joined us. Steve had been in Oxford a couple of years but had never brought us a single case. We used to joke about whether he even worked there. We should have known of course that he was the full-time FCI (foreign counterintelligence officer) for our district, and we didn't even know it. That is just how uncoordinated our intelligence gathering was before 9/11.

Rich and Steve explained that for the past several months, they had been running FISA (Foreign Intelligence Surveillance Act) wiretaps on Ashqar's phone and fax machine. They had hundreds of hours of audiotapes and boxes of fax copies with lots of large numbers, which appeared to be bank and other financial records. They were frustrated, however, and stymied from using it because the FBI had too few Arabic translators to cover any cases outside of obvious targets like New York and L.A. The local FBI had a lot of stuff but didn't know what it was or how to evaluate it.

They had, however, not been passive. From the numbers on the documents, and a few translated phone calls and a handful of calls in English, they'd compiled enough probable cause to get a national security enter-and-search warrant, sometimes called a "sneak and peek." One weekend when the Ashqars were out of town, a team of agents had surreptitiously entered, searched, and photographed the entire apartment. Again they were stuck with a lot of untranslated documents in Arabic. Under the circumstances they could not just hire some Arab graduate student off the street to translate them. The agents had better luck with a different strategy, however. Feeling they were onto something major, they rented the vacant apartment next door and installed a video camera and recorded every visitor to the Ashqar apartment. When they sent copies to FBI HQ in Washington, the response was immediate: "Holy shit! You've got big-time terrorists coming and going there every month."

Once Rich and Steve cut us in on their investigation, we moved quickly to subpoena secretly Ashqar's bank records, telephone toll records, credit card receipts, and, by court order, his tax returns. When the Hamas connection became clear, Rich and I flew to Washington to meet with the FBI antiterrorism unit. They immediately sent us a native Arab speaker from Yemen to work full time translating our tapes. He was great, but it unnerved us a little when he informed us that under no circumstances would he ever testify in a trial involving Hamas. "Those guys would kill me and all my family too." It was a sobering thought. We were in a new world.

The translator immediately found us a gem. Hidden amongst the Arabic conversations were two extremely clear tapes in English in Ashqar's deep voice and unmistakable accent. Speaking to a man he called "Constantine," Ashqar ordered two men killed. Members of Hamas, they had disobeyed orders to wait and had gone ahead and killed two Palestinians suspected of being informers for the Israelis. Hamas later determined that the men were innocent, so those who killed them, against explicit Hamas orders, were themselves to be executed. We passed on the names, places, and dates to the investigators at Shin Bet, the Israeli version of the FBI. They confirmed the facts for us and invited us to Israel to gather evidence for a prosecution of Ashqar in Oxford.

We consulted frequently with the Terrorism Section of DOJ in Washington. My partner there was Mark Bonner, the brilliant, wise-cracking son of a retired Navy admiral. Working with Mark was alone worth all the trouble the case eventually caused me. It appeared that the best statute to use was RICO, which at the time was just about the only law which fit our facts. Later, after 9/11, Congress passed stacks of statutes dramatically expanding U.S. jurisdiction to reach anti-U.S. terrorist acts around the world.

Then our problems began. The Manhattan U.S. Attorney's Office, legally named the Southern District of New York, but because of their power were known across DOJ as the "Sovereign" District of New York, learned about our case and demanded to take it over, treating us like country cousins. One day, by accident, I ran into Mary Jo White, the fabled U.S. Attorney for the Sovereign District at Main Justice. I went up to introduce myself. I didn't need to. She said, "I know you. You're that guy from Mississippi who is trying to steal my case on Ashqar and Marzook." It was true they had jurisdiction over Marzook and that most of Ashqar's transfers went through big New York banks, but I still thought there was plenty of case to go around for everyone. "No way. They are all ours, and you're out of it." She stomped off, a short, stocky, combative woman wobbling on her high heels. I had to admit she was not wishy-washy. Fortunately, from long associations with her assistants, Pat Fitzgerald, Ken Karras, and Baruch Weiss, I knew we would cooperate and work together even if the trial portion went to them. After all, they needed us and our agents and our insider knowledge of Ashqar.

From the outset we had consulted with Ashqar's student adviser, Nancy Rogers, who had entertained the idea that Ashqar might one day help us. It sounded crazy, but Nancy loved the Ashqars and said they were honest and honorable people. One day Nancy called me out of the blue. "John, if you ever want to talk to Ashqar, this is the moment. They've rented and packed a U-Haul truck and are leaving school and moving to New York to teach in a militant mosque." She said the last straw was when agent Steve Taylor, who had an impish sense of humor and hated Ashqar and his self-righteous ways, had decided to harass him where it hurt Ashqar most. Knowing Ashqar's puritanical wife Asmaa often handled the family banking, Steve had used Ashqar's credit card to charge a batch of X-rated sex videos and had them sent to their apartment. Ashqar had intercepted the videos, but not the bill. It was late morning on a Saturday. Nancy said, "I've told Ashqar you're a man of honor and will not lie to him. He's not sure he wants to go but doesn't know what to do. I can keep him here for an hour or so if you'll agree to meet with him."

I called Rich and Steve and a couple of other FBI agents, but everyone was on the Gulf Coast at firearm training. Rich risked his neck and told me to go ahead alone. Worried about what sort of bureaucratic nightmare this might get Rich into, I nevertheless headed for Nancy's office. She introduced us and left us alone. Following Arab custom, which resembles ours in Mississippi, we exchanged pleasantries and talked about our childhoods for a good fifteen minutes. When I told him I grew up eating kibbe and baba ghanoush at the Syrian deli of my grandmother's best friend and that my daughter was living with a respected Saudi family in Oxford, he relaxed a little and said we could talk business.

I told Abdel I had an indictment drafted charging him with raising funds to support terrorism. He remained silent. I told him there was another alternative. I stressed that he had accepted for several years American hospitality and as our guest he was obligated to respect us and not to cause harm to Americans. He readily agreed, saying, "If you know Hamas, you know their charter vows never to use violence outside of Palestine. If you will recall, Hamas has never taken any violent action in America." I'd never thought of it that way but had to agree—so far.

He asked point-blank what we wanted. I told him he had valuable sources of information not available to us. We wanted him to warn us if anything was about to happen in America. He seemed not displeased. "What about Hamas? I am not saying I am associated with them myself, but as a Palestinian patriot, I totally share their views." I decided to compromise for the moment. "We won't ask you to violate your conscience. We ask you to *follow* your conscience by protecting us, your American hosts, among whom you have many friends." He looked thoughtful. "This could put me and my family in great danger. Your subtle distinctions between groups will not impress them. To them, a traitor is a traitor."

I asked him who he could help us with. He responded quickly: "The Islamic Jihad. They kill indiscriminately. Many of them are former Hamas supporters who were expelled for being bad people." I agreed that was a place to start. Then I addressed the immediate problem, his proposed move to New York. I played a card I knew I might regret later but thought would work. "You know the Jews control New York. There are many Zionists there. You will not feel at home there. In Mississippi, the Jews will understand you better." He laughed. "You really are a lawyer. You think like a Jew." We laughed together. Little did I know that later, after he left Oxford for good, Ashqar would choose as his lawyer a feisty, eccentric Jewish lawyer named Stanley Cohen. We shook hands. "There is no rush to move. I will talk to Asmaa. We will remain here until we can see if this arrangement will work."

The FBI, usually jealous of its jurisdiction, was this time flexible, allowing me to do the questioning of Ashqar as long as local FBI supervisor

Rich Calcagno participated. Since Ashqar spoke almost entirely of eso-teric Middle Eastern and Islamic issues, there was no way Rich could do the questioning. I, therefore, did most of the questioning, dictated a draft of a report of interview, which Rich would then reword in the approved FBI format. However unorthodox, it worked perfectly.

One surprise for me was the required participation by a veteran member of Quantico's behavioral unit. Before and after each meeting, an agent would brief us by phone on what the bureau wanted to know, how to broach subjects, what subjects to avoid, and similar issues. The pre-meeting telephone briefings usually lasted an hour, the post-meetings sometimes two hours. At first I was skeptical, but he knew his stuff and was not overly controlling. His positive feedback encouraged us when we felt like we were spinning our wheels.

For our first meeting we had no idea what to expect. Rich rented the best suite at a motel. We had two agents on surveillance just in case Abdel had backup or was followed unbeknownst to him. There were no prob-lems. He came alone as promised. The behaviorist thought Ashqar liked order, so we arranged to meet on a strict schedule, every Thursday after-noon at 2:00, always at the same motel, but always in a different room. We promised Ashqar the rooms would not be bugged and we would not secretly tape-record him, and we kept our word. We met every Thursday from September 17 through November 4, 1996, at which time FBI brass in Washington decided to send in a specialist in handling antiterrorism informants, which ended our role.

In our first interview, we learned Ashqar was not leaving Oxford because he was unhappy there, but because his well-educated wife had been offered a teaching job at the wealthy Al-Massein mosque in Pat-terson, New Jersey. Ashqar himself had both legal and health problems. The previous winter, he had fallen on the ice and shattered his tailbone. Botched surgery had made it worse, and he was in substantial pain, often standing and pacing during our interviews, apologizing for doing so. Two hours would pass quickly, and at the end he joked that this was nothing like being interrogated in his homeland, by either side.

Rich Calcagno sent off his report the next morning, which appar-ently caused quite a stir. On September 30, Rich and I found ourselves in Washington with not only Steve Taylor and his supervisor, Avery Rol-lins, and Jackson agent in charge Jim Frier but lead New York terrorism prosecutor Pat Fitzgerald (now the U.S. Attorney in Chicago) and two of his assistants plus the FBI and INS case agents from New York and Washington. We were joined by two prosecutors from the Main Justice terrorism section and its chief, Jim Reynolds, plus representatives of the secretive OIPR (Office of Intelligence Policy Review), the inner sanctum DOJ agency that approves the legality of covert counterintelligence operations. Presiding was veteran deputy assistant attorney general Mark Richard, a tough cancer survivor and one of the most respected professionals in DOJ history. Fortunately it was a big conference room. It was also a SCIF (Secure Compartmentalized Intelligence Facility), impervious to parabolic intercepts (known on the old *Get Smart* TV show as a "cone of silence" room).

Apparently having an informant from inside Hamas was a unique development. Mark asked me to brief the group, which I did nonstop for an hour or more, after which there was a wide-ranging two-hour discussion of possibilities and pitfalls. We were unanimous in deciding to pursue Ashqar as far as we could as an informant. If that failed, we would sort out later who would prosecute him and where. DOJ's keenest interest lay in Ashqar's intimate ties to Abu Marzook, whom they considered the No. 1 active leader of Hamas.

When the meeting concluded, we agreed for the same group to meet monthly at the same place to share information and coordinate our moves. As the meeting broke up, Washington FBI case agent Jim Casey called me aside and said, "There's somebody you need to meet." Jim had arranged for me to meet the legendary Robert "Bear" Bryant, perhaps the most respected figure of the entire bureau—with the possible exception of Deputy Director Weldon Kennedy, who had been our SAC in Jackson during Operation Pretense and was asked to stay on well past retirement age by FBI Director Louis Freeh. Bryant was perhaps the most legendary FBI agent since J. Edgar Hoover himself. A native of Arkansas, he allegedly got his nickname before the Alabama coach because of his personal ferocity in football scrimmages. He was known for biting his opponents on the leg during scrambles for loose balls. Bryant gave us his private number and offered us complete help, whenever and wherever we needed it.

FBI undercover operations always have code names and Avery Rollins chose to call this one "Pale Horse" from the biblical Book of Revelations, later used by Clint Eastwood for his movie *Pale Horse, Pale Rider*.

But Ashqar was in no condition to ride. He could barely walk. We had the bureau contact friends at the Mayo Clinic for further evaluation and reconstructive surgery if needed. Ashqar was grateful but fearful. For the first time, I saw that he realized he might be getting in too deep. He was especially concerned about his wife and her two sisters, who were also living in the United States and could be in danger if his cooperation became known.

We arranged a different meeting with Ashqar, this time with his wife and her friend Nancy Rogers present. SAC Jim Frier presided, explaining everything from financial incentives, witness protection, and relocation with medical care. Asmaa Ashqar, an usually independent Muslim wife despite her nun-like demeanor, explained to us about fatwas of death, Islamic religious commands like the one Ayatollah Khomeini put on writer Salman Rushdie. She said both she and Abdel were under fatwas by the Grand Mufti of Jerusalem never to cooperate with Israelis or harm innocent Muslims. We asked whether "innocent" included terrorists inside the United States. She said they were not protected, and she and Abdel would help us with what we had asked for.

After Mrs. Ashqar left, to cement the deal I outlined for Abdel some of our proof, even showing him the first page of a draft RICO indictment with his name at the top and quotes from the transcripts of his call to "Constantine" ordering two rogue Hamas members murdered, which Mississippi jurors would be able to hear in English in his own unmistakable accent. He smiled at this with a twinkling expression in his deep eyes I hadn't seen before. There was clearly another Ashqar I'd not known. I mentioned another taped conversation he'd had in Arabic with an operative named "Abu Hammam," whom Ashqar had called in Syria to confirm the successful hit. In this conversation (which I did not mention had been translated for us by the Israelis), he confirmed that one of the men, named Ibrahim, had been caused to "disappear" in Gaza.

After that meeting, things went well, Ashqar became so relaxed he began telling us jokes from inside his culture. Many focused on the alleged lack of intelligence of Egyptian president Hosni Mubarak. They were reminiscent of ethnic jokes prevalent in the U.S. when I was a teenager growing up in the 1950s. Ashqar's favorites were rural humor like those you still hear about sex with farm animals in the remote parts of our district. His versions usually involved the mad leader of Libya, Muammar

Gaddafi, and his love of camels. Then in the first week in November, just as we were really beginning to get good information, Ashqar turned cool and aloof. I asked him in a roundabout way if someone had contacted him or threatened him. As always, when answering a question that would have caused him to lie, which he had sworn not to do, he would lower his eyes and remain silent till Rich or I changed the subject. This happened just as he had been outlining valuable details on the roles and conflicts among the varied Palestinian factions.

Coincidentally, this was the week some FBI bureaucrat decided it was not kosher, if that's the word, to have an AUSA in the middle of such sensitive terrorist debriefings, especially where the only FBI agent present was a novice in Middle Eastern affairs. Rich, with his dark Italian good looks, could have passed for an Arab, and had done some great and scary international work in Colombia, but the bureau wanted somebody with official training who knew Arab lingo. They chose John Atkins, an Ole Miss graduate and grandson of former Mississippi governor Ross Barnett. A smart, smooth guy, John had handled at least one other Palestinian informant and was eager to come back to Oxford. But the bureau never gave him a fair chance. They flew him to Oxford on such short notice that Rich and I had no chance to brief him or Ashqar properly on this dramatic change. He'd read Rich's reports, but that was about it. We were ordered to meet Ashqar on an hour's notice at the motel, introduce John to him cold turkey, then excuse ourselves without any explanation, violating every conceivable tenet of Arab etiquette and honor, not to mention common sense.

Ashqar looked shocked and betrayed as we expected. Since I was out of the loop and not permitted to work with John or help him, the next thing I heard was that Ashqar had abruptly moved to New York to work at a mosque. As soon as he got there, the New York team served him with a grand jury subpoena and an immunity order requiring him to testify against Hamas. Perhaps that was the secret purpose of the switch all along. New York now had him, one way or the other. He had to have felt totally betrayed, which he was. He refused to talk and was jailed for months for civil contempt. As recounted in great detail in the New York and Washington press, Ashqar went on a hunger strike. When doctors testified his heart was affected and he was near death, a sympathetic judge ordered him released on house arrest. He and Asmaa moved to the suburbs of Washington, and he got a job teaching at Howard University, where I had once put on seminars myself as a stand-in for my former mentor and law partner Gilbert Hahn.

In his last year at Ole Miss, a benevolent administration awarded him a Ph.D. in business administration, despite protests from agent Steve Taylor, who contended wiretaps revealed he'd purchased his dissertation off the Internet from a source in Michigan for $600. That allegation may not have been true, but from then on Abdel was "Dr. Ashqar," to his supporters, a professional martyr for the Palestinian cause.

After several years of trips to and from federal jails for contempt, Dr. Ashqar finally faced trial, not in New York, but in Chicago. Pat Fitzgerald, the New York AUSA, had become Patrick Fitzgerald, U.S. Attorney for Chicago, later famous for his prosecution of Governor Rod Blagojevich and others. In 2003, his targets were Ashqar, his paymaster Mousa Abu Marzook, and an old Chicago associate named Salah. Ashqar and Salah had exchanged numerous wire transfers of cash, thus giving Chicago jurisdiction to prosecute the original RICO charges I'd drafted nearly a decade earlier.

By this time, Avery Rollins and Jim Frier had retired, and Rich Calcagno had moved to Knoxville to be near the family of his wife, also an FBI agent. Steve Taylor, suffering from severe burnout from his years chasing Ashqar and fighting the bureaucracy, resigned from the bureau. One day subpoenas for the Chicago Ashqar trial arrived for Avery and Jim Frier and me, issued not by the prosecution but by the defense. They also asked us where they could find Steve Taylor to serve him as an adverse witness. We had no idea. He had disappeared. DOJ insisted that I be represented by counsel at trial because so much of the evidence was then either national security information or classified top secret. They let me choose my attorney, so I chose AUSA Tom Dawson. I owed him a trip ever since 1979, when I went to Geneva in his place in a bank fraud case, not to mention his taking over the Parchman warden beating case so I could go to Paris for training.

His payback was not bad. The defense put us up at the elegant Palmer House Hotel, where I had stayed with my parents as a child. We were in walking distance of the courthouse. Like most federal witnesses, we sat for days in stuffy windowless rooms, swapping war stories while the prosecution finished its case. It worried me that no one from

Chicago had interviewed any of us, not even Rich Calcagno, about our Mississippi investigation, since nearly all their evidence came from that case. Pat Fitzgerald greeted us warmly, however, and said one of his best and most experienced assistants had the case well in hand. When I met him the next day, I thought the AUSA looked pale and exhausted from the long trial. Nancy Rogers had been kept in a separate hotel and a separate witness room. Under the rules we were not allowed to compare our testimony, and it was probably just as well; the temptation to talk with her would have been too great. She testified as a witness to Ashqar's good character. None of the FBI agents was ever called. The two Chicago FBI agents assigned to us were great, good-humored, generous, and confident. They seemed to feel better about the case than the prosecutors, which was encouraging. But then they were not in the courtroom watching the jurors like the prosecutors were.

One morning a U.S. Marshal came to take me to the courtroom. When he ushered me in, I saw that the judge was Amy St. Eve. Tom Dawson had worked with her for independent counsel Ken Starr on the Bill Clinton investigation and said she was said to be a strong and independent judge who brooked no nonsense. She told me she had dismissed the jury, so the defense could question me in open court out of their presence to decide if they wanted to put me before the jury as their witness.

The first thing that struck me was how calm and confident Ashqar's attorneys were. Seeing Abdel, I asked the judge's permission to greet him, which she granted. He smiled and shook my hand like a long-lost friend. "It is so cold here. I wish I were back in Mississippi, even at that hotel." I badly wanted to talk more with him and he with me, but it was definitely not a social occasion. The lead defense attorney, a black Virginian named Bill Moffitt, had a smooth confident demeanor. He took me through my history with Ashqar, concluding on my opinion of his character. I was torn. I wanted to help my fellow prosecutors convict Ashqar because of how he had taken advantage of our country and because he was involved in financing violence. At the same time, I respected him as a man of principle who fought for what he believed to be right. Unlike so many leaders in the Middle East, he seemed to have no real desire for power (belied later by a crazy episode when he announced from prison he would run against Yasser Arafat for President of Palestine). Given the choice, he just wanted to go home.

Then defense counsel asked the question I had hoped I could hold back and spring on them for the first time before the jury: "Did you ever hear Dr. Ashqar speak in English to a man named Constantine?" I was caught. I told him of the conversation, even of accent studies that concluded that Constantine, a Muslim militant who did not know Arabic, was likely a Bosnian. My answer of course settled it. The defense announced, "We will not be calling Mr. Hailman."

Tom Dawson and I flew out of Chicago the next morning. From the Chicago papers and the internet we learned that the jury had acquitted Ashqar of the RICO and all other serious charges except criminal contempt of court for refusing to testify against his comrades in Hamas. Judge St. Eve, clearly not agreeing with the jury verdict, applied the federal sentencing guidelines strictly, in light of all the evidence presented, and sentenced Ashqar to eleven years in federal prison just for contempt, which she had the power to do.

While he served his time, Asmaa's younger sister, the one who lived in New Orleans and whom Asmaa had stayed in the U.S. to protect was murdered. Ashqar and Asmaa, childless, adopted her little boy. It was a bittersweet conclusion to a curious and unsettling case. Hamas now rules Gaza, while Ashqar sits in prison.

The Oxford Anthrax Scare

One memorable weekend not long after September 11, 2001, someone sent letters containing little bags of the deadly powdered poison anthrax through the U.S. mail to several locations, including the U.S. Senate. Several people died. The U.S. Senate was closed for months while they decontaminated it. At the Justice Department, all mail was shut down during the same period. We had to use FedEx or UPS and sent all our letters and packages to off-site private addresses and had special screening procedures for all our own incoming mail. We were grateful the problem had not reached Oxford, although we were deeply concerned for our friends and colleagues in D.C.

Then during the weekend of the Ole Miss–Alabama football game in October 2001, the problem came home to us. Two Ole Miss students drank too much as part of their regular "beer marathon" run and decided to scatter little baggies of white powder along their route. One of the students looked to locals like an Arab, and some citizens who saw the bags being dropped decided it was anthrax and called the police. Although we were confident it was a prank, it was a crazy time, and no one could be sure. Oxford police chief Steve Bramlett, a funny, articulate, and highly proficient officer who was responsible for the safety of the more than seventy thousand visitors to Oxford, a town of ten thousand, told his officers someone needed to drive the bags of white substance to the state crime lab in Jackson, the only place with the facilities to test it properly. Several officers looked at their feet, but one lady officer stepped forward and took the bags and headed for Jackson.

Then the real problems began. Should we inform the public? A quick meeting resulted in a unanimous decision that no one had been exposed to the powder that we could tell. Making a public announcement of a possible anthrax attack could have caused a panic leading to a mass exodus from Oxford which could have caused injuries and possibly deaths. We decided to intensify the search for the students, whom several people had seen drop the bags. If we could question them, we'd probably learn the whole thing was a hoax. If not, we had a big problem on our hands.

Chief Bramlett notified FEMA, the Federal Emergency Management office in Jackson, who deferred to MEMA, the state office. Despite the terrorist threats nationally and our heightened state of alert, the MEMA staff for the entire state consisted of just four people, none closer than Jackson. We had met them earlier right after 9/11 and seen the big chart of all their supposed offices around the state with their supposed employees but knew they had no money to hire staff and that most offices, if they even existed other than on paper, were unstaffed. Phantom offices, in effect.

The MEMA officers on duty took their responsibilities seriously and called Chief Bramlett and told him to evacuate Oxford completely. Steve called together our team of federal, state, and local officials and asked for our advice. Which was worse, risk the anthrax being real and let someone die from a bag not yet found, or try to get everybody out of the football stadium and out of town without anyone panicking or being seriously hurt? This time we were the ones looking at our feet. Finally Steve took over and said there was no way he was evacuating the city over what clearly appeared to be a hoax. We agreed to sit tight.

Within a couple of hours, local officers had tracked down the culprits, who had sobered up and were a little contrite about possibly causing a panic but tended to take the whole thing much too lightly. We decided to make an example of them and I agreed we'd prosecute them federally. Having just been through multiple training sessions on federal terrorism laws, I felt sure we would have some tough laws to use. But as I began drafting a criminal complaint, it seemed no one had thought to make it a federal crime to *fake* a terror attack. I called the DOJ emergency operations center and they said the same thing.

They agreed to authorize us to stretch the terrorism statutes and charge the students with offenses that carried the death penalty. That clearly was overkill, so I called the local DA and my friends in the state Attorney General's Office—at home—to see if they had any state law about making a false claim to use chemical weapons. Amazingly, they could find no state law the students had violated either. Finally, we just went with what the officers had told the boys orally and agreed to let them out on bond in the custody of their parents and sort it out before a federal judge on Monday.

Not long thereafter, the state crime lab called and said the powder was harmless baking soda. The huge football crowd had their good time, there was no panic, and we worked out a deal for the boys to go on federal pretrial diversion with some community service. It was all we could do. Besides, having sobered up and thought about it, they finally seemed sorry. We still wanted to make an example of them but couldn't. All we could do was pressure DOJ to pressure Congress to enact a law posthaste outlawing terrorist hoaxes. Congress fell all over itself trying to see who could sponsor the toughest punishments. Then a backlash set in: How could you send someone to prison for life for a prank? The legislation dragged on. Fortunately the State of Mississippi and its legislature proved wiser. They quickly passed a statute and the governor signed it, making it a felony to fake a terrorist attack by phony drugs or otherwise but leaving state judges considerable leeway on punishment depending on the circumstances. The mighty U.S. Congress finally did likewise many months later.

The siege of Oxford was over. In the meantime other offices had it far worse than we did. The FBI office at Little Rock received scores of phony terrorism reports to the point that my old friend Michael Johnson, the criminal chief there, said the FBI could hardly work any other cases for chasing terrorist shadows and that he had three of his prosecutors chasing their tails with the agents trying to find something to charge people with. Then, as quickly as it began, it was over, and people soon forgot about the threat. Now hardly anyone remembers it ever happened.

CSI Oxford: A Godfather from Yemen Sets Up Shop in Our District[3]

We used to wonder how the twenty-first century would begin. For most Americans, the biggest worry was that our computers would crash because they might not accept 2000 dates instead of 1900s. We'd all heard of terrorism, but it seemed far away unless it was done by some American like Timothy McVeigh or Ted Kaczynski, the Unabomber. September 11, 2001, changed all our assumptions, especially in the Department of Justice. Although shocked, Washington acted quickly. On September 20, DOJ ordered every U.S. Attorney's Office to form its own antiterrorism task force made up of federal and state prosecutors and investigators. These task forces were meant to supplement the Joint Terrorism Task Forces (JTTFs) which existed only in major cities like New York and L.A. Our district had no JTTF. No one knew where or when the next attack might occur. Large public gatherings like malls or football games seemed likely targets. Having recently returned from multiple training missions in Muslim countries including Tunisia, Morocco, Indonesia, and Oman, which is beside Yemen and guards the entrance to the Persian Gulf and its oil, I drew the short straw and was named lead task force attorney for our district. In less than a week, our Oxford task force was up and running.

My selection was not based solely on my recent training missions for prosecutors in Muslim countries. I also grew up with Arab culture. My grandmother's best friend was a Syrian lady whose family ran a Middle Eastern deli a block from her house. I was eating kibbe before I started school, and my lunch boxes often had more hummus and baklavas than hot dogs and twinkies. My older daughter had just lived for a whole year with a Saudi Arabian professor's family in Oxford, whose relatives had once employed the Bin Laden family before they became rich. I'd also taken a semester of Arabic and spent a summer while in college hitchhiking (foolishly) through Algeria and Morocco. Despite what I thought was a fair knowledge of Arab and Muslim culture, I'd never heard of Osama Bin Laden. Ever since the presidency of the first George Bush, each U.S. Attorney's Office also had one attorney designated as "National Security Coordinator." I had also held that position since it was created. Our main job was to coordinate cooperation against criminal organizations that operated across countries, especially drug smugglers. We had once done what they call an "extraordinary rendition," i.e., an "informal" extradition by tricking a corrupt former Mexican police chief wanted for several murders into flying back to Mexico voluntarily. He had been working as headwaiter at a Mexican restaurant in Oxford.

At first, we had little idea what to do to help in the struggle against terrorism. Reading the federal laws on the subject, such as "Offering Material Support to Terrorists," sounded as remote as climbing a mountain in Tibet. Then, in the first week of November, came a letter from Attorney General John Ashcroft, which noted that the federal agencies primarily responsible for pursuing terrorists—the FBI in the United States and the CIA outside the United States—were overwhelmed with leads from the four Trade Center plane-bombs and other terrorist plots. DOJ had a list of over five thousand foreign nationals residing in the United States, mainly students, who had not made the contacts or appointments required to continue in the U.S. on their visas. The letter stated that these persons were not suspected of terrorism but needed to be found and interviewed. Each U.S. Attorney's Office was asked to help locate several such foreign nationals in their districts because the usual federal investigators had more serious suspects to pursue. A second purpose was the hope was that the students would furnish us useful information on possible terror plots or persons who warranted investigation.

A follow-up memo informed us that five such persons either resided in our district or had listed someone in our district as their contact person. I quickly found four of them, who had simply failed to notify INS of changes of address. All were cooperative. Two even offered to work for us to gain information. The fifth proved different. A native of Yemen, he had enrolled at a university in New Mexico but gave a backup address in far away Byhalia, Mississippi. When I went to talk to the chief of police in Byhalia, an old friend, AUSA Jimmy Warren from Marshall County went with me. The address turned out to be a trailer on the DeSoto County line. The residents, who'd lived there all their lives, had never heard of such a person but suggested we try three or four local convenience stores, all of which were owned and run by persons of Arab or Muslim origin. We did. To our surprise, every store had a back room full of young, nervous-looking Arab males. The managers, all of whom spoke good English and were friendly and cooperative, said they'd never heard of the guy we were looking for but volunteered to ask about him throughout the community. We recontacted them several times, but they never heard of him. I reported this to DOJ, who never asked us to do anything more.

I mention the Interview Program just in case anyone may have read the book *Fall of The House of Zeus*, which alleges at p. 153 that it was not DOJ but "a lone and dubious confidential informant" in Byhalia who prompted our office to unfairly target Arab-American convenience store owners there, issuing grand jury subpoenas and calling for tax investigations of individuals never suspected of any illegal activity. None of that ever happened. Ironically, at p. 353 the book cites as the only basis for those serious allegations certain "confidential sources." This serious factual error doubles the irony because, as a career prosecutor, I have been wary all my life of relying too much on confidential sources. In this case the sources were dead wrong. The only contact we ever had with Byhalia was to look for the one missing student and we never had any confidential source there.

The confusion obviously arose from an open and public investigation by the FBI and other agencies in which we later prosecuted a large number of Yemeni convenience store owners, mainly for drug, food stamp, and contraband cigarette offenses. That case began when the FBI convened in New Orleans a nationwide meeting of agents and prosecutors from at least eight states, from New York to California, prominently including Louisiana and Mississippi. The most I can say is that a foreign intelligence service had told U.S. agents that "sleeper" cells were being established across the United States, primarily in Yemeni-operated convenience stores, to be activated as needed should further terrorist attacks be launched. We were ordered by DOJ to assist the FBI, the lead anti-terror agency, in locating and legally disrupting any such operations. We received training on prior Yemeni terror operations in the United States from North Carolina investigators who successfully infiltrated them. (See "Blood Money" in the bibliography.)

After several months of secret attempts to gain information, we could find nothing indicating any ties to terrorism or even sympathy with anti-American groups in our district by the Yemenis. We did, however, find plenty of other illegal activity. We found many instances of food stamp fraud. Most of the stores checked out by ATF also dealt in contraband cigarettes. The stores' real illegal profits came from huge sales of cases of ephedrine, the necessary precursor for making the deadliest and most addictive drug in our district, methamphetamine, or crystal meth.

There being no terrorist connections, the FBI withdrew from the case, which was pursued undercover by the MBN and DEA, assisted by ATF and the Department of Agriculture. In those days of classified antiterror investigations, every undercover operation had a code name. We tried to keep our names low-key and anonymous. When I began the Abdel Ashqar case, we labeled the boxes of evidence "AA" but had to change that when secretaries began asking if someone in our office had joined "Alcoholics Anonymous." To make the convenience store operation more bland, we named it simply "CSI" (for Convenience Store Initiative) after the popular TV series *CSI* (Crime Scene Investigation) as in *CSI New York* and *CSI Miami*. The name seemed commonplace and drew attention away from the undercover operation, which turned out to be quite successful. The main targets of the investigation were two brothers from Yemen: one in Louisiana nicknamed "Grandfather" and one in Columbus in our district who called himself the "Godfather." Not lacking in heavy-handed humor, and operating mainly in minority neighborhoods, he had a big sign stating, "The Godfather, the real nigger." In the end we obtained a thirty-nine-count federal indictment against eleven store owners and clerks for selling contraband cigarettes and thousands of ephedrine doses knowing they would be used to make meth, and for buying federal food stamps for cash for fifty cents on the dollar.

Twenty-two other defendants were arrested by local police, sheriffs and MBN agents, ten of them in Columbus and others in Holly Springs, West Point, and Starkville. MBN director Marshall Fisher announced the state arrests in partnership with the local district attorney's office, which prosecuted all those cases under state law. The state part of the operation was code-named Operation 607 after the anti-meth law sponsored in 2005 by Governor Haley Barbour, which was House Bill #607. In an excellent, in-depth article summarizing the state convictions, *Columbus*

Packet owner/editor Roger Larson noted that although most of the defendants had lived in the U.S. for years, most needed interpreters to understand the court proceedings. (*Columbus Packet*, January 25, 2007)

Leesha Faulkner of the *Daily Journal* wrote several thorough and fair-minded articles stressing the successful integration of many law-abiding, legal-resident Yemenis in our district (*Daily Journal*, January 29, 2007). Those defendants, who spoke good English, had all acquired American nicknames such as "Ed, Nick, and Mike." Defense attorneys filed numerous motions challenging the indictments, but by July 2007 all our defendants had pled guilty. Most received relatively modest sentences under federal guidelines tailored to fit the offenses. Mastermind Hamzah Ahmed, however, the self-styled "Godfather" of the multistate criminal enterprise, was sentenced to 138 months or eleven and one-half years. The case was ably prosecuted by AUSA Curtis Ivy Jr. of our Drug Task Force. Given the recent tumultuous events in Yemen, many of the defendants might well have been better off doing short sentences in the U.S. and remaining here afterward rather than being engulfed in a bloody civil war in their native Yemen. And there was certainly no anti-Yemen discrimination by our office as alleged in *Zeus*.

A Reluctant Terrorist: Adnan "Captain Joe" Awad[4]

One day in 1993, acting U.S. Attorney Al Moreton came into my office and said, "John, I've got a case you're going to love. It's not a bank robbery, but may be even better." Since there is nothing better than a good bank robbery, I wondered why the usually calm and collected Al Moreton seemed so excited. "Is it a kidnapping?" I asked, going for my next favorite. He told me to be patient. "First the bad news: It's a civil case." Was it some emergency thing that the civil guys don't want to handle, like a TRO (temporary restraining order), one of those high noon shootouts with none of that boring pre-trial discovery that usually ruins civil cases?

"It's better than that. The name of the case will tell you something." He put the complaint on my desk. It was entitled *Sealed Plaintiffs v. Sealed Defendants*. I'd never heard of such a thing. "Before you even read the thing, you have to sign a statement agreeing to abide by a secrecy order. It is a federal tort claim against the FBI, the U.S. Marshals, and the U.S. Attorney in Hawaii by a former Arab terrorist who is now in the federal Witness Protection Program, whose director is also a defendant. Since you loved that other civil case where you defended the head of the Witness Protection Program, and you are our antiterror coordinator, it has you written all over it." Al was right. The case where I had defended Gerald "Gerry" Shur, head and founder of the Witness Protection Unit, a hero of mine, against serial murderer Marion Albert "Mad Dog" Pruett, had been one of my all-time favorites. Also, Washington had recently sent me to Tunisia twice as part of our Anti-Terrorism efforts.

Al had me hooked. I signed the form and opened the file. I saw Gerry Shur's name and was excited. I also saw that one of the accused FBI agents was Ed Needham, with whom I'd recently worked on the Ashqar case. Defending Ed and Jerry would be a pleasure. Then I noticed a potential downside. Because of its sensitive nature, the lead counsel would not be the local U.S. Attorney but DOJ in Washington. My experiences with the lumbering national bureaucracy had not always been positive. Individual attorneys were often excellent, but there were always three or four tiers of career-minded superiors who had to review and initial everything you did. You couldn't blow your nose without several bureaucrats initialing your handkerchief.

The complaint alleged that the plaintiff, whose name was Adnan Awad, a native of Palestine, and his American wife Lynn, were residents of our district, residing near Guntown. The complaint was written by Bill Beasley, a fine lawyer from Tupelo who was partners with Pete Mitchell, a well-known and distinguished former district attorney. The complaint was concise, claiming government agents, including Dan Bent, U.S. Attorney for Hawaii, had subpoenaed Awad to testify in Athens, Greece, at the trial of members of the infamous May 15 organization about a terrorist bomb which went off on a Pan Am Flight from Tokyo to Honolulu in 1982. The bomb wounded 15 passengers and killed one and nearly brought down the whole giant airliner and killed everyone on board. The gist of the complaint was that agents of the government had failed to obtain U.S. citizenship and a U.S. passport for Awad, as they had allegedly agreed to do, even after he testified twice, at great risk to his own life, resulting in several convictions, including that of terrorist Mohammed Rashid, a top leader of the May 15 group under the protection of Iraqi dictator Saddam Hussein. Of course I wanted the case.

Upon further reading, it appeared that the case might take years to complete. The witnesses were scattered everywhere. There were serious questions whether the legal theories underlying it were valid. The claims sounded far-fetched. But most important was the secrecy. Any time you deal with national security documents, you can expect excruciating years of squabbles. All attorneys have to pass background checks and take security oaths. Federal agencies often refuse, not surprisingly, to give up their most sensitive documents. Nevertheless, I looked forward to handling the case. As it turned out, things went even slower than I imagined. Poor U.S. Magistrate Jerry Davis, who had also handled the discovery in the endless *Ayers* lawsuit to desegregate Mississippi's universities, which I handled for the U.S. Attorney for over twenty-five years, also caught the *Awad* case, presiding with Chief Judge Glen Davidson, our former U.S. Attorney, over the motion and discovery squabbles in *Sealed Plaintiffs*. It would be a decade before the *Awad* case came to trial.

In the meantime, we got a new U.S. attorney, Calvin "Buck" Buchanan, a native of Okolona, an Ole Miss graduate, and former U.S. Army JAG attorney. One day early in his term while we were reviewing the printout of my caseload, he saw *Sealed Plaintiffs*. "What is this?" he asked. I explained. "This thing may not go to trial in our lifetime. You're my criminal chief and lead prosecutor on all kinds of cases. Let's reassign this to Felicia Adams." A new hire, Felicia was a sharp lawyer and a good writer and could handle the civil motion practice just fine, but Buck could tell how much I wanted to try the case, so he added, "If this baby ever does go to trial, Felicia can brief you on it quickly, and you can jump back in and do the trial with her." That was all I needed to hear. Felicia later transferred to the U.S. Attorney's Office in Jackson and was thus not around for the *Awad* case. Then in 2011 President Obama returned Felicia Adams to us, naming her U.S. Attorney for the Northern District.

In early 2001, we received notice that the case had been set for trial by Judge Davidson in Aberdeen. The attorney from Main Justice was asking that we get active in the case immediately. New U.S. Attorney Jim Greenlee asked if I would mind handling the case. He did not have to ask twice. I called the assigned DOJ attorney, who was named Joe Shur. A veteran of years of important trials, Joe was open and friendly and in no way condescending to a country cousin lawyer from Mississippi. He asked me not only if I would voir dire the jury but take some of the key witnesses. He had the good judgment to know from experience that the folks in Aberdeen, Mississippi, were not necessarily well-disposed toward Washington lawyers. Some people locally referred to the Clinton administration as our "Second Reconstruction." The following week we were to interview the plaintiff's psychiatrist on Awad's claim that mistreatment by agents had damaged his mental health and marital relations with his wife. That promised to be an interesting interview. I had plenty of experience with shrinks and enjoyed them and their way of thinking.

To bring me up to speed, Joe brought down the remaining defendants, all FBI agents and U.S. Marshals, for me to interview. The years of motions had thinned the ranks of defendants, but the case was still critical to FBI agent Ed Needham and the others. They were sued not only as agents acting in their official capacities but also individually for acts allegedly exceeding their legal authority as agents. Under a Supreme Court decision called *Bivens*, if the jury found they acted without proper authority, they could be ordered to pay damages out of their own pockets, probably bankrupting them. Nothing is more scary to a government agent than the prospect of financial doom from a lawsuit.

To prepare me, Joe Shur suggested I read a book about the case, which was out of print, but available in libraries. I checked it out of the Ole Miss Library using my adjunct law professor's card. The book was entitled *Terrorist: The Inside Story of the Highest-Ranking Iraqi Terrorist Ever to Defect to the West*, and was written by Steven Emerson, whom I'd watched many evenings on the PBS News Hour. The book did not mention the lawsuit, but told in great detail the facts of Awad's background and detailed his testimony in the Rashid case. I had an intern Xerox me two copies and devoured it, writing all over one of them, keeping the other one clean for possible use on cross examination.

Awad's story was intriguing. Born in a village in the uplands of Palestine, he had an idyllic childhood with a warm and loving extended family. They divided their time between months in the forested mountains and weeks on the beaches of the Mediterranean. The only irritant was the endless conflict with the Israelis, who blocked the roads with checkpoints and searches. Later, during recesses in the trial, Awad told me his family taught him that the Israelis were their enemies but not to hate them, that hate destroyed the hater. He said they told him the problem was so old it would never be resolved in his lifetime. They said it was simple: "They have what we want, and we want what they have. We will kill each other for it till one gets it for good. It is not religion that divides us. It is the land. We both worship it and will readily die for it."

At the end of Awad's primary schooling, the Mideast wars persuaded his parents they had to leave Palestine for a time, but would one day return victorious. Their educational system was breaking down, and the violence was never ending. They moved first to Lebanon, which he loved and where he thought he saw a workable solution to the ethnic and religious conflicts, where groups could tolerate each other. Then Lebanon had its own vicious civil war, and his family sent him on to school in Damascus, Syria. He received a good education there but began to run with a bad crowd. He joined a gang of tough Palestinian teenagers who made their spending money shaking down café owners. If the owners refused to pay the teenagers' petty extortion demands, their businesses were trashed, tables turned over, glasses and plates smashed. The gang never assaulted people, and the police seemed to assume the damages were the result of business rivalries, so Awad was never even arrested.

As Awad matured, he became physically powerful, and local representatives of Yasser Arafat's Palestine Liberation Organization (PLO), recruited him for their military wing, the Palestine Liberation Army, a relatively professional unit. They sent him to training camps, where he learned military discipline, how to fire automatic weapons and handle explosives. He loved the military life and rose to the rank of captain. He declined to talk about what he actually did operationally, but was good at repeating what might be called the politically correct line of Arab militancy: "We don't hate Jews. We exist to oppose the oppression of Zionism, the destruction of Palestine and its people by militant Zionists. They are the ones who hate us. They started this by driving us from our ancestral lands."

After five years as a PLO officer, Awad became restless. He was not really a political animal and wanted a family and a real home, wherever it took him. He had also discovered his true interest in life: chasing women. He heard that life was good in Baghdad, and with his training in engineering, he thought he could build a life for himself in Iraq, then one of the most modern, advanced, and secular of Arab countries. In Baghdad he landed a choice job as foreman on a series of jobs for a Japanese company which was building palaces for Saddam Hussein. Successful and well liked, the suave and urbane Awad began to receive invitations to parties which included members of Saddam's inner circle. He developed a fatal attraction (the first of several) for a beautiful Iraqi woman connected to the inner circle. He spent more and more time with them to be near her. The group began talking politics, which he did not enjoy, but went along to be with the woman.

Because of his background with the PLO, they began to share with him some of their plans to liberate Palestine. Before he knew it, he was compromised and knew too much. Friends told him he had made a big mistake, because he was now part of the group and could never leave it. He thought of fleeing, but had no credentials to get to the West and there was no place to hide in the Middle East. They would track him down and kill him. He realized too late how naïve he had been.

One night the hammer finally fell on him at a party at the house of a friend of Saddam Hussein. He was summoned into a back room where a fair, slim man with a thin moustache showed him a sophisticated laboratory. There were tables with beakers of chemicals and elaborate bomb-making materials. "We know you know bombs and thought you might be interested." Awad said he actually knew little about bombs except how to place them and detonate them. The slim man laughed: "We make them. All you have to do is put them where they need to be." Awad tried not to look afraid, but woke up later in a cold sweat. He thought of heading for the border, leaving all his possessions behind, but he was frozen, his mind numb, unable to act or think. For a week he was like a zombie and called in sick to his job several times.

Then he got the dreaded call. The slim man, whose name was Mohamed Rashid, wanted to meet with him that same evening, at the same house, but alone. With a feeling of doom, Awad went there in a taxi. Ushered quickly into the laboratory, he was greeted warmly by Mohamed and his plotters. "We have a mission for you. Come into the next room." Beside the lab room was a second, quite different chamber. Lined with shelves on three walls, it looked like a storage room for luggage at a large hotel. Everywhere were suitcases and hang-up garment bags.

Mohamed explained. "You know what a plastic explosive is, of course?" Awad nodded. "This is a very secret, very dangerous place. In every bag here there are plastic explosives hidden somewhere, usually in the lining. None of these bags has any metal. Everything is leather, wood, or plastic: no X-ray will detect any problem with any of these bags. Certain chemicals in which they have been soaked will prevent dogs from alerting on them. We would hate for you to get caught because they suspected you were a drug courier." Awad felt empty and helpless. He didn't dare ask what they wanted him to do.

Rashid resumed. "We have taken care of all details. You will be a Lebanese businessman who is combining business with pleasure. You will fly to Athens and have a pleasant vacation at our expense. Then you will fly on to Geneva on business where a first-class suite is reserved for you at the Hilton Hotel." Mohamed lifted an expensive-looking hang-up bag from a rod. "You will be a well-dressed, rich businessman. They are never suspected. You will check in, leave this bag filled with plastic explosive, set its timer, and walk out of the Hilton hotel forever. We have prepared a second set of identity papers for you as well as reservations on a different airline to return circuitously back here."

Awad knew he had to say something, so he asked why put the bomb in Geneva, and why in the Hilton? "The Swiss think they are too smart, immune to us Arabs. It will terrify them and all the West and show them there are no safe havens from us. The Hilton is owned by Jews, and many Jews stay there. It will show them they are never safe anywhere."

Stunned, Awad went along, trying not to look terrified. He wore the elegant clothes they bought for him. With his good looks, good manners, and military posture, he looked the part of a rich Lebanese businessman. In Athens, he had lots of opportunities to meet attractive women and plenty of money to seduce them, but was too nervous and depressed to think of women and spent most of his time locked up in his expensive hotel suite, miserable. When the day came to fly to Geneva, he panicked. He thought of fleeing to Turkey or Iran, where he might work as a displaced Palestinian laborer. But his nerve failed him. He plodded on according to Rashid's directions. When his taxi pulled up at the Hilton in Geneva, he let the bellman carry the bomb bag up to his suite. Once inside, he broke down completely, sobbing uncontrollably. There was no way he could kill all those people. Perhaps the best way was to set the timer for one minute and blow himself up with all the others. His life was nothing anyway.

Then a strange mood, like a trance from the Arabian nights, overtook him. He began to think of the bomb as alive, like a genie. He talked to it, sharing his fears, asking its advice. Of course the bomb never answered. Awad finally thought about more practical ways out. He knew bombs. Rashid had explained this one to him in detail. Perhaps he could disarm it in such a way as to make it not go off. He would simply walk away, go back to Baghdad, pretend he'd done his part but that the bomb failed to explode. It sometimes happened—wires came loose, timers failed to function. But Rashid was a professional. They would not believe Awad, and would probably torture him horribly. He could never take it and would tell the truth and be tortured to death.

In the end, he decided to go with his heart. He just could not kill people under these cowardly circumstances. He'd take his chances with the West. He called the Swiss police. The officer on the desk thought it was a hoax, or just another "crazy Arab." Who would help him? He had noticed scores of Saudis in their flowing robes and headdresses in the lobby. He called the Saudi embassy. They were more supportive, but did not want to be involved. They passed him up their chain of command until a high-ranking diplomat finally told him, "Go to the Americans. Tell no one you have talked to us. The Americans will handle it."

Awad called the American embassy. They seemed dubious, but sent a man right over. Awad showed him the bag. The American said, "This is no bomb." Awad then showed him the disguised timer and detonator and cut open the lining of the bag. The American called a different branch of the Swiss police. They immediately recognized it as a bomb and took it to their lab. The Americans handed Awad over to the Swiss but remained in daily contact with him. He told them everything. With remarkable skill he drew a very accurate pencil portrait of the bomb room and even of Rashid himself. Trained as an engineer, Awad was an excellent draftsman.

After long discussions, the Swiss and the Americans decided to place Awad in the Swiss version of Witness Protection. They gave him a new identity and a Lebanese passport and relocated him to a city on the coast of Morocco. They gave him a handsome living allowance and a red convertible sports car. After all, he had prevented the worst terror attack in history on Swiss soil. And he was a good source for all sorts of information not just on May 15 but on PLO structure and militant activities from Baghdad to Damascus.

To Adnan Awad, he had made it to paradise. He had saved his life and probably hundreds of others. He had money, status, leisure, and, most important, everything he needed to pursue the beautiful and Westernized women of coastal Morocco. He lived like a minor prince. He began to hope it would never end. But his paradise only lasted a few months. Awad tended to enjoy himself to excess and the Moroccan police began to wonder who he really was and if they really wanted him in their country. Official wiretaps and visual surveillance are widespread there, and his frequent contacts with Swiss and American police were not consistent with his pose as a Lebanese businessman.

After consultations, the Swiss persuaded the Americans to put him into the U.S. Witness Protection Program and move him to the U.S. with yet another identity. Awad agreed. He'd always dreamed of visiting America. Agreements were signed, and he was relocated to a large city in the Northeast. Problems arose immediately. The U.S. program was infinitely more bureaucratic than the Swiss, and his handlers seemed to know nothing of Arab culture and what it took for him to be comfortable. The food was strange, the climate cold. He had lost his sports car, his fancy hotel, his familiar clothes. To be inconspicuous in America, he had to appear to be a poor Arab immigrant.

Worst of all, American women seemed turned off by him. His tales of adventure, which had seduced the women of Morocco, Baghdad, and Damascus, went nowhere with the women in the bars he frequented. One night, to impress a woman who'd finally shown some interest in him, he told her his true life story, especially the bomb-in-Geneva part. She was fascinated. But after a few weeks together, his macho and domineering Arab-male ways aggravated her. He "disciplined" her. She called the police. When Awad told his U.S. Marshal handlers what he'd done, they moved him again, this time to Boston, and gave him yet another new identity.

This time things worked better. His identity as a Lebanese businessman suited him, and there was an Arab community with familiar food and cultural ways. He met a Lebanese businesswoman, moved in with her, and worked in her business. He was happy, if still cold, and still a valuable terrorism informant. Then came the usual domestic conflicts and crises. She was suspicious of his frequent absences and strange meetings and accused him of seeing another woman. For once faithful, Awad was hurt and decided the only way to explain himself was to tell her the truth and trust her to keep it secret. She did not. His past life scared the bejeebers out of her and she threw him out.

The marshals told him they'd move him one more time, but if he breached security again, he was out of the Witness Program for good. He agreed to make things smoother, and politely asked them to please move him to someplace warm where he'd feel at home. After a year in America, studying the culture, he thought he'd found the perfect place, an Old World city on the water with a mild climate, fine seafood, and a sophisticated culture comfortable with exotic strangers. He wanted to relocate to Charleston, South Carolina.

The Marshals agreed. It should be a good fit. The paperwork was done and a brand new Adnan Awad was ready for Charleston and happily flew away. When he landed, however, there seemed to be some mistake. It was freezing cold with snow on the ground. The sign at the airport said nothing about South Carolina. It said, "Welcome to Charlotte, North Carolina, banking center of the New South." Someone had screwed up. That night, sad beyond belief, Awad drowned his sorrows in the nearest bar. An attractive blond accepted his offer of a drink. By then his English had become quite good and his knowledge of American culture, especially American women, was much improved. Wasting no time, he launched right into his story, which captivated the woman. She found him handsome, charming, romantic, a real gentleman. He found her beautiful and feminine.

He decided right then he liked southern women better than the northern version. Their voices were softer, they paid more attention to their looks, and most of all they seemed to defer to men more than the aggressive women he'd known in the north. The woman told him her name was Lynn, and she was working in Charlotte but was about to move back to her native Mississippi. Lynn and Adnan quickly became a couple. The marshals learned that Adnan had blown his cover again, this time for the last time. By mutual agreement, he left the Witness Protection Program and moved with Lynn to the Tupelo area, where they were married.

With this dramatic story as background, I drove to Tupelo for the interview with the psychiatrist. An employee of the Regional Mental Health Center, Louis Masur was impressive. Unlike most psychiatrists

I'd known, he was able to explain esoteric psychiatric theories in plain English. The fact that he was Jewish surprised me a little. "Does Awad know that?" I asked him. Dr. Masur said that was one of the first things he told him, just in case, but Awad seemed sincere when he said he was not anti-Semitic. "We Arabs all want Jewish lawyers, so why not a Jewish psychiatrist?"

After a couple of hours, we figured we were ready to take Dr. Masur's testimony. While technically a witness for Awad and quite sympathetic to his situation, he could honestly find nothing the FBI or marshals had done personally to make things worse for him mentally. Adnan had even admitted it to him. His entire problem was with their anonymous bureaucratic superiors, who had failed to get him the American citizenship he'd been promised. They also refused to give him back his old Lebanese passport the Swiss had given him, substituting only a green card work permit, which Awad felt made him a second-class citizen. He wanted to vote and serve on juries and be a real American. There was some justice in his complaints. I just wished he hadn't put the honest, hardworking FBI agents and marshals through such stressful personal legal hassles.

We got the list of jurors, which looked good. Selecting jurors for such a case was trickier than it looked. Although Awad had been a member of the PLO, he had never really been a terrorist. He was a military man, and it showed. What some people might think would be a rural U.S. prejudice against a foreigner might not hold. For one thing, in this case he was the underdog, always an appeal to American jurors, especially Mississippians, who often feel put down by the government and the richer states of the North. Mississippi is also perhaps the most pro-military of all U.S. states, with an old warrior culture. Mississippi also has a long history of accepting Christian Lebanese and Syrian immigrants as exemplified by Robert Khayat, the grandson of a Lebanese immigrant who went on to be Chancellor of the University of Mississippi. Its provost was Carolyn Ellis Staton, also of recent Lebanese origin. A prominent state senator was Ali Mohamed, who knew enough of local sensibilities to change his first name from Ali to "Ollie" and take on a good old boy Delta accent. Especially in the Delta, Mississippi still has good traditional Lebanese restaurants, with everything from raw kibbeh to luscious baklavas. An elder in my own rural Oxford church, College Hill Presbyterian, is Samir Husni, a native of Lebanon and former chairman of the Journalism

Department at Ole Miss. He and his wife have had two fine Lebanese restaurants in Oxford, one across the street from the federal courthouse. I suspected Awad might prove an attractive character to a Mississippi jury, contrary to what outsiders would assume.

Islam was a different issue. Muslims were seen, even before the 9/11 plane bomb attacks, as foreign and strange. But Awad was not religious and was a witness *against* them, and had risked his life for us testifying against violent Islamists. In the end we decided just to pick a regular jury as if the civil trial were about a car wreck or a broken contract. What we wanted was enough intelligence to follow the evidence and people who did not have any grudges against the federal government. Interestingly, neither side challenged many jurors. We both felt we would get a fair trial of a unique case.

Security for the case was like nothing I'd seen before. The place was crawling with marshals, seemingly one for every witness. Judge Davidson, a military veteran with great respect for security and order, had carefully researched handling such cases with judges from around the county. As a representative for U.S. district judges on the prestigious U.S. Judicial Conference, which met regularly at the U.S. Supreme Court in Washington, he had access to the latest techniques in balancing openness of public trials with the need for security in terrorist cases and the anonymity necessary for the marshals who guarded them.

To establish certain technical elements of the case, Bill Beasley had to call Witness Protection marshals to establish the time periods, places, signed documents, and cities where Awad had been under protection. Judge Davidson required opaque screens in front of those officials, hiding them from public view during their testimony. Black construction paper was taped over windows on the public doors to the courtroom, just enough to prevent viewing, but not enough to attract special attention. The day before trial, the file was unsealed and the parties' names were revealed. But since it was a civil case and sounded technical, few people seemed to notice it. Federal files were not yet fully computerized under the current PACER system, which is now searched online daily by reporters and bloggers alike. As for the press, only one reporter that I recall covered the trial, Marty Russell of the *Daily Journal*.

There was one near mishap. By pure coincidence, a vanload of political science students from Mississippi State stopped by to visit the federal courthouse. The judge told the marshals to let them in. Fortunately for security purposes they came during a particularly boring time in the trial while Bill was putting in a series of documents. Finding nothing interesting in the case, the students moved on to their next visit and never inquired further about it.

The main witness at trial would of course be Awad himself. I had learned a lot about him from our frequent chats in the hall during the many recesses that make up federal trials. I always made sure Awad's attorney Bill Beasley was around when we chatted, and we talked about everything else in the world but the case. We swapped stories about Morocco, where we had both spent considerable time and had similar experiences. We talked about the Sultanate of Oman on the Persian Gulf facing Iran, where I'd done missions and where he had always wanted to vacation. My interest in him was sincere, and although there was an obvious tactical advantage to us in my knowing something of his character and temperament, the personal empathy was sincere on both sides.

Adnan was a complex, colorful, and emotionally volatile character. In movie terms he would have been more at home in *Casablanca* than in *Lawrence of Arabia*. He looked like a Turk, with a shaved head, military bearing, and was always impeccably dressed. He was both aggressive and humorous. One of our discussions concerned what I should call him. My practice as a prosecutor was always to be formal and correct with defendants, invariably calling them "Mr." whatever their name was. A rare exception was chief deputy sheriff Ray Bright of Marshall County, whom we prosecuted three separate times for various acts of corruption. By the time of the third trial, we knew him so well we called him "Cousin Ray." Naming Awad was a challenge. Having had at least ten different official aliases as he moved from Baghdad to Athens to Geneva to Morocco and several U.S. cities, he was a man of not only many names, but many identities. One day, as we bantered about how we should address each other, the issue came up as to which of us, under Arab rules of courtesy, was due more respect. He said prosecutors were high officials. I reciprocated by saying that patriotic witnesses were just as worthy. Finally, he asked for my date of birth. Agreeing that we both looked younger than our real ages, we determined that I was senior by two months and entitled to be senior man in terms of etiquette and precedence. "What then will I be to you?" I told him his witness status was better left unspoken for security seasons. He asked me, quite seriously: "How do you perceive me as a man, Sir, truly?"

Considering his appearance and attitude, I told him to me as an American he looked like a retired military officer. Recalling his last rank in the PLO and the easiest to remember of his aliases, I suggested I call him "Captain Joe." He liked it right away. "It is respectful and also sounds American. It will be our little secret what *sort* of captain I was. From now on, I am Captain Joe. But what should I call you?" Relying on old southern ways, I proposed that because I was his elder, he should call me by the friendly but deferential southern phrase "Mr. John." He liked it. "I love your southern ways. Now we are friends."

Later, when the trial was over, I handed Captain Joe a Xerox copy of Stephen Emerson's book about him to autograph. His spoken English was very good, but he'd never bothered to learn to write English. He therefore inscribed the inside cover of the book for me in Arabic and had his wife Lynn translate it into English right below it. The inscription read: "To John, my enemy in court, but my friend in life." He had captured perfectly the spirit of the case and our relations. When the trial ended, I looked for Ed Needham and the U.S. Marshal defendants to inscribe the book as well, but couldn't find them, which I still regret.

Joe Shur had been so good to me as a partner in the trial that I was tempted to ask him the favor of letting me cross-examine Captain Joe because I felt I knew him better. Joe had already asked me to cross-examine Lynn Awad and psychiatrist Louis Masur, so taking Captain Joe too was asking a lot. I tiptoed up to the subject. "John, I'm sure you'd do a great job, but Washington would have my head if you took *all* the main witnesses. In our case, you prepare and take Ed Needham, and I'll take the marshal. I'll plan to take Adnan, but just in case, you be prepared for him, too." I've never had a better Washington trial partner than Joe Shur.

Bill Beasley did the best he could on direct with Lewis Masur, bringing out the significant psychological pain and suffering Adnan had endured. But my cross was more like a direct. I never had to confront Lewis at all, just asked him what caused all Adnan's problems. It was simply the trauma which his life had inflicted on him, much of which he brought on himself. None of it could fairly be blamed on the federal agents. The only stress Lewis thought the government brought on was the long delay in giving him his promised citizenship and their refusal to get him a U.S. passport or return his old Swiss-issued Lebanese one.

Captain Joe himself hurt his case on the stand. Despite valiant efforts, Bill simply could not control his volatile client. Captain Joe the American turned back into Adnan Awad, Damascus shakedown artist and womanizer. He erupted on the stand into angry fits of temper, at times admitting what to Americans were serious mistreatment of his wife and other women. As if cross-examining himself, he rebutted his own case. Every time Bill got him to make a point, Adnan would ramble on about it, undermining the good points with volunteered bad points of his own. Finally, Bill said, "No further questions."

We took a recess, as is normal to prepare for cross of a key witness. Joe asked me if I wanted to take him. In a rare moment of uncertainty, I told Joe my adrenalin level was high and there was a lot to ask, but I didn't know where to begin. I asked Joe what he thought. "I feel like you do, and when I feel that way, maybe it means there is nothing to ask. What if I just stood up and said, 'No questions'?" I asked to think about it for a minute. A very few times in my entire career have I done the same thing with criminal defendants who made such wretched witnesses that I knew the jury didn't believe them. But to this jury it might seem arrogant and overconfident. And yet, thinking back to the cases when I did ask no questions on cross, I recalled jurors nodding and even smiling, as if to say, "Thanks for not wasting our time." I told Joe to go for it.

"Your Honor, in light of the statements under oath of the plaintiff, we have no cross-examination." The jurors looked at each other, some nodding as we'd hoped. There was really nothing we could have elicited that would have made our case any stronger. Hoping to recover quickly from a really bad moment, Bill Beasley immediately called Lynn Awad to the stand. She was an attractive woman but looked exhausted, totally worn down by the ordeal. Bill got from her the details of their courtship and marriage, the terrible fears and pressures she and her husband had been under, both inside and outside the Witness Program. She shared her husband's suspicions that their phones had been tapped and that even their marital bedroom had been bugged, but had no proof of it. She seemed truthful, even sympathetic, but did not really help their case. She too had nothing but praise for Ed Needham and the marshals and other

FBI agents with whom she had dealt personally, complaining only of the faceless people in Washington who had refused to keep their bargains with her husband.

As I watched the jury look at Lynn, my impression was that they were thinking, "Why did this educated dentist's daughter from Tupelo marry such a man? He has his good points surely, but a husband? What was she thinking?" My idea for cross was to treat her as a sympathetic victim of circumstances and a clash of cultures, not a victim of our clients, who had treated her better than anyone else. On direct she had mentioned several incidents, including Adnan being violently angry at the agents. I asked her about those. I asked her if any agent had ever hit Adnan or her. She said definitely not. They had never threatened them in any way at any time. What about Adnan? Had he ever threatened the agents when he was angry?

Her reply caught me off guard: "No, he took it all out on me. When he was mad at them, he beat me. He told me it's part of his culture. He was always sorry later, and we always made up, but it was hard. He blacked my eyes, busted my lips. He didn't really mean it, that was just his way." I asked her if she'd ever told Dr. Masur about this as part of their therapy. "No, that was strictly private between us." The jurors first stared at her, then began looking away. Rather than pressing her, I sat down. Bill Beasley had no redirect. In my mind, the case was over. They never really had a case against these good men.

Bill Beasley then announced he rested his case. After making a standard oral motion to dismiss the case, not expecting it to be granted, Joe Shur asked for a recess for us to decide the order of our witnesses. There had been motions to dismiss on file for years, which were always denied as to our clients, although many other defendants had been dismissed. To our surprise, Judge Davidson called on Bill to answer our oral motion for dismissal, a good sign, although many times trial judges do that just to make a record of reasons to deny the motions and to protect their rulings from reversal later on appeal. This time it felt different.

Bill argued gamely that his case was proved. After Bill finished, Judge Davidson announced to our surprise that he did not need to hear from us. He explained succinctly that the plaintiffs had no case against these named defendants and ordered them dismissed immediately. He then raised his eyebrows as if to say, "Not so fast" and went on. "As to what might be termed contractual violations, however, the court finds that plaintiff Adnan Awad may have a case. That matter has not really been presented in the proper forum, however. Such claims may only be considered under the Tucker Act, the federal law under which the United States waives its sovereign immunity against suits on contract claims. This Court therefore orders the contract portion of this case be transferred to the U.S. Court of Federal Claims in Washington, D.C., under the Tucker Act."

Lynn and Captain Joe seemed, if anything, relieved. Joe told me in the hall he thought the judge was a wise man and asked if I would follow the case to Washington. I told him normally not, that I knew little about that law and specialists from there would no doubt handle it. "They will not be like you," he said.

Captain Joe and Lynn divorced shortly after trial, and he moved to Gulfport and opened a little shop selling his drawings and colorful metal sculptures. I would have liked one as a keepsake, but before I learned of it from an old friend in Gulfport, the shop had closed. My friend, himself a graphic designer with his own ad agency, said, "Some of his stuff was really good. Too bad he left." On the other hand maybe not, because if he'd stayed on, Hurricane Katrina would have gotten him a couple of years later.

The Court of Claims also ruled against Adnan on fairly technical grounds, but since then his case has been taken up by others administratively. The best argument for his case appeared in the *Stanford Law Review* of November 2005. Written by Michelle Visser, then the law clerk for Judge Bruce Selya of the First U.S. Circuit Court of Appeals, it was entitled "Sovereign Immunity and Informant Defectors: The United States' Refusal to Protect Its Protectors." The article makes an excellent case for improving our system for handling the sensitive issues of terrorism informants and witnesses. It also gives rich details, too long for me to repeat here, stressing how Adnan did finally receive a $750,000 reward for his assistance to the United States.

Captain Joe perhaps got the greatest measure of recognition he had wanted all along from Judge Glen Davidson in his published opinion on the case where he said:

Despite the government's promises, Awad did not receive United States citizenship and a passport until June of 2000, over fifteen years after his arrival. And even then he appears to have received his citizenship and passport primarily as a result of his own persistent and extensive efforts.

Thus, Captain Joe did indeed finally become a real American, and in a uniquely American way—by doing it himself.

Notes

The notes which follow are mainly for reference purposes for any reader who might wish to consult the file for a particular story in depth. The contents of many files have now been routinely shredded, usually ten years after the file was closed. The files which still exist will be in the clerk's office of the U.S. District Court in Oxford or at the Fifth Circuit in New Orleans, but many will have been shipped to a faraway federal record storage center.

The variety in the case numbering systems comes mainly from the evolution of computer record keeping. The citations to news stories do not reflect undue interest in publicity but an interest in how our cases were presented to the public. In retrospect, the news stories now seem even more useful in the way they encapsulate in brief terms what happened, free of the numbing legal jargon of official court records. Newsmen apparently do a better job of preserving history than lawyers.

Preface

1. As I suspected, the "best" criminal careers are in the white-collar area, which require more education, carry shorter prison terms, and promise fewer chances of a violent death. Near the top of the criminal hierarchy, not surprisingly, are identity thieves (fourth), telemarketing scammers (fifth), and counterfeiters (tenth). Number 1 is a type of criminal I encountered only once: drug counterfeiters. They tend to operate mainly from outside the United States, selling bogus Viagra and the like. They are therefore rarely seen, much less caught. We did, however, have one big score out of Clarksdale, another home of the blues, where a couple got rich selling a "natural" product which promised both larger breasts (by two cup sizes) and larger penises. The couple ended up, in addition to being prosecuted by us, as defendants before an outraged Judge Judy on nationwide TV under the title "Bustin' Loose."

The number 2 "best" crime we also encountered only toward the end of my career. Like most successful crimes it is hard to detect, expensive to investigate, and rarely prosecuted: smuggling contraband cigarettes on the black market. This scam is actually a complex of crimes which can involve everything from substituting cheap tobacco from China for expensive Carolina leaf, but always involves in some way avoiding the heavy federal and state taxes on cigarettes, which can amount to several dollars a pack and millions of dollars a truckload. A brisk trade in counterfeit cigarette stamps has also developed. Add in the tax-free enclaves of Native American reservations, which are legally foreign nations not subject to state taxes, and you have a career richer than untaxed casinos.

Chapter 1. Bank Robbers I've Known

1. *U.S. v. Shabazz*, CRG-75-54, CRG-75-55; *U.S. v. Walker (Shabazz)*, 530 F. 2d 975 (5th Cir. 1976).
2. *U.S. v. Washam*, CRW-74-89.
3. *U.S. v. House*, CRG-80-37.
4. *U.S. v. Craft*, CRD-82-2-WK-0; *U.S. v. Craft*, 691 F. 2d 205 (5th Cir. 1982).
5. *U.S. v. Lewis*, CRW-91-05-B.
6. *U.S. v. Porterfield*, 3:02 CR-134; *U.S. v. Porterfield*, CRW-88-85.
7. *U.S. v. Mitchell*, 2:94 CR-12-GHD; *U.S. v. Mitchell*, 3:94 CR-66.
8. *U.S. v. Nathaniel Johnson*, CRG-82-29-K.
9. *U.S. v. James Keith Johnson*, 2:95 CR-49.
10. *U.S. v. Kelly*, CRE-84-50-LS; *U.S. v. Kelly*, 783 F. 2d 575 (5th Cir. 1986).
11. *U.S. v. Franks*, 1:93 CR-116; 5th Cir. 94-60132.
12. *U.S. v. Webb*, 1:02 CR-10.
13. *Northeast Mississippi Daily Journal*, March 16, 2006.
14. *U.S. v. Wilson et al.*, 2:04 CR-114; 5th Cir. 94-60132.

Chapter 2. Corruption in Positions of Trust:
Lawyers, Judges, Supervisors, and Sheriffs

1. *U.S. v. Freshour*, 1:99 CR-0015-NBB-1.
2. *U.S. v. Nunley*, 1:94 CR-00125-NB-B-1.
3. *U.S. v. Shuffield*, 3:06 CR-127-P-A; *Oxford Eagle*, October 12, 2006, January 29, 2007.
4. *Jackson Clarion-Ledger*, January 14, 2000.
5. *U.S. v. Pickett*, 2:99 CR-8; *U.S. v. Ellington*, 2:03 CR-100; *U.S. v. Starks et al.*, 2:98 CR-0092-GHD.
6. *Oxford Eagle*, December 13, 1996.
7. *U.S. v. Jones*, CRG-88-39-B.
8. *U.S. v. Costilow*, CRE-82-34-K-P.
9. *U.S. v. Burke, Pegues, & Sims*, 3:03 CR-120; 5th Cir. 04-60973; *U.S. v. Barksdale*, 3:03 CR-0083-001; *U.S. v. Mitchell*, 3:02 CR-151.

10. *U.S. v. Miller*, 3:03 CR-106; *Holly Springs South Reporter*, October 16, 2003.

11. *U.S. v. Hamilton*, CRD-78-36-K; opinion *sub nom U.S. v. Bright*, 630 F. 2d 804 (5th Cir. 1980).

12. For the full text of his *Rose* report, see an outstanding law review article by Professor Ron Rychlak at pp. 889-1051 of the *Mississippi Law Journal*, Vol. 68, No. 3 (Spring 1999).

13. *U.S. v. Hamilton*, CRD-78-36-K; *U.S. v. Reed*, CRD-78-37-K.

14. "Dirty Dozen? Tampering with Juries Appeals to Defendants Facing Steep Sentences," *Wall Street Journal*, January 30, 1995.

15. *U.S. v. Renfro*, CRD-79-34-K; *U.S. v. Renfro*, 620 F. 2d 497 (5th Cir. 1980); *U.S. v. Renfro*, CRD-80-28-WK-P; *Memphis Commercial Appeal*, September 9, 1980.

16. *U.S. v. Wallace*, CRD-79-10-5; *U.S. v. Riley*, CRD-81-3.

17. *U.S. v. Grisham*, CR-90-172.

18. *Jackson Clarion-Ledger*, October 9, 1988.

19. U.S. v. Miller, CRE-87-8.

20. *U.S. v. Little*, 3 CR-87-0000105; *U.S. v. Little*, 687 F. Supp. 1042 (N.D. Miss. 1988), affirmed 889 F. 2d 1367 (5th Cir. 1989).

21. *U.S. v. Spradling, Crayton*, CRE-82-58-WK-P; Itawamba *County Times* "The Only Paper in the World That Cares Anything about Itawamba County," October 21, 1982; *Northeast Mississippi Daily Journal*, March 9, 1983; *Memphis Commercial Appeal*, March 9, 1981–March 28, 1984.

22. *U.S. v. Jones et al.*, 3:93 CR-087-D; 5th Cir. 95-60236; *Holly Springs South Reporter*, February 2, 1995; *U.S. v. Tatum*, 4:00 CR-100, 3:05 CR-001.

23. Although usually held confidential under Federal Rule 7, Judge Keady gave me special permission to reveal what happened in the grand jury in this and certain other cases to present to lawyers and students as cautionary tales as long as names were withheld.

24. *U.S. v. Glenn*, CRE-86-61-LS-D.

25. *U.S. v. Stewart*, 2:03 CR-48.

26. *U.S. v. Hall*, 3:06 CR-023-B; *Oxford Eagle*, August 17, 2007; *U.S. v. Carothers*, 3:07 CR-001-B-A; *Oxford Eagle*, August 2, 2007.

27. *U.S. v. Caywood, Morehead, Moultrie*, 3:08 CR-014; *Northeast Mississippi Daily Journal*, March 26, June 25, 2008, January 9, 2009; *Oxford Eagle*, August 14, 2008.

28. *Jackson Clarion-Ledger*, August 19, 2008.

29. Ibid., August 13, 2008.

30. *Northeast Mississippi Daily Journal*, October 11, December 4, 2011; Jeff Amy, "Mississippi Settles Beef Plant Case for $3.9 Million," Associated Press, April 17, 2012.

31. *U.S. v. Scruggs, Scruggs, & Backstrom*, 3:07 CR-192-B; Peter Boyer, "The Bribe," *New Yorker*, May 19, 2008.

Chapter 3. Civil Rights and Civil Wrongs

1. *U.S. v. Beard et al.*, 1:95 CR-116-GHD.

2. *U.S. v. Clayton*, 172 F. 3d 347 (5th Cir. 1999).

3. *U.S. v. Harrison*, CRD-80-17-LS-P; *Memphis Press-Scimitar*, April 18, 1980; *Jackson Clarion-Ledger*, April 17, 1980; *Memphis Commercial Appeal*, July 3, 1980.

4. *U.S. v. Dorman et al.*, CRG-84-12-LS; *Jackson Clarion-Ledger*, February 17, 1984.

5. *U.S. v. Skaggs*, 2:93 CR-187-B-O.

6. On July 7, 1996, the *Jackson Clarion-Ledger* weighed in heavily about the horror of this new scourge, hoping it was not "recreational racism," as some suggested.

7. Michael Kelly, "Playing with Fire," *New Yorker*, July 15, 1996, offers an excellent in-depth analysis of motive. See also Gary Fields and Richard Price, "Church Arsons One Year Later: Out of the Ashes: A Sense of Unity," *USA Today*, December 23, 1996.

8. *U.S. v. Ballinger and Wood*, 9948-CR-01-BF. DOJ press releases dated November 9, 1999, and July 11, 2000, detail the charges and districts best. See also a follow-up in the *Jackson Clarion-Ledger*, December 11, 2010.

9. *Jackson Clarion-Ledger*, April 17, 1998.

10. *U.S. v. Butler*, CRW-86-56-GD; 5th Cir. 87-4322; *Jackson Clarion-Ledger*, May 8, 1987; *Memphis Commercial Appeal*, May 8, 1987.

11. *U.S. v. Cummings*, CRW-82-18-WK-P.

12. *U.S. v. Winters et al.*, 4:94 CR-65-LS; *U.S. v. Winters*, 105 F. 3d 200 (5th Cir. 1997); *U.S. v. Winters*, 174 F. 3d 478 (5th Cir. 1999); *Jet*, July 4, 1994.

13. Morris, *Ghosts of Medgar Evers*, 116.

14. Ibid., 119.

15. http://www.justice.gov/archive/ag/speeches/2007/ag_speech_070227.html.

16. Shaila Dewan, "After Inquiry, Grand Jury Refuses to Issue New Indictments in Till Case," *New York Times*, February 28, 2007; "No Indictment in '55 Emmett Till Slaying," USA Today, February 27, 2007.

17. A longer version of the summary, including a complete transcript of the trial, is available at http://vault.fbi.gov/Emmett%20Till.

Chapter 4. Killers and Wannabes

1. U.S. Senate, Committee on Armed Services, *Transcript of Trial Proceedings*.

2. *North Carolina v. Alford*, 400 U.S. 24 (1970).

3. *Brady v. U.S.*, 397 U.S. 742 (1970).

4. *U.S. v. Walton*, CRE-72-48-S. "Walton Found Sane," *Oxford Eagle*, December 4, 1975.

5. *U.S. v. Lampkin*, CRE-78-1-K; *Starkville Daily News*, September 10, 1976, April 10, 1979; *Paxton (Ill.) News Gazette*, April 6, 2009.

6. *U.S. v. Gaines*, CRW-76-117-S.

7. *U.S. v. Hutcheson, Hinson*, 3:95 CR-15-B.

8. *U.S. v. Fort*, CRE-83-50-LS-P; *Memphis Commercial Appeal*, August 19, November 12, December 3, 17, 1983; *Jackson Clarion-Ledger*, November 6, December 7, 1983, June 7, 1992, June 5, 1993; "Fort Pleads Guilty, Fails to Appear for Sentencing, U.S. Marshal Service Declares Him Top 15 Fugitive," U.S. Marshal Press Release, December 6, 1983; "Fort Has Courtroom Full of Spectators under His Spell," *Chicago Tribune*, October 18, 1988; Jeffrey Toobin, "Capone's Revenge: How Far Can a Prosecutor Go to Secure Crucial Testimony from Plea Bargainers?" *New Yorker*, May 23, 1994.

9. *U.S. v. Harold Shaw*, CRG-90-19-B.

10. *Taitt v. U.S. et al.* [Pruett], District of Colorado 82-M-1731, deposition on March 23, 1983, at the Law Library at Parchman, Mississippi.

11. *U.S. v. Leedom*, 2:96 CR-136-D-B; *Leedom v. State*, 1999-KA-1754-SCT.

12. *U.S. v. Dillard et al.*, 1:02 CR-038-P-D.

13. *U.S. v. Tohill et al.*, CRE-89-37-D.

14. *U.S. v. Ronald Shaw*, CRE-81-2-S; *U.S. v. Ronald Shaw*, 701 F. 2d 367 (5th Cir. 1983).

Chapter 5. Faraway Places with Strange-Sounding Names: The Age of Terror

1. *U.S. v. El-Sarji*, 2:00 CR-120; William Finnegan, "The Secret Keeper," *New Yorker*, October 19, 2009.

2. *U.S. v. Marzook, Salah, Ashqar* (N.D. Illinois), 03-CR-978-3.

3. *U.S. v. Ahmed*, 1:03 CR-030.

5. *Awad v. U.S.*, 1:93 CV-376-D-D; *Awad v. U.S.*, 2001 WL741638 (N.D. Miss. April 2001); 5th Cir. 99-60042; *Awad v. U.S.*, 301 F. 3d 1367 (Fed Cir. 2002); Steven A. Emerson, "Journey into Fear," *Penthouse*, March 1991; *Northeast Mississippi Daily Journal*, May 12, 1992; Emerson, *Terrorist*; Michelle Visser, "Sovereign Immunity and Informant Detectors: The United States' Refusal to Protect Its Protectors," *Stanford Law Review* 58 (November 2005). *Daily Journal* reporter and current Ole Miss journalism professor Marty Russell wrote an excellent series of stories on our trial that appeared on February 27 and March 1, 2, 6, 7, and 8, 2001. See also *U.S. v. Rashid*, 234 F. 3d 1280 (D.C. Cir. 2000); *Awad v. U.S.*, 301 F. 3d 1367 (Fed. Cir. 2002); and *Awad v. U.S.*, 61 Fed. Cir. 281 (2004), as well as Douglas Pasternak, "Squeezing Them, Leaving Them," *U.S. News and World Report*, July 8, 2002.

Bibliography of Related Readings

Baca, Keith. *Native American Place Names in Mississippi*. Jackson: University Press of Mississippi, 2007.

Bachleda, F. Lynne. *Guide to the Natchez Trace Parkway*. 2nd ed. Birmingham: Menasha Ridge, 2005.

Baldwin, Joseph. *Flush Times of Alabama and Mississippi: A Series of Sketches*. 1853; New York: Sagamore, 1957.

Ball, Howard. *Justice in Mississippi: The Murder Trial of Edgar Ray Killen*. Lawrence: University Press of Kansas, 2006.

Bicentennial History of the United States Attorneys, 1789–1989. Washington, D.C.: DOJ, 1989.

Biden, Joseph. *Promises to Keep: On Life and Politics*. New York: Random House, 2007.

Bin Laden, Carmen. *Inside the Kingdom: My Life in Saudi Arabia*. New York: Warner, 2005.

Bing, Stanley. *One Hundred Bullshit Jobs*. New York: Collins, 2006.

Bridges, Tyler. *Bad Bet on the Bayou: The Rise of Gambling in Louisiana and the Fall of Governor Edwin Edwards*. 1st ed. New York: Farrar, Straus, and Giroux, 2001.

Brieger, James. *Hometown Mississippi*. 3rd ed. Jackson: Town Square, 1997.

Buchanan, Minor Ferris. *Holt Collier: His Life, Roosevelt Hunts, and the Origin of the Teddy Bear*. 4th ed. Jackson: Centennial Press of Mississippi, 2002.

Burke, James Lee. *Jolie Blon's Bounce*. New York: Pocket Star, 2003.

Cash, W. J. *The Mind of the South*. New York: Vintage, 1941.

Clark, Victoria. *Yemen: Dancing on the Heads of Snakes*. New Haven: Yale University Press, 2010.

Cobb, James. *The Most Southern Place on Earth: The Mississippi Delta and the Roots of Regional Identity*. New York: Oxford University Press, 1992.

Cooley, Armanda, Carrie Bess, and Marsha Rubin-Jackson. *Madam Foreman: [The O.J. Jurors Speak] A Rush to Judgment?* Beverly Hills, Calif.: Dove, 1995.

Crockett, James. *Operation Pretense: The FBI's Sting on County Corruption in Mississippi*. Jackson: University Press of Mississippi, 2003.

Crowley, Michael. "Blood Money." *Reader's Digest*, February 2004, 190–209.

Cullen, John B. *Old Times in Faulkner Country*. Baton Rouge: Louisiana State University Press, 1976.

Dabney, Joseph Earl. *Mountain Spirits: A Chronicle of Corn Whiskey from King James' Ulster Plantation to America's Appalachians and the Moonshine Life*. New York: Bright Mountain, 1984.

Daley, Robert. *The Prince of the City: The True Story of a Cop Who Knew Too Much*. Boston: Moyer Bell, 1988.

Daly, Sherrie. *Teed Off: My Life as a Player's Wife on the PGA Tour*. New York: Gallery, 2011.

Dean, John. *Blind Ambition: The White House Years*. New York: Simon and Schuster, 1976.

DeLaughter, Bobby. *Never Too Late: A Prosecutor's Story of Justice in the Medgar Evers Case*. New York: Scribner's, 2001.

Denton, Sally. *The Bluegrass Conspiracy: An Inside Story of Power, Greed, Drugs, and Murder*. New York: Doubleday, 1990.

Dillmann, John. *The French Quarter Killers*. New York: Macmillan, 1987.

Earley, Pete, and Gerald Shur. *WITSEC: Inside the Federal Witness Protection Program*. New York: Bantam, 2003.

Emerson, Steven A. *Terrorist: The Inside Story of the Highest-Ranking Iraqi Terrorist Ever to Defect to the West*. New York: Villard, 1991.

Enzweiler, Stephen. *Oxford in the Civil War: Battle for a Vanquished Land*. Charleston: History Press, 2011.

Faulkner, William. *Big Woods*. New York: Random House, 1931.

———. *The Viking Portable Faulkner*. Ed. Malcolm Cowley. Rev. and exp. ed. New York: Penguin, 1978.

Freeh, Louis J., with Howard Means. *My FBI: Bringing Down the Mafia, Investigating Bill Clinton, and Fighting the War on Terror*. New York: St. Martin's Griffin, 2006.

Graham, Fred. *The Alias Program*. Boston: Little, Brown, 1977.

Greene, Robert. *The Sting Man: Inside ABSCAM*. New York: Dutton, 1981.

Grisham, John. *Ford County: Stories*. New York: Bantam, 2009.

———. *The King of Torts*. New York: Doubleday, 2003.

———. *A Time to Kill*. New York: Wynwood, 1989.

Guralnick, Peter. *Careless Love: The Unmaking of Elvis Presley*. Boston: Little, Brown, 1999.

———. *Last Train to Memphis: The Rise of Elvis Presley*. Boston: Little, Brown, 1994.

Humes, Edward. *Mississippi Mud: A True Story from a Corner of the Deep South*. New York: Pocket, 1995.

Huntington, Samuel. *The Clash of Civilizations and the Remaking of World Order*. 1st ed. New York: Simon and Schuster, 1996.

Jeff Fort, Angel of Fear [video]. NBC News Chicago, 1988.

Keady, William C. *All Rise: Memoirs of a Mississippi Federal Judge*. Boston: Recollections Bound, 1988.

King, Katherine, and Margaret King. *Y'all Twins?* Marietta, GA: Deeds, 2012.

Lange, Alan, and Tom Dawson. *Kings of Tort*. 2nd ed. Battle Ground, Wash.: Pediment, 2010.

Levitt, Matthew. *Hamas: Politics, Charity, and Terrorism in the Service of Jihad*. New Haven: Yale University Press, 2006.

Lewis, Michael. *The Blind Side: Evolution of a Game*. New York: Norton, 2006.

Lindsay, Paul. *Witness to the Truth: A Novel of the FBI*. New York: Random House, 1992.

Lott, Trent. *Herding Cats: A Life in Politics*. New York: Easton, 2005.

Lynch, Timothy, ed. *In the Name of Justice: Leading Experts Reexamine the Classic Article "The Aims of the Criminal Law."* Washington, D.C.: Cato Institute, 2009.

McGee, Jim, and Brian Duffy. *Main Justice: The Men and Women Who Enforce the Nation's Criminal Laws and Guard Its Liberties*. New York: Simon and Schuster, 1996.

McPhail, Pam. *No Room for Truth*. Chapel Hill: Spring Morning, 1995.

Moody, Anne. *Coming of Age in Mississippi*. New York: Dell, 1968.

Morris, Willie. *The Ghosts of Medgar Evers: A Tale of Race, Murder, Mississippi, and Hollywood*. New York: Random House, 1998.

Naipaul, V. S. *A Turn in the South*. New York: Knopf, 1989.

Nelson, Jack. *Terror in the Night: The Klan's Campaign against the Jews*. Jackson: University Press of Mississippi, 1996.

O'Brien, Darcy. *Power to Hurt: Sexual Assault inside a Judge's Chambers: Sexual Assault, Corruption, and the Ultimate Reversal of Justice for Women*. New York: HarperCollins, 1996.

Orey, Michael. *Assuming the Risk: The Mavericks, the Lawyers, and the Whistle-Blowers Who Beat Big Tobacco*. Boston: Little, Brown, 1999.

Oshinsky, David M. *Worse Than Slavery: Parchman Farm and the Ordeal of Jim Crow Justice*. New York: Free Press, 1996.

Percy, William Alexander. *Lanterns on the Levee—Recollections of a Planter's Son*. New York: Knopf, 1964.

Quan, Robert Seto. *Lotus among the Magnolias: The Mississippi Chinese*. Jackson: University Press of Mississippi, 1982.

Reid, Stephen. *Jackrabbit Parole*. Toronto: Seal, 1986.

Rhodes, Richard. *Why They Kill: The Discoveries of a Maverick Criminologist*. New York: Knopf, 1999.

Simenon, Georges. *Maigret in Court*. San Diego: Harcourt, Brace, Jovanovich, 1983.

Snow, C. P. *The Masters (Strangers and Brothers)*. New York: Macmillan, 1951.

Solotaroff, Ivan. *The Last Face You'll Ever See: The Private Life of the American Death Penalty*. New York: HarperCollins, 2001.

Taylor, William Banks. *Brokered Justice: Race, Politics, and Mississippi Prisons, 1798–1992*. Columbus: Ohio State University Press, 1993.

Temple, John. *Deadhouse: Life in a Coroner's Office*. Jackson: University Press of Mississippi, 2005.

Till-Mobley, Mamie, and Christopher Benson. *Death of Innocence: The Story of the Hate Crime That Changed America*. New York: Random House, 2003.

Toole, John Kennedy. *A Confederacy of Dunces*. New York: Wings, 1980.

U.S. Senate. Committee on Armed Services. *Transcript of the Trial Proceedings Relating to the Attempted Murder of Senator John C. Stennis in the U.S. District Court for the District of Columbia*. October 1973.

Watson, Jay. *Forensic Fictions: The Lawyer Figure in Faulkner*. Athens: University of Georgia Press, 1993.

Weary, Dolphus, and William Hendricks. *I Ain't Comin' Back*. Wheaton, Ill.: Tyndale, 1990.

Weinberg, Michael. *Careers in Crime: An Applicant's Guide*. Kansas City: Andrews McMeel, 2006.

Wells, Samuel J., and Roseanna Tubby, eds. *After Removal: The Choctaw in Mississippi*. Jackson: University Press of Mississippi, 1986.

Weston, Greg. *The Stopwatch Gang*. Toronto: Macmillan Canada, 1992.

White, Neil. *In the Sanctuary of Outcasts*. New York: White, 2009.

Wilkie, Curtis. *The Fall of the House of Zeus: The Rise and Ruin of America's Most Powerful Trial Lawyer*. New York: Broadway, 2011.

Winokur, Jon. *Encyclopedia Neurotica*. New York: St. Martin's, 2005.

Woodward, Bob. *The Secret Man: The Story of Watergate's Deep Throat*. New York: Simon and Schuster, 2005.

Wright, Simeon, with Herb Boyd. *Simeon's Story: An Eyewitness Account of the Kidnapping of Emmett Till*. Chicago: Hill, 2010.

Acknowledgments

A project as ambitious as this book, with its multitude of stories and characters, could only be completed with the generous help of an army of friends. It began several weeks before I retired from the U.S. Attorney's Office with Anita McGehee, secretary to the U.S. Attorney, and Joan Allen, administrative officer, who led this computer-illiterate dinosaur to the basement where I copied unindexed drawers of large-format docket sheets which held the key facts of my hundreds of old cases. Once I was retired and decided which cases were worth retelling, I turned to district court clerk and former U.S. Marshal David Crews, whose excellent staff, led by Sherryln "Judge" Adams and his secretary Connie Armstrong and several intelligent and diligent deputy clerks, helped me over several months lift dozens of old leather-bound docket books and xerox their oversized pages. What a task it was.

With those records in hand, I turned to chief probation officer Danny McKittrick to retrieve more detailed records. Danny, himself a notorious teller of colorful war stories, furnished many useful insights into his more interesting clients. I turned next to the U.S. Marshal's Office where their recently retired stalwart, the aptly named Inspector Eddie Rambo, helped me recall the details of our most memorable cases together. The marshals' partner in running the Oxford Jail, known locally as the Buddy East Hotel, has been for the last forty years the wise and always reliable Buddy East, the only ten-term elected sheriff I know, who was an invaluable resource for details of old cops-and-robbers stories.

In addition to those sources, I added thirty-five bankers boxes of my own files, memos, briefs, affidavits, indictments, and other documents I'd squirreled away, and finally began writing the book. I was ably assisted by the energetic Dawn Jeter, director of operations at the Overby Center at Ole Miss, where I was a writing Fellow. Dawn and her staff did the hard work of typing my first drafts, hand-written on traditional yellow legal pads, which seemed fitting for such old cases. Joining Dawn were my most dedicated helpers of all, the Ole Miss law students who brainstormed, critiqued, and typed multiple drafts. Spencer Ritchie, Stephen Smith, Caleb Ballew, Doug Maines, and Taylor McNeel racked up hours of creative work as researchers, sounding-boards, and fact-checkers. To complete the book, I had the brilliant and wonderfully enthusiastic Caroline Eley, Joanna Frederick, Drew Tominello, and Laci Bonner. These wonderful students made a pleasure of the grueling work of finishing this volume. The personal relationships with these law students, whose only reward for their work was one hour per semester of law school directed study credit, were easily the best part of writing the books. Their attitudes have strongly reinforced my opinion that this new American generation will be one of our finest ever. My gratitude to them is total, as is my gratitude to University Press editor-in-chief Craig Gill, director Leila Salisbury, cover designer Todd Lape, marketing manager and idea man Steve Yates, keen-eyed production editor Shane Gong Stewart, and all my other comrades at the Press, one of America's finest publishers.

Index

About the Author

John Hailman attended both the Sorbonne in Paris (two years) and the Universite Laval in Quebec, Canada. Then he received his B.A. from Millsaps College in Jackson, Mississippi, his M.A. from Tulane University in New Orleans, Louisiana, and his J.D. from the University of Mississippi in Oxford, Mississippi. He was a Prettyman Fellow in Trial Practice at Georgetown and received the International Law Certificate from the National School for Magistrates in Paris, France. He is one of the rare prosecutors elected to the exclusive American Board of Trial Advocates and was a Founding Bencher of American Inn of Court III.

Hailman has received numerous commendations from a series of FBI directors and from attorneys general from Griffin Bell and Janet Reno to Edwin Meese and Alberto Gonzalez, including the Justice Department's highest honor, the Attorney General's Distinguished Service Award. He was the only Justice Department employee to receive, for his tenure as the nation's longest-serving U.S. attorney criminal chief, the Senior Executive Service Leadership Award.

Hailman taught for many years at the FBI Academy and the Justice Department Advocacy Institute in Washington, D.C., and Columbia, South Carolina. He has been an adjunct professor of law at the University of Mississippi for over twenty-five years and still teaches trial advocacy and law and literature there.

Hailman and his wife Regan have two children, Dr. Allison Hailman Doyle of Meridian, Mississippi, and Lydia Hailman King of Baltimore, Maryland, and one granddaughter, Abbey McGrew Doyle, age two. The Hailmans divide their retirement time between homes in Oxford, Mississippi, and a village in the Charente region of southwest France near Bordeaux.